CHAUCER

Modern Essays in Criticism

CHAUCER

MODERN ESSAYS IN CRITICISM

edited by

EDWARD WAGENKNECHT

OXFORD UNIVERSITY PRESS

LONDON   OXFORD   NEW YORK

OXFORD UNIVERSITY PRESS
Oxford   London   Glasgow
New York   Toronto   Melbourne   Wellington
Ibadan   Nairobi   Dar es Salaam   Cape Town
Kuala Lumpur   Singapore   Jakarta   Hong Kong   Tokyo
Delhi   Bombay   Calcutta   Madras   Karachi

Library of Congress Catalogue Card Number: 59-6854
First published by Oxford University Press, New York, 1959
First published as an Oxford University Press paperback, 1959

This reprint, 1978

Printed in the United States of America

PREFACE

THE idea of putting together a collection of papers on Chaucer, growing out of my own needs in teaching that poet, long antedated the decision of my publishers to embark upon the series of anthologies which they inaugurated in 1957 with Leonard F. Dean's *Shakespeare: Modern Essays in Criticism.* Nearly all my material has been drawn from the learned journals in the modern language field, and this has been done deliberately, not only because most of the important new material about Chaucer comes out in these journals but also because I wished to make learned journal material more easily available to students than is at present the case. Few of the smaller American colleges have really adequate files, but even when they have they often find it necessary to restrict their use by undergraduates.

I have tried to illustrate Chaucerian investigation in as many aspects as possible, striking a reasonable balance between criticism and historical scholarship. As anyone who has any familiarity with the field knows, historical scholarship has long predominated; most of the critical articles included have been written during recent years. I have, however, excluded highly technical articles, such as considerations of textual problems, date, sources, etc., thinking that these would be of little interest except to the most advanced students, who might safely be trusted to dig them out of the files.

If only because my contributors frequently disagree with each other, it ought not to be necessary to remark that I do not agree with all of them, but I do believe that every one of them has something to say that is worth pondering. Manly's paper on the Knight, dating from 1907, is interesting as the first fruits of a method of investigation which, as developed later in his *Some New Light on Chaucer* (Henry Holt and Company, 1926), opened up a whole new field. Though J. Leslie Hotson's paper on 'The Nun's Priest's

Tale' represents a type of inquiry in whose presence I am generally inclined to be somewhat wary, I must confess I find it more worthy of credence than some Chaucerians have pronounced it. But it really will not make much difference whether the reader 'agrees' with Hotson or not; so exhilarating a performance simply could not be left out.

Most of the giants of Chaucerian scholarship are here, as well as some others. Kittredge is represented by two articles, both widely influential and of great historical importance. I greatly regret the absence of John Livingston Lowes, but I finally reconciled myself to it on the ground that probably all users of this volume will have access to his stimulating book, *Geoffrey Chaucer and the Development of His Genius* (Houghton Mifflin Company, 1934). I considered many articles by Lowes but none of them seemed quite right for such a book as this. At one time I contemplated printing the famous article in which Frederick Tupper argued that *The Canterbury Tales* were constructed on a framework suggested by the Seven Deadly Sins (*PMLA*, XXIX [1914], 93–128), together with Lowes' reply to it (*PMLA*, XXX [1915], 237–371). Lowes' argument has, however, been so generally accepted that it seemed hardly worth while to fight this battle all over again. It was different with the articles by Kittredge and Hinckley about the 'Marriage Group,' which I have printed, for this question is still open, though it is true that a great many teachers of Chaucer are so much under the spell of Kittredge's persuasive writing and speaking that they have never discovered it. In a much more personal way, I also regret the absence of my dear friend, Edith Rickert, the greatest teacher I ever had and the only person I ever encountered who was both a great teacher and a great scholar. Insofar as they were devoted to Chaucer, most of Miss Rickert's energies went into editing and teaching; she wrote comparatively few articles. I pondered using her persuasive argument on *The Parlement of Foules* (*Modern Philology*, XVIII [1921], 1–29), but finally concluded that it would be better to print the much more recent article by Charles O. McDonald which gives a wider survey of scholarship in this area (incidentally summarizing Miss Rickert's own article).

I have given *The Canterbury Tales* the lion's share in this book because that is what they get in most of the courses in which the volume will be used, but I have tried not to neglect the *Troilus*. I wish I could have printed at least one article on each tale and/or pilgrim, but this obviously was impossible. If it be asked why, then, I have given so much material on the Pardoner and the Wife of Bath, the answer must be not only that these are the greatest characterizations among the pilgrims but also that I believed that at some point the reader of this volume must be permitted to look at problems of interpretation from a number of different angles and to savor different views. I must confess that I wish I might have had space to give more material about the minor poems, but I have tried to atone for my paucity here by choosing articles that are as comprehensive and as perspicacious as possible.

It remains only to thank the many editors and publishers who have graciously permitted the materials in this book to be reprinted (specific acknowledgements are made at the bottom of the page on which each article begins) and to ask the reader to keep in mind the fact that in their original appearances many of these articles were much more elaborately documented than they are in these reprints. For deciding which notes to retain and which to drop the editor alone is responsible. I have been careful, however, to retain a great many notes in which reference is made to other articles on the subjects herein considered. If this volume turns out the be- and end-all of its readers' investigations in Chaucerian scholarship, it will have realized only a portion of its usefulness; I hope it may also serve as a guidepost pointing toward further explorations. I have not attempted to make the form of such annotation as I have retained uniform throughout the volume. In a very few instances I have cut long quotations from Chaucer's own writings in the text of the articles themselves.

EDWARD WAGENKNECHT

Boston University
August 28, 1958

CONTENTS

ix

CHAUCER

Modern Essays in Criticism

W. H. CLAWSON

The Framework of *The Canterbury Tales*

For the purpose of this article, a framework or framing story is to be understood as a narrative which, however interesting in itself, was composed for the primary purpose of introducing and connecting a series of tales, which are the *raison d'être* of the whole work. Though it is outside my plan to trace the origin and growth of this literary genre, a few examples may be given. In the oriental collections entitled *The Thousand and One Nights* and *The Seven Sages,* the stories are told in order to postpone the execution of a condemned person. In the first case, this is done by the device of interrupting each story at a crucial point, with a promise to conclude it if the execution is put off for a day. In *The Seven Sages,* a work known in various forms in mediaeval Europe, a young prince, the son of a Roman emperor, has resisted the amorous advances of his stepmother and has been accused by her of assault and of plotting his father's death. Because she has put a spell upon him which makes it impossible for him to speak for seven days without losing his life, he is unable to refute the charge; but his seven wise tutors come to his assistance. Each evening the stepmother relates to the emperor a story that recalls the wiles of counsellors, and each morning one of the tutors tells a tale illustrating a woman's cunning. They thus succeed in putting off the execution from day to day until the period of the spell is com-

Reprinted, by permission, from *The University of Toronto Quarterly,* xx (1951), 137–54.

pleted. When the prince can speak, he convinces the emperor of his own innocence and his stepmother's guilt and she suffers the fate she had planned for him. Both framing stories gain interest through suspense and the second imposes unity and didactic purpose on the tales it encloses.

There are other collections of stories of didactic intention which lack the element of suspense in the framing tale. Among these, *The Fables of Bidpai* and the *Disciplina Clericalis*, both of oriental origin, were accessible to mediaeval English readers. Here, moral precepts are imparted to a pupil by a wise teacher, and are illustrated by a series of tales. A very ingenious example of this type of framing story is to be found in the *Confessio Amantis* of John Gower, completed in 1390, when Chaucer was still at work on *The Canterbury Tales*. Gower's framework is based on a skilful combination of two allegorical themes, the seven deadly sins and courtly love. The poet makes his petition to Venus, under whose direction he confesses his sins to her priest, Genius, and is warned against each sin by a series of tales. This schematized allegory is worked out with great precision and gives admirable unity to the poem as a whole, the pleasing effect of which is increased by the neatness of the versification and the unpretending clarity of the style. Chaucer made a somewhat similar use of love-allegory in his *Legend of Cupid's Saints*, a martyrology of famous classical heroines who died for love. In an introductory vision the task is imposed on him by the god of love as penance for his alleged offence in relating the disloyalty of Criseyde. But there are no links between the stories, and after nine had been written Chaucer gave up the plan and began *The Canterbury Tales*.

We are now to consider the type of frame-story in which a series of tales is related by a member or members of a social group for purposes of entertainment. Among the many devices employed by Ovid as a setting for the stories of his *Metamorphoses* there are several examples of stories told by members of a group. At the beginning of Book IV, the three daughters of King Minyas of Thebes, who disbelieve in the divinity of Bacchus, have met in their house on the day of his festival to defy his authority by spinning and weaving. To pass the time, each relates a story: the death of Pyramus and Thisbe, the love of Mars and Venus, the transformation of Hermaphroditus. There is some discussion between the stories. In the end, the girls are transformed into bats by the angry god. The episode might have suggested to Boccaccio and Chaucer the device of stories told by a group.

Such a device appears as an episode in Boccaccio's earliest work, the *Filocolo*, a long prose version of the French romance of *Floris and Blanchefleur*, which he addressed to his mistress, Marie d'Aquino. Florio, son of the king of Spain, has been separated by his parents from his beloved Biancofiore, a Saracen captive. Travelling under the name of Filocolo in search of her, with several companions, he is detained by storms at Naples, where he and his friends are invited to join a gay company of ladies and gentlemen assembled in a garden. The leader of the group, Fiametta (Boccaccio's name for his lady) suggests that the thirteen members of the company shall each in turn propose a problem of love. A presiding officer is to discuss and give the answer to each problem, and Fiametta is unanimously chosen. It is clear that this episode was the preliminary sketch from which Boccaccio developed the framework of the *Decameron*. The pleasant garden, the gracious social background, the presiding queen, the stories or situations presented in turn by each of the company, connected by discussion, and unified by a common theme, follow essentially the same scheme as that of the more famous work.[1] Two of the stories were retold in the *Decameron*, and one of these, on the theme of the Lady's Rash Promise, as told in the *Filocolo*, is held by many scholars to be the source of the tale of Chaucer's Franklin. In fact, Chaucer's detailed acquaintance with the *Filocolo* and his indebtedness to it, not only for this story, but also for many details of the meeting of Troilus and Criseyde at the house of Pandarus, seem to have been definitely established by the studies of Young, Lowes, and Tatlock.[2] It is therefore conceivable that Chaucer derived the general idea of a series of framed tales from Boccaccio's youthful work.

It should be noted, however, that a closer parallel to Chaucer's scheme exists in an episode of Boccaccio's pastoral romance, the *Ameto*, written about 1341. Here a company of seven nymphs meet in a wooded meadow to entertain one another by a series of tales on a common theme, under the direction of a presiding officer, the huntsman Ameto; and they are brought together by a special religious occasion, a festival of Venus. Ameto calls on each nymph in turn, and in the intermissions he comments on each story. Five of the nymphs relate tales of their unhappiness in marriage to an unloved husband and of the consolation each obtained by an affair with a youthful lover. The confession of one nymph definitely resembles the marital experiences of the Wife of Bath and of the ill-assorted couple of the Merchant's Tale, but in view of the widespread occurrence of this theme in mediaeval literature, the similarities are not close enough to prove Chaucer's indebtedness.[3]

Except for the limited number of the tales and their restriction to a single day, the *Ameto* episode resembles the *Decameron* framework, resembling it in four ways: the tales are told in succession by members of an organized group; this group is brought together by special external circumstances; there are narrative and conversational links between the tales; there is a presiding officer. Now in these four essential features, the *Decameron* is in agreement with *The Canterbury Tales*. The general tone of the framing narrative and the general topics of its tales are very similar to those of Chaucer: four of Boccaccio's tales are analogues to four of Chaucer's; and in Boccaccio's apology for the impropriety of some of his stories he makes the same defence as that offered by Chaucer for the same fault—that he must tell what happened, that the reader may skip any tale he wishes, and that such stories are purely for entertainment and are not to be taken too seriously. However there are no verbal parallels, and the resemblances might be due to coincidence.[4]

The majority of Chaucer scholars hold that the indebtedness of *The Canterbury Tales* to the *Decameron* is not established. There is no convincing evidence that Chaucer derived his Clerk's Tale from any source but Petrarch's Latin version and a French translation of this.[5] He attributes the tale only to Petrarch; and, though he must have possessed and closely studied manuscripts of the *Filocolo, Filostrato,* and *Tesieda,* he never mentions Boccaccio's name. There is no evidence that Chaucer met Boccaccio during his brief visit to Florence in 1373, and even had the meeting taken place, it is doubtful whether the Italian author would have mentioned the *Decameron,* with which for many years he had been out of sympathy, and which he seems to have endeavored to suppress. There is some reason to believe that Chaucer never saw a copy of the *Decameron,* and his indebtedness to it must at most be regarded as not proven.[6] However, an examination of this famous work, so close to Chaucer in point of time, so similar in structure, content, and spirit, and so comparable in artistic achievement, should aid us in forming an estimate of Chaucer's narrative art in the Canterbury framework.

The framing narrative of the *Decameron* is superbly constructed. It begins with a grimly realistic description of Florence during the great plague of 1348, recounting in sober detail the symptoms of the disease and its fatal effects not only on men but on animals, the fruitless search for remedies, the abandoning of the sick and dying in their houses through fear of infection, the break-down of moral restraints, the collection of bodies, the mass funerals by torchlight, the heaping of the corpses in common graves. At the height of this disaster, seven young ladies of birth and breeding, all of them friends and some related, happen to meet after morning service in the church of Santa Maria Novella. After some conversation, the eldest, Pampinea, points out that in their desperate situation, bereaved of their relatives, and exposed to the danger of infection and the disorders of the city, both nature and reason prompt them to save their lives. She proposes that they retire in a body to one of their country estates, taking such servants as they may still have. These villas are well stored with supplies, and there the isolation and the fresh country air will save them from the plague and fortify their spirits. All consider the plan reasonable, but they hesitate to adopt it without male advice and protection. At this point, three young men of their own social circle enter the church; and since they are known to be honorable and trustworthy, they are invited to join the venture. Next morning at dawn the party sets out, accompanied by three maid-servants and four men-servants, seventeen persons in all.

A walk of two short miles brings them to a palace at some distance from the road, with spacious halls and chambers and surrounded by meadows and gardens. Here, on the initiative of Pampinea, it is decided to choose each day a king or queen, with authority over the party for that day. The director is to nominate a successor, who shall rule from that evening to the next, and so on until all have shared the honor and responsibility. After Pampinea has been elected the first queen, and crowned with a wreath of laurel, the morning is spent in amusements and an early dinner. Then follows a midday rest, and in the afternoon all assemble in a shady spot, where they pass the heat of the day in the telling of stories. Each of the ten contributes a tale when called upon, and on this day the queen's tale comes last. The evening ends with supper, instrumental music, dancing, and the singing of a *canzone* by one of the company. The same programme is continued on each day on which stories are told, until each of the party has held the office of king or queen and each has told ten stories. It is then proposed and agreed upon that they return to their responsibilities in Florence.

From the preceding outline, we note the neatness and symmetry of Boccaccio's plan. One hundred stories are told in ten days, ten on each day, one by each member of a group of ten. The events of each day follow a general pattern. The whole gracious and charming picture is framed by the horror and distress of the stricken city, which form a powerful contrast to the beauty and freshness of the sheltered gardens and the gaiety of the company.

It has sometimes been said that in comparison to the framework of *The Canterbury Tales* that of the *Decameron* lacks movement, that it is a static and monotonous account of a group that sits in a circle and tells stories from day to day. We find, however, that the story-tellers do not remain in the same place, but transfer their headquarters more than once, so that their expedition involves a number of short journeys. Moreover, they are absent from Florence two full weeks and do not spend every day in story-telling. They set out on Wednesday and tell stories that afternoon and the next. Friday is spent in religious devotions, and on Saturday the ladies wash their hair. On Sunday morning, lest they be disturbed by other refugees from the city, they move to another palace, two miles west of the first. They then dine and tell stories beside a marble fountain in a walled garden. Here are related the tales of the third, fourth, fifth, and sixth days, from Sunday to Wednesday. On Wednesday evening, the tales having been finished early, the ladies walk a mile to explore a delightful valley, surrounded by wooded hills and watered by a stream which expands into a small lake. In this lake all bathe before returning to the palace. After supper the three gentlemen also visit the spot, and one of them, who is king for the next day, directs that the whole company shall dine and tell stories there. On Friday and Saturday, as in the former week, no stories are told. On the second Sunday of their absence, all attend mass at a little neighboring church, after which the usual routine is followed, and also on Monday and Tuesday, the ninth and tenth days. On Wednesday morning, a fortnight from their departure, all return to Florence.

These short journeys give life, charm, and variety to their narrative. The minor events and the conversation to which they give rise help to characterize the members of the company. There is some differentiation of these persons, but only a few emerge with any vividness or individuality. Dioneo adds vitality to the narrative by his daring jests and comments and his lively good humor. He obtains the privilege of telling any tale he pleases no matter what subject has been assigned, and after the first day he is allowed to speak last, because it is realized that he wants to maintain the spirits of the company by ending each day with a merry tale. When it is his turn to sing a *canzone,* he persists in offering to sing various ribald songs, instead of the courtly love-song that is required, until he is sharply called to order by the queen. Low comedy is provided by a quarrel between two of the attendants in which an elderly woman, something like the Wife of Bath, pungently rebukes one of the men-servants for professing to understand the wiles of her sex. There is nothing resembling the characterizing portraits of Chaucer's General Prologue, though there is a slight but charming sketch of one of the ladies, Fiametta, of which Marie d'Aquino was probably the model; the love-stricken Filostrato may be Boccaccio himself.

Though the characters of the *Decameron* framework are not

well-rounded personalities, they are sufficiently individualized to provide a measure of variety. The social background, on the other hand, helps to give the framework unity. The tale-tellers are all of one social class, members of the same circle, intimate friends. The manners and ideals are those of gentlefolk; there is an inherent graciousness and courtesy in speech and 'action. In spite of occasional liberty in discussing some of the stories and in spite of the coarseness of many of them, the general tone of conversation is decorous and conduct is unexceptionable. The stories themselves supply vivid pictures of every social class in every part of Italy, and they range also over France, England, and many Mediterranean countries.

Unity and symmetrical arrangement are supplied by the grouping of the stories. Except on the first and ninth days, each tale-teller (with the exception of Dioneo) is required to relate his or her story to a single theme. Day II, with stories treating of unfortunate persons who unexpectedly achieve happiness, is devoted mainly to tales of separation and recovery, after the style of the Greek romances. Day III is occupied with successful love-intrigues; several are of the fabliau type; others, such as the story of Giletta of Narbonne and the Count of Rousillon (related again in Shakespeare's *All's Well*) belong to the category of romance. The tales of Day IV, 'on those whose love had an unhappy ending,' are romance with a tragic cast, such as those of Tancred and Ghismunda and Isabella and the Pot of Basil. As a relief from these, Day V introduces stories that begin in misfortune and end happily, such as the noble one of Federigo degli Alberghi and his sacrifice of his favorite falcon in the service of his lady. The anecdotes of Day VI include the delightful one of the preaching friar displaying his relics, like Chaucer's pardoner, to a country congregation. On Days VII and VIII, the story-tellers, with their tricks played by wives on husband and husband on wives, return to the fabliau themes. Day X ends the series on a lofty moral plane with stories of heroic virtue such as the nobility of husband and lover in the tale of the Lady's Rash Promise and the superhuman resolution of Griselda.

To sum up, the framework of the *Decameron* is characterized by unity, balance, and symmetry. Variety is supplied by action and movement, by some individualization of the tale-tellers, and by a wide range of content in the tales. The narrators are all of one class, the gentry of Florence, though all classes and all regions of Italy appear in the stories. The charming surroundings of the tale-telling are framed by the sombreness of a great disaster. The prevailing tone, however, is one of gaiety and good breeding and the freedom of language and content in some of the stories is tempered by reason and self-control. The style is occasionally formal, but usually clear, natural, and spontaneous. The tales are sufficiently connected, not only by grouping into themes but also by brief comments and the occasional suggestion of a story which precedes.

Before proceeding to *The Canterbury Tales*, we must consider another collection of stories, the *Novelle* of Giovanni Sercambi of Lucca. In its original form, the *Novelliero*, now lost, it included 100 stories and was composed in 1374. The later version, extant in one incomplete manuscript of the fifteenth century, was completed not earlier than December 19, 1385. It contains 155 stories with a *proemio* and *intermezzi*. It has not yet been edited as a whole, though most of the tales are in print and the *proemio* and parts of the *intermezzi* have been included in Bryan and Dempster's *Sources and Analogues of Chaucer's Canterbury Tales*.

This collection is an imitation of the *Decameron*, but certain features bring it closer to Chaucer's *Canterbury Tales*. A large company of people of many callings and social classes sets out on foot from the city of Lucca on a journey through the principal cities of Italy in order to avoid the pestilence that has attacked their city. At a meeting in the principal church, a certain wealthy citizen, Aluisi, proposes the election of a leader and is at once chosen by all for that office. He makes arrangement for their food, lodging, and entertainment, and calls on various members of the company for tales, music, and moral instruction. The tales are sometimes told as the travellers walk along the road and sometimes at the inns after the evening meal. This is a more realistic arrangement than Chaucer's device of tales told to a band of twenty-nine pilgrims on horseback. A second difference from Chaucer's scheme is that all the tales are related by the same person, Giovanni Sercambi himself, while Chaucer modestly assigns to himself only 'Sir Thopas' and 'Melibeus.' Another difference is that in the *Novelle* there are no characterizing portraits of the travellers and scarcely any entertaining incidents on the way that might bring out character by action. The framing story is in part a tedious and detailed narrative of routine events. Its chief merit is that of a contemporary account of travel in fourteenth-century Italy with some description of the ancient buildings, churches, and shrines of the principal cities. There is little humor except for the occasion on which Aluisi falls asleep during the telling of a tale and, being roused by the laughter of the travellers, calls for another tale that will keep him awake. Not infrequently the tale-teller directs his story to one group of the pilgrims such as merchants, judges, despairing lovers, jealous husbands, but in a general and impersonal way. In short, the framing narrative has none of the sparkle and charm exhibited by Boccaccio and Chaucer, and the resemblances to Chaucer are broad and general.

Whether Chaucer was indebted to Sercambi for any of these parallels is a question that cannot be answered. He passed through Lucca on his first Italian journey in 1373 and could there have met Sercambi—a not unimportant person—and have heard of his plan; and he could have heard of or seen the first form of the work during his second journey in 1378, since he was then in Milan, which had political relations with Lucca; or he might have seen the second form of the work between 1385 and 1387, when he is thought to have begun *The Canterbury Tales*. A few of Sercambi's tales are analogues to tales in Chaucer (e.g. the Shipman's), but the resemblances are insufficient to prove indebtedness. We must conclude that, while a connection is not impossible, Chaucer, who lived in Kent for some time after 1385–6, did not need suggestions from anyone for the idea of tales told by pilgrims on the road to Canterbury.

This idea of a pilgrimage as the occasion for the telling of a sequence of stories was one of the happiest devices of Chaucer's *Canterbury Tales*. The religious motive of a pilgrimage made possible the coming together on a friendly footing of representatives of many social classes; and the relative safety and cheapness of such a form of travel, especially to so famous and long-established a shrine as Canterbury, promoted a holiday spirit which encouraged music and story-telling and led to the free exchange of opinions and confidences. Thus through his adoption of the pilgrimage device Chaucer was enabled to make of his General Prologue an unsurpassed social document and of his framing narrative a true human comedy.

The General Prologue presents a social group of thirty persons, larger and more diversified than the ten gentlefolk of the *Decameron,* smaller and more manageable than Sercambi's indefinitely large company. Chaucer's group of pilgrims is not schematically representative of English society but covers well enough the main social elements. The nobility and the lowest class of laborers are excluded as unlikely to travel in the fashion of this group; but the knights, the learned professions, the landed gentry, the mediaeval manor (through its miller and reeve), and the free agricultural laborers are all represented. The rising middle classes are well exhibited by the London merchant, preoccupied with foreign commerce, the five tradesmen with aldermanic ambitions, Harry Bailey, solid citizen and innkeeper of Southwark, and by the London cook and manciple. From the provinces come the expert cloth-weaver, Alison of Bath, and the daring sea-captain of Dartmouth. The portraits of the clergy (nearly one-third of the company) are significant for the tolerance with which Chaucer points out the foibles of the monastic orders in describing the Monk and Prioress; his greater severity in satirizing the worldliness of the Friar; and his open attack on the corrupt Summoner and the fraudulent Pardoner. His ideal portraits of the Clerk of Oxford and the Parish Priest, along with his equally favorable descriptions of the Knight and the Ploughman, perhaps reflect his own admiration at a time of changing standards of the basic ideals of earlier mediaeval society, as they had found expression in its fundamental classes—the men of prayer, the men of war, and the men of labor.

An even more distinctive feature of the General Prologue is its method of characterization. Each of the pilgrims who is described is revealed in such sharp and clear detail that we feel personally acquainted with him or her as an individual, and at the same time we recognize him as representative, not only of a social class, but of a type of character which may be recognized in any country and in any age. Nothing like this series of portraits had ever appeared in literature. It is the main reason for the perennial appeal of the General Prologue. Any analysis of these portraits must be inadequate to account for their extraordinary charm. They range from sixty-two lines (the Friar) to nine lines (the Cook), and the average is thirty lines. Within this space, not a word is wasted: details of physical appearance, dress and equipment, social rank, and character evoke the whole man or woman by powerful suggestive strokes.

No small part of the realism of these portraits is their informality, their lack of regular order. We find now a detail of dress or equipment: 'His bootes souple, his hors in greet estaat'; now an habitual significant action: 'And evere he rood the hyndereste of our route'; now a significant speech: 'He wolde the see were kept for any thyng / Bitwixe Middleburgh and Orewelle'; now a sharply drawn physical detail: 'His nekke whit was as the flour-de-lys'; now a brief statement of character: 'And al was conscience and tendre herte.' Yet such apparently haphazard details were certainly deliberately planned to produce the effect of spontaneity that creates a sense of intimate acquaintance with each pilgrim. Manly has established the point that Chaucer drew some of the portraits from real persons of his acquaintance; he has put forth a convincing argument in the case of the Host, the Prioress, the Sergeant of the Law, the Franklin, the Reeve, and the Shipman, and he has established a probability for the Knight, the Miller, the Summoner, the Friar, the Pardoner, and the Wife of Bath. He carefully guarded himself from asserting that these characters were mere photographs of individuals, but he opposed the idea that they were artificial compilations, intended to present a schematized picture of mediaeval society. 'From the experiences and observations of his life, his imagination derived the materials for its creative processes.'[7]

Chaucer's characterizations of the pilgrims is carried still further in the continually moving narrative of the links between the tales. The devices by which Chaucer maintains the freshness, variety, and liveliness of this background are natural and entertaining; and most important of all is the role of the Host. He dominates almost every episode along the road to Canterbury. His dignity, his independence, his experience as an innkeeper, his geniality, his tact admirably qualify him for the leadership of a personally conducted tour; and the way in which he meets the various minor and major crises of the journey gives continuous dramatic interest to the links. His sense of social values prompts him to arrange that the Knight shall tell the first tale and call on the Monk to follow; but when the Miller insists on being heard instead, the Host yields the point to avoid a disturbance because he sees that the man is drunk. Yet ordinarily he maintains a firm rein, warns against loss of time, and stops any pilgrim who wanders from the point. He adapts his tone to the person he addresses, is respectful to the Knight and Man of Law, courtly to the Prioress, encouraging to the shy and aloof Clerk, bluff with the Cook. In order to keep the company entertained he jests good-humoredly with the Monk and the Priest, and he ridicules Chaucer in order to dissipate the sober mood created by the Prioress's Tale. Alert to prevent quarrels, he checks the bickering of the Friar and Summoner and reconciles the Manciple and Cook; and when he becomes involved in an angry exchange of abuse with the Pardoner he readily yields to the Knight's intervention as a peacemaker.

The Host does not let the company forget that he is the judge of the tales:

> And wel I woot the substance is in me,
> If any thyng shal wel reported be.

His comments on the tales keep the general scheme in mind, and further reveal his personality. His literary tastes are conservative. He cannot understand the delicate and whimsical irony of Chaucer's parody of the romances in 'Sir Thopas': 'Now swich a rym the devel I beteche!'; and he demands the substitution of a tale, 'in which ther be some murthe or some doctryne.' The Man of

15

Law's Tale, which included both entertainment and instruction, had suited him exactly: 'This was a thrifty tale for the nones!' And he is well pleased with the moral allegory of Chaucer's 'Melibeus' —partly, however, because the peace-loving Dame Prudence offered such a pleasing contrast to his own formidable wife, Goodelief.[8] The Host prefers humorous to tragic stories. The Shipman's and the Nun's Priest's Tales are highly commended; but he strongly supports the Knight's interruption of the Monk's tragedies, agreeing with his preference for stories with a happy ending. Indeed he is so distressed by the Physician's story of Virginia that nothing can restore him but a drink or a ribald tale.

Another dramatic element of the framing narrative is the constant introduction of quarrels and disputes. These are sometimes motivated by occupational jealousy as in the case of the Miller and the Reeve, who are often brought into conflict through their duties in connection with the mediaeval manor, and of the Cook and the Manciple, who are rival caterers. The Friar and Summoner are also natural rivals, in that both are expert in winning money from the laity in various unscrupulous ways. The chief item of dispute that runs through several stages of the journey is the age-old war of the sexes, which perhaps begins with the Host's allusion to his wife's love of domination, is lightly touched on in the Nun's Priest's tale of Pertelote and Chauntecleer, and rises to the importance of a discussion or debate in the Wife of Bath's frank statement of her heretical opinions on matrimony and the different replies that these call forth from the Clerk, the Merchant, and the Franklin.

Still another dramatic artifice employed in the links and prologues is what might be called the confession. Based perhaps on a literary convention which appears in the *Roman de la Rose* and in the Elizabethan soliloquy, the device is here made natural through the confidential mood inspired by the pilgrimage. The Franklin as well as the Host reveal their domestic troubles on one or two occasions; but the outstanding examples of this form of self-revelation are the Wife of Bath's Prologue, the Pardoner's Prologue, and the Canon's Yeoman's Prologue, with the first part of his tale. In each case a strongly individualized personality intimately reveals his or her principles and practice, however contrary to accepted morality; each then enforces these statements of experience by the authority of a tale by way of exemplum; and each evokes a dramatic response from the other pilgrims. The Wife of Bath's account of how she won the mastery of her five husbands, with its accompanying tale of woman's sovereignty, precipitates the different kinds of irony displayed by the Clerk and the Merchant. The Pardoner's cynical confession of avarice, lechery, and gluttony, contrasted with his eloquent sermon against these sins, ends in a scene variously interpreted by the critics but accepted by all as tensely dramatic. In the Canon's Yeoman's Prologue and the preliminary part of his tale, this semi-learned confederate of a shabby alchemist, who has joined the pilgrims in the hope of getting some money to realize his dream of achieving the transmutation of elements, finally sees that his sales talk will never convince the Host or the other pilgrims. He then breaks down and frankly describes in copious detail the constant failure of their experiments and the hopelessness of attaining their end. His tale itself is not about his own master, who seems to have been a deluded enthusiast, but about another alchemist who swindled an unsuspecting priest; at the end, he declares that the secret of alchemy will never be revealed except by the will of God.[9]

To show that the personalities so clearly brought before us in the Prologue and the links are further revealed in the tales would take us beyond the limitations of our subject. It must suffice to note that only two of the tales are definitely known to have been written before the work was undertaken; that all the tales are sufficiently appropriate to their tellers; and that a good many of them—such, for example, as the Miller's and Reeve's, the Prioress's, the Wife of Bath's, the Friar's, the Summoner's, and the Pardoner's —were certainly written with the purpose of more fully illustrating these characters. It may be added that Chaucer's tales even more than Boccaccio's afford illustrations of every important genre in mediaeval literature, including not only fabliau and romance but also saint's legend, sermon, and mediaeval tragedy. (Saint's legend and sermon appear in Boccaccio satirically, not seriously.)

It remains to consider the over-all structure of *The Canterbury*

Tales, with some reference to that of the *Decameron.* Boccaccio's work, we have seen, is admirably organized. On the other hand, Chaucer's *Canterbury Tales* is unfinished; and this fact may not be due only to pressure of business or illness. Chaucer began several works that he left uncompleted, sometimes with no clear indication how he would have worked them out. Kemp Malone says: 'Chaucer was not the man to worry much about loose ends, and he was not always careful to make things neat and tidy.'[10] He adds, however, that 'the easy conversational effect would infallibly be missed if everything was in order.' Perhaps Chaucer was not much concerned because he was leaving his tales without having fitted them all neatly together; nevertheless, it is reasonable to suppose that had he lived he would have imposed on them some consecutive order. In none of the fifty-seven complete or nearly complete manuscripts is there a continuous narrative of the whole journey. Instead, they present a number of connected narratives of certain stages of the journey, in which are incorporated one or more of the tales. In some of these units or fragments there are indications of time and of places passed on the road. In such an unfinished state the work was left by Chaucer at his death in 1400, and the manuscripts that we have show the efforts of various editors and copyists to piece the fragments together.[11] There is an extraordinary variety in the placing of these fragments, but they may be divided roughly into two orders. The first is that of the Ellesmere manuscript and a number of others, and is followed in the edition of Professor F. N. Robinson. This order is perfectly consistent, as far as time references go, with the realities of a journey to Canterbury, which would occupy three or perhaps four days, but it involves one error as to places. The sequence that begins with the Wife of Bath refers to the approach of the pilgrims to a place called Sittingbourne, which is about forty miles from London; and a later fragment, extending from the Shipman's Tale to the Nun's Priest's Tale, says that the company is approaching Rochester, only thirty miles from London. It seems incredible that Chaucer would have allowed this inconsistency to stand had he lived to complete the work.

In another and larger group of manuscripts the place references are even less satisfactory, the marriage-debate sequence beginning with the Wife of Bath is broken into its elements and rearranged in various ways, and, moreover, many of the links between tales are distorted or spurious. Most scholars regard these differences as the work of copyists.[12] However, there is one link, not occurring in the first order of manuscripts, that connects the Man of Law's Tale with that of the Squire. The Host has just called on the Parson to follow the Man of Law with a tale, but is rebuked by the Parson for enforcing his request with an oath. The Host, in annoyance, calls him a Lollard:

> 'I smelle a Loller in the wynd,' quod he.
> 'Now! goode men,' quod oure Hoste, 'herkeneth me;
> Abideth for Goddes digne passion,
> For we shal have a predication;
> This Loller here wol prechen us somwhat.'
> 'Nay, by my fader soule, that shal he nat!'
> Seyde the Squyer; 'Here shal he not preche;
> He shal no gospel glosen here ne teche.
> We leeven alle in the grete God,' quod he;
> 'He wolde sowe som difficulte,
> Or springen cokkel in oure clene corn.
> And therefore, Hoost, I warne the biforn,
> My joly body shall a tale telle,
> And I shal clinken with so mery a belle
> That I shal waken al this companie.
> But it shal be of no philosophie,
> Ne phisylas ne termes queynte of lawe.
> Ther is but litel Latyn in my mawe.' [13]

Now these dramatic lines are certainly Chaucer's, but he cannot have assigned such a rude speech to the exquisitely courteous Squire. They must have been intended for one of the rougher members of the company, and indeed in a few manuscripts they are assigned to the Summoner; but this must also be a scribal mistake, since the Summoner was fond of quoting legal terms in Latin. However, one manuscript, the Selden, of no great authority, it is true, assigns the speech to the Shipman, and it must be admitted that it perfectly fits the character of that bluff, daring seaman; moreover it has been noted acutely that there is no other pilgrim whose name begins with an S, except the sergeant of the Law, who has just finished his tale. The Chaucer Society editors therefore assumed that the Selden scribe had hit on Chaucer's intention. They accordingly attached the Shipman's Tale and its whole sequence to the Man of Law's Tale, thus correcting the place references of the Ellesmere group by bringing in Rochester before Sittingbourne and at the same time giving the tale an appropriate prologue. The resulting order of the tales is that found in the Skeat and Globe editions, and though it is doubtless ba<ed on subjective instead of strict textual criticism it does afford a reasonable view of the plan of *The Canterbury Tales* as Chaucer was gradually working it out on the basis of the preliminary sketch of the General Prologue.

The Chaucer Society editors had less ground for shifting the Physician-Pardoner sequence from a position towards the end of the journey to one immediately preceding the Wife of Bath's Tale. This shift was made in an effoit to fit their theory as to the number of days occupied by the pilgrimage, but there is little evidence to support the change. Chaucer has not really supplied enough time references to indicate whether two or three nights were spent on the road, and he might not have considered this necessary. He did achieve, however, a very effective ending.

In the General Prologue the Host proposes and all agree that each of the twenty-nine pilgrims shall tell two stories on the road to Canterbury and two on the return journey and that he who is judged to have told the best story shall be awarded a supper at the Tabard Inn. Had Chaucer completed the work we may assume that he would have given an account of the stay of the pilgrims at Canterbury as well as of the final supper in Southwark. It may be noted that two of Chaucer's fifteenth-century followers wrote accounts of the Canterbury visit. Lydgate, in the preface to his *Siege of Thebes* in 1420, brought himself into the company, telling how he joined them in Canterbury and related the Theban story as the first tale of the return journey.[14] An unknown monk of Canterbury, in a narrative found in the Northumberland manuscript of *The Canterbury Tales,* gives a detailed account of the devotions of the pilgrims at the shrine, of their sight-seeing in the town, and of certain other farcical adventures of the Pardoner at the inn; and he follows this with the Merchant's Tale of Beryn, as the first tale of the return journey.[15] Chaucer, however, ended his work as the pilgrims approached Canterbury, with his original scheme not half completed. Only one of the company, Chaucer himself, had told two stories; twenty-one others had told one story apiece (one of these unfinished); one story, the Canon's Yeoman's, had not been provided for in the Host's scheme; and seven pilgrims (the Yeoman, the Ploughman, and the five burgesses) had told no stories at all. The last story in all the complete manuscripts is that of the Parson. In calling on him the Host remarks, 'Every man, save thou, hath toold his tale.' The Parson refuses to entertain the company with vain fables, but offers 'a myrie tale in prose,' which is, however, a moral and religious discourse on penitence and the seven deadly sins. The whole company agrees that a sermon will be an appropriate close to the taletelling and the Host bids him proceed. It has been suggested that the Manciple's Tale, which precedes, was really intended by Chaucer for the first of the return journey and the Parson's Tale for the last before the arrival at London. But there is little in the text to support this view, and it has been urged that the solemnity of the Parson's Tale does not suggest that it was to be followed by a convivial supper at the Tabard. A more reasonable view is that Chaucer, finding that he would be unable to complete his original plan, reduced it to one tale for each pilgrim on the way to Canterbury. If illness was the cause of this decision, we can understand why he ended the work on a serious note and appended the famous Retraction, in which he expresses repentance for writing those tales that tend to sin as well as his other works of worldly nature. However this may be, Chaucer has given his work a dignified and effective conclusion, in fine contrast to its light-hearted beginning. The Canterbury pilgrimage becomes symbolic

> Of thilke parfit glorious pilgrymage
> That highte Jerusalem celestial!

NOTES

1. See Pio Rajna, 'L'Episodo delle Questioni d'Amore nel *Filocolo* del Boccaccio,' *Romania*, XXXI (1902), 28–81.

2. Karl Young, *The Origin and Development of the Story of Troilus and Criseyde*, Chaucer Society, Second Series, 40 (London, 1908); J. L. Lowes, ' "The Franklin's Tale," the *Teseide*, and the *Filocolo*,' *Modern Philology*, XV (1918), 689–728; J. S. P. Tatlock, *The Scene of the Franklin's Tale Revisited*, Chaucer Society, Second Series, 51 (London, 1914). See also Pio Rajna, 'Le Origini della novella narrata dal "Frankeleyn" nei *Canterbury Tales* del Chaucer,' *Romania*, XXXII (1903), 204–267.

3. See Pratt and Young, in W. F. Bryan and Germaine Dempster, *Sources and Analogues of Chaucer's Canterbury Tales* (Chicago, 1941), pp. 11–13; Bryan and Dempster, *ibid.*, pp. 339–340; J. S. P. Tatlock, 'Boccaccio and the Plan of Chaucer's *Canterbury Tales*,' *Anglia*, XXXVII (1913), 69–117.

4. See Tatlock, *ibid.*; L. Morsbach, 'Chaucers Plan der *Canterbury Tales* und Boccaccios *Decameron*,' *Englische Studien*, XLII (1910), 43–52; Hubertis M. Cummings, *The Indebtedness of Chaucer's Works to the Italian Works of Boccaccio, University of Cincinnati Studies*, Series 2, 10 (1915–1918), 33–42; other references by Pratt and Young, in Bryan and Dempster, *op. cit.*

5. See J. Burke Severs, in Bryan and Dempster, *op. cit.*

6. See W. E. Farnham, 'England's Discovery of the Decameron,' *PMLA*, XXXIX (1924), 123–129; Pratt and Young, in Bryan and Dempster, *op. cit.*

7. J. M. Manly, *Some New Light on Chaucer* (New York, 1926), p. 263.

8. See Edith Rickert, 'Goode Lief, My Wyf,' *Modern Philology*, XXV (1927), 79–82.

9. See S. Foster Damon, 'Chaucer and Alchemy,' *PMLA*, XXXIX (1924), 782–728.

10. Kemp Malone, 'Style and Structure in the Prologue to the *Canterbury Tales*,' *ELH*, XIII (1946), 43–44.

11. See John M. Manly and Edith Rickert, *The Text of the Canterbury Tales* . . . (Chicago, 1940), II, 474–794, 'The Order of the Tales'; J. S. P. Tatlock, 'The *Canterbury Tales* in 1400,' *PMLA*, L (1935), 100–139.

12. But see Carleton Brown, 'The Evolution of the Canterbury Marriage Group,' *PMLA*, XLVIII (1933), 1041–1059; 'Author's Revision in the *Canterbury Tales*,' *PMLA*, LVII (1942), 29–50.

13. This extract from the Man of Law's end-link is quoted (with modern punctuation) from J. M. Manly's *Canterbury Tales* (New York, 1928), p. 571.

14. See Lydgate's *Siege of Thebes*, ed. Axel Erdmann, Chaucer Society, Second Series, 46 (London, 1911).

15. *The Tale of Beryn, with a Prologue of the Merry Adventure of the Pardoner with a Tapster at Canterbury*, ed. F. J. Furnivall and W. G. Stone, Chaucer Society, Second Series, 17, 24 (London, 1887).

J. R. HULBERT

Chaucer's Pilgrims

IN no other part of his writings was Geoffrey Chaucer more
original than in the series of sketches of the pilgrims in the prologue
to the *Canterbury Tales*. Though the *Sources and Analogues* is
able to provide the source or at least an analogue for every complete tale, it gives no information of any similar series earlier than
Chaucer's time.[1] Clearly the plan was the result of 'inspiration.'
Much has been written, however, on the sources of particular
elements in the prologue. It may be worth while to consider in one
place these and other features which contributed to the success of
Chaucer's design.

Certain features of the plan strike the reader at once and hence
need only be mentioned. The sketches were devised to provide
representatives of the chief classes of English society under the
higher nobility. No one ever supposed it chance that there are
one knight, *one* lawyer, *one* monk, etc. Moreover the sketches not
only give typical traits of temperament, appearance, and manners,
but incorporate the essentials of medicine, law, scholarship, religion, the theory of knighthood, and also satire on faults in social
life; they summarize the noblest ideals of the time and the basest
practices. The result therefore is a conspectus of mediæval English
society; it would be possible to use the prologue as basis for a
survey of fourteenth century English life; indeed that is the effect,
in a somewhat limited way, of the modernization made a hundred

Reprinted, by permission, from *PMLA*, LXIV (1949), 823-8.

years ago by John Saunders and, more fully, by Miss Bowden's recent book.

Furthermore, the development is not discursive. The sketches are models of compression in expression and selection of significant details. Often the expression has an epigrammatic pointedness which reminds modern readers of Pope: 'Nowher so bisy a man as he ther nas, And yet he semed bisier than he was'; sometimes this is combined with an idealism rare in Pope: 'Sownynge in moral vertu was his speche, And gladly wolde he lerne and gladly teche.' In many instances there are exuberant lines which sharpen the effect desired: e.g. of the Squire, 'He was as fresh as is the monthe of May'; of the Monk, 'His eyen stepe, and rollynge in his heed, That stemed as a forneys of a leed'; of the Friar, 'And in his harpyng, whan that he hadde songe, His eyen twinkled in his heed aryght as doon the sterres in the frosty night.'

Aside from these obvious merits, the effectiveness of the sketches is enormously enhanced by the fact that they are not mere assemblages of general traits, composite photographs, types in the Theophrastian sense, but contain many individual details. This has long been recognized. Thus more than forty years ago Professor Root wrote:

It is by their successful blending of the individual with the typical that the portraits of Chaucer's *Prologue* attain so high a degree of effectiveness. The Wife of Bath is typical of certain primary instincts of woman, but she is given local habitation 'bisyde Bathe,' and is still further individualized by her partial deafness and the peculiar setting of her teeth. A wholly different type of womanhood, the conventional as opposed to the natural, is furnished by the Prioress. The description of the gentle lady abounds in minute personal, individual characteristics, physical and moral; yet all these individualizing traits are at the same time suggestive of that type which finds fullest realization in the head of a young lady's school—What is true of these two is true of all the personages of the *Prologue*. The details enumerated nearly always *suggest* at once the individual and the type.[2]

In 1907 and more extensively in 1925 Professor Manly presented specific evidence of the individual elements in the sketches.[3] It had long been recognized that Harry Bailey was an actual innkeeper; but it could be alleged that he is outside the series of pilgrims. In 1933, however, it was proved, as Root had surmised in 1907, that there was a cook of London named Roger of Ware.[4] Manly's data showed a great likelihood that other characterizations include details derived from actual people. The two pilgrims who are named are quasi-public figures—a hotel-keeper and a restaurateur. The others whose connections with actual people Manly pointed out are not. Perhaps Chaucer aimed at a kind of actuality in the former (to give verisimilitude, as in his mention of a real inn and real places en route), but in the latter, though willing that his readers should perceive allusions to actual persons, felt that the effect would be less typical and less artistic if the figures were positively identified.

Naturally in presenting his material Manly emphasized individual traits rather than typical ones, but of course he did not mean to imply that the pilgrims were not presented as types of mediæval society. He understood quite well the significance of what he was pointing out—i.e., that in large part Chaucer's success in these sketches, the difference between his characterizations and those of Overbury and Earle, was due to the fact that, whether by conscious intent or happy inspiration, he combined individual features with typical ones in such a way as to gain vividness and realism, not to be found in type delineations before him. As far as I can see, it may be that Chaucer introduced the references to Baldeswelle, the good ship Maudelayne of Dertemouthe, and the Temple merely to entertain his friends with 'hits' on current scandals. Certainly they must have produced such an effect on Bukton and the others. But no doubt most readers will suppose that he used the references to gain the effect of realism that they produce on us.

Before proceeding further, it would be well to point out that probably we shall never know the full extent of Chaucer's individual references. Mention of particular places, such as Baldeswelle, beside Bathe, the scenes of the Knight's engagements, Dartmouth, certainly are individual details. *Perhaps* the proper names, Hubert, Eglantine, Oswald, Alice, have the same significance. The physical details such as the Miller's wart and black nostrils, the Franklin's forked beard, the Monk's protruding eyes, are derived from specific observation; but can one be sure that Chaucer had seen a *Miller*, who had such a wart and nostrils, and a *Monk* with 'eyen stepe'? Perhaps so; surely he could not have ascribed to Roger of Ware a mormal unless the Cook had one. It may be that in all such cases except the Cook Chaucer used such details for suggestion of character, as Professor Curry has shown to be likely in the case of the Miller.[5] At any rate there is bound to be uncertainty as to the significance of this type of descriptive detail.

Yet more difficult to interpret is a third form of descriptive matter. Had Chaucer encountered a Pardoner who was a *eunuchus ex natura*, a Summoner who suffered from alopicia or salt phlegm? If he had, no doubt he expected some of his readers to recognize those pilgrims as actual persons. But it is quite possible that in characterizing two types whom he wished to seem disgusting, he aimed to strengthen the effect by ascribing to one an unpleasant disease and to the other an unhappy physical constitution. On readers after Chaucer's day, the impression produced is certainly as if he had worked in the way just mentioned. But we can never be sure that even when he is writing most typically he had not individuals in mind, and was not expecting his contemporary readers to recognize them. For example, though the Squire seems merely a type, there may have been one young dandy whom all the details fitted so perfectly that he would have come instantly to the mind of any person familiar with the gentry about the royal court.

Concerning two of the sketches it seems desirable to add further comment. After referring to Manly's and Cook's articles on the historical background of the Knight, Professor Robinson remarks: 'It is not likely that any single historical figure is represented by Chaucer's Knight. But the career which is sketched is typical, and the events referred to might have been witnessed by a contemporary of the poet.'[6] Of course Professor Robinson has a right to express the opinion that the Knight is not based on an actual person; but his last clause is in no way a justification for the opinion. If it were not possible for a contemporary to have fought in those campaigns, the poet would have been guilty of an elementary fault. Consideration of the list shows that the Knight had fought only in religious wars. If the list is meant to be merely typical, it is extraordinary that it does not include Creçy, Poitiers, or any campaigning in France or Spain. Evidently it is possible to interpret the facts in different ways; Robinson regards them as typical; Manly wrote: 'As the portrait is far from being merely typical, it may well be that of some real knight, or, more probably, a composite picture based upon the adventures of more than one knight.' To my way of thinking it is most reasonable to suppose that it is based on the career of a single knight known to Chaucer; it has a perfect consistency not likely to be found in a composite; why, if it was a composite, introduce the specific detail of fighting with the lord of Palatye against another heathen in Turkey? It is not surprising that no one has been able to identify the Knight; the Scrope-Grosvenor Roll, which is our chief source of information on the careers of individual knights, surely does not include the full career of *every* late fourteenth century English knight. The gentle reader should recognize that Robinson and Manly are greater authorities; I merely state my opinion.

Since Manly published no evidence of individual traits in the characterization of the Monk, it may be pertinent to comment on that sketch as an instance of the problems still unsolved. Miss Bressie was quite right, I think, in believing that Chaucer had in mind an actual person; but the identification she proposed was far from convincing. When one considers that the Monk is a man of wealth (the references to the cost of his hunting and his expensive dress), keeper of a cell, lover of hare-hunting, and likely to become an abbot, one recognizes elements which are not generally typical. They mean either that Chaucer had in mind an actual person or perhaps that in order to indicate his impression of the wealth and worldliness of monks he elected to include special details which, though not very rare, were decidedly not typical.

Finally, the success of the sketches and especially their readability are due in considerable part to the variety in method and attitude in the different characterizations. The realization of this fact was brought home to me long ago by my constant contact with the text in the course of teaching. More recently it has been pointed out by Mr. G. H. Cowling, but it can bear more development than he gives it. He writes:

> The portraits of the pilgrims are not all drawn in the same way. It is true that Chaucer endeavored to picture individuals with an outstanding peculiarity—a physical trait like the Miller's wart, a humour like the Franklin's love of rich dishes, or a passion like the Knight's love of prowess and troth; but the portraits differ in kind, as well as degree. Some of the portraits are idealized . . . other portraits are so realistic that they must have been drawn from life.[7]

A sketch may be entirely general; e.g., as far as I can see the accounts of the Yeoman, Physician, and Burgesses are quite in the Theophrastian manner. It may join realistic details to typical statements—e.g. the Man of Law, Franklin, Merchant, Cook and Shipman—or specific details to idealism; thus the sketch of the Knight expresses the finest concepts of chivalry but joins to them the list of campaigns and the detail that he was not 'gay.' It may be purely ideal, the aim to express in the highest degree the qualities desirable in a certain rank of life, e.g. the Clerk, the Plowman, the Parson. It may represent an entirely individual character, who at most is typical of a general class of human beings—the Wife of Bath. It may join satire to typical statements and possibly individual traits, e.g. the kindly satire of the Squire and Prioress, the slightly more serious satire of the Monk, the sharper satire of the rogues, especially the Summoner, Pardoner and Friar. Any sketch may be lightened by humor, e.g. the Squire, the Prioress, the Manciple, the Man of Law; or it may be made more serious by suggestion of moral disapproval as in the cases of the Friar, the Summoner, and the Pardoner.

Perhaps the reader may disagree with one or another of the analyses implied in the preceding paragraph. Complete agreement among all readers is not to be expected or perhaps desired. But the fact of variety in elements and method is hardly to be challenged. Chaucer's success in the characterizations is due to many factors—the range of classes which his pilgrims represent, the compression resulting from a high degree of selection of details and pithiness of utterance, the use of individual details together with typical statements, and the varying ways in which he combined the elements in the different descriptions.

NOTES

1. (Chicago, 1941), esp. pp. 4–5. Cf. also Lowes' illuminating comments in his *Geoffrey Chaucer* (Boston, 1934), pp. 198 ff., and the admirable discussion in F. N. Robinson's *Complete Works of Chaucer* (Boston, 1933), pp. 2 ff.
2. *The Poetry of Chaucer* (Boston, 1906), p. 161.
3. *Transactions American Philological Assn.* (1907), pp. 89 ff.; *Some New Light on Chaucer* (New York, 1925).
4. See Miss Rickert's note in the *London Times Literary Supplement,* 1932, p. 761.
5. *Chaucer and the Mediæval Sciences* (New York, 1926), pp. 79 ff.
6. *Op. cit.,* p. 753.
7. *Chaucer* (London, 1927), p. 152.

ARTHUR W. HOFFMAN

Chaucer's Prologue to Pilgrimage:
The Two Voices

CRITICISM of the portraits in Chaucer's General Prologue to *The Canterbury Tales* has taken various directions: some critics have praised the portraits especially for their realism, sharp individuality, adroit psychology, and vividness of felt life; others, working in the genetic direction, have pointed out actual historical persons who might have sat for the portraits; others, appealing to the light of the medieval sciences, have shown the portraits to be filled, though not burdened, with the lore of Chaucer's day, and to have sometimes typical identities like case histories. Miss Bowden,[1] in her recent study of the Prologue, assembles the fruits of many earlier studies and gives the text an impressive resonance by sketching historical and social norms and ideals, the facts and the standards of craft, trade, and profession, so that the form of the portraits can be tested in the light of possible conformities, mean or noble, to things as they were or to things as they ought to have been.

It is not unlikely that the critics who have explored in these various directions would be found in agreement on one commonplace, a metaphor which some of them indeed have used, the designation of the portraits in the General Prologue as figures in a tapestry. It is less likely that all of the critics would agree as to

Reprinted, by permission, from *ELH, A Journal of English Literary History*, XXI (1954), 1–16.

the implications of this metaphor, but it seems to me that the commonplace deserves to be explored and some of its implications tested. The commonplace implies that the portraits which appear in the General Prologue have a designed togetherness, that the portraits exist as parts of a unity.

Such a unity, it may be argued, is partly a function of the exterior framework of a pilgrimage to Canterbury; all the portraits are portraits of pilgrims:

> At nyght was come into that hostelrye
> Wel nyne and twenty in a compaignye,
> Of sondry folk, by aventure yfalle
> In felaweshipe, and pilgrimes were they alle,

But the unity of the Prologue may be also partly a matter of internal relationships among the portraits, relationships which are many and various among 'sondry folk.' One cannot hope to survey all of these, but the modest objective of studying some of the aesthetically important internal relationships is feasible.

If one begins with the unity that is exterior to the portraits, the unity that contains them, one faces directly the question of the nature of pilgrimage as it is defined in this dramatic poem. What sort of framework does the Prologue in fact define? Part of the answer is in the opening lines, and it is not a simple answer because the definition there ranges from the upthrust and burgeoning of life as a seasonal and universal event to a particular outpouring of people, pilgrims, gathered briefly at the Tabard Inn in Southwark, drifting, impelled, bound, called to the shrine of Thomas a Becket at Canterbury. The pilgrimage is set down in the calendar of seasons as well as in the calendar of piety; nature impels and supernature draws. 'Go, go, go,' says the bird; 'Come,' says the saint.

In the opening lines of the Prologue springtime is characterized in terms of procreation, and a pilgrimage of people to Canterbury is just one of the many manifestations of the life thereby produced. The phallicism of the opening lines presents the impregnating of a female March by a male April, and a marriage of water and

earth. The marriage is repeated and varied immediately as a fructi-
fying of 'holt and heeth' by Zephirus, a marriage of air and earth.
This mode of symbolism and these symbols as parts of a rite of
spring have a long background of tradition; as Professor Cook[2]
once pointed out, there are eminent passages of this sort in Aeschy-
lus and Euripides, in Lucretius, in Virgil's *Georgics,* in Columella,
and in the *Pervigilium Veneris,* and Professor Robinson cites
Guido delle Colonne, Boccaccio, Petrarch, and Boethius. Zephirus
is the only overt mythological figure in Chaucer's passage, but,
in view of the instigative role generally assigned to Aphrodite in
the rite of spring, she is perhaps to be recognized here, as Professor
Cook suggested, in the name of April, which was her month both
by traditional association and by one of the two ancient etymolo-
gies.[3] Out of this context of the quickening of the earth presented
naturally and symbolically in the broadest terms, the Prologue
comes to pilgrimage and treats pilgrimage first as an event in the
calendar of nature, one aspect of the general springtime surge of
human energy and longing. There are the attendant suggestions of
the renewal of human mobility after the rigor and confinement of
winter, the revival of wayfaring now that the ways are open. The
horizon extends to distant shrines and foreign lands, and the attraction of the strange and faraway is included before the vision
narrows and focusses upon its English specifications and the pilgrimage to the shrine at Canterbury with the vows and gratitude
that send pilgrims there. One way of regarding the structure of this
opening passage would emphasize the magnificent progression
from the broadest inclusive generality to the firmest English specifi-
cation, from the whole western tradition of the celebration of spring
(including, as Cook pointed out, such a non-English or very doubt-
fully English detail as 'the droghte of March') to a local event of
English society and English Christendom, from natural forces in
their most general operation to a very specific and Christian manifestation of those forces. And yet one may regard the structure in
another way, too; if, in the calendar of nature, the passage moves
from general to particular, does it not, in the calendar of piety,
move from nature to something that includes and oversees nature?
Does not the passage move from an activity naturally generated

and impelled to a governed activity, from force to *telos*? Does not the passage move from Aphrodite and *amor* in their secular operation to the sacred embrace of 'the hooly blisful martir' and of *amor dei*?

The transition from nature to supernature is emphasized by the contrast between the healthful physical vigor of the opening lines and the reference to sickness that appears in line 18. On the one hand, it is physical vitality which conditions the pilgrimage; on the other hand, sickness occasions pilgrimage. It is, in fact, rather startling to come upon the word 'seeke' at the end of this opening passage, because it is like a breath of winter across the landscape of spring. 'Whan that they were seeke' may, of course, refer literally to illnesses of the winter just past, but, in any event, illness belongs symbolically to the inclement season. There is also, however, a strong parallelism between the beginning and end of this passage, a parallelism that has to do with restorative power. The physical vitality of the opening is presented as restorative of the dry earth; the power of the saint is presented as restorative of the sick. The seasonal restoration of nature parallels a supernatural kind of restoration that knows no season; the supernatural kind of restoration involves a wielding and directing of the forces of nature. The Prologue begins, then, by presenting a double view of the Canterbury pilgrimage: the pilgrimage is one tiny manifestation of a huge tide of life, but then, too, the tide of life ebbs and flows in response to the power which the pilgrimage acknowledges, the power symbolized by 'the hooly blisful martir.'

After line 18 the process of particularizing is continued, moving from 'that seson' just defined to a day and to a place and to a person in Southwark at the Tabard, and thence to the portraits of the pilgrims. The double view of pilgrimage is enhanced and extended by the portraits where it appears, in one aspect, as a range of motivation. This range of motivation is from the sacred to the secular and on to the profane—'profane' in the sense of motivations actually subversive of the sacred. All the pilgrims are, in fact, granted an ostensible sacred motive; all of them are seeking the shrine. The distances that we are made aware of are both *within* some of the portraits, where a gulf yawns between ostensible and actual motivation, and *between* the portraits, where the motivation of the Knight and the Parson is near one end of the spectrum, and the motivation of the Summoner and the Pardoner near the other end. There is such an impure but blameless mixture as the motivation of the Prioress; there is the secular pilgrimage of the Wife of Bath, impelled so powerfully and frankly by Saint Venus rather than drawn by Saint Thomas, and goaded by a Martian desire to acquire and dominate another husband; in the case of the Prioress, an inescapable doubt as to the quality of *amor* hesitates between the sacred and secular, and in the case of the thoroughly secular Wife of Bath, doubt hesitates between the secular and the profane while the portrait shows the ostensible motive that belongs to all the pilgrims shaken without ever being subverted, contradicted perhaps, brazenly opposed, but still acknowledged and offered, not, at any rate, hypocritically betrayed. In the area of motivation, the portraits seem to propose, ultimately, a fundamental, inescapable ambiguity as part of the human condition; prayer for the purification of motive is valid for all the pilgrims. And the pilgrims who move, pushed by impulse and drawn by vows, none merely impelled and none perfectly committed, reflect, in their human ambiguity, the broad problem of origins and ends, the stubbornness of matter and the power of spirit, together with ideas of cosmic resolution and harmony in which source and end are reconciled and seen to be the same, the purposes of nature and supernature found to be at one, the two restorative powers akin, the kinds of love not discontinuous, Saint Venus and Saint Thomas different and at odds yet not at war, within the divine purpose which contains both.

The portraits of the Knight and the Squire have a particular interest. The relationships between these two portraits are governed by and arise out of the natural relationship of father and son. Consanguinity provides the base for a dramatic relationship, and at the same time is the groundwork for a modestly generalized metaphor of age and youth. Each portrait is enhanced and defined by the presence of the other: the long roll of the Knight's campaigns, and the Squire's little opportunity ('so litel space'), a few raids enumerated in one line; a series of past tenses, a history, for the Knight, and for the Squire a present breaking forth in active participles; the Knight not 'gay,' wearing fustian soiled by his coat of mail, 'bismotered,' the Squire bright and fresh and colorful; the Knight meek and quiet,—or so the portrait leaves him—beside the Squire, who sings and whistles all the day. The Knight's love is an achieved devotion, a matter of pledges fulfilled and of values, if not completely realized, yet woven into the fabric of experience (ideals—'trouthe,' 'honour,' 'fredom,' 'curteisie'). The Squire is a lover, a warm and eager lover, paying court to his lady and sleeping no more than the nightingale. In the one, the acquired, tutored, disciplined, elevated, enlarged love, the piety; and in the other, the love channelled into an elaborate social ritual, a parody piety, but still emphatically fresh and full of natural impulse. One cannot miss the creation of the Squire in conventional images of nature, the meadow, the flowers, the freshness like May, the lover like the nightingale,—comparisons that are a kind of re-emergence of the opening lines of the Prologue, the springtime surge of youthful, natural energy that animates the beginning. 'Go, go, go,' the bird's voice, is a major impulse in the portrait of the Squire and in the Squire's pilgrimage; the Knight's pilgrimage is more nearly a response to the voice of the saint. Yet the Squire is within the belt of rule, and learning the calendar of piety. The concluding couplet of the portrait

> Curteis he was, lowely and servysable,
> And carf biforn his fader at the table.

has the effect of bending all the youth, energy, color, audibleness, and high spirit of the Squire to the service of his father, the Knight, and to attendance on his pilgrimage, with perhaps a suggestion of the present submitting to the serious and respected values served and communicated by the past, the natural and the imposed submitting of the son to his natural father, and beyond him to the supernatural goal, the shrine to which the father directs his pilgrimage.

The portraits of the Knight and the Squire represent one of the ways in which portraiture takes into account and develops the double definition of pilgrimage which is established at the beginning. The double definition of pilgrimage is involved in a different way in the portrait of the Prioress; there it appears as a delicately poised ambiguity. Two definitions appear as two faces of one coin. Subsequently, when the portrait of the Prioress is seen together with the portraits of the Monk and the Friar, a sequence is realized, running from ambiguity to emphatic discrepancy, and the satire that circles the impenetrable duality of sacred and secular impulse in the case of the Prioress, knifes in as these impulses are drawn apart in the case of the Monk and strikes vigorously in the still wider breach that appears in the case of the Friar. What is illustrated within the portraits is amplified by a designed sequence.

The delicate balance in the picture of the Prioress has been generally recognized and has perhaps been only the more clearly exhibited by occasional seesawing in the critical interpretation of the portrait in which the satiric elements are sometimes represented as heavy, sometimes as slight, sometimes sinking the board, and sometimes riding light and high. There is, perhaps, no better illustration of the delicacy of the balance than the fact that the Prioress's very presence on a pilgrimage, as several commentators have pointed out, may be regarded as the first satiric touch. The very act of piety is not free from the implication of imperfection; the Prioress is obligated to a cloistered piety that serves and worships God without going on a journey to seek a shrine, and prioresses were specifically and repeatedly enjoined from going on pilgrimages. Prioresses did, nevertheless, go as pilgrims, so that Chaucer's Prioress is not departing from the norm of behavior of persons in her office so much as she is departing from the sanctioned ideal of behavior. In the case of the Prioress, the blemish is sufficiently technical to have only faint satiric coloring; it is not the notable kind of blemish recognized in all times and all places. Nevertheless, it is precisely this kind of hint of a spot that places the Prioress at one end of a sequence in which the more obviously blemished Monk and Friar appear. If we pose a double question— What kind of woman is the Prioress, and what kind of prioress is the woman?—the portrait responds more immediately to the first part of the question, and leaves the answer to the second part

36

largely in the area of implication. The portrait occupies forty-five lines, and more than three-fourths of the lines have to do with such matters as the Prioress's blue eyes, her red mouth, the shape of her nose and width of her forehead, her ornaments and dress, her table manners, her particular brand of French, her pets and what she fed them, and her tenderness about mice. It is, of course, one of the skilful arts of these portraits to work with surfaces and make the surfaces convey and reveal what lies beneath, but it should be observed that in the case of the Parson—or even in the case of the Knight—a character is arrived at almost entirely without physical and superficial detail. One need not take the emphatic surface in the portrait of the Prioress as necessarily pejorative in its implication; it need not follow that the Prioress is a shallow and superficial person, and, in consequence, sharply satirized. But the portrait does seem, by means of its emphasis on surfaces, to define the Prioress as woman, and strongly enough so that tension between the person and her office, between the given human nature and the assumed sacred obligation is put vividly before us, and rather as the observation of a fact than as the instigation of a judgment. In the cases of the Monk and the Friar, the tension is so exacerbated that judgment is, in the case of the Monk, incited, and in the case of the Friar, both incited and inflamed to severity.

In the portrait of the Prioress the double view of pilgrimage appears both in an ambiguity of surfaces, and in an implied inner range of motivation. In the surfaces there is a sustained hovering effect: the name, Eglentyne, is romance, and 'simple and coy' is a romance formula, but she *is* a nun, by whatever name, and 'simple' and 'coy,' aside from their romance connotations, have meanings ('simple' and 'modest') appropriate enough to a nun; there are the coral beads and the green gauds, but they *are* a rosary; there are the fluted wimple and the exposed forehead, but the costume *is* a nun's habit; there is the golden brooch shining brightly, but it *is* a religious emblem. Which shall be taken as principal, which as modifying and subordinate? Are the departures or the conformities more significant of her nature? Are her Stratford French and her imitation of court manners more important than the fact that she sings well and properly the divine service? Do we detect vanity in her singing well, or do we rely on what she sings and accept her worship as well performed—to the glory of God? The ambiguity of these surface indications leads into the implied range of motivation; this implied range has been generally recognized in the motto—'*Amor vincit omnia*'—on the Prioress's golden brooch, and the implications set up in the portrait as a whole seem to be clustered and tightly fastened in this ornament and symbol.

The motto itself has, in the course of history, gone its own double pilgrimage to the shrine of Saint Venus and to sacred shrines; the original province of the motto was profane, but it was drawn over to a sacred meaning and soon became complexly involved with and compactly significant of both. Professor Lowes comments on the motto as it pertains to the Prioress:

> Now is it earthly love that conquers all, now heavenly; the phrase plays back and forth between the two. And it is precisely that happy ambiguity of the convention—itself the result of an earlier transfer—that makes Chaucer's use of it here . . . a master stroke. *Which of the two loves does 'amor' mean to the Prioress?* I do not know; but I think she thought she meant love celestial.[4]

Professor Lowes, presumably, does not really expect to see the matter concluded one way or the other and finds this very inconclusiveness, hovering between two answers, one of the excellences of the portrait. There is, however, a certain amount of illumination to be gained, though not an answer to the question as formulated by Professor Lowes, by asking the question another way and considering an answer in terms that lie outside of the Prioress's motivation. Put the question in this form: Which of the two loves does the *portrait* in the context of the Prologue mean by *amor*? The answer to this question, of course, is *both*. On the one hand, profane love or the love of earthly things does overcome all; the little vanities and pretensions, the love of color and decoration and dress, the affection squandered in little extravagances toward pets, the pity and tender emotion wasted upon a trapped mouse—the multiplicity of secular, impulsive loves threatens to and could ultimately stifle the dedication to the celestial love. This answer is, in fact, a version of the Prioress's character and motivation some-times offered. It actually implies one half of the view of pilgrimage —the natural powers that move people and that may usurp the whole character. But the other answer—celestial love conquers all things—also applies to the portrait, though it is not very easily arrived at in terms of the Prioress's motivation. Here we are deal-ing with the ostensible meaning of the motto, the ideal meaning of the motto as worn by a prioress—what it ought to mean in terms of her office. And, no matter what the impurity of the Prioress's motives, no matter what she means or thinks she means by the motto, the motto does, in the calendar of piety, mean that God's love is powerful over all things, powerful in this case over the vanity that may be involved in the wearing of the brooch, powerful over all the shallowness and limitation and reduction and mis-direction of love that the Prioress may be guilty of, powerful over all her departures from or misunderstandings of discipline and obligation and vow, powerful over all inadequacy, able to over-come the faults of God's human instruments and make this woman's divine office valid. The motto, and the portrait of which it is the conclusion, appreciate both the secular impulses and the sacred redemptive will, but there is no doubt which love it is that is crowned with ultimate power.

Chaucer has found ways, as in the case of the Prioress, of making an ideal or standard emerge within a portrait. The standard may be ambiguously stated or heavily involved in irony, but it is almost always present, and nowhere with greater effectiveness than in the most sharply satiric portraits. This, I take it, is the effect of the formula of worthiness which is applied to so many of the pilgrims. A character is declared to be 'worthy' or 'the best that ever was' of his craft or profession or office, and frequently under circumstances that make the statement jarring and the discrepancy obvious. There is a definite shock, for example, when Friar Hubard is de-clared to be a 'worthy lymytour,' or the Pardoner 'a noble ec-clesiaste.' Even when the satiric thrust has two directions, striking both at the individual and at the group to which he belongs, the implication has nevertheless been lodged in the portrait that there could be, for example, a worthy friar, or a pardoner who was indeed a noble ecclesiastic. The reader is, as it were, tripped in the act of judging and reminded that if he condemns these figures, if they appear culpable, there must be some sort of standard by which they are so judged, by which they appear so.

Chaucer has also adopted the method of including ideal or nearly ideal portraits among the pilgrims. There are, for example, the Knight and the Plowman, figures at either end of the secular range, and among the clerical figures there is the Parson. A host of relative judgments, of course, are set up by devices of sequence and obvious pairing and contrasting of portraits. It is the ideal portraits, however, that somehow preside over all these judgments and comparisons, and it is to them that the relative distinctions are presented for a kind of penultimate judgment. Prioress, Monk, and Friar, and all the other clerical figures are reckoned with the Parson who is, in fact, made to speak in an accent of judgment upon the clerical figures who go astray—'. . . if gold ruste, what shal iren do?' (We may remember the Prioress's shining gold brooch, the Monk's gold pin, and, among the secular figures, the Physician who so doubly regarded gold as a sovereign remedy.)

Chaucer has used an interesting device for undergirding the ideal portrait of the Parson. He employs consanguinity with metaphorical effect. After the assertions which declare that the Parson 'first . . . wroghte, and afterward . . . taughte,' the actualizing of Christian ideals is supported by the representation of the Parson as brother to the Plowman. It is the Parson's Christian obligation to treat men as brothers, and the portrait abundantly affirms that he does so. Making him actually the brother of the Plowman brilliantly insists that what supernature calls for is performed by the Parson and, more than that, comes by nature to him. The achieved harmony both comes from above and rises out of the ground; sacred and secular are linked, the shepherd of souls and the tiller of the soil. This is a vantage point from which the conflicts of secular and sacred, of nature and supernature, are seen in a revealing light, a point at which one sees reflected in the clear mirror of ideal characters and an actual-ideal relationship the fundamental double view of pilgrimage established in the beginning.

The double definition of pilgrimage is differently but nonetheless revealingly illuminated by the portraits of another fraternizing pair, the Summoner and Pardoner, who conclude the sequence of pilgrims. The illumination here is not clarified by way of ideal characters but somehow refracted and intensified by the dark surfaces upon which it falls. The darkness is most visible in connection with the theme of love, which appears here in a sinister and terrible distortion. The hot and lecherous Summoner, the type of sexual unrestraint, is represented as harmonizing in song with the impotent Pardoner, the eunuch; the deep rumbling voice and the thin effeminate voice are singing, 'Com hider, love, to me!' The song, in this context, becomes both a promiscuous and perverted invitation and an unconscious symbolic acknowledgment of the absence of and the need for love, love that comes neither to the grasping physical endeavor of the Summoner nor to the physical incapacity of the Pardoner—nor to their perverted spirits. Love has been treated in the Prologue from the beginning as dual in character, a matter both of the body and the spirit, the *amor* symbolized by Venus, sung by the Squire, equivocally illustrated by the Prioress, lustily celebrated by the Wife of Bath; and the *amor dei,* the love shadowily there beyond all the secular forms of love, a hovering presence among the pilgrims and sometimes close, as to the Knight and the Parson and the Plowman, and symbolized in the saint's shrine which is the goal of all of them. On this view, the song of the Summoner and the Pardoner is a superb dramatic irony acknowledging the full extent of their need and loss, the love of God which they ought to strive for, the love which they desperately need.

The office which each of these men is supposed to fulfill should be taken into account. The Summoner is, ostensibly, an instrument through whom divine justice, in a practical way, operates in the world. There are, in the portrait, a few touches that may be reminders of the ultimate source of his authority and function: his '*Questio quid iuris,*' though it is represented satirically as the sum and substance of his knowledge, and posed as a question, *is* legitimately the substance of his knowledge—his province, is law, especially the divine law; '*Significavit*' is the opening word of a legal writ, a dreaded worldly pronouncement of divine judgment, excommunication; he is physically a fearful figure from whom children run (not the divine love which suffers them to come), and some of the physical details may be reminders of noble and awesome aspects of divine justice—his 'fyr-reed cherubynnes face' and the voice described in a significant analogy as like a trumpet, 'Was nevere trompe of half so greet a soun.' The Pardoner, on the other hand, is the ostensible instrument of divine mercy and love. Many of the pardoners, as Miss Bowden points out, went so far as to pretend to absolve both *a poena* and *a culpa,* thereby usurping, in the pretended absolution *a culpa,* a function which theological doctrine reserved to God and His grace. In any case, their legitimate functions were an appeal for charity and an extension of God's mercy and love. The Pardoner, it should be observed, is, compared to the Summoner, an attractive figure. We may be reminded of the superior affinity of the Pardoner's office by the veil which he has sewed upon his cap, the copy of St. Veronica's veil which is supposed to have received the imprint of Christ's face.

The , istice and love of which the Summoner and Pardoner are emissaries are properly complementary and harmoniously, though paradoxically and mysteriously, related, so that the advances that are being made both of persons and of values are, in a very serious sense, proper to this pair. The radical physical distinctness of Summoner and Pardoner is at this level the definition of two aspects of supernature; there is the same employment of physical metaphor here that there is in the portraits of the Parson and the Plowman, but with the difference that light comes out of darkness, and out of the gravest corruption of nature the supernatural relationship emerges clarified in symbol. The Summoner cannot finally pervert, and the Pardoner's impotence cannot finally prevent; the divine justice and love are powerful even over these debased instruments—*Amor vincit omnia.* Beyond their knowing, beyond their power or impotence, impotently both Pardoner and Summoner appeal for the natural love—melody of bird-song and meadows of flowers—and both pray for the celestial love, the ultimate pardon which in their desperate and imprisoned darkness is their only hope: 'Com hider, love, to me!'

The exterior unity achieved by the realistic device and broadly symbolic framework of pilgrimage is made stronger and tighter in the portraits, partly by local sequences and pairings, but most impressively by the illustration, the variation and enrichment by way of human instances, of a theme of love, earthly and celestial, and a general complex intermingling of the consideration of nature with the consideration of supernature. The note of love is sounded in different keys all through the portraits:

The Knight

> . . . he loved chivalrie,
> Trouthe and honour, fredom and curteisie

The Squire

> A lovyere and a lusty bacheler . . .
> So hoote he lovede that by nyghtertale
> He sleep namoore than dooth a nyghtyngale.

The Prioress

> . . . Amor vincit omnia.

The Monk

> A Monk . . . that lovede venerie, . . .
> He hadde of gold ywroght a ful curious pyn;
> A love-knotte in the gretter ende ther was.

> A fat swan loved he best of any roost.

The Friar

> In love-dayes ther koude he muchel help . . .

> Somewhat he lipsed, for his wantownesse, . . .

The Clerk

> For hym was levere have at his beddes heed
> Twenty bookes, clad in blak or reed,
> Of Aristotle and his philosophie,
> Than robes riche, or fithele, or gay sautrie.

The Frankelyn

> Wel loved he by the morwe a sop in wyn;
> To lyven in delit was evere his wone,
> For he was Epicurus owene sone . . .

The Physician

> He kepte that he wan in pestilence.
> For gold in phisik is a cordial,
> Therefore he lovede gold in special.

The Wife of
Bath

> Of remedies of love she knew per chaunce,
> For she koude of that art the olde daunce.

The Parson

> But rather wolde he yeven, out of doute,
> Unto his povre parisshens aboute
> Of his offryng and eek of his substaunce.

> . . . Cristes loore and his apostles twelve
> He taughte, but first he folwed it hymselve.

The Plowman

> With hym ther was a Plowman, was his brother, . . .

> Lyvynge in pees and parfit charitee.
> God loved he best with al his hoole herte
> At alle tymes, thogh him gamed or smerte,
> And thanne his neighebor right as hymselve.

The Summoner
and
the Pardoner

> . . . 'Com hider, love, to me!'

The theme of restorative power attends upon the theme of love. It is, of course, announced at the beginning and defined in terms both of nature and supernature. Both the Physician, concerned with natural healing, and the Pardoner, the agent of a supernatural healing, appear under the rubric of 'Physician, heal thyself.' The worldly Physician is disaffected from God; the Pardoner is naturally impotent. Serious inadequacy in either realm appears as counterpart of inadequacy in the other. It is the Parson who both visits the sick and tends properly to the cure of souls; he works harmoniously in both realms, and both realms are in harmony and fulfilled in him.

44

The pilgrims are represented as affected by a variety of destructive and restorative kinds of love. Their characters and movement can be fully described only as mixtures of the loves that drive and goad and of the love that calls and summons. The pilgrims have, while they stay and when they move, their worldly host. They have, too, their worldly Summoner and Pardoner who, in the very worst way, move and are moved with them. Nevertheless, the Summoner and Pardoner, who conclude the roll of the company, despite and beyond their appalling personal deficiency, may suggest the summoning and pardoning, the judgment and grace which in Christian thought embrace and conclude man's pilgrimage and which therefore, with all the corrosions of satire and irony, are also the seriously appropriate conclusion to the tapestry of Chaucer's pilgrims.

NOTES

1. Muriel Bowden, *A Commentary on the General Prologue to the Canterbury Tales* (New York, 1948).

2. Albert S. Cook, 'Chaucerian Papers—I: I. Prologue 1–11,' *Transactions of the Connecticut Academy of Arts and Sciences,* XXIII (New Haven, 1919), 5–21.

3. Cook, 5–10.

4. John Livingston Lowes, *Convention and Revolt in Poetry* (Boston, 1919), p. 66.

JOHN MATTHEWS MANLY

A Knight Ther Was

No picture in all the wonderful gallery of portraits through which one passes to reach the Canterbury Tales has awakened more interest or fastened itself more firmly in the minds of men than that figure of the 'verray, parfit, gentil knight' which stands just at the entrance to the gallery. His picturesque career, his devotion to the knightly ideals of 'trouthe and honour, fredom and curteisye,' his simplicity and gentleness, his unfailing tenderness of the feelings of others—'he never yet no vileynye ne sayde in al his lif unto no maner wight,'—his eager haste to perform the pilgrimage he had vowed, which caused him on that unforgettable April morning to join Geoffrey Chaucer and his chance acquaintances, despite his stained gipoun,—all these things live in our memories as the features of one whom we have seen and known. It is not my purpose to erase or alter a single line in this well-known portrait. I have not asked you to listen to me because I have discovered some scandal in the life of the 'gentil knight'—some dark secret which after five hundred years has come to light to make us pity his trustful friends and that guileless poet who chanced to meet and love him on the road to Canterbury. If one knew such a secret, one would hesitate long before admitting the claims of historic truth. But I do not. My task, if not so simple, is at least more agreeable. It seems to me that this portrait—like all the others in this and other

Reprinted, by permission, from *Transactions and Proceedings of the American Philological Association*, xxxviii (1907), 89–107.

ancient galleries—has faded a little, that time has taken away the richness of coloring which was such a wonder and delight to the contemporaries of the artist and left us only line and hints of light and shade. I do not wish to retouch the portrait, to spoil it with crude bright modern colors, but, if possible, to apply to it a 'reviver' made of extracts from certain old documents and restore a part, at least, of the color and tone of the original.

When Chaucer painted this portrait, the figure which served him as model and the ideals which it embodied were already doomed. Gunpowder and cannon had come to take away the occupation and the prestige of the knight, and almost exactly at the same time Genoa and Venice had given the first great demonstration that 'business is business' and that the ideals of chivalry must give way to the ideals of commerce. The doom was, of course, as yet unrecognized. The triumphs of cannon and of commerce seemed only the miserable petty triumphs of the vulgar, the common, the undignified. But the uncanny magic of fate was over the whole doomed system of chivalry, and, as always happens to a doomed system, the flame of devotion flared wider and higher and burned for a moment with unwonted intensity and purity. Knighthood was no longer a mere feudal obligation, it had become an ever-alluring ideal; men fought not because they must, but because they might; and the conditions of the time gave to the ideal all the inspiration of religious fervor and all the enticements of contact with the unknown, the mysterious, the unsearchable.

The battles in which the knight had been engaged were all battles against the infidels. That they had the sanction of the Church was, no doubt, by no means a minor consideration in the fourteenth century, but the prime element in their fascination for Chaucer's audience was undoubtedly that they were all fought, as we may say, on the very confines of the civilized world. The small group of nations who in the west of Europe represented Christian civilization and who, despite their jealousies and quarrels, knew and understood one another so well, were shut in on the west by an apparently infinite ocean which constantly stimulated the imagination to tales of fairy lands beyond or beneath it where women were beautiful and loving and faithful and mortal men became immortal; and on the south and east and northeast were peoples scarcely less romantic and mysterious than the fairy peoples of the 'land of the undying.' On the south and east were Moors and Arabs, possessors of a more elaborate and more highly ornamented architecture, of a finer craftsmanship in swords and armor, in tapestries and silks and carpets, in spices and perfumes and all the luxuries of life, of deeper cunning in mathematics and medicine and philosophy and a world of mysterious sciences derived from Aristotle and Pythagoras and Hippocrates and nameless 'masters of those who know.' Behind the Saracens on the east and already pressing beyond them into Russia on the northeast were the even more mysterious Tartars and Turks, who, coming without warning from the unknown heart of Asia, brought with them all the mysterious associations of India and China. To us the tale which the young squire heard from some knight who had fought in the East, —the tale he left half-told—'the story of Cambuscan bold and of the wondrous steed of brass,' of the magic ring and sword and mirror, is a curious and interesting flight of the oriental imagination; to Chaucer's contemporaries—fresh from the veracious narratives of Sir John Mandeville—it was probably a strange but credible transcript of life beyond the Christian pale. Somewhere in the remote east, they believed, ruled that mysterious sovereign Prester John, and near his empire lay the sandy sea, the floating islands, the lands of the dogfaced men, of the 'anthropophagi and men whose heads do grow beneath their shoulders.'

Associations and ideas such as I have tried to indicate were aroused in the minds of Chaucer's contemporaries by the mere recital of the names of cities and lands where the knight had fought. And in almost every instance the campaigns had not only attracted adventurous spirits from all parts of the Christian world, but had been sufficiently brilliant or long-continued to furnish matter for wonder and admiration for many long years. The two years' siege of Algezir, the sudden capture of Alexandria, were events that could not soon be forgotten even had they occurred in our own day, when the newspapers overwhelm us daily with reports of more events, significant or trifling, than came to the knowledge of Chaucer and his contemporaries in a decade. To the

48

men of that quiet time they furnished recollections and conversation for a whole generation.

The campaigns ascribed to the knight form three groups. The first in order of time is probably the group composed of the siege of Algezir, the raids in Belmarye, and the mortal combats in the lists in Tramissene. All of these, of course, are events in the long struggle to drive the Moors out of Spain and punish their piratical raids from northern Africa upon Christians and Christian commerce. Algezir, the modern Algeciras on the west coast of the bay of Gibraltar, was one of their most important strongholds and for two years stubbornly resisted the siege maintained by Alfonso of Castile with the aid of earls and barons and men-at-arms from the whole Christian world. It is not strange, therefore, that when it finally fell in the spring of 1344, King Edward of England sent to Alfonso a letter of elaborate and jubilant congratulation, a copy of which is still preserved in the Archives of England and published in Rymer's *Foedera*.[1] That Englishmen took part in the siege and were present at the surrender we know to be a fact and not one of Chaucer's poetic fictions. The collection of ancient documents just cited contains a letter of credence[2] dated August 30, 1343, in favor of Henry, Earl of Derby, and William de Montacute, Earl of Salisbury, to Alfonso, King of Castile. The letters of protection for the men who accompanied these earls seem not to have been preserved, but we may presume that the train of each consisted of about thirty men, as similar letters for the trains of Arundel and Derby issued in March, 1344, provide respectively for twenty-nine and thirty-two men.[3]

Whether the expeditions in the African kingdom of Belmarye occurred before or after the siege of Algezir, we have no means of knowing. Rymer[4] prints a letter, dated June 12, 1341, from Edward to Alfonso, congratulating him on his memorable victory over the king of Belmarye (Ad Regem Castellae, super Victoria contra Mauros sub Rege Benemeren, Memoratissima). But after a ten years' truce other expeditions occurred in considerable numbers throughout the century, and Chaucer may have had a later one in mind for his hero.

The dates of the mortal combats in Tramissene (the modern

district of Tlemçen in western Algeria) are also, of course, under the circumstances, unascertainable. The nature of them, however, we may infer with some degree of probability from an interesting passage in Froissart. They were apparently not combats in which he and his opponent were engaged alone. Let us hear Froissart's account of a challenge of a later date, when the army of the Christians (mainly the French) was besieging the City of Africa in 1390:—

'The besiegers and their enemies studied day and night how they could most effectually annoy each other. Agadinquor Oliferne, Madifer de Tunis, Belins Maldages, and Brahadin de Bugia, and some other Saracens, consulted together, and said: "Here are our enemies the Christians encamped before us, and we cannot defeat them. They are so few in number when compared to us, that they must be well advised by their able captains; for, in all our skirmishes, we have never been able to make one knight prisoner. If we could capture one or two of their leaders, we should acquire fame, and learn from them the state of their army and what are their intentions. Let us now consider how we may accomplish this." Agadinquor replied, "Though I am the youngest, I wish to speak first." "We agree to it," said the others. "By my faith," continued he, "I am very desirous of engaging them; and I think, if I were matched in equal combat with one of my size, I should conquer him. If you will, therefore, select ten valiant men, I will challenge the Christians to send the same number to fight with us. We have justice on our side in this war, for they have quarrelled with us without reason; and this right and the courage I feel, induce me to believe that we shall have the victory." Madifer de Tunis, who was a very valiant man, said: "Agadinquor, what you have proposed is much to your honor. To-morrow, if you please, you shall ride as our chief toward the camp of the Christians, taking an interpreter with you, and make a signal that you have something to say. If you be well received by them, propose your combat of ten against ten. We shall then hear what answer they give: and, though I believe the offer will be accepted, we must take good counsel how we proceed against these Christians, whom we consider as more valiant than ourselves."

'This being determined on, they retired to rest. On the morrow, as usual, they advanced to skirmish; but Agadinquor rode on at some distance in front with his interpreter. The day was bright and clear, and a little after sunrise the Saracens were ready for battle. Sir Guy and sir William de la Tremouille had commanded the guard of the night, and were on the point of retiring, when the Saracens appeared in sight about three bow-shots distant. Agadinquor and his interpreter advanced toward one of the wings, and made signs to give notice that he wanted to parley with some one; by accident, he came near the pennon of a good squire-at-arms called Affrenal, who, noticing his signs, rode forward apace, and told his men to remain as they were, "for that he would go and see what the Saracen wanted: he has an interpreter with him, and is probably come to make some proposition." His men remained steady, and he rode toward the Saracen.

'When they were near each other, the interpreter said, "Christian, are you a gentleman, of name in arms, and ready to answer what shall be asked of you?" "Yes," replied Affrenal, "I am: speak what you please, it shall be answered." "Well," said the interpreter, "here is a noble man of our country who demands to combat with you bodily; and, if you would like to increase the number to ten, he will bring as many of his friends to meet you. The cause for the challenge is this: They maintain, that their faith is more perfect than yours; for it has continued since the beginning of the world, when it was written down; and that your faith has been introduced by a mortal, whom the Jews hung and crucified." "Ho," interrupted Affrenal, "be silent on these matters, for it does not become such as thee to dispute concerning them; but tell the Saracen, who has ordered thee to speak, to swear on his faith that such a combat shall take place, and he shall be gratified within four hours. Let him bring ten gentlemen, and of name in arms, on his side, and I will bring as many to meet him." The interpreter related to the Saracen the words that had passed, who seemed much rejoiced thereat, and pledged himself for the combat.

'This being done, each returned to his friends; but the news had already been carried to sir Guy and to sir William de la Tremouille, who, meeting Affrenal, demanded how he had settled matters with the Saracen. Affrenal related what you have heard, and that he had accepted the challenge. The two knights were well pleased, and said, "Affrenal, go and speak to others, for we will be of your number ten." He replied, "God assist us! I fancy I shall find plenty ready to fight the Saracens." Shortly after, Affrenal met the lord de Thim, to whom he told what had passed, and asked if he would make one. The lord de Thim willingly accepted the offer; and of all those to whom Affrenal related it, he might, if he pleased, have had a hundred instead of ten. Sir Boucicaut the younger accepted it with great courage, as did sir Helion de Lignac, sir John Russel, an Englishman, sir John Harpedone, Alain Boudet and Bouchet. When the number of ten was completed, they retired to their lodgings to prepare and arm themselves. When the news of this combat was spread through the army, and the names of the ten were told, the knights and squires said, "they are lucky fellows, thus to have such a gallant feat of arms fall to their lot." "Would to Heaven," added many, "that we were of the ten." '—Johnes' transl., bk. IV, cap. xxii; Kervyn, XIV, 241 ff.

Combats such as this were, we may believe, the three which Chaucer credits to his hero, with the addition that he had 'aye slain his foo.'

The campaigns of the second group are apparently all connected more or less directly with Pierre de Lusignan, King of Cyprus and Jerusalem, and the famous capture of Alexandria. The siege of Alexandria though not long continued, being indeed an assault rather than a siege, was one of the most spectacular events of the century that witnessed the splendid victories of Creçy and Poitiers. The city itself was currently believed in the west to surpass all the other cities in the world each in its peculiar excellence. Those who had seen it declared it to be larger than London, more beautiful than Paris, and richer than Genoa or Venice. Although the assault upon it was sudden and the capture a matter of only a few days, the event had long been prepared for. In October, 1362, the King of Cyprus began a journey through Europe, lasting nearly two years, in the vain attempt to organize the European sovereigns in a crusade against the Saracens. He was himself a most picturesque and attractive figure. He was in the prime of his strength and beauty and endowed with talents of no mean order. Everywhere he was received with princely hospitality and loaded with more than princely gifts of gold and jewels. Everywhere he made friends by his charming personality, his courtesy, his intellectual brilliance, his courage and success in numberless tourneys. He visited the Pope, the kings of France and England, the Emperor, the courts of Franconia, Misnia, Saxony, Bohemia, Poland, Austria. Few were willing to aid him officially, but all were ready to approve his undertaking and to allow their subjects to enlist with him if they wished. Froissart's account of the attitude of King Edward of England may serve to indicate the caution, expressed or unexpressed, of many:—

'It would take me a day were I to attempt relating to you the grand dinners, suppers, and other feasts and entertainments that were made, and the magnificent presents, gifts and jewels, which were given, especially by queen Philippa, to the accomplished king of Cyprus. In truth, he was deserving of them, for he had come a long way and at a great expense, to visit them, to exhort the king to put on the red cross and assist them in regaining countries now occupied by the enemies of God. But the king of England politely and wisely excused himself, by saying: "Certainly, my good cousin, I have every inclination to undertake this expedition; but I am growing too old, and shall leave it to my children. I make no doubt, that when it shall have been begun, you will not be alone, but will be followed most willingly by my knights and squires." "Sir," replied the king of Cyprus, "what you say satisfies me. I verily believe they will come, in order to serve God, and do good to themselves; but you must grant them permission so to do; for the knights of your country are eager in such expeditions." "Yes," answered the king of England, "I will never oppose such a work, unless some things should happen to me or to my kingdom which I do not at this moment foresee." The king of Cyprus could never obtain anything more from King Edward in respect to this croisade; but, as long as he remained, he was politely and honorably feasted with a variety of grand suppers.'—Johnes' transl., bk. I, cap. ccxviii; Kervyn, VI, 384 f.

Many earls and barons and men-at-arms from all parts of Europe did flock to his standard, and, with the aid of the Pope and the Knights Hospitallers, his fleet sailed from Rhodes in September, 1365, on a crusade directed against some unknown point in the East. Pierre himself had not decided upon the exact point of attack, but during the voyage, at the suggestion of one of his council, he determined to try to capture Alexandria by a sudden attack. On Tuesday, October 9, he anchored before the city, and two days later had complete possession of it. The victory was signalized by many notable feats of arms, chief among them those of the king himself, and was celebrated in a poem of nearly nine thousand lines, by Guillaume de Machaut, Chaucer's contemporary, and, to a certain degree, one of his masters in the art of poetry. Less voluminous, but hardly less enthusiastic, accounts of it are given by many chroniclers. It made upon the minds of the men of the time an impression not altogether unlike that made in our own day by the Russo-Japanese naval battle of Tshushima.

With this brilliant event are associated, in this second group of campaigns, the successes at Lyeys and at Satalye and probably also the service under the Lord of Palatye 'ageyn another hethen in Turkye.' Satalye, the ancient Attalia in Asia Minor, was one of the strongest fortresses in the east and a constant menace to Cyprus. The date of its capture from its Saracen lord was, however, not 1352, as is commonly stated, but August, 1361. As this was prior to the visit to Europe made by Pierre in behalf of his crusade, we must infer that Chaucer's gentil knight had sought the east before the east sought him. It is possible, if not indeed probable, that Chaucer conceived him to have been a member of the company attending the Count of Hereford, who is recorded to have been with Pierre on the expedition against Satalye, as well as in the attack on Alexandria. Apparently the knight found the east to his liking, for he took part, as Chaucer tells us, in the capture of Lyeys—a strongly fortified city and harbor on the coast of Armenia the Lesser—which Pierre took from its Turkish lord in 1367, according to the Cypriote chronicle of Strambaldi, though Machaut seems to have thought the expedition unsuccessful. At what time we are to place the service under the lord of Palatye 'ageyn another hethen in Turkye' is doubtful. In 1365, according to Strambaldi (p. 66), the lord of Palatye was a heathen bound in friendly treaty and doing homage to Pierre de Lusignan. How long this remained the case I have been unable to discover.

The third and last group of campaigns we must dispose of more rapidly. All of them belong to the operations of the Knights of the Teutonic Order, whose chief seat was then Marienburg in Prussia. This order, founded at Jerusalem in 1128 by the German Crusaders, removed to Venice and by 1283 had become master of all the territory in north Europe between the Vistula and the Niemen. In 1309 they removed their headquarters to Marienburg, but had Königsberg also as an important centre of operations. Their especial task was to defend the Christian border against the Lithuanians and the Tartars, the latter of whom were masters of most of Russia. The task was difficult and practically incessant. No data are given us by Chaucer for determining the time of the knight's visits. We have records of visits there by some Englishmen in 1362, but our hero seems then to have been in the Orient. A time of equal stress for the Teutonic Order began in 1385, when, according to Assmann, many foreign knights came to their aid. We may well believe that this later period was the time of the knight's campaigns. In support of this, we may note in the first place, that Chaucer says that in Prussia the knight was often given the highest seat at the table—'began the bord'—in recognition of his distinguished character and services. He was, therefore, probably not a young knight at the time in question. If he fought first in 1344 at Algezir, he was probably in 1387, the supposed date of the Canterbury Tales, between sixty and sixty-five. Obviously he was not so old as to be ready to retire, for, says Chaucer, 'he was late ycome from his viage'—the technical term for a military expedition. And this suggests the second reason for dating his career in Pruce, Lettow, and Ruce, or at least one of his campaigns there, immediately before his pilgrimage to Canterbury, namely that, inasmuch as he joined the pilgrims in London, he had not landed at Dover or any port in Kent, but perhaps at some northern port lying nearer to Prussia. This is of course not conclusive, for, had he been returning from the Orient, he would perhaps have landed at Dart-

55

mouth or some other west of England port, as ships from the Orient usually did. But the question of date is not of serious import to our discussion.

We have thus far seen that Chaucer's knight was probably between sixty and sixty-five, that he began his military career in the early forties while Chaucer was still an infant, and consequently would have been a man of mature years and doubtless of much reputation when Chaucer himself as a young squire was in France with the army in 1359, and further, that, although the battles and expeditions ascribed to him are among the most brilliant and adventurous of the age, they fall naturally into three great groups of campaigns. One is tempted to inquire further whether in conceiving his knight Chaucer merely endowed him with the most notable campaigns of the age or whether he may have had in mind one or more men who more or less closely approximated the experiences and exploits of the knight. Chance has provided us with an interesting set of documents which suggest that, though Chaucer may not have given us in the knight a portrait of one of his own friends, he at least knew men of the exact type he has drawn with such affectionate skill.

In 1386, by the order of the crown, testimony was taken to decide a dispute between the Yorkshire family of Scrope and the Chester family of Grosvenor as to which had the right to the arms Azure, a bend Or, which both bore and claimed. Chaucer himself was one of the witnesses in favor of Scrope, and his testimony on this occasion is our principal datum for the time of his birth. Some persons testified concerning tombs and stained windows and other monuments of ancient date that bore the arms in question as those of one or the other claimant. Most of the witnesses, however, were knights and esquires, who testified to the occasions when they had seen the said arms borne publicly in battle or elsewhere. The testimonies by no means give complete sketches of the military careers of the witnesses, but since some of the Scropes themselves nearly duplicated the career of the knight, we get in them hints as to the possibilities of an approximate model among these men whom Chaucer knew. Let us take first the testimony of Nicholas Sabraham, Esq.[5]

56

'Nicholas Sabraham, Esquire, aged sixty and upwards, armed thirty-nine years, said that the arms Azure, a bend Or, were the arms of Sir Richard Scrope, for he had seen the arms of Scrope on banner and coat-armour in the expedition of Sir Edward Balliol in Scotland, also on a banner in the company of the Earl of Northampton, when he chivauchied by torchlight out of Loghmaban as far as Peebles, and had in his company Sir Henry Scrope with his banner. The Deponent also said, that in the assemblage from all Christian countries at the instance of the King of Cyprus, when he meditated his expedition to Alexandria in ships and galleys, one Sir Stephen Scrope was present, armed in the arms of Scrope, Azure, a bend Or, with a label Argent for difference, and immediately on landing, received in those arms the order of Knighthood from the King of Cyprus. He further said that he was armed in Prussia, in Hungary, at Constantinople, "à la bras" of Saint George, and at Messembre, at which latter place there is a church, and therein lieth one of the Scropes buried, and beneath him there are depicted on the wall the arms of Scrope, Azure, a bend Or, with a label, and on the label three "bezants Gules"; he knew them to be the arms of Scrope, and to have borne that name, because the wardens of the said church told him so. The Deponent saw Sir Henry Scrope armed in France with a banner in the company of the Earl of Northampton, and Sir William Scrope, elder brother of the said Sir Richard, in the same company, armed in the entire arms, or with differences, at the battle of Cressy, at the siege of Calais, in Normandy, in Brittany, in Gascony, and in Spain, and beyond the great sea in many places and at many chivalrous exploits: in those places he never heard speak of Sir Robert Grosvenor or of any of his ancestors' (p. 323).

'John de Rither, Esquire, aged sixty-six, armed since the time when the late King made his chivauche to Burenfos in Picardy, deposed that the arms Azure, a bend Or, belonged to the family of Scrope by inheritance. . . . Afterwards the noble King made his expedition before Paris: Sir Henry was there with his banner, and the present Sir Richard Scrope was there also, armed in the entire arms, in the company of the Earl of Richmond; Sir Geoffrey Scrope being then armed in the same with a difference, in company of the late Lord of Lancaster. After that expedition peace was made, when Sir Geoffrey Scrope went, with other knights, into Prussia, and there, in an affair at the siege of Wellon in Lithuania, he died in these arms, and was buried in the Cathedral of Königsberg, where the said arms are painted in a glass window, which the Deponent himself caused to be set up, taking the blazon from the arms which the deceased had upon him' (p. 358).

'Sir Richard Waldegrave, aged forty-eight, armed twenty-five years, deposed that the arms Azure, a bend Or, belonged to the Scropes, who were reputed to be of ancient lineage, as he had heard, in the lifetime of the Earl of Northampton. He saw Sir Richard so armed in the expedition of the late King before Paris, and at the same time Sir Henry Scrope with his banner, on which were the said arms with a white label. And also beyond the great sea he saw Sir William Scrope so armed, with a label, in the company of the Earl of Hereford at Satalia in Turkey, at a treaty which was concluded between the King of Cyprus and "le Takka," Lord of Satalia, when the King of Cyprus became Lord of Satalia' (p. 377).

'Sir Henry de Ferrers, aged forty-six, armed thirty years, deposed that he never heard of any one who had so good right to the arms Azure, a bend Or, as Sir Richard Scrope, and the other branches of his family. He said that he saw Sir Geoffrey Scrope, the son of Sir Henry, so armed in Brittany; also the said Sir Geoffrey so armed in Prussia, and afterwards in Lithuania, before a castle called Piskre, and that he there died, and from thence his body was brought back into Prussia and interred, in the same arms, in the cathedral of Königsberg, where they were placed on a tablet, as a memorial, before the altar. The Deponent saw Sir Henry Scrope before Paris, with his banner, and his body so armed with a white label, and Sir Richard Scrope with the arms entire. The said Sir Geoffrey Scrope was then armed in the company of the late Lord of Lancaster before Paris, and before the time that he went into Prussia' (p. 445).

The significance of these documents is so clear as hardly to need comment. Not only in details, but in its entirety, the career which Chaucer ascribes to his 'gentil knight' is that which actually fell to the lot of more than one of his contemporaries and acquaintances. Sir Harris Nicolas (*The Scrope-Grosvenor Roll*, ii, pp. 105 f.) goes so far as to suggest that Sir William Scrope was definitely in Chaucer's mind as he drew this famous portrait. This is perhaps an exaggeration, but we have unmistakable evidence that Chaucer was painting no picture of fancy, but giving us a figure at once realistic and typical of the noble and adventurous idealists of his day.

If you will indulge me a few seconds more, I should like to repeat a suggestion I made several years ago in regard to the sources of *The Squire's Tale*. After showing that the only literary source suggested were out of the question—and my argument has been accepted universally—I suggested that Chaucer may have heard the story from some knight or esquire who had fought in the Orient, and promised to write some day of the possibility that he actually knew persons who might well have brought the story from the East. I hope I have in this paper redeemed my promise. I have shown you that among Chaucer's fellow-witnesses—men doubtless well known to him—are several whose opportunities for hearing and transmitting such a story were all that could be desired. It may be interesting, and perhaps not altogether without significance, to recall the well-known fact that the English translation of the romance of William of Palerne was made at the command of Humphrey de Bohun, Earl of Hereford,—not the one above recorded as taking part in the capture of Satalye and Alisaundre, to be sure, but his uncle and immediate predecessor as Earl of Hereford.

NOTES

1. v, 415 (orig. ed.). The letter dated May 30, 1344, is headed: Ad Regem Castellae, super Aigezira Conquistata, Gratulatoria.

2. *op. cit.* v, 383.

3. *op. cit.* (Record. ed.) iii, 1, 10, and 11.

4. *op. cit.* (orig. ed.) v, 257.

5. This and the other testimonies in the Scrope-Grosvenor case are given in the edition of the roll published by Sir Harris Nicolas. The first volume contains the documents, the second contains translations of them and Nicolas's introduction and notes. I quote the translations, giving the page references to vol. ii.

CHARLES MUSCATINE

Form, Texture, and Meaning in Chaucer's
Knight's Tale

I

DESPITE the fact that the interpretive literature on Chaucer's *Knight's Tale* is extensive, the poem has remained one of the most baffling of the *Canterbury Tales*. It has resisted satisfactory interpretation where poems of much more complicated structure—as the *Merchant's Tale*—and much more varied style—as the *Nun's Priest's Tale*—have yielded brilliant results to criticism. The critics of the past fifty years have lacked neither learning nor ingenuity, but somehow their interpretations remain marked by a characteristic indecisiveness—made particularly evident where equally acute analyses produce conflicting and contradictory results—and by a simplicity that does not do justice to the poem and its five hundred years of popularity. It is possible that this critical unsuccess is owing to an error of perspective, that the poem has been generally examined and evaluated in the light of assumptions which are not central to its method. It is the purpose of the present essay to establish this as more than a possibility, and to suggest a viewpoint from which the poem may be seen to have a coherence and fullness of meaning which the traditional critics have hardly touched upon.

The *Knight's Tale* is almost universally taken to be a love poem—a mediæval romance—with philosophical appendages, but the

---

Reprinted, by permission, from *PMLA*, LXV (1950), 911–29. This essay appears in a different form in the author's book, *Chaucer and the French Tradition* (Berkeley, University of California Press, 1947).

particular location of its value is the subject of considerable disagreement. There are many who find the differentiation between Palamon and Arcite to be a central feature of the poem. But among these, there is little agreement as to either the nature of the characterization or the moral to be drawn therefrom. For instance, Fairchild, following a suggestion by Root,[1] sees Palamon as the contemplative, idealistic man and Arcite as the more practical, earth-oriented one. In this view the poem becomes a quasi-allegory of the Contemplative Life versus the Active Life, with the moral superiority given to the former. The premature death of Arcite and the winning of Emelye by Palamon have, then, the air of poetic justice.[2] But against this interpretation, there stands a respectable body of argument to urge that Palamon is the shabbier of the two characters, Tatlock going so far as to suggest that the success of Palamon is an ironic twist in the very absence of any serious moral justification for it.[3] And one persuasive critic has demonstrated that it is perfectly possible—given the assumption that characterization is a main issue—to show that Arcite is the more profound and contemplative, and Palamon the more active and impulsive.[4]

In the face of such possibilities for confusion, other critics have turned elsewhere in the poem. J. R. Hulbert, paying particular attention to Chaucer's source, casts serious doubt on the existence of any meaningful characterization in Chaucer's poem:

> In the *Teseide* there is one hero, Arcita, who loves and is eventually loved by Emilia, a young woman characterized by a natural coquetry, an admiration for a good-looking young knight, and love and sympathy for the wounded hero. Palemone is a secondary figure, necessary to the plot because he brings about the death of Arcita. The story is a tragedy, caused by the mistake of Arcita in praying to Mars rather than to Venus. In Chaucer's story there are two heroes, who are practically indistinguishable from each other, and a heroine, who is merely a name. In the Italian poem it is possible to feel the interest in hero and heroine which is necessary if one is to be moved by a story. . . . In Chaucer's version, on the other hand . . . it is hard to believe that anyone can sympathize with either hero or care which one wins Emelye.

Hulbert calls this lack of characterization the story's greatest weakness, and, faced with the apparent perversity of Chaucer's adaptation of Boccaccio's poem, finds in the *Knight's Tale* only an elaborate and now archaic game:

> . . . Chaucer saw in the *Teseide* a plot which, with some alterations, could be used effectively to present one of those problems of love which the votaries of courtly love enjoyed considering . . . which of two young men, of equal worth and with almost equal claims, shall (or should) win the lady? Stated in such simple terms, the problem may seem foolish, but to readers who could be interested in such questions of love . . . this problem would be no doubt poignant.

> Obviously in so far as the ideas of courtly love have passed into oblivion since the middle ages, narratives in which they are basic cannot appeal to modern taste.[5]

This second approach has been in turn questioned; Paull F. Baum, for instance, suggests that the poem should not be judged on the basis of characterization, and he turns to yet another feature of it: 'If Chaucer has weakened such characterization as Boccaccio gave his principal figures, he has compensated by emphasizing the necessitarian element of the story and very obviously made plot more important than the characters.' But in order to defend the primacy of the 'plot,' Baum is forced to conclude that Chaucer takes the whole 'with a certain air of jocosity,' and would even send us 'back to look for the possible smile behind the description of the worthy and perfect knight himself.'[6] He uncovers glaring breaches of probability, situations so ridiculous ('the heroes fighting ankle deep in their own blood') and infelicitous, that were one not to follow Baum in taking Chaucer to be satirical, one would perforce have to question the poet's command over the most elementary techniques of storytelling. Putting aside the second possibility, and recognizing that Baum is not the only one who has found cross-currents of satire in the poem,[7] few of us will be willing to accept the notion that in the context of the *Canterbury Tales*, this *noble storie*, as all of Chaucer's gentlefolk call it, contains anything which is more than incidentally satirical. At any rate, it is clearly possible that Baum's interpretation suffers by the same kind of fallacy that may be inherent in those of his predecessors: that of seeking fine distinctions in what may not be meant as distinct, of seeking realism of action (or of characterization), for instance, in a poem not written under the assumption of realism of method.[8]

This possibility was long ago suggested by Root:

> If we are to read the *Knight's Tale* in the spirit in which Chaucer conceived it, we must give ourselves up to the spirit of romance; we must not look for subtle characterization, nor for strict probability of action; we must delight in the fair shows of things, and not ask too many questions. Chaucer can be realistic enough when he so elects; but here he has chosen otherwise.

The notion that Chaucer did choose otherwise is, as we shall see, a sensible one. Nevertheless, we may be justifiably reluctant to give ourselves up wholly to the spirit of romance; we may wish to ask questions. Root's interpretation avoids many critical pitfalls, and gives important recognition to the poem's texture, but at serious expense to the poem's meaning. There is a certain narrowness in his conclusion that 'The *Knight's Tale* is preëminently a web of splendidly pictured tapestry, in which the eye may take delight, and on which the memory may fondly linger,' that 'It is not in the characterization, but in the description, that the greatness of the *Knight's Tale* resides.'

This narrowness is, indeed, characteristic of all the approaches that have been mentioned. Each one disregards important aspects of the tale; together they indicate that it has generally not been dealt with as poetry, that is, as an organization whose fullest meaning is dependent on the interplay of a variety of elements. None of them suggests, much less demonstrates, the depth and complexity which we have a right to expect in a work of art that has worn so well for so long. To make a new approach in this direction, it will be necessary first to analyze the structure of the poem, which has heretofore received too little attention, and to reëxamine the nature of its materials, over which traditional criticism has perhaps too fondly lingered.

II

When we look at the poem's structure, we find symmetry to be its most prominent feature. By 'symmetry' I do not mean 'unity,' but rather, a high degree of regularity and order among parts. The poem does fulfil our demand for unity; however, it is not unity in itself, but *unity through regularity* that has particular meaning in the *Knight's Tale*.

The character-grouping is symmetrical. There are two knights, Palamon and Arcite, in love with the same woman, Emilye. Above the three and in a position to sit in judgment, is the Duke Theseus, who throughout the poem is the center of authority and the balance between the opposing interests of the knights. In the realm of the supernatural, each of the knights and the lady has a patron deity: Venus, Mars, and Diana. The conflict between Venus and Mars is resolved by the elder Saturn, with no partiality toward either. In the tournament each knight is accompanied by one hundred followers, headed by a particularly notable king, on one side Lygurge, on the other Emetrius:

> In al the world, to seken up and doun,
> So evene, withouten variacioun,
> Ther nere swiche compaignyes tweye;
> For ther was noon so wys that koude seye
> That any hadde of oother avauntage
> Of worthynesse, ne of estaat, ne age,
> So evene were they chosen, for to gesse.
> And in two renges faire they hem dresse.[9]

This arrangement of the two companies *in two renges* is one of many details of symmetry of scene and action in the poem. At the very beginning of the poem we find a uniformly clad company 'of ladyes, tweye and tweye,/Ech after oother.' When Palamon and Arcite are found in the heap of bodies by Thebes, they are 'liggynge by and by,/Booth in oon armes.' We find that they are cousins, 'of sustren two yborn.'

In the scene following the discovery of Emilye, each offers a lyric on the subject. When Arcite is released from prison, each delivers a complaint in which even the vocabulary and theme are symmetrical:

> 'O deere cosyn Palamon,' quod he,
> 'Thyn is the victorie of this aventure.'
>
> 'Allas,' quod he, 'Arcita, cosyn myn,
> Of al oure strif, God woot, the fruyt is thyn.'

In part two, the narrator divides his attention between them, in alternate descriptions; and in the fight subsequent to their meeting, they are evenly matched:

> Thou myghtest wene that this Palamon
> In his fightyng were a wood leon,
> And as a crueel tigre was Arcite. . . .

Theseus appears, 'And at a stert he was bitwix hem two.' He sets the conditions of the tournament in round numbers: 'And this day fifty wykes, fer ne ner, / Everich of you shal brynge an hundred knightes. . . .' In the third part the narrator describes the making of lists, in the same place as where the first fight occurs. The lists are circular in shape, a mile in circumference. They are entered from east and west by identical marble gates. The altars or temples of Mars and Venus are situated above these gates. Northward (and equidistant from the other two, no doubt) is the *oratorie* of Diana. The three temples are described in succession, and each description is subdivided in the same way: first the wall-painting with its allegorical figures, and then the statue of the deity itself.

The symmetry of description continues with parallel accounts of the two rival companies, each containing a portrait of the leading king. Then follow the prayers of the principals: Palamon to Venus, Emilye to Diana, Arcite to Mars. The prayers are made at the hours dedicated by astrology to those deities, and each prayer is answered by some supernatural event. Internally, too, the three prayers show a striking similarity of design, each beginning with rhetorical *pronominatio*, and continuing with a reference to the deity's relations with the opposite sex, a self-description by the speaker, a humble assertion of incompetence, a request for assistance, and a promise to worship. The spectators enter the lists and are seated in order of rank. The combatants, Palamon and Arcite, with banners white and red respectively, enter the field through the gates of Venus and Mars.

After Arcite's death, his sepulchre is described. It is erected 'ther as first Arcite and Palamoun/ Hadden for love the bataille hem bitwene.' As R. A. Pratt notes, this is also where the lists were built.[10] The funeral procession, like the procession to the lists, is characterized by precise order, and the details of the funeral are full of the same kind of ordering:

> . . . the Grekes, with an huge route,
> Thries riden al the fyr aboute
> Upon the left hand, with a loud shoutynge,
> And thries with hir speres claterynge;
> And thries how the ladys gonne crye . . .

Further elements in the poem's symmetry of structure and scene could readily be brought forward.

Turning now from structure to pace, we find the *Tale* deliberately slow and majestic. Random references to generous periods of time make the story chronologically slow. Though Chaucer omits a great deal of the tale originally told by Boccaccio in the *Teseida*, he frequently resorts to the rhetorical device of *occupatio* to summarize in detail events or descriptions in such a way as to shorten the story without losing its weight and impressiveness. Further, there is an extraordinary amount of direct description in the poem, all of which slows the narrative. The description of the lists is very detailed, and placed so as to give the impression that we are present at their construction, an operation that appears to consume the full fifty weeks that Theseus allows for it. The narrator's repetitious 'saugh I,' and his closing remark, 'Now been thise lystes maad,' cooperate to this effect.

We can hardly fail to note, too, that a great deal of this descriptive material has a richness of detail far in excess of the demands of the story. At first glance, at least, many passages appear to be irrelevant and detachable. To take a well-known instance, we have sixty-one lines of description of Emetrius and Lygurge; yet so far as the action of the poem is concerned, these two worthies do practically nothing.

Like the descriptions and narrator's comments, the direct discourse in the *Tale* contributes to the poem's slowness. There is virtually no rapid dialogue. Speeches of twenty-five or thirty lines are the rule, and one, the final oration of Theseus, is over a hundred lines in length. More than length, however, the non-dynamic *quality* of the speeches is characteristic of the whole poem's style. Many of them have only a nominal value as action, or the instruments to action. Formal, rhetorical structure, and a function comparatively unrelated to the practical necessities of the dramatic situation, are the rule. This is true even where the speech is addressed to another character. For instance, when old Saturn is badgered by his granddaughter Venus to aid her in her conflict with Mars, he replies as follows:

> 'My deere doghter Venus,' quod Saturne,
> 'My cours, that hath so wyde for to turne,
> Hath moore power than woot any man.
> Myn is the drenchyng in the see so wan;
> Myn is the prisoun in the derke cote;
> Myn is the stranglyng and hangyng by the throte,
> The murmure and the cherles rebellyng,
> The groynynge, and the pryvee empoysoning;
> I do vengeance and pleyn correccioun,
> Whil I dwelle in the signe of the leoun,
> Myn is the ruyne of the hye halles,
> The fallynge of the toures and of the walles
> Upon the mynour or the carpenter.
> I slow Sampsoun, shakynge the piler;
> And myne be the maladyes colde,
> The derke tresons, and the castes olde;
> My lookyng is the fader of pestilence.
> Now weep namoore, I shal doon diligence. . . .

And finally, the remainder of the speech, a mere eight lines, is devoted to promising Venus his aid. We can safely assume that Venus knows all about her grandfather. The long, self-descriptive introduction, therefore, must have some function other than the dramatic.

Going on now to the nature of the action, we find that, while the chivalric aspects of the scene are described with minute particularity, there is very little in the *Knight's Tale* of the intimate and distinctive details of look, attitude, and gesture that mark some of Chaucer's more naturalistic poems. The *Tale* is replete with conventional stage business. There are swoons and cries, fallings on knees, and sudden palenesses; there is a symphony of howls, wails and lamentations.

These general and inescapable observations on the nature of the *Knight's Tale* make clear how the poem must be approached. The symmetry of scene, action and character-grouping, the slow pace of the narrative and large proportion of concrete description, the predominantly lyric and philosophic kind of discourse—along with a lack of subtle discrimination in the stage business—all indicate that the tale is not the best kind in which to look for either delicate characterization or the peculiar fascination of an exciting plot.

Chaucer's modifications of the *Teseida* all seem to bear this out. He found much of his material in the long Italian work. By selection and addition he produced a poem much more symmetrical than its source. Chaucer even regularizes the times and places of the incidents in Boccaccio, and many further instances of an increase in symmetry could be cited. The crowning modification, however, is the equalization of Palamon and Arcite. We have seen that this has caused some consternation in the critical ranks. It should now be clear that the critic is not on safe ground when he calls this lack of characterization the story's greatest weakness. The point is rather that subtle delineation of character is neither called for in the poem's design nor possible of achievement through the technical means Chaucer largely employs. There is neither rapid dialogue, nor psychological analysis, nor delicate and revelatory 'business' in the poem. The general intention indicated by the poem's materials and structure lies in a different direction.

But to recognize that the element of characterization is justly minor in the tale does not justify turning to the plot, and making it, in turn, the center of interest. For the fact is that even as bare plots go, as story interest goes, the *Knight's Tale* does not amount to much. The value of the poem depends little on the virtues that make a good story: a swift pace, suspense, variety, intrigue. Its main events are forecast long before they occur. The structure of the poem, indeed, works against story interest. Symmetry in character-grouping, movement, time and place supports the leisurely narrative and description in producing an over-all sense of rest and deliberateness.

With these traditional possibilities eliminated, and under the principle that a poem should be read on the basis of its own assumptions, it seems reasonable to conclude that the *Knight's Tale* is of a kind having a much closer affinity to the mediæval tradition of conventionalism than to realism. We can neither examine nor evaluate it according to canons by which it patently was not written and could never satisfy. Its texture reminds one more of the *Roman de la Rose* than of the *General Prologue*. Its grouping and action, rather than existing for any great interest in themselves, seem constantly to point to a non-representational, metaphorical method. Indeed, there is such a close correlation among all its elements on this level as to give decisive support to such an approach.

III

I would suggest, then, that the *Knight's Tale* is essentially neither a story, nor a static picture, but a poetic pageant, and that all its materials are organized and contributory to a complex design expressing the nature of the noble life,

> That is to seyn, trouthe, honour, kynghthede,
> Wysdom, humblesse, estaat, and heigh kynrede,
> Fredom, and al that longeth to that art. . . .

The story is immediately concerned with those two noble activities, love and chivalry, but even more important is the general tenor of the noble life, the pomp and ceremony, the dignity and power, and particularly the repose and assurance with which the exponent of nobility invokes order. Order, which characterizes the framework of the poem, is also the heart of its meaning. The society depicted is one in which form is full of significance, in which life is conducted at a dignified, processional pace, and wherein life's pattern is itself a reflection, or better, a reproduction, of the order of the universe. And what gives this conception of life its perspective, its depth and seriousness, is its constant awareness of a formidably antagonistic element—chaos, disorder—which in life is an ever-threatening possibility, even in the moments of supremest assuredness, and which in the poem falls across the pattern of order, being clearly exemplified in the erratic reversals of the poem's plot, and deeply embedded in the poem's texture.

The descriptive sections of the *Tale* support this interpretation perfectly, not only in the long passages that come immediately to mind, but also in the short flights that interrupt the narrative to an extent unwarranted by what little information they add to the mere story. By contributing to currents that run continuously throughout the poem—currents that make up the main stream of the noble life—these superficially 'irrelevant' descriptions achieve a secure position in the poem's pattern, and ultimately contribute in an important way to its meaning.

The portraits of Emetrius and Lygurge, for instance, have this kind of poetic relevance although their contribution to the surface narrative is slight. Emetrius has 'A mantelet upon his shulder hangynge,/ Bret-ful of rubyes rede as fyr sparklynge.' Lygurge wears

> A wrethe of gold, arm-greet, of huge wighte,
> Upon his heed, set ful of stones brighte,
> Of fyne rubyes and of dyamauntz.

Unlike the portraits in the *General Prologue*, here the imagery is organized around no central conception of personality, but rather connotes the magnificence that befits nobility. We have noted that after all the description of these two kings they hardly figure in the narrative. The inference, however, is not that the portraits are a waste and an excrescence, 'merely decorative,' but that they perform a function not directly related to the action and independent of the question of character. They contribute first to the poem's general texture, to the element of richness in the fabric of the noble life. More specifically, Chaucer solves the problem of describing the rival companies by describing their leaders; not Palamon and Arcite, but their supporting kings. Their varicolored magnificence, like Theseus' banner, makes the whole field glitter up and down—black, white, yellow, red, green and gold. Their personal attributes—the trumpet voice of Emetrius, the great brawn of Lygurge, their looks, like lion and griffin—give both a martial quality that we are to attribute to the whole company. About the chariot of Lygurge run great, white, muzzled hunting dogs, big as bullocks. Emetrius' pet animals are a white eagle, lions and leopards. The fact that these animals are tame only makes the comparison with their masters the more impressive. And practically every other detail is a superlative, the quality of which contributes to martial or royal magnificence.

In some of the descriptions in the *Knight's Tale*, Chaucer is at his very best as a poet:

> The rede statue of Mars, with spere and targe,
> So shyneth in his white baner large,
> That alle the feeldes glyteren up and doun;
> And by his baner born is his penoun
> Of gold ful riche, in which ther was ybete
> The Mynotaur, which that he slough in Crete.
> Thus rit this duc, thus rit this conquerour,
> And in his hoost of chivalrie the flour. . . .

Even in so short a passage, the power bestowed on this description suggests a function deeper than mere ornament. It links with a score of other passages as an expression of Theseus' preëminence in war and chivalry. Thus the very opening of the poem, with its compressed but powerful description of the conquest of the Amazons and the marriage of Ypolita, is devoted to this end, and the texture of the following incident of the mourning women of Thebes, which acts as a kind of prologue to the *Knight's Tale* proper, widens and perpetuates our notion of Theseus as variously the ruler, the conqueror, the judge, and, not least, the man of pity. Among other subsequent details, the magnificence of the lists and of Arcite's funeral is directly associated with Theseus' dispensations.

The establishment of this preëminence is essential to the meaning of the poem and is carried out on the multiple levels characteristic of Chaucer's whole method in the *Tale*. There is an obvious correspondence between the quality of these descriptions and the position of Theseus as the central figure in the poem's pattern of characters. And like the descriptions, the speeches in the poem have a great deal of metaphoric value. If they do not operate very effectively in the interest of plot and characterization—Theseus has been likened to Polonius!—it is because they serve other and more poetic ends; they too contribute to the pattern of tones and values which is the real substance of the poem. Those of Theseus again show him as representative of the highest chivalric conceptions of nobility. From the point of view of design he is the central figure in the poem. As the most powerful human figure he presides over the events and interprets them. His final oration is a masterpiece of dignity. Theseus assembles his parliament, with Palamon and Emilye, to make an end of the mourning for Arcite. The speech is carefully and formally introduced:

> Whan they were set, and hust was al the place,
> And Theseus abiden hadde a space
> Er any word cam fram his wise brest,
> His eyen sette he ther as was his lest,
> And with a sad visage he siked stille,
> And after that right thus he seyde his wille. . . .

The commentators tell us that the speech itself is adapted from Boethius. It is a monologue of *sentence* and doctrine in the mediæval manner. The progress of the speech is logical and orderly: Theseus takes up first principles, then general examples from nature, and finally the matter in hand. Chaucer makes no effort to conceal its scholastic character. As a parliamentary address it is not outside the realm of possibility, but this is the least justification for it. A deeper reason for its suitability is its beautiful agreement, in organization and content, with the principle of order which Theseus both invokes and represents throughout the tale. In a sense the representative of Fate on earth, the earthly sovereign interprets the will of the divine one:

> 'Thanne may men by this ordre wel discerne
> That thilke Moevere stable is and eterne.
>
> What maketh this but Juppiter, the kyng,
> The which is prince and cause of alle thyng,
> Convertynge al unto his propre welle
> From which it is dirryved, sooth to telle?
> And heer-agayns no creature on lyve,
> Of no degree, availleth for to stryve.
> Thanne is it wysdom, as it thynketh me,
> To maken vertu of necessitee,
> And take it weel that we may nat eschue. . . .'

The king is an inveterate enemy to rebellion: 'And whoso gruccheth ought, he dooth folye,/ And rebel is to hym that al may gye.' The principal representative of chivalry espouses a highly idealistic conception of the value of a good name:

> 'And certeinly a man hath moost honour
> To dyen in his excellence and flour,
> Whan he is siker of his goode name;
> Thanne hath he doon his freend, ne hym, no shame.
> And gladder oghte his freend been of his deeth,
> Whan with honour up yolden is his breeth,
> Than whan his name appalled is for age,
> For al forgeten is his vassellage.
> Thanne is it best, as for a worthy fame,
> To dyen whan that he is best of name.'

The actions and speeches by the central figure are the normative ones in the poem. Those of Palamon and Arcite are lesser and contributory, in the sense that they only provide the questions and the elements of variety whose resolution Theseus expounds and interprets. They are, in fact, exemplary of life as it is lived. In this light, it is important to differentiate carefully between the balance of tone that Chaucer preserves in his treatment of them, and the more or less direct evidences of satire and of tragedy which many critics have seemed to find there. Theseus' speech on the loves of Palamon and Arcite, for instance, has prompted the suggestion that here Chaucer revolts against the courtly code which the knights represent.[11] First of all, it must be seen that the poet is not here dealing with courtly love *per se*, but only with love, on a par with chivalry, as one of the persistent facts of the noble life. The tournament is held, we remember, 'For love and for encrees of chivalrye.' The emphasis, however, is not as in the courtly romance, where the inner psychological life is explored and where the action revolves about the pursuit and defense of the lady's rose. The lady in the *Knight's Tale* is merely a symbol of the noble man's desires. And the question of love is never in debate here. We take love in this society for granted, and then go on to discover how faithfully experience in love exemplifies the partial blindness of all earthly experience. Love, we find, can create dissention between sworn brothers, can make a man lament his release from prison, forsake safety and native land, and, after unending toll of time and strength, it can leave him bloody and desirous of death. Theseus' speech on love, as his speech on Arcite's death, is normative and judicial; and to the noble, the mature mind, the paradoxically impractical quality of love is both laughable and admirable. The rivalry and consequent exploits of Palamon and Arcite are so impractical, and yet so much a reflex of their knightly spirits, that there is something to be said on both sides. Theseus' speech, therefore, is a mature appraisal, not an adverse criticism, of courtly love; certainly not a reflection of Chaucer's 'strong revolt against the code.'

The leavening, balancing element of common sense in Chaucer is very often, as here, signalized by a lapse of the high style and the introduction of colloquialism:

> 'But this is yet the beste game of alle,
> That she for whom they han this jolitee
> Kan hem therefore as muche thank as me.
> She woot namoore of al this hoote fare,
> By God, than woot a cokkow or an hare!'

With all this humorous ventilation of the subject, however, the real power of love is not denied:

> 'But all moot ben assayed, hoot and coold;
> A man moot been a fool, or yong or oold,—
> I woot it by myself ful yore agon,
> For in my tyme a servant was I oon.
> And therefore, syn I knowe of loves peyne,
> And woot hou soore it kan a man distreyne,
> As he that hath ben caught ofte in his laas,
> I yow foryeve al hoolly this trespaas. . . .'

This kind of balance, if it precludes satire, does not of course rule out the possibility of irony. Indeed, such a tone is consonant with Theseus' maturity and dignity. But the several touches of this sort in the poem, and the tensions within its structure that in modern critical parlance might also be called ironic, neither point to the moral superiority of one knight, nor support a tragic attitude toward either of them. It is true that, while Chaucer equalized the Palemone and Arcite of the *Teseida,* he carefully preserved a certain difference between them. One serves Venus, the other Mars. One prays for Emilye, the other for victory. But it does not appear that by preserving this distinction Chaucer implies any moral preference. As the whole background of the *Tale* shows, the worship of Mars is no less an important aspect of the noble life than the worship of Venus. To Arcite goes the honor in war, the magnificent funeral, and the intangible rewards brought out in Theseus' oration. To Palamon goes Emilye; in her are described the rewards that accrue to him as the servant of Venus. That the differentiation between the knights is ultimately a source of balance rather than of conflict can be seen even at the beginning of the poem. Palamon sees Emilye first, and prays to her as if to Venus, in a lyric monologue:

> 'Venus if it be thy wil
> Yow in this gardyn thus to transfigure
> Bifore me, sorweful, wrecched creature,
> Out of this prisoun help that we may scapen.

> And if so be my destynee be shapen
> By eterne word to dyen in prisoun,
> Of our lynage have som compassioun,
> That is so lowe ybroght by tirannye.'

This is followed by the lyric of Arcite, 'The fresshe beautee sleeth me sodeynly', and the distinction between them is expressed by Arcite in his argument for his claim to the lady:

> 'For paramour I loved hire first er thow.
> What wiltow seyn? Thou wistest nat yet now
> Wheither she be a womman or goddesse!
> Thyn is affeccioun of hoolynesse,
> And myn is love, as to a creature. . . .'

Now this distinction is not clearly carried out beyond the passage in question, although it has been expanded by critics to allegorical and morally significant proportions. And even if it did exist as a sustained and fundamental difference between the knights, it would not create a moral *issue* in the poem. In the passage in question Arcite's argument clearly serves to balance Palamon's claim to priority, and thus to restore the equality of the two knights. The validity of Arcite's position is further supported in his contention that love is a law unto itself, that

> '. . . positif lawe and swich decree
> Is broken al day for love in ech degree.
> A man moot nedes love, maugree his heed.'

This is a fact substantiated by the events of the poem, and elaborately expounded in Theseus' speech on love, where it is again a question of conflict of authorities.

What further deadens any possibly moralistic or tragic implications in the fate of Arcite is a touch of Chaucer's lightness. Were Arcite's death ultimately attributable to some moral disjointedness of his own, we should expect it to be made abundantly clear. But in a literature where the advent of death is one of the most powerful instruments of moral exemplum, Chaucer goes far out of his way to stifle any such construction. In describing Arcite's death, he involves the reader not in moral conclusions, but in complicated *physical* data whose connotations are so cold and scientific that no moral conclusion can possibly be drawn. The spirit of moral non-commitment is brought out clearly in the final lines of the narrator's comment, where again we see the leavening, commonsensical element expressed through colloquialism:

> Nature hath now no dominacioun.
> And certeinly, ther Nature wol nat wirche,
> Fare wel phisik! go ber the man to chirche!
> This al and som, that Arcita moot dye. . . .

The critic must be on his guard here not to exaggerate the meaning of this digression, not to convert a deftly administered antidote for tragedy into an actively satiric strain. This would be to mistake Chaucer's balance for buffoonery. Immediately following this passage comes Arcite's most elevated speech. Were the narrator's remarks to be read as a satiric comment on Arcite's death, the whole noble fabric of the speech, and of the poem too, would crumble.

The lines immediately following Arcite's death are the same kind of countercheck to tragedy, a non-committal disposal of the question of heaven or hell by drawing attention again from the character to the narrator:

> His spirit chaunged hous and wente ther,
> As I cam nevere, I kan nat tellen wher.
> Therfore I stynte, I nam no divinistre;
> Of soules fynde I nat in this registre,
> Ne me ne list thilke opinions to telle
> Of hem, though that they writen wher they dwelle.
> Arcite is coold, ther Mars his soule gye!

Again the light irony of the digression is followed by a resumption of the narrative in full seriousness—here the description of the funeral—without loss to Arcite's dignity.

If Palamon and Arcite exemplify legitimate attitudes of equal value, and balance or supplement each other in providing not moral conflict but variety, we must not look at the relationship between them, but rather to their common position in relation to the universe, to find the real moral issue in the poem. And Chaucer expresses this issue not only through a tension between the poem's symmetrically ordered structure and the violent ups and downs of the surface narrative—too plainly to be seen to require elaborate analysis—but also through a complication of texture, in the weaving of darker threads among the red and gold.

I have already suggested that the poem's speeches, like its descriptions, are largely part of its texture; many of them are less important as pointing to specific psychological characteristics that issue in direct action than as elements in broader organizations, with deeper and more ulterior relevance to what goes on in the poem. Thus we have from Palamon and Arcite a considerable number of lyrics, some of them contributing only to the poem's general background of conventional love and chivalry, and others, more important, in which love-lament melts into poetry of a more philosophical kind, and brings us to the heart of the issue. This latter characteristic of the poem's texture supports the view that love, which has been too often regarded as the poem's central theme, is used only as a vehicle of expression, a mode of experience of the noble life, which is itself the subject of the poem and the object of its philosophic questions. Thus, in the magnificent death-speech of Arcite the lyric of love merges with the philosophical, the lady addressed becomes part of the speech's descriptive imagery, and the theme of love itself is subsumed in the category of all earthly experience:

> 'Naught may the woful spirit in myn herte
> Declare o point of alle my sorwes smerte
> To yow, my lady, that I love moost;
> But I biquethe the servyce of my goost
> To yow aboven every creature,
> Syn that my lyf may no lenger dure.
> Allas, the wo! allas, the peynes stronge,
> That I for yow have suffred, and so longe!

> Allas, the deeth! allas, myn Emelye!
> Allas, departynge of oure compaignye!
> Allas, myn hertes queene! allas, my wyf!
> Myn hertes lady, endere of my lyf!
> What is this world? what asketh men to have?
> Now with his love, now in his colde grave
> Allone, withouten any compaignye.'

Similarly, the speech of Arcite after his release from prison shifts from personal outcry to general speculation. Here, although Arcite mentions the paradoxical nature of men's designs with reference to the irony of his *own* position, he sounds a note which reëchoes throughout the poem:

> 'Som man desireth for to han richesse,
> That cause is of his mordre or greet siknesse;
> And som man wolde out of his prison fayn,
> That in his house is of his meynee slayn.'

The parallel lament of Palamon in prison is a variation on the same theme:

> 'O crueel goddes that governe
> This world with byndyng of youre word eterne,
> And writen in the table of atthamaunt
> Youre parlement and your eterne graunt,
> What is mankynde moore unto you holde
> Than is the sheep that rouketh in the folde?
> For slayn is man right as another beest,
> And dwelleth eek in prison and arreest,
> And hath siknesse and greet adversitee,
> And ofte tymes giltelees, pardee.
> What governance is in this prescience,
> That giltelees tormenteth innocence?'

The motive of misfortune and disorder is extended in ever-widening circles of reference in the descriptions of the three temples:

> First in the temple of Venus maystow se
> Wroght on the wal, ful pitous to biholde,

79

> The broken slepes, and the sikes colde,
> The sacred teeris, and the waymentynge,
> The firy strokes of the desirynge
> That loves servantz in this lyf enduren. . . .

On the walls of the temple of Diana are depicted the stories of
Callisto, Daphne, Actaeon, and Meleager, all of unhappy memory.
In the description of Mars' temple, the narrator is most powerful.
He sees

> . . . the derke ymaginyng
> Of Felonye, and all the compassyng;
> The crueel Ire, reed as any gleede;
> The pykepurs, and eek the pale Drede;
> The smylere with the knyf under the cloke;
> The shepne brennynge with the blake smoke;
> The tresoun of the mordrynge in the bedde;
> The open werre, with woundes al bibledde. . . .

In this context, the monologue of Saturn is the culminating expression of an ever-swelling undertheme of disaster:

> 'Myn is the drenchyng in the see so wan;
> Myn is the prison in the derke cote;
> Myn is the stranglyng and hangyng by the throte,
> The murmure and the cherles rebellyng,
> The groynynge, and the pryvee empoysonyng. . . .'

In Theseus' majestic summary there is a final echo, the continuing
rhetorical repetition as insistent as fate itself:

> 'He moot be deed, the kyng as shal a page;
> Som in his bed, som in the depe see,
> Som in the large feeld, as men may see. . . .'

This subsurface insistence on disorder is the poem's crowning
complexity, its most compelling claim to maturity. We have here
no glittering, romantic fairy-castle world. The impressive, pat-
terned edifice of the noble life, its dignity and richness, its regard
for law and decorum, are all bulwarks against the ever-threatening

forces of chaos, and in constant collision with them. And the crowning nobility, as expressed by this poem, goes beyond a grasp of the forms of social and civil order, beyond magnificence in any earthly sense, to a perception of the order beyond chaos. When the earthly designs suddenly crumble, true nobility is faith in the ultimate order of all things. Saturn, disorder, nothing more or less, is the agent of Arcite's death, and Theseus, noble in the highest sense, interprets it in the deepest perspective. In contrast is the incomplete perception of the wailing women of Athens:

> 'Why woldestow be deed,' thise wommen crye,
> And haddest gold ynough, and Emelye?'

The history of Thebes had perpetual interest for Chaucer as an example of the struggle between noble designs and chaos. Palamon and Arcite, Thebans, lovers, fighters and sufferers, through whom the pursuit of the noble life is presented, exemplify through their experiences and express through their speeches this central conflict.

NOTES

1. R. K. Root, *The Poetry of Chaucer* (Boston, [1906]), p. 170; H. N. Fairchild, 'Active Arcite, Contemplative Palamon,' *JEGP*, xxvi (1927), 285–293.
2. Fairchild, pp. 290–292. See also P. V. Shelly, *The Living Chaucer* (Phila., 1940), pp. 236–237; C. D. Baker, 'A Note on Chaucer's *Knight's Tale*,' *MLN*, xlv (1930), 460–462; Hubertis M. Cummings, *The Indebtedness of Chaucer's Works to the Italian Works of Boccaccio*, Univ. of Cincinnati Studies, Ser. ii, Vol. x (Cincinnati, 1916), pp. 139, 141; William Frost, 'An Interpretation of Chaucer's Knight's Tale,' *RES*, xxv (1949), 295–297.
3. J. S. P. Tatlock, *The Development and Chronology of Chaucer's Works* (London, 1907), pp. 232–233; W. G. Dodd, *Courtly Love in Chaucer and Gower* (Boston, 1913), pp. 238–239, n. 1; H. R. Patch, *On Rereading Chaucer* (Cambridge, Mass., 1939), p. 206.
4. Albert H. Marckwardt, *Characterization in Chaucer's Knight's Tale*, Univ. of Michigan Contributions in Modern Philology, No. 5 (Ann Arbor, 1947). Similarly H. B. Hinckley, *Notes on Chaucer* (Northampton, Mass., 1907), p. 53, mentions 'the madcap Palamon and the equally ardent but more rational Arcite.'
5. 'What was Chaucer's Aim in the *Knight's Tale*?' *SP*, xxvi (1929), 375, 377, 380, 385.

6. 'Characterization in the "Knight's Tale," ' *MLN*, XLVI (1931), 302, 303, n. 2.

7. Tatlock, pp. 232–233; Hulbert, p. 385, n. 20; Patch, *op. cit.*, pp. 208–209; see '1949 Research in Progress,' *PMLA*, LXIV (1949), 121, no. 807.

8. Two clear examples of the application of the canons of rigid realism to the poem are Henry J. Webb, 'A Reinterpretation of Chaucer's Theseus,' *RES*, XXIII (1947), 289–296; and F. Torraca, 'The Knightes Tale e la Teseida,' in his *Scritti Vari* (Milan, 1928), pp. 89–107.

9. Quotations are from *The Complete Works of Geoffrey Chaucer*, ed. F. N. Robinson (Boston, [1933]).

10. 'Chaucer's Use of the *Teseida*,' *PMLA*, LXII (1947), 615, n. 60.

11. Agnes K. Getty, 'Chaucer's Changing Conceptions of the Humble Lover,' *PMLA*, XLIV (1929), 210–212.

A. C. EDWARDS

Knaresborough Castle and
'The Kynges Moodres Court'

IN Chaucer's *Man of Law's Tale* there is an omission of a place name which probably indicates the poet's sensitiveness to the politics of his time. In this tale, the court of King Alle's mother, Donegild, is twice the scene where treason occurs. Donegild, jealous of her daughter-in-law, Constance, twice dupes a messenger, and brings about the banishment of the Queen and her son.

As to the exact location where the exchanges of messages take place Chaucer is noncommittal. On the journey northward the messenger rides to 'the kynges mooder,' and returning, he stops at 'the kynges moodres court.' Yet Trivet, Chaucer's source for the *Man of Law's Tale,* explicitly states that the exchanges occurred at Knaresborough, a castle between England and Scotland:

> A cel temps estoit Domulde, la mere le Roy, a Knaresbourgh entre Engleterre & Escoce, . . . A-vint que le Messager, maunde par Elda & lucius, ala par knaresburgh pur porter & nuncier a la mere le Roi bone nouele, com il quidoit par resoun.[1]

Gower too, who borrowed perhaps from Chaucer, in retelling the same story in the *Confession Amantis,* was willing to accept Knaresborough as the scene of Donegild's duplicity:

Reprinted, by permission, from *Philological Quarterly,* xix (1940), 306-9.

> The messager, to Knaresburgh,
> Which toun he scholde passe thurgh,
> Ridende cam the ferste day.
> The kinges Moder ther lay
> Whos rigte name was Domilde,[2] . . .
> In alle haste ayein he goth
> Be Knaresburgh, and as he wente,
> Unto the Moder his entente
> Of that he fond toward the king
> He tolde.[3]

Later, Knaresborough Castle and the treason which was perpetrated there is again brought out by Gower when the messenger is summoned before the king for questioning:

> The messager . . . began to seie . . .
> At Knaresburgh be nyhtes tuo
> The kinges Moder made him duelle.
> And whan the king it herde telle,
> Withinne his herte he wiste als faste
> The treson which his Moder caste;[4]

Finally, in a fifteenth century version of Trivet's tale we find the translator again designating Knaresborough Castle as the habitat of Donegild and the scene of the treasonous exchange of messages:

> And than at that tyme was Domild the kynges moder at knaresburgh . . . hit happed than that the messanger, the which was sent to Olda and Lucius, wente to knaresburgh, for to bere tidinges, and to telle the kynges moder Joyful spede and good deliverance of the quene.[5] . . . Than with theese letteres come ageyn that foole the messanger with an evell be Domyld unto the Castell of Knaresburgh ayene.[6]

Like Gower, the translator insists on linking the castle with treason:

> And so that messager was called forthe, the whyche answered utterly, and sayde that he was never knowing neyther culpable nowise in that treason. Nevertheless he knowledged weele of his

drunkenesse in the court of Domyld, the kynges moder, at knaresburgh; And yef there were any treasoun do, hit was purposed there.[7]

Not without good reason did Trivet, Gower, and the fifteenth century translator place the wicked stepmother and treason at Knaresborough. For since the murder of Thomas a'Becket in 1170, an opprobrium had attached itself to the castle when Hugh de Morville, the owner at the time, fled there with his fellow-murderers[8] and remained in hiding behind the castle's walls for a year.[9] The murderers were regarded with horror by the natives of the shire, and the castle itself must have been given a wide berth if we are to accept the word of a chronicler of the period:

> . . . in occidentales Angliae partes secesserunt usque ad Cnaresburgum, villam Hugouis de Morevilla, et ibi tamdin remanserunt donec viles habiti fuerant a compatriotis illius provinciae. Omnes enim illorum vitabant alloquia nec aliquis cum eis manducare vel bibere voluit. Soli enim manducabant et soli bibebant, et fragmenta cibariorum suorum canibus projiciebantur. Et cum inde gustassent, nolebant inde quiquam comedere.[10]

The fact that even today 'local tradition still points out the hall where they [the murderers] fled for refuge, and the vaulted prison where they were confined after their capture'[11] would indicate that the Dominican monk, Trivet, 'moral Gower,' and probably the later translator of the tale were all aware of the castle's connection with the murder of Thomas a'Becket, and that it was an ideal location for the treason episodes in their tales.

Moreover, the reputation of Knaresborough was not improved in the years following Becket's murder. Far from the seat of government, the castle had a history which was punctuated through the fourteenth century with incidents ranging from trespass to rebellion against the king.[12] At one time the castle was the personal property of the infamous Queen Isabella who, with her consort Mortimer, had been suspected of being all but treasonous to England in her dealings with the Scots.

One would suppose then that Chaucer, who sent his pilgrims to the shrine of Thomas a'Becket, would have been as explicit as his source, and would have recalled the Saint by placing Donegild and her treachery at the castle of one of his murderers, Hugh de Moreville. Why then was Chaucer silent?

The answer seemingly is to be found in the fact that John of Gaunt, Chaucer's patron or at least his benefactor, owned Knaresborough;[13] and in the early 1380's an interesting series of events took place which made it almost mandatory that Chaucer locate Donegild's treason not at Knaresborough but rather at the ingenuous 'kynges moodres court'. Gaunt, at the time when the Savoy was being destroyed by the peasants, was safe within the castle walls of Knaresborough[14] and had just concluded 'by the offer of liberal terms' a truce with the Scots.[15] When the rebellion broke out, his wife, *Constance*, first tried to find shelter in Pontefract castle, and failing to gain admittance, rode on the same night to Knaresborough by torchlight.[16] When he heard of the rebellion Gaunt started to march south to aid his king, but learned on the way that he had been accused of treason by the Government. He was obliged to turn therefore, and to flee to Scotland for refuge.[17]

Chaucer, the court poet, keeping a weather eye on patronage and political disputes, was probably following a wise course when he refrained from naming his patron's own property as the home of treason and the unnatural Donegild.

NOTES

1. Chaucer Society, *Originals and Analogues* (London: Trübner and Co., 1888), 2nd series, Nos. 7, 10, 15, 20, 22, p. 27.

2. G. C. Macaulay, *The Complete Works of John Gower* (Oxford: Clarendon Press, 1901), 11, p. 155. Professor E. P. Kuhl first called my attention to the inclusion of the castle in Gower's tale.

3. *Ibid.*, p. 157.

4. *Ibid.*, p. 164.

5. Chaucer Society, *op. cit.*, p. 236.

6. *Ibid.*, p. 238.

7. *Ibid.*, p. 242.

8. Benedict of Petersborough, *Gesta Henrici II et Ricardi I* (London: Longmans, Green, Reader and Dyer, 1867), I, 13.

9. A. P. Stanley, *Historical Memorials of Canterbury* (2nd American ed., Philadelphia, 1899), p. 121.

10. Benedict of Petersborough, *op. cit.*, I, 13–14.

11. A. P. Stanley, *op. cit.*, p. 121.

12. *Calendar of Patent Rolls*, Edward II, A. D. 1317–21, pp. 46, 123, 176, 544; Edward III, A. D. 1330–34, pp. 55, 321; Richard II, Feb. 16, 1379, p. 357.

13. S. Armitage-Smith, *John of Gaunt* (New York: Charles Scribner's Sons), p. 202.

14. *Ibid.*, p. 250.

15. *Ibid.*, p. 251.

16. Knighton, II, p. 144.

17. *Ibid.*, pp. 145–6.

MARIE PADGETT HAMILTON

———

Echoes of Childermas in the Tale
of the Prioress

THE tantalizing description of Madame Eglentyne intoning the divine service gains additional, if adventitious, interest from the fact that on the way to Canterbury she does recite and allude to various passages from the Canonical Office and the Mass. That her Prologue is reminiscent of both the Office and the Little Office of the Virgin has been suggested. It has not been pointed out that *The Prioress' Tale* and Prologue taken together, either quote or refer to all the chief portions of the Mass for 28 December, Childermas or the Feast of the Holy Innocents.

The connexion, to be sure, has not been entirely overlooked. For *Prioress' Tale* 627, where the weeping mother of the dying child is called a new Rachel, Professor Robinson cites Matthew ii, 18 and adds:

> Mr. Joseph Dwight has pointed out to the editor that this passage, along with the Psalm *Domine Dominus noster*, occurs among the portions of Scripture read at the Mass on the Feast of the Holy Innocents. This might account for their association in Chaucer's mind, though the comparison of the bereaved mother to Rachel would be natural in itself.[1]

In view of all the parallels, however, it seems clear that Chaucer had the Mass of the Innocents in mind when he wrote the tale of

Reprinted from *The Modern Language Review*, xxxiv (1939), 1–8, by permission of The Modern Humanities Research Association. The article has been revised by the author for this reprint.

the Prioress, that for him and his contemporary readers the story was enriched by association with one of the most appealing feasts of the Church. The purpose of this paper is to illustrate that point, and to suggest that Chaucer's original source for the legend might have been a sermon on Innocents' Day and, in that event, probably a sermon preached by a boy bishop, a little clergeon.

In the first place, the hero of *The Prioress' Tale* is not merely a little child but, as it were, the representative of childhood itself on the threshold of accountability. To his own generation, nurtured in the melancholy lore of the climacteric ages,[2] Chaucer suggested as much when he changed the age of the boy from ten years or more, as it appears in the other extant versions of the story, to seven years. Modern readers must turn for an explanation to such antecedents of Jaques' soliloquy as *The Mirror of the Periods of Man's Life or Bids of the Virtues and Vices for the Soul of Man.*[3] There the Good and Bad Angels began to contend for mastery over little Everyman

> Whanne the child was vii yeer olde,
> Passyng sowkyng of milke drewis.

The author explains their choice of that particular year by the commonplace that 'at vii yeer age childhood bigynnes,' that afterward, at fourteen, it 'blynnes,' and 'than knowliche of manhode he wynnes.'

For this as for other reasons the legend of Chaucer's little clergeon lends itself to association with Childermas, and the more so since in the fourteenth century the ceremonies of the feast were conducted by children, 'the schoolboys or the choir-boys, or both,'[4] under the leadership of a boy bishop. The custom flourished in every country of Western Europe, and especially in England and France.[5] In England, according to ecclesiastical records from the thirteenth to the sixteenth centuries, the boys usurped the places of the deacons and priests for the whole twenty-four hours from Vespers on the eve of the feast to Vespers on Innocents' Day. The custom prevailed, with variations, not only in cathedrals and in collegiate and parish churches, but also in schools and religious houses.

The fact that the feast to which Chaucer seems to have related his story was conducted partly by children gives heightened significance to the initial stanza of the Prioress' Prologue:

'O Lord, oure Lord, thy name how merveillous
Is in this large world ysprad,' quod she;
'For noght oonly thy laude precious
Parfourned is by men of dignitee,
But by the mouth of children thy bountee
Parfourned is, for on the brest soukynge
Somtyme shewen they thyn heriynge.'

This is a rendering of Psalm viii, 2–3, as the caption of the Chaucerian manuscripts, *Domine dominus noster,* would indicate; but, as Mr. Joseph Dwight realized, it is also a translation of the Introit of the Mass for the Holy Innocents:

Ex ore infantium, Deus, et lactentium perfecisti laudem propter inimicos tuos. Domine, Dominus noster, quam admirabile est nomen tuum in universa terra.[6]

By changing thus the order of the verses in the Psalm, the liturgy at once strikes the keynote of the feast and places emphasis on the phrase 'Out of the mouth of babes,' as Chaucer also does by mentioning it again in the story proper, lines 607–8:

O grete God, that parfournest thy laude
By mouth of innocentz, lo, heere thy myght!

The Prioress more than once calls the little clergeon 'this innocent,'[7] as in lines 565–6:

Fro thennes forth the Jues han conspired
This innocent out of this world to chace.

Her narrative gains in pathos and dimension through the analogy here to Herod's attempt to kill the infant Jesus, an analogy made unmistakable by the further comment, 'O cursed folk of Herodes

al newe.' As might be expected, the Gospel for the Innocents' Mass
is Matthew ii, 13–18, the account of the flight of the Holy Family
into Egypt and of Herod's slaying the male children in Bethlehem
'of two years old and under.' Chaucer's reason for laying his scene
in Asia, a departure from all extant analogues, may have been to
suggest once more the similarity between his story and the account
of those earlier Asiatic martyrs.[8]

A further connexion between the two was noted by Mr. Dwight,
this reference of the Prioress to the dying boy's mother:

> Unnethe myghte the peple that was theere
> This newe Rachel brynge fro his beere

The Innocents' Gospel closes with the prophecy of Jeremiah, now
fulfilled in the grief of the bereaved mothers, who are typified by
Rachel: 'In Rama was there a voice heard, lamentation and great
mourning: Rachel bewailing her children, and would not be comforted, because they are not.' The Church had decreed that the
Feast of the Innocents be kept with purple, and that the Mass be
stripped of the *Te Deum,* the *Alleluia,* and the *Gloria,* 'out of
compassion, as it were, for the sorrowing mothers of Bethlehem';[9]
and the Communion of the Mass again commemorated their grief
by repetition of the verses about Rachel: *Vox in Rama audita est,*
etc. Like the ranting of Herod, played 'upon a scaffold hye,' the
beautiful passage from Jeremiah laid hold on the mediaeval imagination, and the figure of the archetypal Rachel, refusing to be
comforted, had a central place in the liturgical dramas dealing
with the Slaughter of the Innocents.[10]

As the Gospel for Innocents' Day tells of the murder of the
babes, so the Epistle for the Mass records their triumph over
death. It is Apocalypse xiv, 1–5, the description of the Celestial
Lamb and his followers, the 144,000 virgins. Because St. John calls
these 'the first fruits to God and to the Lamb,' they were identified
with the earliest Christian martyrs, the victims of Herod, and
consequently in the Middle Ages it was held that Herod had killed
144,000 male children in little Bethlehem.[11] The immaculate procession of the Lamb was central in the Canonical Office for Chil-

dermas, and the liturgical plays in celebration of the feast usually opened the scene of the Slaughter of the Innocents with the doomed children carrying or following a lamb and singing the *Ecce Agnus Dei* or the *Emitte Agnum.*[12]

No student of Chaucer need be reminded that Apocalypse xiv, 1–5 was also the inspiration for one of the most affecting stanzas of *The Prioress' Tale*. There the little boy is said to have joined the Holy Innocents, where without fear of persecution he may sing a new song:

> O martir, sowded to virginitee,
> Now maystow syngen, folwynge evere in oon
> The white Lamb celestial—quod she—
> Of which the grete evaungelist, Seint John,
> In Pathmos wroot, which seith that they that goon
> Biforn this Lamb, and synge a song al newe,
> That nevere, flesshly, wommen they ne knewe.

So much for the Mass, of which the Introit, the Gospel, the Epistle, and the Communion are paraphrased or directly alluded to by the Prioress. Some details of the liturgy for the mediaeval service conducted by the children on the eve of Innocents' Day also may be pertinent. The one at Salisbury Cathedral [13] began with a procession during which the boys, as at all other observances of the Canonical Office for Childermas, sang the *Centum Quadraginta,* an arrangement of those verses from the Innocents' Epistle which Chaucer adapted for describing the celestial triumph of his little schoolboy. The remainder of the liturgy for that service was chiefly in praise of 'Cristes mooder deere,' comprising passages from the Mass of the Blessed Virgin for the season from Christmas Day to Candlemas.[14] The fact that schoolboys took part in Childermas ceremonies, where Mary was especially honoured in the observances of the Canonical Hours, would help to explain why the older schoolmates of Chaucer's little clergeon 'lerned hire antiphoner' at the approach of Christmas, with particular attention to Marian anthems like the *Alma Redemptoris Mater.*[15] Naturally the little seven-year-old would wish to imitate the older boys who, we may suppose, were preparing to sing at the Innocents' services;

and hence his anxiety to learn the *Alma Redemptoris* 'er Cristemasse be went.'

The little fellow's readiness to learn is compared to the precocity of St. Nicholas:

> Thus hath this wydwe hir litel sone ytaught
> Oure blisful Lady, Cristes mooder deere,
> To worshipe ay, and he forgat it naught,
> *For sely child wol alday soone leere.*[16]
> But ay, when I remembre on this mateere,
> Seint Nicholas stant evere in my presence,
> For he so yong to Crist dide reverence.

Skeat and Professor Robinson gave no explanation of this reference beyond the fact, recorded in the Roman Breviary and elsewhere, that Nicholas as an infant at the breast fasted on Wednesdays and Fridays. Hence we may digress to note that Chaucer may also have been thinking of such passages about him as this from the *Vita Sancti Nicholai* in the *South English Legendary*:

> Ðo he was sethþe of grettore elde: to scole he was i-set;
> So wel he leornede: þat man nuste, no child leorni bet.
> Sethþe þo he more couþe: al his studie he tok
> to guodespelles ant to holi writes: and alle oþere bokes for-sok.[17]

Allusions to St. Nicholas, though their appropriateness to Chaucer's narrative needs no justification, are especially germane to the echoes of Childermas in *The Prioress' Tale;* for the Feast of St. Nicholas, 6 December, was closely related to Childermas. The boy bishop usually was elected on Nicholas' Day,[18] sometimes officiated at the Feast of Nicholas as well as at the Feast of the Holy Innocents, and hence sometimes was called the Nicholas Bishop or Bishop Nicholas.[19] Plays about St. Nicholas were regular features of the less solemn festivities of Childermas,[20] and on the eve of the feast the child bishop and his companions marched first to the altar of Nicholas where one was available.[21]

Granted that Chaucer related his story to the Feast of the Innocents 'of ful avysement,' why did he do so? The heightened appeal of his narrative would be reason enough. To the trained mediaeval ear his legend of the little martyr had rich overtones, through association with an ancient ceremonial which honored the charm and innocence of all childhood and symbolized the grief of all bereaved motherhood, the universal Rachel:

> Whan seyd was al this miracle, every man
> As sobre was that wonder was to see.

Yet I suspect that a connection between the 'miracle' and the feast may have antedated Chaucer's handling of the theme. It is clear that martyred children, and more particularly those who were said to have been slain by Jews, were associated with the babes of Bethlehem. In Brewer's *Dictionary of Miracles*, familiar analogues of *The Prioress' Tale*, the allegedly historical accounts of the youthful martyrs Richard of Pontoise, William of Norwich, and the little St. Hugh of Lincoln whom the Prioress invokes, are treated in the section on 'Herod and the Innocents'; and the body of Richard, supposedly murdered by Jews in the year 1182, is said to have been enshrined in the Church of the Holy Innocents in Paris. There is also the legend from Vincent of Beauvais of the child who shared his bread with an image of the weeping Christ Child and was speedily rewarded by death and beatitude; 'wherefore,' says the narrator, 'he doth now most undoubtedly feast among the Innocents of Bethlehem.'[22]

Among those who retold the widespread legend of the martyred choirboy or schoolboy, it remained, however, for Chaucer to deepen its perspective and heighten its evocative power by relating it not merely to St. Matthew's account of Herod's victims, but also to the liturgy of the Mass in which the Church commemorated their martyrdom. The association, nevertheless, may already have been made in some other context, and the most likely one would be the services of the Church themselves. The story of the little clergeon, with its allusions to the precocious sanctity of St. Nicholas, would have made an ideal exemplum for a Childermas sermon. As in *The Pardoner's Tale*, the narrative might have been used as the framework for the whole homily, and the more likely if it had been designed for delivery by a boy bishop.

That the theme of *The Prioress' Tale* was employed in sermons is certain. It appears in the *Promptuarium* (or storehouse of *exempla*) which Johannes Herolt appended to his *Sermones de Tempore et de Sanctis,* a collection much in demand during the fifteenth and sixteenth centuries.[23] Professor Woodburn Ross, in *Modern Language Notes* for May 1935,[24] gives the text of a hitherto neglected analogue to Chaucer's story from Bromyard's popular manual for preachers, the *Summa Predicantium,* composed in England, apparently shortly after 1370. On the evidence of that version, of another from the *Speculum Exemplorum,* and of still another from a book containing sermons, Professor Ross concludes that the story of the chorister or schoolboy murdered by Jews was 'very likely in fairly frequent use as a pulpit exemplum.'

This circumstance would help to explain the wide diffusion and popularity of the legend, and also, perhaps, Chaucer's associating it with Childermas, if perchance he heard the story in a sermon on that occasion. While we are indulging in pure speculation, we might picture the scene as Lincoln Cathedral, where an analogue to the legend of 'yonge Hugh of Lincoln,' invoked by the Prioress, would have been especially fitting as an exemplum for the Feast of the Innocents. Chaucer, we are told, 'had various reasons for interest in Lincolnshire.'[25] His sister-in-law, Katherine Swynford, had a manor there; and Philippa Chaucer in February 1386 was admitted to the society of patrons of the cathedral.[26]

Finally, if Chaucer did hear the story of the Prioress in an Innocents' sermon, it not improbably was from the lips of a boy bishop.[27] 'In various places in England,' says Professor Young, 'the Boy Bishop, as part of his assumption of mature responsibility, preached a sermon at Mass.'[28] Chambers speaks in particular of the custom at St. Paul's, where the boy did not write his own sermon.[29] William de Tolleshunte, almoner of Paul's, bequeathed to the almonry copies of 'all the quires of sermons for the Feast of the Holy Innocents'[30] preached by boy bishops in his time, the early part of the fourteenth century. Dean Colet, as late as 1512, specified that the boys of St. Paul's School should 'every Chyldre-masse day come to paulis Church, and here the Chylde Bishoppis sermon and after be at hye masse, and eche of them offre a 1d to the Childe Bishopp.'[31] A discourse on the infant Jesus written by Erasmus for delivery by a boy at Colet's school has been preserved, as have sermons unmistakably designed for boy bishops.[32]

The echoes of Childermas in *The Prioress' Tale* demand no explanation beyond the literary tact and inventiveness of Chaucer, but it is pleasant to conjecture that he may have heard the story at an Innocents' Mass, *ex ore infantium*.

NOTES

1. Students' Cambridge Edition of *Chaucer's Complete Works* p. 841.

2. 'The ancient sages by curious notes have found out, that certain yeeres in mans life be very perilous. These they name climacterical or stayrie yeares, for then they saw great alterations. Now a climactericall yeare is every seaventh yeare. . . . Hence it is that in the seaventh yeere children doe cast and renew their teeth. In the fourteenth yeere proceedeth the strippling age,' etc. (from W. Vaughan's *Natural and Artificial Directions for Health*, 1602, as quoted by Furnivall in his edition of *The Mirror of the Periods of Man's Life*. See note 2, p. 2).

3. In *Hymns to the Virgin and Christ, The Parliament of Devils, and Other Religious Poems*, ed. by Furnivall, EETS, O. S., 24, 1867, pp. 58–78.

4. Leach's phrase. His essay 'The Schoolboy's Feast,' in *The Fortnightly Review* (January 1896), pp. 128–41, still is one of the best short accounts of the boy bishop in England. Chambers gives an ampler account in *The Mediaeval Stage*, vol. i. chap. 15. See also Young, *The Drama of the Mediaeval Church*, I, 104–11, and Gayley, *Plays of Our Forefathers*, pp. 54–61. Unfortunately I have not seen Canon Fletcher's pamphlet, *The Boy Bishop at Salisbury and Elsewhere*, 1921.

5. Young, *Drama of the Mediaeval Church*, I, 106.

6. Since the Mass for Innocents' Day is essentially the same today as in Chaucer's time (*Catholic Encyclopaedia*, under 'Feast of the Holy Innocents'), my quotations are from the Roman Missal in present use. As Robinson's note reminds us, Psalm 8 is prominent in the Matins service, which would have been familiar to the Prioress, but in view of the various echoes of the Mass of the Holy Innocents in the story itself, it is reasonable to suppose that Chaucer had in mind the Introit of the Mass in this passage.

7. The boys who took part in the Childermas ceremonies quite naturally were known as Innocents (Chambers, I, 347).

8. It would be pleasant to assume that the alien setting was designed to avoid the issue of local prejudices, or that it was meant to suggest that for the Lady Prioress the ugly anti-Semitism of her tale was an academic concern of distant times and places, but her final invocation to the martyred Hugh of Lincoln precludes any such charitable interpretation.

9. *Catholic Encyclopaedia*, under 'Feast of the Holy Innocents.'

10. See especially Karl Young, *Ordo Rachelis*, University of Wisconsin Studies in Language and Literature, IV, and his *Drama of the Mediaeval Church*, vol. II, chap. 20.

11. *Catholic Encyclopaedia*, 'Feast of the Holy Innocents.'

12. Young, *Drama of the Mediaeval Church*, I, 102–7, 110–14.

13. The Sarum Office (in use there) is reproduced by Chambers, vol. II, appendix M, and is the basis of my summary.

14. The Offertory, *Felix namque est, sacra Virgo*, etc., and the Gradual, *Speciosus forma prae filiis hominum*, etc.

15. The *Alma Redemptoris* is the Marian anthem now sung during Christmas week. According to Skeat, the Roman Breviary for 1583 designated it for use at that time—i.e. from Advent to Candlemas. Since the Mass for the Innocents was essentially the same in Chaucer's time as now, and since the mediaeval ritual for the other Innocents' services at Salisbury Cathedral was composed of passages of liturgy still in use by the Roman Church during the Christmas season, the presumption is that the *Alma Redemptoris*, which was very popular in the Middle Ages, was sung from Advent to Candlemas, then as now. But see Carleton Brown, 'Chaucer's Litel Clergeon,' in *Modern Philology*, III (April 1906), 9–13.

16. My italics.

17. EETS 87, 240, lines 13-16.

18. Young, *Drama of the Mediaeval Church*, I, 106; Chambers I, 369.

19. Leach, *op. cit.*, p. 133.

20. Gayley, *Plays of Our Forefathers*, p. 61.

21. Leach, p. 133.

22. *Speculum Historiale* 6, col. 99, translated by G. G. Coulton, *Life in the Middle Ages* 1.52.

23. See Herolt's *Miracles of the Blessed Virgin Mary*, translated by C. C. Swinton Bland (London, 1928), especially pp. 1–2, 92–3.

24. 'Another Analogue to *The Prioresses Tale*,' pp. 307–10.

25. See Robinson's note 684, on p. 841 of the Cambridge Chaucer, citing Manly.

26. Cowling, *Chaucer*, pp. 18–19.

27. Lincoln was one of the cathedrals where the boy bishop held sway. See above, p. 3, note 5.

28. *Drama of the Mediaeval Church* 1.110.

29. Chambers, I, 355–6.

30. Owst, *Preaching in Mediaeval England*, p. 220, quotes the phrase from Tolleshunte's will. See also Chambers, I, 354–5.

31. Chambers I, 356; quoted from Lupton's *Life of Colet*.

32. *Ibid.*, p. 356 and note 3. It is not certain that Erasmus' sermon was designed for a boy bishop.

J. LESLIE HOTSON

Colfox *vs.* Chauntecleer

'GEOFFREY CHAUCER,' says Professor Kittredge, 'is nearer to us than Alexander Pope.' This is true, not only of the spirit of his times, but also of the man. Chaucer is more like us than Pope is: we feel more mental, moral, and spiritual kinship with the writer of the *Nun's Priest's Tale* than with the author of the *Essay on Man*. But, though this is true, we are not to think that therefore we understand him more thoroughly. In reality, we comprehend nearly all of Pope, and some of him we don't like; *per contra,* we like all of Chaucer that we comprehend: yet there are moods and meanings in him hard to fathom.

Though the modern reader finds some of his meanings obscure, we may be sure that they were clear to his contemporaries. We can draw no other conclusion from the evidence of his firm, compact style, and his unfailing choice of the right word. When Chaucer's meaning is not plain to us, the fault lies in our ignorance either of his speech and education or of the smaller and more interesting facts of his life and times. Often we are baffled by a passage which we feel contains more meaning or humor than we can get from it. What would we give to appeal to the author in the words of Criseyde:

> For al this world ne can I reden what
> It sholde been; som jape, I trowe, is this;
> And but your-selven telle us what it is,
> My wit is for to arede it al to lene;
> As help me god, I noot nat what ye mene.

Reprinted, by permission, from *PMLA*, XXXIX (1924), 762–81.

Chaucer's mood complicates his meaning; and his most intricate mood is humor. The greatest rub in the path of understanding it is *partial appreciation.* Our satisfaction at having seen something, one or two points, perhaps, quite prevents us from seeing more. In exploring Chaucer's humor we are sailing on perilous seas; yet it is true that we are in more danger of not seeing his whole meaning than we are of misrepresenting what we see. We lose more than we distort.

With these considerations in mind, let us turn to the tale of the Nun's Priest. Here we are in the midst of Chaucer's humor; here we have his skill at its finest and his genius at its height. Harry Bailly has ordered the priest to tell a tale, and to be merry about it. 'Yis, sir,' replies the goodly man, 'But I be merry, y-wis I wol be blamed.' This gives the note; but the preacher, from force of habit, casts his whole fable into homiletic form, adds long illustrations, or *exempla,* and uses the main episode to point a serious moral. Yet all this covers the story only as the robe covers the priest. Inside is the 'large breest,' swelling with fun and ironic humor, and unfolding the irresistibly comic tale in admirable periods of eloquence.

Its most delightful quality is the mock-heroic. Royal Chauntecleer's grim forebodings; Dame Pertelote's contempt for his cowardice; her common-sense prescriptions for his diet; Chauntecleer's defense of the significance of dreams, and his long appeal to grave authorities; his supercilious rejection of homely remedies, and his ironical praise of woman, which restores his good humor—what glorious fun! Yet, even though the general tone of the story is sympathetic and not satirical, and though we like to think that Chaucer wrote it solely as a perfect bit of comic narrative, to judge it properly we must put ourselves in the place of his audience.

Now the medieval readers did not understand 'art for art's sake'; they preferred useful stories: stories that taught, that satirized, or that pointed an excellent moral. The authors were of the same mind; the attitude of even the most 'artistic' of them is exposed by Pandarus:

> How-so it be that som men hem delyte
> With subtil art hir tales for to endyte,
> Yet for al that, in hir entencioun,
> Hir tale is al for som conclusioun.

Chaucer, of course, does point a moral at the end of his fable; yet I question whether the medieval reader, although delighted with the mock-heroics and pleased with the moral, was satisfied with the very general nature of the satire on human frailty in the rest of the tale. Moreover, the thing is told with such *verve* and high spirits, that it is hard not to suspect that author and audience saw something further in it to amuse them: something besides the main comic dialogue, the characters, and the stock situation, which time has hidden from us.

This suspicion gathers weight when one considers the origin of the *Cock and the Fox*. It is drawn from an incident in the *Renart* epic. The *Renart*, in its allegorical sense, was a satire on contemporary society. Are we sure that Chaucer's selection departed completely from this tradition of contemporary satire, and took perennial human nature as its province? Furthermore, the *Cock and the Fox* is a *fable*. Fables, in the Middle Ages, were commonly-used engines of satire. In the hands of Marie de France, the animal figure always concealed a man. It is evident that Chaucer's readers were educated to expect satirical hits and some more than didactic pieces of allegory in their beast epic and beast fable. The *Nun's Priest's Tale*, we must remember, is Chaucer's first and only fable; it deserves closer study than it has received. We must look beneath his lively pictures of human character for sly contemporary hits.

Indeed, after the moral has been pointed, the narrator gravely announces that the tale is, in fact, something more than

> a folye
> As of a fox, or of a cok and hen.

This homiletic assurance, while thoroughly in character, seems nothing but anti-climax; but there is no anti-climax if we catch Chaucer's solemn wink.

Let us turn to the story, then, to see if there are any grounds in fact for our suspicion. In the first place, the date of the poem has not been fixed. The maturity and finished excellence of its execution, however, lead most scholars to place it in the later period of the Canterbury Tales, or, roughly, 1390–1400: a decade which included the last years of the reign of Richard II, and the usurpation of Henry IV.

The natural places in which to look for possible inner meanings are, as we have seen, the passages in which the sense is unclear, in which Chaucer added to his original, or varied from it. One of the particulars in which Chaucer seems somewhat obscure, and also differs from his originals, is in his use of names. The fox in the originals is called *Reinicke* or *Renart;* Chaucer, although he uses the name *Renard* for the fox in the *Legend of Good Women*, introduces him here as a *colfox*, and later calls him *daun Russel*. What is the purpose in these changes?

Let us look first at the word 'colfox,' which is found in English only in this passage from Chaucer. It is worth while to give Skeat's note on it in full:

> *col-fox;* explained by Bailey as a 'coal-black fox'; and he seems to have caught the right idea. *Col-* here represents M. E. *col*, coal; and the reference is to the *brant-fox*, which is explained in the New E. Dict. as borrowed from the G. *brand-fuchs*, 'the German name of a variety of the fox, chiefly distinguished by a greater admixture of black in its fur; according to Grimm, it has black feet, ears, and tail.' Chaucer expressly refers to the black-tipped tail and ears in 1. 4094 above. Mr. Bradley cites the G. *kohlfuchs* and Du. *koolvos*, similarly formed; but the ordinary dictionaries do not give these names. The old explanation of *col-fox* as meaning 'deceitful fox' is difficult to establish and is now unnecessary.[1]

Skeat is correct in showing that the probable meaning of the word coincides with the description of the fox given by Chaucer in ll. 4094–5; but *in this very description* Chaucer also varies from all the other versions of the story. In the *Renart,* and also in *Reinhart Fuchs* Chantecler dreamed that he saw a beast clothed in a red fur coat, with an opening at the neck made of bone. This he made

Chantecler put on.[2] Chaucer's Chauntecleer, on the contrary, has no allegory in his dream, but hard fact. A reddish-yellow beast, something like a dog, tipped with black at both ends, with murder in his glowing eyes, came after him.

It seems evident that Chaucer had some purpose in view in making his fox a *colfox*, and in carefully describing him later in the story:

> And tipped was his tail and bothe his eres
> With blak, unlyk the remenant of his heres.

Let us examine this animal more closely. Why 'colfox'? 'Colfox,' as a common noun, occurs, we know, only in this passage from the *Nun's Priest*. But Colfox is also a proper name, a surname; and is found in England from Chaucer's time to ours.

Of the Colfoxes living in the period 1360–1400, two, Nicholas and Richard Colfox, were prominent men, and were known at court. Both were at one time or another closely associated with the castle at Barton-Segrave, co. Northampton, which belonged to Thomas Mowbray, Duke of Norfolk.

Richard, undoubtedly the younger of the two men (and perhaps the son of Nicholas), appears in the records as an intimate associate of the most prominent Lollard knights, and later as prince's esquire under Henry V. We find him first in 1395, when King Richard granted him a moor called *Overmershe*, in Cheshire. This was followed by another gift in the next year. When Henry IV usurped the power in 1399, Richard Colfox evidently enjoyed the especial favor of Henry, Prince of Wales (Bluff Prince Hal), for the latter confirmed the grant and made sure that the land was his. By 1404, however, Colfox had associated himself too closely with the Lollard knights to please the prince, who seized his property. In this year also we find Richard Colfox as an executor of the will of Lewis Clifford, the knight and Lollard who, as Professor Kittredge has shown[3] was one of Chaucer's friends. Four years later, in 1408, the keeping of Barton Segrave Castle was taken out of the hands of Richard Colfox, now an esquire, and he was found not responsible for its deterioration. By 1413 we find him in partnership with that protagonist of Lollardry, Sir John Oldcastle; they have sold the king a jewel, and are dunning him for the unpaid balance. But the next winter sees the arrest and trial of the Lollards. Richard Colfox, Esquire, was examined at Winchester and tried at Westminster in January, 1414. In March, the King issued the following 'pardon':

> The King orders the several sheriffs to proclaim pardon for Lollards, except Sir John Oldcastle, Sir Thomas Talbot, Richard Colfox, and nine others, those in sanctuary, and those already arrested.

For a year this Colfox was an outlaw or a prisoner; then on May 23, 1415, he was pardoned and reinvested with his lands. After nine years he was still in favor, and in 1428 he received a grant. Six years later, he died.

So much for Richard Colfox, Prince's Esquire, sometime of Barton-Segrave, Northamptonshire. As we have seen, he was in the closest association with Sir Lewis Clifford, a friend of Chaucer, and must have been well known to the poet. Is he the Colfox aimed at in the *Nun's Priest's Tale*? Before we can decide, we must examine the other Colfox.

Nicholas Colfox was probably born in Nantwich, co. Chester, of a family which had been prominent there for at least a century. Some of the entries of the name 'Nicholas Colfox of Nantwich' are, however, so early, that we are forced to postulate one, or even two earlier namesakes. Even when we are sure that the documents fall within the active life of our Colfox, it is hard to tell which Nicholas is meant, although the records at times specify 'the younger' or 'Nicholas Colfox, senior.'

The first unmistakable reference to the man whom we are tracing comes immediately after Henry Bolingbroke's seizure of the throne in 1399. In open Parliament, Colfox was implicated, as chief coadjutor, in the murder of a man whose mysterious death two years before had deeply stirred the people of England. In 1397, Mowbray, who was Colfox's master and a creature of Richard II, at the King's secret order, had arrested the duke of Gloucester, taken him to Calais, and there secretly murdered him. Gloucester, a prince of the blood, was uncle to Henry Bolingbroke, and had long led the popular opposition against the detested king. The murder, prearranged and coldly accomplished, of such a powerful man, could not remain hidden. Almost at once the truth was suspected, and popular feeling ran high against Mowbray. In challenging him at Shrewsbury (in 1398, five months after the crime), Henry publicly accused him of the murder. A year later, as we have said, in the Parliament held after Henry had driven Richard from the throne, a circumstantial story of the dark affair was told by an eye-witness. It is the confession of John Hall, formerly valet to Mowbray, who guarded the door of the Prince's Inn at Calais during the murder. Hall's account relates that on that night in September, 1397,

> le dit Duc de Norffolc & un Johan Colfox Esquier du dit Duc, viendrent al Chaumbre de dit Johan Halle, en la Ville de Caleys. Lequel Johan Colfox appella le dit Johan Halle hors de son lyt, luy comaundant de venir à dit Duc son Seigneur; lequel Johan Halle soy leva de son lyt, & veigna as ditz Duc & Johan Colfox. Et le Duc luy demaunda, Purquoy avez atant demure; & luy demaunda s'il oiast rien del Duc de Gloucestre? Quel Johan Hall respontist, Qu'il supposa qu'il fuist mort. Et le dit Duc de Norffolc disoit, noun; nepurquant de dit nadgairs Roy luy avoit charge pur mourdrer le dit Duc de Gloucestre: Et que le dit nadgairs Roy, & le Duc d'Aumarle, adonqes Count de Roteland, avoient envoiez certains leurs Esquiers & Vadlets pur estre illoeques . . .

And, later, having gathered more men—

> . . . soy alèrent ovesque le dit Duc de Norffolc toutz ensemble vers l'Ostell appelle le Princes In. Et quant ils furent illeoqes, le dit Duc de Norffolc metta les ditz Johan Colfox, William Hampsterly, — Bradeston, William Serle, — Fraunceys, William Roger, William Denys, — Cok del Chaumbre, & Johan Halle, en une maison deinz le dit Hostell, et ala son chemyn . . .

Then he tells how they brought the duke of Gloucester to this house, where Colfox and the others were placed in wait for him, and how they murdered him. Let us stop here to glance back at our text.

> A Colfox, ful of sly iniquitee
>
> . . . .
>
> Wayting his tyme on Chauntecleer to falle,
> As gladly doon thise homicydes alle,
> That in awayt liggen to mordre men.
> O false mordrer, lurking in thy den!

That the name *Johan* of the Colfox who acted as Mowbray's right-hand man in this Calais business is merely a blunder for *Nicholas,* is demonstrated beyond a doubt by later documents:

> 1404. Mar. 31. Pardon, out of reverence for Good Friday last, to Nicholas Colfox, 'chivaler,' for the death of Thomas, late Duke of Gloucester, the king's uncle.

An ancient petition shows that Colfox had earnestly sued Henry for this pardon. It was granted, as we see, a little less than seven years after the murder had taken place. In that time he had risen from esquire to knight.

All the other parties to the murder did not escape as easily as Colfox. John Hall, immediately after his confession, was put to death with the peculiarly savage refinements which the law reserved for traitors. William Serle, another of the murderers, one of the Gentlemen of Richard's Bedchamber, and an executor of his will, was captured in 1404, and condemned as a traitor for the murder of the Duke of Gloucester. His death was considerably prolonged and made a deep impression on the country. It is recorded in many chronicles. Even the authorities admitted that he had suffered 'more and severer penalties than other our traitors have endured before these times.'

But to return to Colfox. Less than three weeks after Hall's confession, Henry seized Colfox's property.

> 1399. Nov. 3. Grant to the king's esquire Henry Lyvermer of the lands, rents, and services which *Nicholas Colfox* had of the grant

of Thomas Mowbray, late duke of Norfolk, in Barton Segrave, co. Northampton.

His pardon for murder was followed in 1405 by another: this time for 'treasons, insurrections, rebellions, and felonies.' The remaining references to him are of little importance: a mention of his rental, a pardon for not appearing to be sued for debt, and a tax assessment on his property in Gloucester. So much for the documents.

We have found, then, in this man, a plausible reason why Chaucer departed from all the variants of the beast fable to make the villain of his piece a 'Colfox.' The killing of Gloucester, a prince of England and youngest son to Edward III, was more than murder: it was treason. Hall and Serle, as we have seen, were executed as traitors. It is worth noting that Chaucer likens the Colfox not to murderers, but to famous *traitors*:

> O newe Scariot, newe Ganilon!
> False dissimilour, O Greek Sinon,
> That broughtest Troye al outrely to sorwe!

Besides throwing light on the mysterious Colfox, this notorious murder may also explain the presence of one of Chauntecleer's *exempla*. These illustrative anecdotes, as we know, were borrowed from Cicero or Valerius Maximus, and added by Chaucer to the fable. The first and longer of them (which constitutes one-eighth of the entire poem) is a harrowing tale of a secret murder, done in a foreign town. Near the end of it, Chaucer digressed from his *exemplum* original to apostrophize God the just, and to reflect on the discovery of hidden murder:

> O blisful god, that art so just and trewe!
> Lo, how that thou biwreyest mordre alway!
> Mordre wol out, that see we day by day.
> Mordre is so wlatsom and abhominable
> To god, that is so just and resonable,
> That he ne wol nat suffre it heled be;
> Thogh it abyde a yeer, or two, or three,
> Mordre wol out, this is my conclusioun.

If this emphatic aside, coupled with the anecdote of the secret murder done in a foreign town, be compared with the hidden murder of Gloucester at Calais; and if the vigorous characterization of the traitorous, murdering, and unique *colfox* be placed beside the Colfox of John Hall's confession, it seems more than possible that Chaucer, in writing the *Nun's Priest's Tale*, was touching contemporary history.

On this hypothesis, the work must have been written after September, 1397. Furthermore, it is likely that Chaucer wrote the tale when some little time had elapsed after the crime. We cannot think that such a spirited and humorous performance, if it made the slightest reference to a revolting murder, could have been composed while the country was still shocked by the news.

But, taking the reference for granted, and leaving the question of date aside for the moment, let us ask a question: was Chaucer, in this passage, aiming at Colfox personally, or through him at some man or party which he represented? Dryden, in modernizing the *Nun's Priest's Tale*, naturally did not grasp the meaning of *colfox*; yet he was not blind to the shining opportunity which the passage offers for political satire:

> A Fox, full-fraught with seeming sanctity,
> That feared an oath, but, like the devil, would lie;
> Who looked like Lent, and had the holy leer,
> And durst not sin before he said his prayer;
> This pious cheat, that never sucked the blood
> Nor chewed the flesh of lambs but when he could. . . .

The analogy between Chaucer and Dryden is significant. Both were the greatest writers of their time; both wrote for the Court; each of them saw a king of England dethroned and another set up; each lived in an intensely political age, when bitter partisanship was the rule. In his *Cock and Fox*, Dryden aimed at a party. Did Chaucer select a relatively unimportant, but notorious knight for his butt (since his name was miraculously apt), or was Colfox a stalking-horse for higher game?

To answer this question, we must reconsider the whole tale in the light of what we have found. In the first place, did Chaucer launch this *mock-heroic* poem without inspiration or stimulus from some actual *heroic* incident? The murder of a duke, we may be sure, was not an occurrence which would suggest the writing of a mock-heroic. We remember that the central episode is an encounter between a cock and a fox, in which neither is killed, but in which both are damaged by their own folly: the cock through his love of flattery, and the fox by chattering when he should hold his tongue.

An encounter took place in 1398, the year after the murder of Gloucester: an encounter which every reader of Shakespeare or of English history is familiar with. This was the famous quarrel of Henry Bolingbroke, then Duke of Hereford, with Thomas Mowbray, Duke of Norfolk, followed by their duel at Coventry. Richard stopped the proceedings just before blows were struck, and exiled the antagonists: Henry for ten years, and Mowbray forever.

Such an heroic encounter, ending a bit ingloriously, but without hurt, for both combatants, furnishes an excellent occasion for a *sympathetic,* humorous fable, done in a grave and gay mock-heroic style. Let us go a bit further in search of confirmation or disproof of this conjecture.

Chaucer adds to his original in his description of the antagonists. While none of the other variants gives Chantecleer any color, Chaucer lavishes colors on him, until the lordly cock seems more splendid than Nature warrants:

> His comb was redder than the fyn coral,
> And batailed, as it were a castel-wal.
> His bile was blak, and as the jeet it shoon;
> Lyk asur were his legges, and his toon;
> His nayles whytter than the lilie flour,
> And lyk the burned gold was his colour.

This description is so heightened as to give rise to suspicion. I have yet to see or hear of a rooster who combines a black bill, white claws, and azure legs with a gold plumage. Moreover, there are terms here which give a strong heraldic tint to the picture: '*gold* color,' '*azure* legs,' '*battled* comb.'

Henry of Bolingbroke's coat of arms, when he entered the lists at Coventry, was emblazoned on his armor. His bearings at this time were· 'England and France ancient; impaling: azure, a cross fleury between five martlets or; over all a label of five points: three points ermine, and two azure, floretté or.' The predominant color is gold: the fleurs de lys, the cross, the martlets, and the leopards of England. The fields are azure and gules (red). The label is white and azure; its teeth form crenelated or battlement-like shapes on the red field. The ermine-spots are, of course, black, and are shaped like arrowheads (compare Chauntecleer's bill). This rough description is enough to show the striking similarity between Chauntecleer's colors and Henry's arms. All the colors on Henry's coat and no others, are found on Chauntecleer; and several of them Chaucer calls by their heraldic names.

Contemporary literature lends strength to the surmise that Henry was here represented under the guise of a fowl. The curious satirical popular poetry of the times constantly refers to him as a bird: 'an *eron,' 'aquila,' 'egle,' 'falcon,' 'blessid bredd,' 'beu brid.'*

To turn from Chauntecleer to the Colfox, we find that the careful description of his colors is also added by Chaucer:

> His colour was bitwixe yelwe and reed;
> And tipped was his tail, and bothe his eres,
> With blak, unlyk the remenant of his heres.

Now, as we have said, it was not Colfox, but Colfox's master, Mowbray, Earl Marshal of England, who met Henry in the lists. On his appointment as Earl Marshal in 1397, the office had been made hereditary in his family; and he and his heirs male had received permission from the king in Parliament to 'have, wear, and carry' as a sign and badge of their high station, a *golden truncheon tipped with black at both ends.*

To draw these likenesses together, on the one hand we have Chauntecleer, splendid in gold, azure, red, white, and black; a musical, eloquent, courteous bird, 'royal as a prince.' Beside him let us put Henry of Bolingbroke, the best knight in England, wearing colors identical with Chauntecleer's; brilliant in music, learned in logic, referred to as 'hende egle,' 'beu brid,' and the like, in contemporary poems; son to John, King of Castile and Leon, and grandson to Edward III of England.

On the other hand we have a unique type of fox, a *colfox*: as treacherous and bloodthirsty as those who 'lie in wait to murder men'; his color is a golden-orange, and he is tipped at each end with black; he is Chauntecleer's adversary. Beside him let us place Thomas Mowbray, whose right-hand man in the dastardly murder at Calais was Colfox; his badge of office is a gold truncheon, tipped at each end with black; he is Henry of Bolingbroke's adversary.

So much for the colors and general description; but the striking likeness between the fable and the duel goes even further. We remember that the fox was tricked and defeated by talking at the wrong time. The duel found its origin in some wild words concerning the king's faithlessness, which Mowbray dropped into Henry's ear in confidence when they were riding to London. Henry wrote the indiscreet words down, took them to the King in Parliament, and, accusing Mowbray of treason, challenged him to fight. The duel ended, as we know, in Mowbray's exile for life.

> 'Nay,' quod the fox, 'but god yeve him meschaunce
> That is so undiscreet of governaunce,
> That jangleth whan he sholde holde his pees.'

Chauntecleer, on the other hand, fell through vanity and blindness caused by flattery. Now we have no evidence that Henry of Bolingbroke, like Chauntecleer, was more susceptible to flattery than other men; we do know, however, that if ever riches, accomplishments, and good looks made a man a target for flattery, Henry was that man. Chaucer, we must remember, was a beneficiary of the lords of Lancaster: John of Gaunt had shown him great favor, and Henry, his son, was not lacking in generosity to the poet. It is very possible that the apostrophe, which is out of place in the mouth of the priest, may come with real feeling from Chaucer himself:

> Allas, ye lordes, many a fals flatour
> Is in your courtes, and many a losengeour,
> That plesen yow wel more, by my feith,

> Than he that soothfastnesse unto yow seith.
> Redeth Ecclesiaste of flaterye;
> Beth war, ye lordes, of hir trecherye.

The striking similarity between the circumstances of the famous duel and those of the fable make certain other of Chaucer's additions to his originals suspect. For example, when the King had stopped the duel, and had proclaimed to the threatening multitude, which idolized Henry, that he was banished for ten years, and had as yet not announced the punishment of Mowbray, whom they hated, the crowds made such an outcry and tumult that nothing could be heard.

To the 'pursuit of the fox' motif, which Chaucer found in his originals, he adds a lively account of the deafening noise which was made at the fox:

> They yelleden as feendes doon in helle;
>
> . . . .
>
> So hidous was the noyse, a! *benedicite!*
> Certes, he Jakke Straw, and his meynee
> Ne made never shoutes half so shrille,
> Whan that they wolden any Fleming kille,
> As thilke day was maad upon the fox.

Again, Chaucer heightens to heroic proportions the weeping and lamentation which the hens made at the sight of Chauntecleer. When Henry left London to go into exile,

> . . . more than forty thousand men and women . . . were crying and weeping after him so piteously that it was pity to see and hear, and kept saying, 'Ah, gentle Earl of Derby! will you leave us, then? There will never be joy nor good in this land until you come back to it; . . . through envy, through tricks, and treason they drive and send you out. And why do you leave us, gentle Earl of Derby?' Then men and women wept so violently that greater grief could not be. The Earl of Derby was not convoyed nor escorted with trumpets, shawms, nor instruments out of the city, but with tears, cries, and lamentations so utterly dolorous that there was no heart so hard that it did not feel pity.

Though we have gone far from our first mention of the Colfox, it will be remembered that later in the tale, Chaucer calls him *daun Russel*. In her investigation, Miss Petersen was puzzled by the use of the name *Russel* instead of the traditional *Renart*. She could see no apparent reason for the change, since the 'word *Renart* is just as pliable in iambic meter as the word Russel.' An adequate political reason for the use of the word exists. Sir John Russel was one of five hated minions of Richard II. When Henry came back in triumph from exile, he executed three of them at Bristol: Wiltshire, Bushy, and Green, as traitors; Bagot fled, and Sir John Russel got off by feigning madness.

Such are the similarities between contemporary history and the *Nun's Priest's Tale*. It is immediately evident that much is left unexplained; that some of the passages which I have not dealt with appear to deny the probability of my suggestions. The Coventry duel took place on a Monday; yet the poem says of the sorrows of Chauntecleer that 'on a Friday fil al this meschaunce.' The duelling date was September 16, 1398; yet the equivocal date given in the tale can be read April 2, if reckoned mathematically, or May 3, on the zodiacal computation, but never as September. Again, Henry at this time had no wife; Mary Bohun was dead. If Chauntecleer represents Henry, who then is Pertelote? Moreover, if this poem is a political satire, why has the author delightfully drawn the character of a skeptical woman, and inserted a learned discussion of the significance of dreams, another on predestination and free will, and an invective against Friday?

To arrive at any tenable conclusion, we must restate our conception of the purpose and main interest of the tale.

As it stands it is a mock-heroic poem, whose richness and strength center in the characters and conversation of Chauntecleer and Pertelote. The satire, in the main, is general and sympathetic. High burlesque lightens the homiletic tone. Terrible *exempla,* when placed in the mouth (or bill) of a barnyard fowl, lose much of their ponderousness.

The main interest, then, is character, and not incident. Yet though this is true, it is no proof that Chaucer conceived the tale from the beginning as a character study of Chauntecleer, the proud, impractical, vain man, and of Pertelote, the skeptical level-headed woman. It is more probable that he began with some *occasion* for writing a version of the beast fable, with amplifications; and that his interest was attracted only later to elaborating the first part into matchless character-drawing and dialogue.

The evidence of Colfox, the colors of the adversaries, and the rest, warrant us in forming a tentative hypothesis at least for the date of composition, if not also for the meaning of the inserted details.

Granting, for this purpose, that the striking similarities between the actual events and the incidents of the tale were intentional on Chaucer's part, when was the work composed? Long after the duel, or almost at once? Obviously, the latter. In a scambling and unquiet time, such as Richard's reign, or indeed in any time, topical hits must be prompt. The duel, as we know, occurred on September 16, 1398. On October 3, the two exiles left England. The *Nun's Priest's Tale* was composed, let us say, shortly after their departure, in October or November, 1398.

To present the theory in a direct, connected manner, it is desirable to recapitulate the movement of events. Richard's rule had never been good; but, as it drew near the catastrophe, it sank lower and lower into depths of corruption and anarchy. The literature of the period abounds in lamentations on the times, and in censure of evildoing. Richard's misrule is condemned in unmeasured terms. Even Chaucer, whom we have never considered as being a direct critic of contemporary things, joins the chorus with a strong exhortation to King Richard, worthy of one of the minor prophets:

> O prince, desyre to be honourable,
> Cherish thy folk and hate extorcioun! . . . .
> Shew forth thy swerd of castigacioun,
> Dred God, do law, love trouthe and worthinesse,
> And wed thy folk agein to stedfastnesse.

But censure and lamentation quickly lose their force. Chaucer must have known this as well as any man of the Middle Ages. His common sense must have told him, too, that lamenting only increases woe.

Let us put ourselves as nearly as possible in his place in 1397. The rumor spreads that the Duke of Gloucester has been murdered. People at the Court, and many of the citizens, are sure that Mowbray and Colfox, who took the Duke to Calais, were the vile tools. Henry of Lancaster is now the only leader that the people have left; and, though not above plotting in the dark against the King, and betraying confidences, Henry is popular. He makes up his mind to avenge his murdered uncle, and tricks Mowbray by catching up his rash words and bearing the tale to the King. A duel is arranged with the greatest of pomp; the popular excitement is extreme, and all England flocks to Coventry. Richard fears for his safety, and brings a bodyguard of a good twenty thousand archers and plenty of men-at-arms. The people, to a man, are for Henry and against Mowbray, and feeling runs high. Richard is advised not to risk the duel, with its possible consequences. It goes forward, however; but at the last moment, his courage fails. He gives the signal, and the heralds cry 'Ho! Ho!'

> O! when the king did throw his warder down,
> His own life hung upon the staff he threw:
> Then threw he down himself.

Thus all the preparation comes to naught, and the mighty combat ends for both antagonists in wretched banishment. They go; and the people curse Mowbray, and weep for Lancaster.

What an excellent opportunity for John Gower heavily to moralize on the evils of the times; or to write a 'tragedie' picturing the sudden fall of the two nobles from their high estate into misery! As Chaucer says of Chauntecleer:

> But sodeinly him fil a sorweful cas;
> For ever the latter end of joye is woe.
> God woot that worldly joye is sone ago;
> And if a rethor coude faire endyte,
> He in a cronique saufly mighte it wryte
> As for a sovereyn notabilitee.

But Chaucer is wise enough to let others endite 'sovereign notabilities.' For his part, he will touch the affair lightly and surely; doing more with his grave smile than could be done with all the long faces in Christendom. For material, he needs not look far; a fable from the Beast Epic is apt to his hand. In creating his mock-heroic masterpiece on this frame, he is not so stupid as to plan a complete allegory of the recent affair. He knows that a few well-chosen strokes, scattered through, are more delightful to the reader than a weary parallelism. He will mask his batteries, too; he will give his episode a fanciful, contradictory date. He will use the favorite Friday, instead of the actual Monday. Yet when he begins to introduce his characters, their artistic possibilities are so fascinating that he studies them with all his mature skill. Deeply interested, as we know from the *Troilus,* in the character of a skeptical woman, Chaucer transfers the skeptical rôle to Pertelote, and develops Chauntecleer into a splendid creature, admirable in beauty, learning, speech, in everything, in short, but his natural fear of the fox, and his unthinking love of flattery.

We are not to think that Chaucer intended Chauntecleer to represent Henry Bolingbroke throughout, nor that there was an original to Pertelote, any more than we are to suppose that Dryden meant the behavior of his fox throughout to be taken for that of the typical Puritan. A hit is a hit, and must never be pressed too far. Mowbray is only shadowed forth in the person of the fox: this fact is thoroughly demonstrated by the use of names. *Colfox,* to be sure, is a fox; but he is also Mowbray's esquire. *Daun Russel* is a fox, too; at the same time, he is another of Richard's detested officers. Fugitive, deft, these allusions are the kind that tell, without exposing the author to actions for libel! Moreover, the tale, in spite of its serious passages, is so merry that no one could possibly take offense: least of all Henry, with whom Chaucer was on familiar terms.

If the tale was written in 1398, we have a most interesting corroboration of the feeling, which many scholars share, that Chaucer's powers did not wane towards the close of his life. Here is perhaps his most delightful work, done in the maturest style, two years before his death. Why need we suppose that his powers decayed? *The Compleint of Chaucer to his Empty Purse*, written in 1399, shows no loss of power and humor.

This explanation of the *Nun's Priest's Tale*, then, makes an effort at a rational historical explanation of the obscure meanings, the lively apostrophes, and the variations and additions which are found in Chaucer's mock-heroic masterpiece.

This would take nothing from the dramatic interest of the main story, nothing from the grave dignity of the characters, nothing from the rich, humorous treatment. On the contrary, it would add a subtlety of touch-and-go allusion to contemporary events of the first order, and give the matchless tale a new zest.

NOTES

1. *Notes*, p. 255.
2. Kate O. Petersen, *Sources of the Nonne Prestes Tale*, p. 53.
3. *Modern Philology*, I, 1. (cf. *Cal. Pat. R.* 1405–8, 165).

GEORGE LYMAN KITTREDGE

Chaucer's Pardoner

CHAUCER, the critics tell us, possessed a genius eminently dramatic, and a matchless talent for story-telling, but frequently allowed his mediæval love of moralizing to defeat, for the moment, his narrative powers, and now and then grossly violated dramatic propriety, whether carelessly or from the exigencies of satire. As instances of the first of these sins are usually cited the self-satisfied speech of Nature in The Doctor's Tale, and the long soliloquizing excursus on free will and predestination in the Troilus. The most flagrant offense under the second head is commonly supposed to be the harangue of the Pardoner.

In The Doctor's Tale, Nature is produced in person, exhibiting her artistic masterpiece Virginia, and boasting of her in a showmanlike address to the public. The device may be granted absurd, and it certainly interferes with the flow of the narrative. But there is a further consideration, the character of the doctor. The doctor is a very formal person, from whom a degree of prosiness is to be expected. It was Chaucer's artistic duty, in the Canterbury Tales,—as it has clearly been his purpose,—not only to select stories appropriate to the several pilgrims, but to make the method of delivery correspond to the character of the teller. The offending passage in the Troilus must be justified, if at all, on other grounds. A long soliloquy on the foreknowledge of God, absolute necessity, necessity conditional, and free will is not quite what one expects

---

Reprinted from *The Atlantic Monthly*, LXXII (1893), 829-33.

from a Trojan prince whose love is going to the Grecian camp. But though a great anachronism, and though rather unskillfully brought in, the soliloquy is by no means an impertinence. The idea of fate is subtly insistent throughout the poem,—it is perhaps even the key to Cressida's character; and surely, at this juncture, if ever, Troilus may have his thoughts about the mysterious inevitableness that is governing his life.

These and other considerations make it worth while to look with some scrutiny at what passes for Chaucer's great sin against dramatic propriety, the confessions of the Pardoner.

The Pardoner, it is said, exposes himself with unnaturally frank cynicism. He might properly indulge in a sly sneer at the pretenses of his vocation; but to proclaim that his relics are a sham; to declare that his

> 'intent is only for to win,
> And nothing for correction of sin,'

and that when once the penitents' money is in his pouch he does not care if their 'souls go a-blackberrying' after death; to avow in a coolly casual way that he is himself 'a full vicious man,'—all this is dramatically impossible. But this is not all: after the tale is finished, the Pardoner, according to the usual view, is so foolish as to try his impostures on the very audience which he has just enlightened as to his own vices and the tricks of his trade.

An attempt is sometimes made to account for these absurdities by a reference to the Roman de la Rose. The character of the Pardoner is in part a reproduction of the False-Semblant of that poem, and False-Semblant, as an allegorical personage, is not bound by dramatic law. It is a convention of satire, illustrated in a drastic way by Garnet's speech in Oldham, to make an odious character describe himself unsparingly,—a trick absurd in itself, but no more absurd than such conventions as the long 'aside' in the drama. This defense, or explanation, has always been felt to be unsatisfactory. Chaucer is not a reformer. He is not even, if rightly taken, a satirist. His aim is not to reconstruct the Church or to ameliorate humanity, but to depict certain characters, and to let them tell stories. He has no right to resort to conventions which, permissible to one who depicts a character *ad hoc*, are unjustifiable in one who depicts a character for its own sake. It is an equally weak defense to allege that the Pardoner is drunk. One draught of ale, however 'moist and corny,' would never fuddle so seasoned a drinker. Besides, he manifests none of the signs of intoxication. Unless, then, it can be shown that the character of the Pardoner is consistent with itself and with nature, the poet has blundered; and the gravity of his blunder is increased by the excellence of the Pardoner's Tale, perhaps the best short narrative poem in the language. In general, Chaucer shows exquisite delicacy in fitting the various Canterbury tales to the characters of the tellers. In the present case, we have a beautiful story, wonderfully told, put into the mouth of a vulgar, prating rascal, not only destitute of moral and intellectual dignity, but so lacking in common sense that he cannot hold his tongue about his own impostures. Yet the prologue, the tale, and the epilogue all show Chaucer at the height of his powers. It is possible that an explanation of the problem may be found by considering all the available evidence as to the Pardoner's character. It may appear from such an examination that his character is consistent throughout, and of a kind to make the apparent impropriety of the introductory confession in conformity to nature.

In the first place, then, we may be sure that the Pardoner is a thoroughpaced scoundrel. His bulls of popes and cardinals may be genuine,—it would in any case not do for him to confess to the felony of forging the pope's seal,—but his relics are counterfeit, and he has no illusions about the holiness of his mission. He preaches for money, and has no concern for the reformation of morals or for genuineness of repentance on the part of those who offer to his relics and receive his absolution. He is skillful at his business: it has brought him in a hundred marks (almost seven hundred pounds in our values) a year since he first took it up. Like all clever impostors, he is proud of his dexterity. Under ordinary circumstances, prudence would constrain him to suppress the exhibition of this pride; but the circumstances are not ordinary. He is not on his rounds. The pilgrims are a company associated by chance, and likely never to assemble again after their return supper at Harry Bailly's. If they repeat his words, it will not much matter. He cannot labor in his vocation while he is with them, and none of them are likely to cross his path in the future. They are not of the kind among whom he is used to ply his arts. His best field is the country village. To be sure, the parson and the ploughman are from the country; but the character of the parson makes the parish which he administers a forbidden region to such loose fish as the Pardoner. One of the ordinary restraints on freedom of self-revelation, then, is wanting: he need fear no disagreeable consequences.

Further, the unsoundness of the Pardoner's morals is known to the company before he begins his cynical confessions. He may pose as a holy man when he is swindling the peasantry of some remote hamlet; but hypocritical airs and graces would be absurdly futile among his present companions. That there has been no attempt at such posturing is made clear enough by the host, the gentles, and the Pardoner himself. The host calls on the Pardoner for a merry tale; the Pardoner assents with an alacrity which warrants vehement suspicion, and the gentles protest that they want no ribaldry, and insist on something elevated and instructive. This is significant enough of the impression the Pardoner has made on his traveling companions. The Pardoner easily adapts himself to the temper of his audience. It is his business to know moral tales. He has his sermons by heart, and most of these, as a matter of course, contain an *exemplum*, an anecdote which can be 'improved' to the edification of a churchful of laymen. But before beginning he feels the need of refreshment.

> 'I graunte ywis,' quod he, 'but I moot thynke
> Upon som honest thyng whil that I drynke.'

Not that he has 'to think awhile before he can recollect some decent thing,' as has been suggested. He is honestly thirsty, and glad of an excuse to quench his thirst, no doubt; but, being a man of ability and eloquence, he must have plenty of 'honest things' at his tongue's end.

Perhaps we have now facts enough to explain the self-revelation of the Pardoner's prologue. He knows what his fellow-travelers think of him; he has just consented to tell an over-facetious story; he is now about to preach a highly edifying sermon. There is no opportunity to pull wool over the eyes of his hearers, even if there were any motive for it. Sure that they will perceive the enormous discrepancy between his character and his teaching, the Pardoner is impatient of occupying the position of a futile hypocrite. He is too clever a knave to wish others to take him for a fool. Hence these cynical confessions at the outset, the dramatic purpose of which is now clear. The Pardoner is, in effect, saying to the pilgrims: 'I am about to tell you a moral tale. I am going to preach you one of my sermons. You will find the sentiments of this sermon unexceptionable. Do not think, however, that I expect you to believe me in earnest. You know what kind of fellow I am, and this is my trade.'

With these feelings, then, the Pardoner begins his tale or sermon. Knowing it by heart, as he tells us himself, and being accustomed to preach with great unction, he is soon rapt into the same mood of conventional earnestness that he has found so effective in the pulpit. By the time he arrives at the ejaculations on the wickedness of sin and the horrors of homicide, gluttony, lechery, and gambling, which (though marked 'auctor' by the officious stupidity of some scribe) form the 'application' of the whole discourse, he is at a white heat of zeal. Forgetful of his surroundings, he does not stop with the 'application,' but goes on to the exhortation with which he regularly concludes his harangues:—

> 'Now, good men, God foryeve yow your trespas,
> And ware yow fro the sinne of avarice!
> Myn holy pardoun may yow alle warice,
> So that ye offre nobles or sterlinges,
> Or elles silver broches, spones, ringes.
> Boweth your heed under this holy bulle!
> Cometh up, ye wyves, offreth of your wolle!
> Your name I entre heer in my rolle anon,
> Into the blisse of heven shul ye gon;
> I yow assoile, by myn heigh power,
> Yow that wol offre, as clene and eek as cleer

As ye were born. — *And lo, sirs, thus I preche;*
And Jesu Crist, that is our soules leche,
So graunte yow his pardoun to receyve,
For that is best, I wol yow nat deceyve!'

The last four lines of this passage are particularly significant.
The Pardoner's invitation to come up and offer to the relics and
receive absolution is glaringly out of place in a speech to his
fellow-travelers, to whom he has already made full confession of
the emptiness of his pretensions. 'Come up, ye wives, and offer of
your wool!' has no appropriateness when addressed to the pilgrims.
Perceiving the absurdity, the speaker pulls himself up with the
explanatory 'This is the kind of sermon I am in the habit of deliver-
ing.' ('And lo, sirs, thus I preche.')

So far, all is plain sailing. We might suppose the preacher carried
away by professional enthusiasm, and forgetting just where he
ought to have stopped. We might suppose, on the other hand, that
he wished to give his hearers a complete specimen of his discourses, final invitation and all. But what shall we think of his
next words?—

'And lo, sirs, thus I preche;
And Jesu Crist, that is our soules leche,
So graunte yow his pardoun to receyve,
For that is best, I wol yow nat deceyve!'

It may be that these words, apparently so out of consonance with
anything we have yet heard from the Pardoner, furnish the key to
his character. May we not believe that the beautiful and impressive
story that he has just told—a story that no one can read without
emotion—has moved even him, though he has told it a thousand
times before in the way of his profession? The unusual circumstances under which he has preached his sermon may have assisted
in producing this effect. For once, perhaps, the hideous incongruity
between his preaching and the profligate invitation to come up and
be pardoned through the efficacy of his trumpery relics has appeared to him. Possibly we may venture to think that the Pardoner, moved by his own tale, went on mechanically to this profes-

sional invitation, perceived its absurd inopportuneness with a start, and thus had its hypocritical villainy suddenly projected in his own mind against the beauty and impressiveness of his tale. This would still further increase his emotion, which, after an explanatory 'And lo, sirs, thus I preche,' finds vent in an ejaculation profoundly affecting in its reminiscence of the Pardoner's better nature, which he had himself thought dead long ago. 'My pardon,' he says, 'is of no account, as you know. God grant that you receive Christ's pardon, which is better than mine. I will not deceive you, though deceit is my business.'

Of course this better mood can last but a moment. There is no question of repentance or reformation, for the Pardoner is a lost soul. The reaction comes instantly, and is to the extreme of reckless jesting. Aware that the pilgrims know him thoroughly by this time, for he has even taken pains to reveal himself, he nevertheless impudently urges them to kiss the relics and make offering and receive pardon. The invitation has sometimes been taken as given in dead earnest; but this is inconceivable. It would imply superhuman folly on the speaker's part to try to deceive the pilgrims when he has just warned them against his own deceit. Besides, we have evidence that the Pardoner hurries into this strain of reckless jocularity to escape from the serious mood that has surprised him.

'But, sirs, o word forgat I in my tale,'

are the words with which he begins the closing passage, and these very words indicate his confusion. For he has not forgotten his relics. On the contrary, he has just been talking about them, and praising their efficacy. The whole passage is jocose. At the end, he turns to the host, and pointedly suggests that *he* begin, as being the most sinful of the company. This remark alone would suffice to indicate how little serious purpose there is in the proposition of the Pardoner. The host is the last person to yield to seductive suggestions of this sort in any case, and it would be idle to expect him to do so after the full revelation of himself that the Pardoner has made.

The host, who of course has no knowledge of the conflict of

feelings through which the Pardoner is passing, naturally replies in a strain of coarse raillery. Under ordinary circumstances, the effect of this jesting on the Pardoner would be to evoke a still more scurrilous response. He must often have bandied words in all good nature with persons of the host's freedom of speech, and there is no reason to suppose that he is constitutionally thin-skinned. Under ordinary circumstances, too, so fluent a man as the Pardoner, if he got angry, would have plenty of words in which to vent his wrath. On the present occasion rage makes him dumb.

> 'This Pardoner answerede not a word:
> So wroth he was no word he wolde seye.'

The inference seems to be plain. The contest of feelings in the Pardoner's mind, the momentary return to sincerity, which must have been accompanied by profound emotion, the revulsion of feeling indicated by his jesting proposition to his fellow-travelers, are too much for his equanimity. When the host replies with a scurrile jest, he is simply too angry to speak. That this is the correct interpretation of the course of events is further substantiated by the surprise which the host feels at this, to him, inexplicable anger on the part of the Pardoner. He has not noticed the Pardoner's moment of emotion; he has, therefore, supposed the jesting to be of the ordinary sort, and he feels injured that his reply is taken in ill part.

> ' "Now," quod our host, "I wol no lenger pleye
> With thee, ne with no other angry man." '

The knight makes up the quarrel, which of course neither party wishes to prolong, and the company rides on as before.

If these considerations are sound, we have in Chaucer's treatment of the Pardoner no violation of dramatic propriety, but, on the contrary, the subtlest piece of character delineation the poet has ever attempted. The Pardoner is an able and eloquent man, a friar, very likely, who had entered his order with the best purposes, or, at any rate, with no bad aims, and with possibilities of good in him, and had grown corrupt with its corruption. His debasement seems to be utter, for one must not forget the picture in the general prologue. Nothing but a ribald story appears possible from him. But, by showing us the man in a moment of moral convulsion, Chaucer has invested him with a sort of dignity which justifies the poet in putting into his mouth one of the most beautiful as well as one of the best told tales in the whole collection.

If the considerations referred to be not sound, there is no explaining away the difficulties: the cynical prologue remains a monstrous absurdity; the error in tact involved in giving a despicable fellow a magnificent tale to tell seems ultimate; the earnest remark of the Pardoner that Christ's pardon is better than his is a piece of impertinence; the Pardoner's anger at the host's jesting is improbable; the dumbness of his wrath is out of character; and the surprise of the host at his losing his temper is nugatory. The interpretation suggested seems not only to be in harmony with all the phenomena, but even to explain some phenomena otherwise inexplicable except as blunders. That a fortuitous collection of blunders should combine to make up a subtle piece of character delineation is not impossible, perhaps, but is hardly what one would expect. Is it not reasonable, then, to accept an interpretation of the prologue and the tale which brings them into harmony with what we know of Chaucer's exquisite delicacy of portraiture, and wonderful power of dramatically adapting his stories to their tellers, particularly as the Pardoner's Tale must have been written when all his powers were at their height?

G. G. SEDGEWICK

The Progress of Chaucer's Pardoner, 1880-1940

UNDER date of 12 June, 1880, Jusserand remarked that the picture of Chaucer's Pardoner was 'indeed too familiar,' that 'its very strangeness [had] partly come to be overlooked.'[1] And as he no doubt intended, his famous essay on 'Chaucer's Pardoner and the Pope's Pardoner' had or seems to have had a two-fold issue. First, it may be credited with revealing to readers of Chaucer a rich interest latent in the Pardoner and his performance. At any rate it set moving a long line of researches that have exploited the wealth. More specifically, it proved the poet's 'minute accuracy . . . so far as the most monstrous and, so to speak, unlikely of his heroes is concerned.' The Pardoner, *qua* pardoner, was thus amply revealed in all essential respects sixty years ago, and the significance of the revelation was clarified and deepened by a chapter in *English Wayfaring Life in the Middle Ages*.

But even Jusserand may not have guessed in 1880 or 1884 how very accurate and complex that portraiture was. Ever since he wrote, research and criticism and interpretation have been busy with the noble ecclesiast. For the Wife of Bath and the Pardoner exercise a fascination not so much over the unregenerate as over God's elect. If the latter do not bourd and play as the unregenerate do, they certainly become astonishingly vocal in the presence of that ungodly pair in whom William Blake saw the 'scourge and

Reprinted, by permission, from *Modern Language Quarterly*, I (1940), 431-58.

blight' of every age. An explanation of those hard words in the
light of Blake's philosophy may prove to be the last judgment on
the Pardoner. Lacking that, I have tried, in reviewing the chief
judgments of these last sixty years, to sort out the established from
the doubtful and to see the Pardoner afresh as he appears in 1940.
Of necessity, such a review must cover ground that is very familiar;
but its examination of certain details and its general picture of the
Pardoner are, I believe, not usual.

I

Research and criticism are pretty generally agreed about the
Short Story to which the Pardoner gave classic shape. Its 'analogues' are now counted in legions, as perhaps they were in Chaucer's own day. Tyrwhitt spotted an Italian specimen a hundred
and sixty years ago, in 1881 Richard Morris noted the earliest
known form of the tale,[2] parallels have been cropping up everywhere ever since, and no doubt they will continue to appear as
long as there are new stocks of folk-lore to examine. No one any
longer expects to find Chaucer's precise original. As far back as
the 13th century,[3] the story had filtered from the Orient into the
deep well of European exempla from which all ecclesiasts could
draw. We may choose to fancy that Chaucer himself first heard it
from the mouth of a preacher. At some time, as we now see, somebody—whether Chaucer or another—enriched the tale by fusing
into it a mysterious personage engaged in the Quest for Death.[4]
Ten Brink long ago believed,[5] and Professor Carleton Brown now
believes, that this figure is the Wandering Jew casting his shadow
over the Three Robbers; but the strange shape of the Old Churl
as evoked by the Pardoner—if shape he might be call'd—has
seemed to others even more portentous. Whatever meaning you
put upon him, surely in this particular tale he is an emanation of
Chaucer's art alone. For one thing, folklore and homilist together
could hardly account for the appearance of Roman elegy in a
pardoner's sermon or for its transfiguration into notes so exactly
pitched and so disturbing:

And on the ground, which is my moodres gate,
I knokke with my staf, bothe erly and late,
And seye 'Leeve mooder, leet me in!' [6]

But praise of the Pardoner's narrative art is not relevant to this study, and indeed it has now become superfluous. In 1886, W. A. Clouston remarked that Chaucer tells the tale 'in a manner that is superior to any other version in prose and verse'[7]—a moderate judgment that no one will question, even after enjoying the glitter of 'The King's Ankus.'[8]

Unhappily, a sense of proportion has too often been lacking in admirers of the prize exemplum—for it was an exemplum, and nothing more, to Chaucer's Pardoner. Sometimes you wish his narrative art had not been so impressive, since then no one could have lifted a 'perfect short story' out of its context or thought of it as an end in itself. Chaucer never meant it to be so taken. Reading it in and out of context are two quite different things. But the 'riotoures thre' seem to hypnotize many readers into overlooking or resenting the fact that Chaucer had other things to do than merely tell a fine story. To Lounsbury, the 'long disquisition in which the Pardoner indulges on the evil effects of drunkenness and gaming' was an 'intrusion of irrelevant learning' which 'breaks the thread of the tale . . . and adds nothing to its effect.'[9] The heresy is still extant. As late as 1935, Mr. Carleton Brown (following the lead of Dr. H. B. Hinckley[10]) felt he had to 'account for' the irrelevant intrusions that Lounsbury reprobated. These troubles will be discussed later. At the moment it is enough to say that they result from misunderstanding of Chaucer's design and may be attributed to the spell cast by the great tale.

Of the 'credibility' of the Pardoner and his revelations, it is safe to say that no responsible critic has really doubted it during the last sixty years. Editors are still bound to warn beginners against the myth of monstrous unlikelihood which Jusserand undertook to dispel in 1880. They must still point out that the Pardoner of Chaucer's fiction is no more strange than the pardoner of historic fact. They must still refer to the convention of the self-confessor in medieval satire which links the Wife of Bath to the

Old Woman in the Romaunt of the Rose and the Pardoner to False Seeming. It is also well to be reminded of the immediate inspiration which the ecclesiast may have got from his moist and corny ale—though I have heard Professor Kittredge say that one drink would hardly account for the result, especially when the Pardoner had a cake for shoeing horn. And, lastly, no one who has listened to intimate autobiography in the smoking-room of a transcontinental train need feel troubled by the Pardoner's abandon. As Ten Brink remarked long ago, the rogue 'unmasks his trade and practices with that shamelessness and bare-faced frankness which the atmosphere of the Canterbury Tales requires.'[11] Jusserand's classic fantasy (which, by the way, must not be taken as literal comment) expands this statement with persuasive eloquence:

> On the further bench of the tavern the pardoner remains still seated. There enter Chaucer, the knight, the squire, the friar, the host—old acquaintances. We are by ourselves, no one need be afraid of speaking, the foaming ale renders hearts expansive; here the secret coils of that tortuous soul unfold to view; he gives us the summary of a whole life, the theory of his existence, the key to all his secrets. What matters his frankness?—he knows that it cannot hurt him; the bishop has twenty times brought his practices to light, but the crowd always troops round him. And who knows if his companions—who knows if his more enlightened companions, to whom he shows the concealed springs of the automaton—will, to-morrow, believe it lifeless.

Later on in this essay, I shall point out how, by skilful manipulation, Chaucer practically leaves his Pardoner with no other choice than to speak exactly as he did.

Various other critical agreements can be reviewed as quickly. The most important of these admits the debt which the whole scheme owes to the medieval sermon. For while Chaucer sees the Pardoner as anything but a parson, he does make him preach a queer sort of exhibition sermon which is undoubtedly a masterpiece in its given setting. It has been, and still is, misunderstood even by some who have a deep and lively interest in the 'medieval mind.' But everybody now understands that somehow or other

Chaucer got himself steeped in all the dyes of traditional preaching before he set about creating the Canterbury Tales and several of the pilgrims in it. We have long known his familiarity with the stores of exempla[12] from which he furnished the Pardoner with other material besides the Three Robbers' tale. Brave attempts, not altogether successful, have been made to exhibit several of the Tales, the Pardoner's among them, as more or less 'typical' medieval sermons.[13] And though this 'sermon' is certainly not 'typical,' Chaucer's very departures from the type imply thorough acquaintance with it. A study of the Parson's tale and the Pardoner's use of it will probably satisfy most readers as to Chaucer's knowledge of the sermon stuff. If it does not, they may fall back on Dr. G. R. Owst's impressive studies of medieval preaching[14] which, extravagant as they are in their general claims of value, do succeed in showing that practically every detail of the Pardoner's practice and utterance can be paralleled in the homilies, the tractates, the sermon manuals, or other records relative to preaching. The 'lost soul' whom Chaucer inflicts on the Pilgrimage fairly reeks of the medieval pulpit: he is a supreme example of the Preaching Fox.

Some of Chaucer's reading was much more secular than sermons, as Professor W. C. Curry has proved to the shocked admiration of scholarship in his essay 'The Secret of Chaucer's Pardoner.'[15] From a study of the physiognomy literature, Mr. Curry shows that the ecclesiast had the physical characteristics of a type of unfortunate known in those writings as *eunuchus ex nativitate*. But no gentle reader need consult the originals in so far as they concern the Pardoner; for there is no 'secret' of this sort about him. Chaucer himself revealed the 'secret' with sufficient clarity, as Mr. Curry points out, in one bleak line:

I trowe he were a geldyng or a mare

—it does not matter which. And this is what everybody, medieval or modern, would 'trowe' him to be from his appearance and voice alone. The fact remains, however, that Chaucer did draw on the Physiognomies, if for no other purpose than to make his figure 'scientific' or to amuse himself otherwise: he was concerned with 'minute accuracy' in respects of which Jusserand was probably unaware. Certainly, he knew those writings, for he mentions one of them; and the 'typical' traits, there set forth, of the *eunuchus ex nativitate* went, beyond dispute, into the Pardoner's portrait. Contrary to Mr. Curry's assumption, I very much doubt that any of the pilgrims (except Chaucer and the Physician) were familiar, or needed to be, with the Physiognomies; and if I agreed with Mr. Curry, I should regret that he came too late to supervise the reading of the Lady Prioress. But there is no need to minimize what he has added to our knowledge of Chaucer's methods if not to our understanding of the Pardoner.

This is perhaps the point at which to speak of Professor J. M. Manly's suggestion that the Pardoner and other pilgrims were drawn from life models. His 'new light on Chaucer'[16] illumines a good many dark corners and re-illumines many familiar ones; it blends with any clear doctrine about Chaucer ever presented. As for the Pardoner, it has localized him more precisely than ever he was before. During the 1380's and 1390's, his House of Rouncivale, an interest of Chaucer's patron, John of Gaunt, was much in the public eye, and not always favourably. We learn, for example, that real pardoners of that house had been notoriously converting collections to their own use, just as their fellow in fiction boasted of doing. Records of this fact, published by the late Professor Samuel Moore[17] before *New Light* appeared, make it 'difficult to believe' that a contemporary audience would not link the person and goings-on of the Pardoner with some actual rogue. Further, 'his new Italian fashions,' as Mr. Manly calls them, are distinctive features that Mr. Curry's physiognomy books obviously cannot account for. If you pause to think of it, a most striking peculiarity of the portrait, not mentioned in *New Light,* is its combination of pardoner and *eunuchus* in one person. This is certainly not 'typical,' as all records and traditions testify decisively. There are good reasons for thinking that, along with many other elements, Chaucer put traits of some well-known individual or individuals into the Pardoner's complex.

II

Chaucerian research, like admiration of the Pardoner's tale, is sometimes afflicted with a faulty sense of proportion. Eaten up with the zeal of discovery, scholars are tempted to see the philosopher's stone in some very ordinary run of the mine. With every deference to Mr. Curry, for instance, one may again point out that his researches do not reveal the 'secret' of Chaucer's Pardoner, as he seemed to think; further, that an oddly naïve view of the Pardoner's last actions is the reward of his mistake. And with every gratitude to Dr. Owst, one cannot agree with him in regarding the study of medieval sermons as the whole duty of man.

Three examples of the scholar's error should be dealt with faithfully. One is perhaps unimportant and innocent enough; but each of the others has proved to be a considerable nuisance; and all three set their ferment working in a mass of valuable information.

The first, which may be called the Flanders Heresy, is based on a single phrase:

In Flaundres whilom was a compaignye.

Why did Chaucer say 'Flanders'? One attempt to answer this question has taught us much about the troubled relations of England with the Low Countries and, particularly, about the Flemish reputation for avarice and hard drinking. If the matter had been left so, there would be no heresy. Flanders, even if mentioned only once, would do as a perfectly good local habitation for three rioters. But is it not too much to 'wonder . . . if in this tale Chaucer is merely telling an idle story [!] to amuse his distinguished audience or if he through the Pardoner, a professional moralizer [!], is not glancing at his own troublous times when he develops this theme of avarice and projects it for its background upon the history of Flanders'?[18] Perhaps this guess at Chaucer's intention is not altogether serious; for surely the poet would not have left a purpose like that to depend on one word used in a conventional narrative opening. Quite certainly it was not the 'purpose' of the Pardoner—all he wanted to do was to make money. And with equal certainty, Chaucer's eye at the moment was fixed on the Pardoner himself, not on international relations. If such a 'purpose' is once referred to the whole pattern which it is alleged to explain, it is rejected instantly. A direct and simple explanation of the apparently mysterious phrase has long been at hand. Skeat said that it probably came from 'an original which is now lost';[19] and one exemplum of a type which, admittedly, Chaucer must have known begins *In marchia flandrie*.[20] For the time being, until we find the poet's precise originals, and in so far as we are interested in his design, that is sufficient answer to the question.

The more pervasive Sermon Heresy, already hinted at in passing, centres attention on the Pardoner's material—or, more exactly, on a part of it—rather than on the Pardoner himself. To do this is to run the risk of overlooking or mistaking Chaucer's 'purpose,' and so to pervert the direction of the material.

Chaucer had no intention of constructing a medieval sermon, 'typical' or otherwise. He did set out to portray a certain remarkable charlatan of a preacher who, in the course of self-revelation, delivers a 'sermon' as a sample of his trade-tricks. Fussy as that statement is, it is not quite meticulous enough. For the whole homily as actually delivered to simple folk 'dwellyng upon lond' is not set down *verbatim*: part of it is *reported*, in satiric vein, to another kind of audience that is listening not so much to the homily as to the self-revelation. Let us say, merely for the sake of convenience, that the Pardoner fits his rural 'sermon' into an 'address' delivered to the Pilgrims. It is a joy to watch his off-hand ease at the job of conveying an exposition within an exposition. Into the 'prologe' which expounds his method to his present audience is woven a long quotation from a past performance; he slips deftly from indirect to direct report, from enveloping 'address' to 'sermon' proper and back again: so that, when he announces 'my tale I wol bigynne,' he knows he can proceed full steam ahead with his prize exemplum, since 'address' and 'sermon' are now running on the same track. He has promised ('I graunte, ywis') to tell a 'moral tale,' and he will pay the debt in full measure. But with a characteristic difference. He will show how a 'moral tale' sounds when told for an immoral purpose:

> By God, I hope I shal yow telle a thyng
> That shal by reson been at youre likyng.
> For though myself be a ful vicious man,
> A moral tale yet I yow telle kan,
> Which I am wont to preche for to wynne.

The 'moral tale,' that is, belongs to both 'sermon' and 'address'— only it is doubly interesting in the 'address.'

So considered, the 'sermon' takes its proper place as one element in the design. No one minimizes the value of knowing what the homiletic material is or how well Chaucer knew it. But to get lost in it, I repeat, is to lose sight of what Chaucer is doing.

One special variety of this Heresy that is more than negatively dangerous has lately been aired again in Mr. Carleton Brown's admirable edition of the *Pardoner's Tale*. Mr. Brown and others have not troubled themselves about the 'sermon' as 'typical,' but with its lack of coherence. There is no necessary relation, they say, between the 'tavern sins,' set forth and illustrated at length, and the theme of Avarice with its superb exemplum. It will be remembered that Lounsbury also condemned the 'intrusion of irrelevant learning' which 'breaks the thread of the tale.' Besides, as Mr. Brown points out, there is a clumsy transition where the 'riotoures thre' suddenly appear; for previously we have heard only of

> a compaignye
> Of yonge folk that haunteden folye.

From all this discrepancy it is plausibly inferred that Chaucer has put together incongruous materials from different sources and failed to cover up the joints. Dr. Hinckley and Mr. Brown have 'accounted for' the trouble by supposing that part or all of the tale was originally written for the Parson and later shifted to its present place.

Clumsiness in introducing the 'riotoures thre' must be admitted at once. And, probably enough, it does indicate that Chaucer has jumped too suddenly from one kind of exemplum to another. But the clumsiness is slight and unimportant, like the inconsistencies in Shakespeare which everyone notices and promptly forgets. It is reasonable also to suppose (in absence of proof) that Chaucer robbed the Parson to pay the Pardoner. But *why* did he do so? Surely not for the express purpose of committing incongruity! One can hardly be grateful for an 'accounting' that involves Chaucer in a major artistic blunder.

Before ratifying the audit, we had better ask if the material is really incongruous. Logically it is, of course. But the Pardoner never set out to achieve logic in preaching to the ignorant. His object 'is alwey oon and evere was'—money. And as an extractor of fool's cash, his 'sermon' cannot be beaten. Flaunting his relics and no doubt his gaudy cross, he practically blackmails every man and woman (especially woman) of his humble congregations into making an offering.[21] His text, *Radix malorum est cupiditas*, gives him a clear pretext for dilating on all *mala* relevant to his hearers, and so a chance to score a bull's eye on every human target in sight. For the so-called 'tavern vices'—gluttony, drunkenness, swearing, gambling—are, regrettably, vices to which all flesh alike is heir. If the preacher can fasten all the probable sins of his congregation on the three rioters of his story, he can make it appear from their fate that the love of money is somehow the root of all mortal ills and that the way of salvation lies along the purse-strings. He is not setting up a logical argument but an emotional barrage. By dilating on the sins of rioters (and of his hearers) with all the arts of the popular orator, he creates an air of 'heavy fear and sin, the mood of a *Danse Macabre*.'[22] After this 'dilatation' he strikes home with his deadly exemplum on *cupiditas*. And then, following close on the account of the robbers' death, comes an iresistible summary and appeal:

> Thus ended been thise homycides two,
> And eek the false empoysonere also.
>
> O cursed synne of alle cursednesse!
> O traytours homycide, O wikkednesse!

O glotonye, luxurie, and hasardrye!
Thou blasphemour of Crist with vileynye
And othes grete, of usage and of pride!
Allas! mankynde, how may it bitide
That to thy creatour, which that the wroghte,
And with his precious herte-blood thee boghte,
Thou are so fals and so unkynde, allas?

Now, goode men, God foryeve yow youre trespas,
And ware yow fro the synne of avarice!
Myn hooly pardoun may yow alle warice,
So that ye offre nobles or sterlynges,
Or elles silver broches, spoones, ringes . . .
Cometh up, ye wyves, offreth of youre wolle!

This is something more potent than 'logic'—it is demagogic genius.
And it 'accounts' for the 'intrusion of irrelevant learning' quite
sufficiently.

The sermon heresies have a close but unexpected relative. Several times I have referred to the 'sins of the tavern.' In Chaucer
criticism this phrase is associated with Professor Frederick Tupper's well-known essay on 'The Pardoner's Tavern,'[23] in which,
with great and learned vivacity, he argued that Chaucer had arranged to have those sins exposed by a preacher who was himself
guilty of them. Further, Mr. Tupper insisted that the preacher
perform *in a tavern,* while the Pilgrims were seated around him.
Such an exposé of the 'tavern sins,' said Mr. Tupper, would play
ironically against a background of clinking canakins and laughing
tap-wenches.

This view was certainly fresh and provocative in 1914. It added
considerably to our knowledge of the 'medieval mind,' and it was
one detail of Mr. Tupper's elaborate scheme wherein each pilgrim
figured as denouncing his own besetting sin.[24] With general consent the scheme has been 'exploded';[25] and consequently part of
Mr. Tupper's argument need not detain us. Evidently, however,
the explosion did not quite disrupt the findings of the special essay,
for one of them is still accepted in criticism, though it seriously
hinders proper understanding of the Pardoner.

Mr. Tupper was certain, I repeat, that the 'tavern vices' were actually exposed *in a tavern*. In fact he dared all and sundry to contradict him and, so far as I am aware, no one has accepted the challenge. But not all readers of the Pardoner's Tale have been so confident. I think Mr. Tupper was mistaken in believing that the pardoner of Jusserand's fantasy—'still seated . . . on the further bench of the tavern'—was meant to be Chaucer's Pardoner in person: to be exact, Jusserand's taverner is a *typical* figure enjoying himself, 'after a well occupied day,' in the company of carefully selected pilgrims. Legouis saw the Pardoner go into the tavern for his drink and come out again: 'il est entré dans la taverne "pour s'aviser d'un sujet honnête tout en buvant," et il en sort décidé à les divertir.'[26] Professor F. N. Robinson is almost but not quite sure; in his view both 'prologe' and tale are 'apparently delivered . . . at the tavern.'[27] 'At least,' Mr. Robinson goes on to say, 'there is no indication that [the Pilgrims] take the road before the Pardoner begins.' There is also, I may interject, no certain indication that they do not. But the editor's final inference is that 'a story which is . . . an attack upon . . . revelry is told in a tavern.'

Now the plain truth is, Chaucer leaves the situation quite ambiguous. At the beginning the Pardoner tells the Host that

> heere at this ale-stake
> I wol bothe drynke, and eten of a cake.

When the gentles protest, he asks for a pause:

> but I moot thynke
> Upon som honest thyng while that I drynke.

Towards the close of his prologue, he remarks,

> Now have I dronke a draughte, of corny ale.

After the tale, when the Knight has quieted things down,

> Anon they kiste, and ryden forth hir weye.

Those four excerpts provide the whole basis on which any guesses about the situation have to rest. In the first and second a distinct pause is indicated. The third may well suggest that the Pardoner has been consuming his ale during the course of the 'prologe'—in which case the Pilgrims may be gathered in front of the booth. The fourth quotation would seem to imply that there was no prolonged hiatus between the kissing and the riding forth. It is at least possible that, after a pause to suit the Pardoner's convenience, the Pilgrims rode on, their entertainer talking to the usual accompaniment of hooves and harness.

But that literal tavern interior of Mr. Tupper's will never do. Only a frivolous person, I suppose, would wonder how the 'tap-wenches' and the proprietor of the ale-stake liked strenuous attacks on their livelihood—especially if delivered on their own premises. And Harry Bailly—he too wanted a drink, but as an innkeeper would he feel justified in being a party to such a disturbance of the peace? Further, it is difficult to enjoy the spectacle of the Lady Prioress standing with the Pardoner at a bar-rail. As for the alleged absurdity of asking the Host to climb down from his horse and kneel on the ground—which is Mr. Tupper's trump-card—*that* is precisely what triumphant impudence might propose, 'Al newe and fressh at every miles ende,' and precisely what the Pardoner saw the Host would never agree to do.

As so very often, a commonplace consideration has been overlooked. If Chaucer had had the slightest interest in providing a 'tavern background,' he would have provided one. Since he did not, we may infer, what should have been obvious from the start, that he was concentrating the whole of his effort on the character and directing his reader's whole attention to the same object. Mr. Tupper's tavern-ironies are irrelevant as well as improbable. Chaucer saw sufficient irony in the spectacle of the Pardoner inveighing against his own sins, perfectly aware that he was doing so. And he provided the required tavern atmosphere in sufficient quantity without any help from the tap-wenches.

The Tavern Heresy, like its fellows, puts stress on the wrong thing—on the sins not on the sinner, on the situation not on the person in it. Certainly Chaucer never meant to do anything of the sort. This time, however, one is grateful to the error for being so attractive and so informing.

III

What follows is mostly 'subjective interpretation' of the Pardoner and his behaviour. A good deal of it has been outlined, in passing, during the course of the review just concluded; and what will now be said is very largely an amalgam of findings which I think have been established by two generations of criticism. There has to be a good deal of conjecture in the amalgam, since all 'interpretation' is, in part, fundamentally conjectural. This, one may insist, does not make the process any the less important or indeed the less imperative. But to say that Chaucer was an artist and usually knew what he was doing is not too brave an assumption. Consequently, when you read on one page of a book that the Pardoner's discourse is a 'work of art' and a few pages farther on that it is chargeable with some glaring inconsistency or excrescence, you suspect a lapse in the critic's own mind. Perhaps, if he had risked a little more 'conjecture,' he would have arrived at a conclusion more consistent. No doubt Chaucer nodded like all other artists, but I think he did not often snore. With that conjecture in mind, I have tried to exhibit the whole Pardoner Scheme as what I firmly believe it to be—a powerfully consistent work of art.

It is convenient to study the Pardoner's development in five stages: (1) his portrait in the General Prologue, (2) his interruption of the Wife of Bath's discourse, (3) the 'head-link,' (4) his 'address,' consisting of a prologue, the 'sermon' proper, and a 'benediction,' (5) the epilogue, consisting of the Pardoner's 'afterthought,' as I shall call it, his quarrel with the Host, and the Knight's peace-making. In spite of debate about the position of (2), I am sure Chaucer must have intended these stages to be considered in that order; and in so considering them I shall try to remember that artistic divisions are not water-tight. The whole scheme outlined above must be studied as in one block.

1. To begin at the very beginning, one should note the first appearance of the word Pardoner:

> Ther was also a Reve, and a Millere,
> A Somnour, and a Pardoner also,
> A Maunciple, and myself.

With due reservations about 'myself' (how blandly impudent it is!), that is the Pardoner's gang: the slums of the Pilgrimage, tellers of harlotries all of them—except 'myself' and the one who would have told the worst harlotry if he had been allowed. Mr. Curry notes that there is no evidence of contact between the Pardoner and respectable folk. There certainly is not. None of the 'gentils' would touch him with the proverbial pole, and even Harry Bailly's final intimate contact was effected under stern duress.

The only Pilgrim who rides with him is the scabby Summoner, 'his freend and his compeer'—an association that quietly insists on attention. In one of the documents quoted by Dr. Owst,[28] Bishop Grandisson flays '*vos archi-diaconorum officiales, vestrive commissarii et registrarii, saeva cupiditate dampnabiliter excecati*,' who wink at unlawful preaching and encourage it for personal profit. As in the partnership of physician and apothecary,

> ech of hem made oother for to wynne—
> Hir frendshipe nas nat newe to bigynne.

Alongside his 'compeer,' the Pardoner leaps to sight as suddenly as a jinni out of the smoke:

> With hym ther rood a gentil Pardoner . . .
> That streight was comen fro the court of Rome.
> Ful loude he soong "Com hider, love, to me!"
> This Somonour bar to hym a stif burdoun;
> Was nevere trompe of half so greet a soun.

Of the companionship so established, Professor H. R. Patch remarks that it is 'the most violent satire in all of Chaucer's poetry.'[29] He means that these lines thrust without warning into the worst corruption of the medieval church in all its branches; and he is justified in using strong words, though he must be thinking of the corruption rather than of Chaucer's verses. Chaucer plainly means those lines to be arresting. But I should prefer to say 'contradiction' instead of 'satire'; and 'broadly comic' instead of 'violent.' That famous first couplet challenges the ear by a heightened pitch of the same cool impudence which has been noticed before and which is everywhere characteristic of Chaucer. The Pardoner would be quite capable of explaining that he learned his ditty from the Pope and of calling on the Summoner for corroboration. Though that would be the Pardoner's joke, not Chaucer's, the couplet does manage to convey something like its temper in a less 'violent' form. Those two lines announce the theme, so to speak, of a whole tone poem, and the 'stif burdoun' of the Summoner supports it with a sort of horribly hearty counterpoint.

I have used the word 'contradiction' advisedly. All interpretations of the Pardoner have to play upon the contradictious theme of 'hypocrite' or 'charlatan' suggested in the ironical couplet. At point after point, as the portrait develops, a duplicity lurks in statements or hints that are apparently plain. Does the walletful of pardons come from Rome all hot, or does the Pardoner merely say so? Is he or is he not in minor orders? Does he believe in the efficacy of relics or is he completely cynical about them? To anticipate a later part of the scheme, is he or is he not capable of reverence? There are, of course, not two opinions about his charlatanism. But there is no final making-up of the mind about the Charlatan himself. Did Chaucer 'hate' him, as Mr. Patch believes, or did he not, or did he 'hate' him only sometimes, or was he nothing more than immensely entertained by him? It is usually sentimental to press or even to put questions like these last, but they do arise without offense in the strange case of the Pardoner. That is why I have thought it worth while to spend so much space on four lines. I might allow Mr. Patch to call them 'startling irony.'

No other portrait in the General Prologue prepares for its outcome in so minute a fashion. Evidently, Chaucer must have seen exactly what he was going to do with the Pardoner by the time he felt able to describe him in such detail and with such complete foreshadowing. Notwithstanding the doubts of Koch[30] and one or two others, there is no real difficulty in reconciling the relics named in the Prologue with those the Preacher showed to the rustics:

one list merely expands the other in perfectly straightforward fashion. Chaucer was not telling his story to children who forbid the teller to 'vary events by so much as one small devil.' But with extraordinary fidelity, as he proceeds with the plan, he does develop every major and minor theme announced in the Pardoner's portrait: irreverence, lust, shameless exhibitionism, physical impotency, avarice, superb skill as charlatan. One theme not announced there—his drinking—is supplied by his association with the Summoner.

2. The Pardoner interrupts the Wife's discourse just where he *would* interrupt it as an expert professional—at the conclusion of one of her numerous little homilies. And he does so in his own surprising manner:

> Up stirte the Pardoner, and that anon:
> 'Now, dame, . . .
> Ye been a noble prechour in this cas.'

The 'cas' is the sexual relation, which naturally interests the singer of 'Come hider, love, to me.' He is later to say he will 'have a jolly wenche in every toun,' but at the moment he is more decorous: 'I was aboute to wedde a wyf.' This is jocosity, of course. But in view of his profession and his House of Rouncivale, it is impudent; and in the light of the portrait, dangerously shameless. This, I take it, is the reason why the Wife of Bath broadly hints that his outburst is due to drink. She speaks firmly, but I think with a certain veiled and allusive moderation which you would not expect from her. 'You had best look out,' she says; 'if you get married, you may drink an ale far more bitter. Take heed or some one will make an example of you.' The Pardoner promptly and wisely withdraws, but not without another bit of impudence:

> . . . teche us yonge men of youre praktike.

The incident is unimportant enough in itself, but it conveys a good deal of suggestion. Beside making one of the little diversions which Chaucer likes, it brings the Pardoner actively upon the stage for a moment, touches up some salient points of the portrait, prepares for a later warning that will be more vigorous, and ever so lightly suggests a possible exposure.

Even if this interpretation be rejected, the very nature of the incident would appear to forbid placing it *after* the Pardoner's main performance; in other words, the Pardoner's tale must follow the Wife of Bath's. Mr. Curry does not place it so, apparently accepting the Chaucer Society's order without question; and he could bring powerful support[31] to his aid if he wished to. I have no desire to thicken the darkness that still envelopes the order of the Canterbury Tales, or indeed to discuss the question at all except in so far as it affects a study of the Pardoner. But unless Chaucer has been guilty of a surprising lapse, the interruption simply cannot follow the tale. In the first place, such an order would involve the flattest kind of anti-climax: for the Pardoner's performance as interrupter is excellent as such, but frightfully feeble as compared with his efficiency as preacher. The minor episode, as I have shown, has value considered as merely preparatory, but next to none at all considered as epilogue. Further, *if* it is an epilogue, it shows the Pardoner up as a complete fool. After the appalling exposé he suffers at Harry Bailly's hands, he would be the last person, as Mr. Curry should agree, to 'entremette' himself into a discussion of marriage or of any question involving sex. Once bitten, twice shy. Now if any view of Chaucer's design is more secure than another, it is that he never imagined the Pardoner as an idiot—as he would be if he courted a second exposure. No doubt Chaucer's general plan changed in the course of development; no doubt he might find that a change involved a wrong disposition[32] of Rouchestre and Sidyngborne on the Canterbury road, or some other similar trouble. But, if he did, he would surely find it better to shuffle two names than to risk a dramatic fatuity.[33]

3. The Pardoner's 'head-link' is worth more attention than it has got or can now get. I think there is a not too subtle dig in Harry Bailly's summons to the new story-teller, 'thou beel amy, thou Pardoner.' *Beel amy* is a 'common form of address,' as the editors stingily say; but this is its only occurrence in Chaucer, and it can

be read as conveying a leer from the Host, whose French is surely rather unexpected. There is also a hint of return thrust, as well as eager zest, in the Pardoner's echoing of Harry's dubious saint:

'It shall be doon,' quod he, 'by Seint Ronyon!'

Other things, however, are more significant than these trifles; and one of them can easily be overlooked.

Harry Bailly would not be sensitive to the Pardoner's abomination, but the gentles were. And their swift outcry—

But right anon thise gentils gonne to crye—

has a double importance. On its surface it recalls the portrait of the rascal as he has appeared to the respectable part of the Pilgrimage: too clever to be predictable, physically abnormal, disturbingly contradictory, scoundrelly beyond words, a clear candidate for interdict. Even the Wife of Bath has eyed him darkly. As for the bawdry which the Miller had already uttered in their hearing without much protest, they had expected he would tell 'his cherles tale in his manere,' and they had known the worst he could do before he began. But they were troubled by the Pardoner's duplicity: altogether too visible on the one hand, and on the other a quite unknown quantity. If the inevitable fabliau came from the visible side, no doubt they could stand it; it was the other quarter they feared. *Ignotum pro horrendo.* This, I believe, is a possible reading of the gentles' mind, or of what Chaucer thought would be there.

The most interesting thing about their protest, however, is its dramatic usefulness. As the text plainly states, it wards off a fabliau and demands doctrine:

Nay, lat hym telle us of no ribaudye!
Telle us som moral thyng.

These commands the Pardoner knows he dare not disobey: 'I graunte, ywis.' But at the same time they have confronted him with a galling choice. He knows plenty of moral things, but to tell one *as such* is completely out of his character and habit; and what

is more, he knows the Pilgrims know that also. To recite the bare
exemplum before *this* audience is to cramp his style intolerably,
for the usual effect is not in view. At the moment there can be only
one effect that will redound to his glory: since he is known to be a
charlatan, he can prove he is the cleverest of his kind from Berwick
unto Ware. In short, he must tell a story at once moral and his
own. No wonder he pauses for a moment:

> but I moot thynke
> Upon som honest thyng while that I drynke.

But only for a moment. We can easily imagine his rapid thinking
as he swallows the ale: 'I have it! The Wife of Bath made a hit with
her confessions. Why shouldn't I follow her example and give an
exhibition, with running comment, of my technique? They have
asked for morality and they shall have it; but it will be morality,
with my special difference, from the mouth of a dark horse. There
can be no risk. Here and now I am perfectly secure.' Much of this
is naked 'assumption,' but it is assumption harmonious with the
immediate context and with the general manner of the Canterbury
cycle. By the device of the 'protest' Chaucer jockeys his Pardoner
into a corner from which he can escape in only one way, and this
he takes after pausing but a moment. The charlatan's self-revelation is, therefore, not only 'credible' on other grounds, it is as near
to dramatic inevitability as it can be made.

4. He loses no time in getting to work:

> 'Lordynges,' quod he, 'in chirches whan I preche,
> I peyne me to han an hauteyn speche.'

Some important aspects of the 'address' that follows have already
been discussed fully enough. Sometimes I think it would be good
sport for a scholar like Mr. C. S. Lewis, who can write Middle
English verse with unashamed skill, to reconstruct the whole of
the 'sermon' which the Pardoner was wont to preach to villagers.
The exploit might help to lay the ghost of the 'typical sermon'; for
if carried out and read intelligently, it might show why Chaucer
did *not* write one. But such a sport may require the services of

another Pardoner. Having only Chaucer's to go by, we must never forget the rascal's dilemma and his effort to escape from it. The way out was not to preach a 'typical sermon' (or one of his own), or to tell a 'perfect short story.' What he did was to fuse two elements diametrically opposed: the sermon and narrative which in themselves faced one way, the self-revelation which faced another. Nothing could be plainer than his own statement:

> Thus kan I preche agayn that same vice
> Which that I use, and that is avarice.
> But though myself be gilty in that synne,
> Yet kan I maken oother folk to twynne
> From avarice, and soore to repente.
> But that is nat my principal entente;
> I preche nothyng but for coveitise.

The Pilgrims were thereby privileged to see a truly marvellous spectacle of the devil calling sinners to repentance, actually achieving that result, and getting pay for his 'assoillyng'!

The Pardoner's 'prologe,' like many other things in Chaucer, is carefully constructed to give an air of improvisation. Apparently it rambles, as if the draught of corny ale were working: the speaker seems to be uttering just what comes into his head. With perfect casualness, he suggests a picture of his rural victims; he digresses to give a graphic imitation of himself at work in front of them—

> . . . it is joye to se my bisynesse;

over and over he rings it out, 'as round as gooth a belle,' that he preaches 'nothing but for coveitise.' For this occasion he shortens or merely reports the display of cheap fireworks by which he awes the yokel, and he takes his immediate audience by the more potent fascination of himself. As soon as this is duly exercised, he can carry out the letter of his promise:

> herkneth, lordynges, in conclusion:
> Youre likyng is that I shal telle a tale. . . .
> For though myself be a ful vicious man,
> A moral tale yet I yow telle kan.

He can now tell his great story as if his two audiences, past and present, were one—as they are in interest, but with what difference in feeling!

The difference is important for two reasons: first, because it affects the closing episode, as we shall soon see, and secondly, because the Pardoner's new audience includes, in a sense, all readers of the tale. Chaucer cannot pause, any more than a dramatist ever can, to display the reaction of the gentles and the others. But if a reader will try to imagine the effect the Pardoner produces on the Pilgrims, he will also be analyzing the effect upon himself. There can be no doubt that the Knight, for instance, is listening intently. To him, the speaker may be loathsome, but he is likewise fascinating. As a devout man, the Knight is revolted by this public exposure of the Church's corruption: if Mr. Patch wishes, he feels the effect as 'violently satiric.' And no doubt, he feels a sort of anger as he imagines what damage these foxes do in the vineyard:

> I rekke nevere, whan that they been beryed,
> Though that hir soules goon a-blakeberyed!

To him, therefore, the exemplum will be all the more shocking because of its very power. The moral tale which 'shal by resoun been at youre likyng'—one of the Pardoner's little ironies—is really as vicious as the teller. The contradiction we noted in the Pardoner at the beginning is the core of his performance at the end.

5. There remain the curious and difficult questions raised by the 'benediction' and the closing episode. What is the state of the Pardoner's mind as he ends the story and goes on in his 'afterthought'? What is the exact significance of the quarrel between Host and Pardoner and of the Knight's intervention?

To the first question, Mr. Carleton Brown proposes a 'simpler solution' than ordinary by declining to raise it. The Clerk, he says, ends a serious tale on 'a becoming note of gravity' and then relapses 'into playful banter': so also the Pardoner. It is hard to see what this parallel, in itself very dubious, 'solves'; and I think one need only state it to find it altogether too 'simple.' If subtleties really exist, they are not 'solved' by waving them aside. And as I have been trying to show, Chaucer's design in this whole affair is very subtly complicated: it extorts 'interpretation,' however much one may shrink from the process. The Pardoner's benediction or 'closing formula' (often so-called) is a most insistent case in point. His 'sermon' is finished:

> And lo, sires, thus I preche.
> And Jhesu Crist, that is oure soules leche,
> So graunte yow his pardoun to receyve,
> For that is best; I wol yow nat deceyve.

Everyone who reads these last three lines finds them moving and strange, and to almost everyone they seem to come in a questionable shape. Lacking Mr. Brown's ability to pass them over, we again ask what impulses lie behind them.

First and most emphatically, they are not the 'closing formula' of the *sermon*, though undoubtedly they have a gravity befitting the superb story and the moving appeal which have just been uttered. But the Pardoner had ended his 'sermon' when he said, 'lo, sires, thus I preche.' He is now speaking to the Pilgrims only, all pretense laid aside, concluding the entertainment which the Host had called on him to furnish, and presumably about to retire to his place alongside the Summoner. At least ten of his fellow-pilgrims conclude their turns with a benediction (in several cases very unedifying); and, of course, medieval narrative generally ends on some such conventional note. Primarily, therefore, the Pardoner is again 'following a tradition.' The point might seem obvious in itself, and it has not gone unnoticed in criticism. But of the two best-known answers to our question, one passes lightly over the obvious and the second neglects it altogether.

In 'The Pardoner's Secret,' Mr. Curry recognizes the element of tradition, yet nevertheless speaks of it as the beginning of a 'masterstroke of deception.'[34] Noting that the Pilgrims may be under his spell, the Pardoner is said to see them as another and fatter flock of victims. Then, to report Mr. Curry, he turns to them suddenly and tells them that this is the way he preaches to *ignorant* people; but *they*, the Pilgrims, are his friends, and he prays that *they* may

receive Christ's pardon; he would never deceive *them;* consequently they are to come and kiss the relics.

This version of the benediction is, I believe, quite untenable.
First, in order to arrive at it, Mr. Curry is compelled to do queer
things with Chaucer's metre. But, what is really important, he
makes the 'sudden turning' come at the wrong place. He forgets
that he has noted the presence of traditional custom; and his
paraphrase obscures the very patent shift which occurs in the
Pardoner's speech and manner at the *close* of the so-called 'formula.' For at this point, as plainly as words and verse can indicate
it, there is a marked transition to what I have called the 'afterthought':

> . . . For that is best; I wol yow nat deceyve—

so closes the benediction. And then follows something in a vein
unmistakably different:

> *But, sires, o word forgat I in my tale:*
> I have relikes and pardoun in my male.

Correct placing of this shift might have been another warning to
Mr. Curry not to regard either the benediction or the 'afterthought'
as deceit. On the contrary, I am very sure, the one is quite serious
and sincere. And as for the other, I am just as sure that it is ironic
banter. Only an utter fool would *seriously* ask the Knight and
the Monk, not to speak of the Host, to kneel down or else give
money 'at every miles ende.' Though the Pardoner is defective
physically, he has his wits about him; there is no need to write
him down an ass, as Mr. Curry does on two separate occasions.
And, in Mr. Brown's phrase, 'an experienced salesman' would
never in one breath twit a buyer with being guilty of both sin and
waistline, especially when the buyer is Harry Bailly. The 'afterthought' cannot be rationally read except as a piece of impudent
horseplay.

Of all comments on the benediction the most important occurs
in an essay on 'Chaucer's Pardoner' by Professor George Lyman

Kittredge, published as long ago as 1893, and substantially repeated in *Chaucer and His Poetry* of 1915. This famous essay still remains by long odds the most complete and satisfying study of the Pardoner ever made. In many respects it seems final. But I agree with Mr. Curry in finding its solution of the final problems unacceptable, though on very different grounds.

Mr. Kittredge believes that the Pardoner 'ought to have stopped' at the close of the exemplum; and that he is carried beyond the proper limits by the histrionic excitement of his preaching. Then (so Mr. Kittredge thinks) realizing that the appeal for repentance and offering, which follows the tale, cannot be directed to the pilgrims, he suddenly cuts it off; and, remembering he once 'preached for Christ's sake,' he utters a solemn benediction in 'a very paroxysm of agonized sincerity.' But the mood of revulsion can be only momentary. In order to cover up his indiscretion he plunges at once into 'a wild orgy of reckless jesting,' in which he describes his presence as 'a regular insurance policy' for the pilgrimage and demands premiums for the same.

This rough summary of two pages from *Chaucer and His Poetry* falls far short of justice to Mr. Kittredge's persuasive argument. The original passage and its context cast a spell very unlike the Pardoner's in intention but nearly equal in effect. It *may* tell the whole truth; and every time I read it, I am tempted to throw overboard every conclusion of my own. But in my cooler moments it appears to me based on a too narrowly selected portion of the text and on a view of the whole document that incurs more difficulty than it resolves.

There is a fallacy concealed not only in the summary given above but in Mr. Kittredge's own pages. His belief that the Pardoner says too much results from what may be called retroactive reasoning. For it could never have occurred to Mr. Kittredge (let alone the ordinary reader) except as a throw-back from the doctrine of benedictory paroxysm. *If* this doctrine is to hold, *then* it is necessary to go back and regard the Pardoner's sermon as too long for his own comfort. But for such a view Chaucer himself gives no warrant in any sign or hint or warning whatsoever. In other words, he must have set about to fool us readers (not to speak

of the pilgrims) just as thoroughly as the Pardoner fooled the ignorant folk. And, in that event, we should almost inevitably be
fooled into missing a sight of the paroxysm also. (Actually, as Mr.
Kittredge notes, everybody in the pilgrimage does miss it.) Such
are the implications of his argument, and somehow we do not like
to believe anything so uncomplimentary to ourselves. Even a
writer of detective yarns drops one or two clues that we could have
picked up if we had been alert enough. No life-line of the sort is
discernible in the 667 lines of verse which Chaucer previously
devotes to the Pardoner. Such deception of an audience is not the
usual habit of an artist; and we may therefore be inclined to doubt
if Chaucer intended any such thing.

What hints *did* Chaucer drop about his intention? They would
seem plentiful enough. First we may revert to the end of the
'prologe':

> A moral tale yet I yow telle kan,
> Which I am wont to preche for to wynne.

Now the 'moral tale' is only one part—admittedly the most highly
coloured—of a whole pattern. But the 'wynning' is another, equally
important in its way. Half-a-dozen times over, the Pardoner says
as much to the pilgrims. No doubt he *could* have stopped at the
point where Death overtook the Robbers, but then the final strokes
of his genius in extortion would have gone unseen. And such a
killing as he always made! One remembers that

> Upon a day he gat hym moore moneye
> Than that the person gat in monthes tweye,

and that he had

> wonne, yeer by yeer,
> An hundred mark sith [he] was pardoner.

Chaucer was exhibiting more than a form of narrative and homiletic art: he was exhibiting also a charlatan's power over folk whose
souls went blackberrying. How utterly irresistible that power was

we have already noted in the terrific summing-up and call to repentance which follows the grim exemplum. If it is true that portrait, 'prologe,' and all must be read as one block, as I believe they must, it is a mistake to say that Chaucer meant the Pardoner to 'preach' too long.

A second difficulty with Mr. Kittredge's view is by this time familiar. The benediction is neither so 'sudden' nor so 'unexpected,' as he says. As we have seen, it was the end, not of the 'sermon,' but of his performance as under contract to the Host; and the Pardoner is following a convention that any story-teller might be expected to observe. Of this simple but important fact Mr. Kittredge makes no mention. The words of the 'formula' are indeed solemn—no more so, by the way, than the Man of Law's benediction—and they ought to be solemn, in order to harmonize with the tone of what precedes. They are, I shall point out, a thoroughly sincere expression of personal feeling, and in a very real sense they may be called surprising. But the surprise is one that needs no previous hint or sign. At any rate, it bears no necessary mark of paroxysm.

Nor can the 'afterthought' be properly described as 'a wild orgy of reckless jesting.' Undoubtedly a critic is bound to call it that if he commits himself to the paroxysm theory; for if there is a paroxysm, there must, I suppose, be some sort of corresponding reaction. One may be excused, however, for finding Mr. Kittredge's prose paraphrase of the wild orgy rather more surprising than Chaucer's verses, which are no more extravagant than anything said about or by the Pardoner elsewhere. Indeed they are the sort of utterance one expects either from the character depicted in the portrait or after his impudence in interrupting the Wife of Bath and the shamelessness of his own 'prologe.' A man who comes straight from Rome to sing a love-song and boast of his jolly wenches needs no orgiastic stimulus to be capable of anything in the 'afterthought.'

Finally, this theory imposes a forward-looking compulsion on the quarrel between Pardoner and Host. Mr. Kittredge sees nothing but 'rough jocularity' in the Host's reply to the *beel amy,* of whose 'emotional crisis' neither Host nor any one else can know;

and he attributes the Pardoner's speechless anger at Harry Bailly to another turn of emotion arising from that crisis. But the text at this point bears a different and painfully obvious meaning. One would hate to face the Host when jocularity steps over the line into mere roughness. As a matter of plain fact—here Mr. Curry and the Portrait come into their own—Harry Bailly flings the Pardoner's impotence full in his face, meaning 'no offense' by it, only 'rough jocularity'! Hamlet had a word for fun like this: 'No, no, they do but jest, poison in jest, no offence i' th' world.' A man may be aware that a member of his company is afflicted with physical defect or deformity; but to mention the fact, in language however moderate, is a fighting offense. And the Host's language has never been accused of moderation. The worst of such 'jocularity' is that it cannot be answered in words. No previous emotional crisis is needed to account for the Pardoner's wrathful silence.

The argument just outlined leads me to reject Mr. Kittredge's interpretation of the episode. The substitute I propose is far less spectacular, but it does represent an attempt to read the document in the light of the whole Pardoner-scheme.

The portrait, it will be recalled, begins with an ironic contradiction and supports this theme by posing a number of irresoluble ambiguities. The scoundrel pictured there is intensely vivid and at the same time curiously baffling; and the disturbance he creates is revolting to physical and moral sense alike. Physically and morally he is charlatanism incarnate. When he interrupts the Wife of Bath, the general effect of the portrait is dramatically though vaguely reinforced. It begins to take on a clear dramatic outline in the Host's leering summons and the protests of the gentlefolk, and it fills out into savage clarity in the 'prologe.' The Pardoner's 'address' is a prolonged working-out of the discord struck at the very beginning. Such, in the view of this study, is a summary of the process up to the benediction.

According to such a view the Pardoner is in control of himself and his speech throughout. No one can deny that he does what he is told to do, but he does it in his own characteristic and shocking way. When his stint has been performed—'Lo, sires, thus I preche'—he prepares to take his leave of the stage. What he now says to the Pilgrims is in a way surprising at the moment but not inharmonious, when you come to think of it, with what went before. Of course a benediction is partly a matter of traditional formula. But in it, if ever at any time, a Pardoner may be allowed to say something at once sincere and stripped of shamelessness. 'I have not deceived you,' he says in effect, 'nor will I do so now. The false "assoillyng" I have just exhibited tends to destruction; but there *is* a cure for souls that is truly efficacious. I have proclaimed myself a charlatan, but I would not have you think me a heretic.' In Chaucer's verse this is no paroxysm but a dignified and eloquent farewell. The teller of the Quest for Death knows what dignity is even if he does not put his knowledge into practice very often; and five centuries of listeners have never denied him eloquence. There is 'some good' in the Pardoner, as two English editors say with commendable restraint.[35] Tomorrow, perhaps, he will even be afraid and tremble 'before that formidable power which he said he held in his hands and of which he has made a toy.'[36]

It would have been well for the Pardoner if this eloquent note had been his last. Here, not earlier, is the point at which he overreached himself; and he did so, I believe, because he was tempted where he was weakest. Chaucer, it seems to me, had made up his mind that this lofty rogue should take a fall—not necessarily that Chaucer 'hated' him but because, in slang phrase, he had been asking for trouble. Of all people in the Pilgrimage, the Pardoner most deserves to be thrown: there can be no clearer case for meting out poetic justice. At any rate, the fall was arranged.

I imagine that a hush has fallen over the pilgrims as the Pardoner brings his 'sermon' to a close. No one, not even the Host, has a word to say. True, there is no basis for this assumption in the text except that a shift is plainly indicated there. The preacher evidently *intends* to stop, does stop in fact—and then goes on. He says he 'forgot one thing'—which he had fully developed only a few lines previously—and then continues in a vein very different from the preceding. I should like to suggest, moreover, that a shift from moral revulsion to wild jesting would also seem to require a second or two for the readjustment. But frankly, my chief basis for the assumption lies in my own experience in reading the poem.

The tale itself is impressive beyond words; the summary and appeal that follow it are appallingly impressive in another way; and the solemn benediction crowns it all with a third emphasis. It is a performance that might well impose silence. The Pilgrims' reaction, already analyzed in the person of the Knight, would not differ in kind from that of the ordinary intelligent reader; probably it would not be feebler. And, except Mr. Curry, every critic who has stopped to comment, no matter how he 'interprets' the benediction, notes a shift in tone as the Pardoner passes on to the 'afterthought.' To my fancy there is a momentary hush where the change occurs.

The Pardoner, as I see him, looks around at the silent pilgrimage with perhaps some surprise and certainly deep satisfaction. Since Harry Bailly has nothing ready to say, he moves on his own behalf as swiftly as he did on a previous occasion. It suddenly occurs to him, 'They have been impressed in spite of themselves! What do they think now of the man forbid? I will get some fun out of their embarrassment.' The hush has flattered the preacher's vanity and so leads to his undoing. Tempted beyond measure, he lets fling at the Pilgrims with his impudently ironic joke, all guards down. His brother, daun Russell, could have given him a warning:

> 'Nay,' quod the fox, 'but God yeve hym meschaunce,
> That is so undiscreet of governaunce
> That jangleth whan he sholde holde his pees.'

Unhappily for the Preaching Fox, there is no one at hand to warn him; and so, in Mr. Curry's pretty pun, he blunders into reckoning without his Host. To tell the truth, Harry Bailly has scarcely reckoned with himself. He is ashamed to have been so impressed; he feels, quite rightly, that the Pardoner of all people is making a fool of *him;* and he is angry. I believe the evidence of anger is plain. The Host is indeed prone to 'rough jocularity,' witness his 'words' to the Cook, the Franklin, the Physician, Chaucer himself, the Monk, the Nun's Priest, the Manciple. But his words to the Pardoner pass the jocular limit. For sheer obscene brutality they have no parallel in the Canterbury Tales—and that is saying a good deal. Then, as the Pardoner is left speechless, he compounds the injury by pointing to his victim's rage.

Even that is not all. The Pilgrims are laughing, relieved to get their own weakness withdrawn to cover, amused at the Host's discomfiture, and more than delighted at the quick deflation of a swollen bubble. It looks to the Knight as if anything might happen, and he therefore steps in to direct the crisis in his usual masterly way. He feels that the Pardoner, thoroughly evil though he is, has provided superb entertainment and has been exposed with a blatancy quite too cruel. He therefore orders the Host to take the initiative in making amends: he says 'ye' to Harry Bailly and 'thee' to the Pardoner. That kiss which they exchange—it will not necessarily be fatal—is a supreme stroke of comic irony. This is the very note which Chaucer struck at the beginning of the Pardoner's portrait in the General Prologue. We are back where we began.

The end should warn us not to inject 'violent satire' into the beginning. Love-song and kiss are widely separated; but they are products of the same temper, which is the temper of Human Comedy and therefore neither violent nor satiric. We begin and end the whole affair with a laugh that need not be either strident or bitter unless we feel inclined to be so in ourselves. Satirists have their own laudable work to do, but Chaucer is not one of them. He cannot be said to 'hate' the Pardoner any more than he 'hates' the Host: Harry Bailly too is 'envoluped in synne' and, as chief offender, he is made to administer the kiss to his *beel amy*. Contrariwise, Chaucer does not 'pity' the Pardoner any more than the Host does: he merely deals with him in a different fashion. Is it possible that words like 'hate' and 'pity' indicate a sentimental wish to make Chaucer a partisan on one's own side?

All this is very far from implying that Chaucer was easily tolerant of evil. That would be silly. Far from tolerating the charlatan, he *presented* him, fully-rounded and without reservation; and the effect is immeasurably more impressive than any satirist can achieve within the limitations of his trade. It was not Chaucer's business to issue warrants against the House of Rouncivale. It *was* his business to *see* one remarkable member of the House and to write down what he saw. Now that the moral issue has been raised, we need only say that Chaucer enables us to sharpen our senses against the scourge and blight of charlatanism. This I

know, for with his help I have watched quacks vending medicine
and politics and religion in our own day.

Such is one view of the Pardoner as he emerges from a progress
through the 'modern mind.'

NOTES

1. *Essays on Chaucer,* Chaucer Society, 2nd series, 1884, 423–436.

2. *Contemporary Review,* IIIIIIII, 738.

3. See Carleton Brown's edition of *The Pardoner's Tale* (Oxford, 1935), p.
xxv.

4. For a summary of research on this point see F. N. Robinson's note on
line C713 of the Canterbury Tales in the Cambridge Chaucer (p. 836). By
the kind permission of the publishers, I have taken my Chaucer quotations
from this edition.

5. *History of English Literature,* II (London, 1893), 171.

6. G. L. Kittredge related these lines to the First Elegy of Maximian
(*American Journal of Philology,* ix [1888], 84 f.). The fact that Maximian
is 'not very respectable' (*The Pardoner's Tale,* ed. Pollard and Barber, London, 1929, p. xii) does not seem relevant.

7. *Originals and Analogues of some of Chaucer's Canterbury Tales,* Chaucer Society, Second Series (1886), p. 436.

8. See H. S. Canby, *Modern Philology,* II (1904), 477–487.

9. Lounsbury, *Studies in Chaucer,* III, 366. Lounsbury does admit defense
on 'the ground of dramatic propriety.' But the admission is obviously half-
hearted.

10. *Notes on Chaucer,* Northampton, Mass., 1907, pp. 157–159.

11. Ten Brink, *op. cit.,* II, 170.

12. See, especially, K. O. Petersen, *On the Sources of the Nonne Prestes
Tale,* Boston, 1898.

13. See C. O. Chapman, *Modern Language Notes,* XLI (1926), 506–509;
XLIII (1928), 229–234; *PMLA,* XLIV (1929), 178–185. Also, C. Jones, *Modern Language Review,* XXXII (1937), 283; *Mod. Lang. Notes,* LII (1937),
570–572.

14. *Preaching in Medieval England,* Cambridge, 1926; *Literature and
Pulpit in Medieval England,* Cambridge, 1933.

15. *Journal of English and Germanic Philology,* XVIII (1919), 593–606;
Chaucer and the Mediaeval Sciences, New York and Oxford, 1926, pp. 54–70.

16. *Some New Light on Chaucer,* Bell (London, 1926[?]), pp. 122–130,
pp. 288–290.

17. *Modern Philology,* XXV (1927), 59–66.

18. D. M. Norris, *PMLA,* XLVIII (1933), 641.

19. *The Complete Works of Geoffrey Chaucer,* v, 275. Skeat's note goes
on to illustrate the abundance of food and drink in Flanders.

20. K. O. Peterson, *op. cit.*, p. 99 n.

21. See W. B. Sedgwick, *Modern Language Review*, XIX (1924), 336–337.

22. See Germaine Dempster, *Dramatic Irony in Chaucer*, Stanford Univ. Press, 1932, p. 77. Dr. Dempster applied the quoted words to 'the specific details of the tavern scene' only. They apply equally well to the discussion of the sins.

23. *Journal of Eng. and Germ. Phil.*, XIII (1914), 553–565.

24. See 'Chaucer and the Seven Deadly Sins,' *PMLA*, XXIX (1914), 93–128.

25. See J. L. Lowes, 'Chaucer and the Seven Deadly Sins,' *PMLA*, XXX (1915), 237–371.

26. *Geoffrey Chaucer*, Paris, 1910, p. 185.

27. Cambridge Chaucer, p. 834.

28. *Preaching in Medieval England*, p. 104 n.

29. *On Rereading Chaucer*, Harvard Press, 1939, p. 164.

30. *The Pardoner's Prologue and Tale*, Chaucer Society, Second Series, 1902, p. XXIX.

31. See S. Moore's article, 'The Position of Group C etc.,' *PMLA*, XXX (1915), 116–122; and J. S. P. Tatlock, 'The Canterbury Tales in 1400,' *PMLA*, L (1935), 100–139.

32. This would occur only if Groups C and B² *must* be joined together. See Moore, *op. cit.*

33. On the other grounds, Koch and Tupper likewise place the Pardoner's Tale after Group D. The manuscripts, I believe, are unanimous in so placing it, along with Group B².

34. *Chaucer and the Mediaeval Sciences*, p. 67.

35. Drennan and Wyatt, *The Pardoner's Tale*, Clive, London, 1911, p. 24.

36. *English Wayfaring Life*, p. 333.

W. J. B. OWEN

The Old Man in *The Pardoner's Tale*

I

THE old man in 'The Pardoner's Tale' has generally been interpreted as Death himself or his representative.[1] This interpretation appears to me to be unjustified by the text and to spoil much of the irony of the Tale. It is true that one of the revellers alleges that the old man is Death's spy; but it is not obvious that we ought to accept the drunken utterance of one of the characters against the author's silence. Chaucer's silence on the subject is indeed significant: generally speaking, his old man is noticeably less particularized than the corresponding figures in the analogues, and it is at least partly by what he may be presumed to have left out that Chaucer has managed to increase the ironic possibilities of this episode of his story.

The old man is not characterized as a hermit or similar figure. This absence of definition emphasizes his seeming triviality: we see him through the eyes of the revellers, as a thing of no account to them; as a man who need not be observed more closely than to reach the conclusion that he is old; whose pitiful attempt to assert his dignity is passed over in crushing silence by the reveller full of wine and arrogance. He seems of no account to them; he is observed by them as cursorily as Chaucer's physical picture of him is vague; yet, ironically, he is of supreme importance to them. A

Reprinted from *The Review of English Studies*, N.S. II (1951), 49-55, by permission of The Clarendon Press, Oxford.

hermit, a philosopher, anyone of obvious spiritual authority, might, we feel, have given them pause: this seemingly insignificant figure has no such authority. He is forgotten, like Death, as soon as the treasure is found; in the analogues the characters corresponding to the revellers sometimes remember him to the extent of thinking him mad.

Thus far, then, there is nothing to suggest that our old man is an allegory of Death. Indeed, certain passages suggest that he is not. He is seeking Death; and that Death or his messenger should seek death is contrary to all the logic of allegory. True, had the old man been presented as immortal, he would have shared his immortality with Death; but he is not so presented. On the contrary, we are told that he wanders about in his old age 'As longe time as it is goddes wille,' which surely does not mean 'for ever'; he wishes to return to Mother Earth, 'But yet to me she wol nat do that grace' (presumably she will later); and that Death should wish to return to the earth seems to have no allegorical meaning. We spoil the point of 'No lenger thanne after Deeth they soughte' by taking the old man as Death. The line is richly ambiguous: the revellers no longer sought *Death*, from their own point of view, because they had found something more interesting; they no longer *sought* him, from the point of view of the story, because they had just found him. This ironical ambiguity is weakened if we suppose that they meet Death in the shape of an old man, pass him by, and meet him again in the shape of the gold: the dual symbol for Death thus imposed on the story confuses and diffuses the irony. Again, it is contrary to the logic of allegory that Old Age as the messenger of Death should appear in a company of young men: when we say that Old Age is the messenger of Death we mean, surely, that when a man becomes old he realizes, or ought to realize, that Death is summoning him and that shortly he will have to obey the summons. Such an allegory can have no meaning in our story, where the only appropriate messenger of Death is Disaster.

Let us suppose, then, that the old man is merely an old man, and examine his conduct from this point of view. His demeanor changes from self-pity to an attempt at dignified reproach which is ignored, and then perhaps to something like fear: plainly, he wants to get away, but his attempt to do it quietly fails. He tries a certain trembling cunning, based on the drunken and blasphemous outburst of the reveller; it succeeds. We return immediately to Chaucer's skill in omission: in the analogues the hermit has seen the gold, has identified it with Death, and is fleeing from it; he leads the revellers to it and points it out directly. There is nothing in Chaucer to suggest that the old man has seen the gold; rather, his failure to proclaim that he has found Death (except in his final speech, where he is obviously taking his cue from the preceding speech of the reveller), and his search for it rather than his flight from it, both suggest the contrary. He does not know, then, what the revellers will find under the tree; for if he does he ought, according to his earlier speech, to have remained with the gold, seeking his death in it. He assumes that they will find nothing; but, once he has directed their attention away from himself, he will have his chance to escape; for it is 'in *that* grove,' under '*that* ook,' which it will take them some little time to reach, that Death 'wol abyde.' He tries a long shot and it finds its mark. Hence Chaucer's omissions: the old man is seeking death, not fleeing from it, for he does not know that it is in the grove; he does not know where it is, much as he would like to know. He does not, indeed cannot, lead the revellers to the gold and point it out to them, for as far as he knows there is nothing there. He does not warn them against it, as his analogues do, for again, as far as he knows, there is nothing there against which they ought to be warned.

The dramatic irony of the old man's almost every utterance is now apparent. He greets the revellers with 'God you see!'; which is what God does not do. He seeks Death: his eagerness to be on his way, the trick he plays to enable him to proceed on his way, lead him away from Death. If the revellers had not spoken 'vileinye' to him, if they had not held him back when he said 'God be with yow' to those who had most need of blessing, he would not have directed them, unwittingly, to the death he sought for himself. His final directions and his final prayer for their salvation reach the height of dramatic irony.

All this achieves its keenest point only if we suppose the old man to be an old man and nothing more; only if we suppose him to be ignorant of the gold and anxious merely to 'go thider as I have to go,' and forced into a sort of senile cunning which devises what he thinks an innocent trick against the revellers. (Who would not humor a drunken and possibly violent man by offering him the first innocent-seeming direction that entered one's head, in order to be rid of his company?) It is out of his aged humanity that there springs Chaucer's main addition to the figure, the self-pitying (and slightly garrulous) speech on his search for death which is to contrast ironically with the revellers' finding of death. Out of the same aged humanity springs the ironical

> Ne dooth unto an olde man noon harm now,
> Na more than ye wolde men dide to yow
> In age, if that ye so longe abyde.

This is pointless as dramatic irony if the old man is an allegory of Death or if he is Death's messenger; for if he is an allegorical figure he knows the meaning of his words and the irony fails. Similarly the reveller's speech which accuses the old man of being Death's spy loses its ironic point if it is true in the sense in which the reveller intends it: the old man is Death's spy, but neither he nor the reveller knows it. He can be ignorant of it only if he is human, and we can appreciate the irony of it only when we know that he is Death's agent unwittingly; in terms of the story, not of himself. Lastly, his farewell prayer is ironical only if we interpret it as humanly intended: it is intended to save the revellers from drunkenness and arrogance, it is needed to keep them from treachery and murder, and, ironically, it serves neither purpose.

II

A sufficient reason for the changed treatment of the story in Chaucer as compared with the analogues can perhaps be found in the gain in irony and the author's originality; yet it is worth considering the possibility that Maximian's First Elegy contributed something more than the idea of a few lines in the old man's main speech.[2] That Chaucer could catch hints from a Latin source which are not necessarily reflected in close verbal borrowing was well demonstrated a few years ago by Karl Young in an acute discussion of the relation to the 'Nun's Priest's Tale' of Geoffrey de Vinsauf's *Nova Poetria*.[3] Something of the same process is perhaps to be seen in Chaucer's use of Maximian here; for in Maximian he could have found already well developed the notion of aged humanity which we have just noted as characteristic of the old man in search of death.

If the interpretation of the old man suggested above is accepted, we have only to search a few lines earlier in the Elegy than the passage originally cited by Kittredge to find a description of him: 'Stat dubius tremulusque senex semperque malorum Credulus. . . .' (195–6). The odd detail of C 718, 'Why artow al forwrapped save they face?', might have been suggested by antithesis to 'Labitur ex umeris demisso corpore uestis' (213): the reveller (or Chaucer with the Latin line in his head) thinks it worthy of note that an old man's garments should fit him so closely. The old man's opening words:

> for I ne can finde
> A man . . .
> That wolde chaunge his youthe for myn age

recall the whole trend of Maximian's lament for lost youth. More specifically, the next lines in Chaucer:

> And therfor moot I han myn age stille,
> As longe time as it is goddes wille.
> Ne deeth, allas! ne wol nat han my lyf

seem to recall

> Nunc quia longa mihi grauis est et inutilis aetas,
> Viuere cum nequeam, sit mihi posse mori . . .
> Nec mori humano subiacet arbitrio!
> Dulce mori miseris, sed mors optata recedit.

C 725–6 correspond generally to 111 in the Latin; C 726 is a Christianized version of 114; and C 727 echoes the second half of 115. The small sermon on politeness towards the aged (C 739–47) possibly had its origin in

> Ipsi me pueri atque ipsae sine lite puellae
> Turpe putant dominum iam uocitare suum

again with the addition of biblical coloring.

Again, for all the attention that his long speech receives, it is approximately true that 'Deficit auditor . . .' and it is certainly true that '. . . non deficit ipse loquendo' (203). Lastly, is not the very length of the speech a reflection of 'O sola fortes garrulitate senes!' (204)?

With these additional parallels at hand it seems easier to believe that the differences between Chaucer's old man and the corresponding figures in the analogues arise rather from Maximian than from the mediaeval poems cited by Mrs. Hamilton. There is no suggestion, as we saw above, that Chaucer's figure is 'destined . . . to go on as long as death and decay shall last.' The most striking difference between Chaucer's character and his analogues is that he seeks death while they flee from it; and, whereas Mrs. Hamilton has not been able, so far as I can see, to find a case in which Elde, the Messenger of Death, is represented as seeking death, this motif is clearly stated in Maximian. 'Maximian,' we are told, 'does not represent his character as symbolic and mysterious'; but this and similar statements beg the whole question discussed above, whether the old man is in fact 'symbolic' or 'mysterious.' To me he is neither. To be sure, there is nothing to prevent the use of the Latin material in the building up of an allegorical figure, as Sackville may have used it in the stanza which Mrs. Hamilton quotes to demonstrate the persistence of the image of knocking at Death's door. But the surrounding context of the Induction, like that of Mrs. Hamilton's mediaeval analogues, is thoroughly allegorical, as that of 'The Pardoner's Tale' is thoroughly realistic. We are bound to interpret the central figure accordingly.

NOTES

1. G. L. Kittredge, *Chaucer and his Poetry* (Cambridge, Mass., 1920), p. 215: 'The aged wayfarer . . . is undoubtedly Death in person. But Chaucer does not say so.' R. K. Root, *The Poetry of Chaucer* (Boston, 1922), p. 229: 'One of the "riotours" accuses him of being Death's spy; we are tempted to believe that he is rather very Death himself. But Chaucer does not say so.' F. N. Robinson, *Complete Works of Geoffrey Chaucer* (Boston, 1934), p. 830. 'The figure in Chaucer becomes . . . a symbol of Death itself, or possibly of Old Age, conceived as Death's messenger.' See especially a more closely argued account in M. P. Hamilton, 'Death and Old Age in "The Pardoner's Tale," ' *SP*, xxxvi (1939), 571 ff., where additional references may be found. Mrs. Hamilton, pointing to contemporary poems on the Three Messengers of Death, Sickness, Disaster, and Old Age, argues that Chaucer had this trio in mind, and that therefore his old man 'must stand for Old Age as the Harbinger of Death.' This reminiscence may perhaps be granted; but Mrs. Hamilton fails to notice that the treatment of the three figures in her main analogue is allegorical, whereas Chaucer's is not: the plague-background is sickness made actual; the end of the Tale is disaster made actual; we should expect, then, that Chaucer's third figure would be, not an allegory of Old Age, but an old man. Similarly, it is possibly to be granted that Chaucer remembered typical features of the Wandering Jew, as is argued by Professor Bushnell (*SP*, xxviii [1931], 450 ff.) and Brown (in his edition, Oxford, 1935), if we bear in mind Professor Bushnell's own caution, that 'It is not likely that Chaucer intended his readers to believe that his old man was the Wandering Jew in person.'

2. See G. L. Kittredge, 'Chaucer and Maximian,' *American Journal of Philology*, ix (1888), 84–85.

3. 'Chaucer and Geoffrey of Vinsauf,' *Modern Philology*, xli (1944), 172–182.

WALTER CLYDE CURRY

The Wife of Bath

I

HE who would enter upon anything like an adequate explanation of the remarkably complex and contradictory character of Chaucer's Wife of Bath must expect heavenly guidance from the stars. Though one may not be entirely prepared to accept the opinion that she 'is one of the most amazing characters . . . the brain of man has ever conceived,'[1] still she is so vividly feminine and human, so coarse and shameless in her disclosures of the marital relations with five husbands, and yet so imaginative and delicate in her story-telling, that one is fascinated against his will and beset with an irresistible impulse to analyze her dual personality with the view of locating, if possible, definite causes for the co-existence of more incongruous elements than are ordinarily found in living human beings. When I first proposed casting the Wife of Bath's horoscope, it was with the supposition that the rules of natural astrology might be used exclusively in the interpretation of certain data, concerning planets and their influence, which Chaucer has furnished us; but it is not entirely so. In the full presentation of the Wife's 'fortune'—her character, personal appearance, and the location and significance of mysterious 'marks' about her body—constant reference must be made to what the mediaeval

---

Reprinted, by permission of the author from *Chaucer and the Mediaeval Sciences* (New York, Oxford University Press, 1926).

mind believed to be truths found in the 'sciences' of celestial physiognomy, metoposcopy, and perhaps of geomancy.

That startling revelation of a woman's experiences in love, the Wife of Bath's Prologue, reaches its climax, I suppose, at the point where Jankin, the unsophisticated clerk of twenty, is selected by Dame Alisoun, aged forty, to fill the recently vacated place and to take up the labors of her fourth husband who has just been packed off to the church-yard. She has wept a little for decency's sake, it will be remembered, and has worn the mourning veil for at least a month out of respect for custom; but her heart has never boon in tho gravo of hor huoband. Evon whilo following tho bior, she tells us, she kept an appraising eye upon the excellent shape of Jankin's leg—she always had a 'coltes tooth.'

> Gat-toothed I was, and that bicam me weel;
> I hadde the prente of sëynt Venus seel.
> As help me god, I was a lusty oon,
> And feire and riche, and yong, and wel bigoon . . .
> For certes, I am al Valerien
> In felinge, and myn herte is Marcien.
> Venus me yaf my lust, my likerousnesse,
> And Mars yaf me my sturdy hardinesse.
> Myn ascendent was Taur, and Mars therinne.
> Allas! allas! that ever love was sinne!
> I folwed ay myn inclinacioun
> By vertu of my constellacioun;
> That made me I coude noght withdrawe
> My chambre of Venus from a good felawe.
> Yet have I Martes mark up-on my face,
> And also in another privee place.

Now from this passage it appears that, to the mind of Chaucer, the cause of Dame Alisoun's peculiarly contradictory character lies not so much in herself as in her stars; possibly she is not to be held morally responsible for all her actions. For at her birth the sign Taurus, one of the 'houses' or 'mansions' of Venus, is said to have been in the ascendent over the horizon, hers being what the exponents of natural astrology would call 'the horoscope in Taurus.'

Her dominant star or ruling planet is Venus—she speaks proudly of the wisdom taught her by 'my dame,' the love-star—which, being posited and at home in its own house Taurus, may be considered 'well-dignified' or particularly beneficent in aspect toward the 'native.' Most unfortunately, however, the combined good influence of the ascendent sign and the dominant star is vitiated by the presence in perhaps platic conjunction of Mars, one of the most 'malefic' and evil of planets. Both Mars and Venus—and if one may put faith in astrologers, the sign Taurus—have left their 'marks' upon her body as well as upon her character. With one eye upon this configuration of stars and with the other upon mediaeval astrological and physiognomical lore, which must have been familiar to Chaucer, let us read and interpret the Wife of Bath's horoscope.

II

Mediaeval astrologers are exceedingly careful in setting up and in drawing figures of the heavens representing horoscopes in all the various signs of the zodiac. Ionnes Tasnier finds that, when Taurus is just rising *in oriente,* Aquarius is discovered *in medio coeli,* Scorpio *in occidente,* and Leo *in imo coeli,* and shows what particular influence each sign in this position exerts upon the native:

> If the horoscope is in Taurus [says he], it may be interpreted in this manner: the native shall be an industrious person, prudent, energetic in acquiring wealth, gaining and losing it with ease, triumphing over enemies.

> Aquarius *in medio coeli* assures favor with princes and presages public acts and offices, perhaps affairs which have to do with water, since this sign is of a watery nature.

> Scorpio *in occidente* indicates that the native will be sagacious, serviceable, and dutiful; he shall lose his wife, if he be masculine, and, if feminine, she shall be deprived of her husband and son.

Leo *in imo coeli* assures the appropriation of inheritances, which shall be gained in spite of insidious obstacles and the claims of children born after the will was made.[2]

So far one may follow with some confidence the technical directions of natural astrology, but no farther; Chaucer has failed to give data concerning the exact positions of sun and moon, and has not indicated the exact hour of the day—whether morning, afternoon, or night—and the day of the year of the nativity in question, all of which is absolutely necessary. But writers on metoposcopy are not silent regarding the supposed influence of Taurus on women—and men—born under that sign. For example, Philippi Finella says:

When Taurus is discovered in the ascendant, the woman born under that sign shall be exceedingly large of face and forehead, rather fleshy with a great number of lines or wrinkles, especially in the forehead, and florid of complexion. She shall have bold eyes, a mobile head inclined more to the right than to the left side, long black hair widely spread over broad shoulders and breast. She shall be slow in her movements, but equipped to perform a maximum of labor with a minimum of aversion. When the first face of Taurus is in the ascendant, she shall be lightly given to affairs of the heart, having a lover for the greater part of her life; often in her amorous affairs she is followed by the reproach of her parents. . . . She shall be inconstant, changeable, speaking (or gossiping) with fluency and volubility, now to this one now to that. . . . This sign shall give her a mole or mark on the neck near its juncture with the shoulders; when this mark is located on the right side, a happy fate may be conjectured, but if on the left side one may reasonably predict dangers. . . . When the line of Venus is observed to be joined to that of Mars, she shall be exceedingly virile, and sagacious in matrimony.[3]

A later writer concerning these matters assures us that 'those born under Taurus are of a cold and dry constitution, inclined to melancholy; one that loves pleasure; . . . once provoked, seldom reconciled; of short stature, but well set; short legs, big buttocks, a bull's neck, wide mouth, and black hair.'[4] And the most scholarly of the students of celestial physiognomy, Baptista Porta, reporting faithfully the opinions of Albohazen Haly, Maternus, and Leopoldus, presents in a passage too long to quote, 'De Tauri formae constitutione, moribus, & physicis rationibus,' [5] much the same conclusions as those cited above.

Still fuller and far more detailed are the prognostications which may be made with certainty regarding the physical form and the disposition of those so fortunate as to be born when Venus, posited in either of her two houses, Taurus and Libra, is the ruling star in a nativity. In a passage headed 'De Veneris forma ad Astrologis descripta,' Porta records the following:

> Venus mistress of a nativity (says Maternus) gives to the native a tall, elegant, white body, pleasing eyes sparkling with splendid beauty, and thick hair agreeably fluffy and sometimes curly or charmingly waving. Venus is similar to Jupiter (says Haly) except that it is her particular province to bestow more charm, greater beauty, and a better conceived, more finely formed, and more alluring and seductive body (seeing Venus is responsible for that grace and elegance peculiar to women); a woman so born is milder and gentler. Others say that she is frail and slender, having dark eyes, delicate eyebrows joined together, tender lips, a full face, a magnificent breast, short ribs, well developed thighs; her general appearance is most attractive, and her figure is refined and elegant. She wantons with her eyes, believing this to be attractive; and her hair is somewhat curly. And Messahala says she has black eyes, in which the dark appears more than in those of other people, beautiful hair, and a face becomingly round and plump but not too full. [6]

Nor does the same author leave us in doubt as to the exact disposition and character of the person born when Venus reigns well-dignified and undisturbed by evil influences in the ascendent sign Taurus. In the section called 'Mores quos Venus largiatur' he continues quoting from his authorities:

> When Venus is the ruling influence in a nativity (says Haly), alone and in a favorable position, the native will be quiet and gentle in disposition, morally upright in character and not in the least depraved or wicked, reflecting always upon right things. She

loves to dance and sing, abhors brawls, disputes, and contentions of all kinds; she delights in dictatorships and intrigues, fine forms and good manners, in truthfulness, and in delicate fancies. She succeeds in making herself loved and esteemed by men; and since she is a devout and pious person engaged in doing right, she is fortunate and happy. Venus makes her children attractive (Maternus agrees), joyous and cheerful of disposition, devoid of constant debaucheries or even of excesses, worthy of love, agreeable, affable, and altogether charming. They are usually lovers of the opposite sex, passionate and voluptuous by nature but religious and righteous. They drink much and eat little; they have a good digestion, which provokes passion and an ardent desire for coition —but they are noble in life and cleanly in act. They cleave with delight to the spirit and practice of music and the arts. They rejoice in sweet-scented baths and in perfumes and fragrances of all kinds, and in poetry inspired by the Muses enriched by choral dance and song. They have finely formed figures, especially the young women, achieve many amatory affairs and happy weddings; temperamental by nature, they show displeasure easily and indulge in complaints, employ crafty devices, and refresh themselves by a return to peace and affection. They have a mutual esteem, the one for another, a fine sense of duty, a ready faith, and a supremacy in good breeding, refinement, and kindliness of heart. Venus makes singers and charming people (says Haly further), ardent lovers of flowers and elegance, taking great care of their fine bodies and splendid, delicate skin and complexion. They are strenuously diligent in the propagation of offspring and in the perpetuation of the race, but are religious and sympathetic. They delight in feminine ornaments and are given to adorning their bodies with elegant and smart attire, most often white in color, have the genteel manners of a courtier, and take pleasure in luxurious flavors and savors. They easily become rulers, performing whatever they undertake with facility. They are given to games and various diversions, to laughter and joyous living, rejoicing in the companionships of friends and in eating and drinking, relying upon others to the point of being often deceived. They are benevolent and utter soft and gentle-voiced words with a small, sweet mouth; they are tender by nature and prone to shed tears.[7]

To this significant passage may be added a pertinent excerpt from the four full pages which Helvetius devotes to the same subject:

> They like to wander and sojourn in strange lands in order that they may enjoy the acclaim of foreign peoples or be accounted cosmopolitan. They love smart, elegant wearing apparel of white, blue, and even black materials, and jewelry of Phyrgian workmanship made of gold, silver, and precious stones for the adornment of their bodies, according to their conception of style and length of purse. In practices and experiences of love, however, they often exceed the measure of good form, and as exhibited in secret their (amatory) services are eager, exceedingly ardent, and glowing with passion. In the marriage relations they are to a high degree volatile, capricious, and inconstant, especially when they are not maintained sumptuously and in grand style; and they are certainly more contented and happy if they are permitted as many separations and divorces as there are numbered principles of love. Their amorous actions bring it about that, while they serve themselves by deceptions and cajoleries, they are pleasing and attractive at the same time, forcing the fascinated will of the lover to surrender.[8]

And still further items may be gleaned from Indagine's account of the influence of Venus when she dominates in the roots of nativities of phlegmatic natures—and she is found only in such nativities:

> Venus makes her children playful, passionate, joyous, beautiful, loving and fearing God, just; . . . they shall be great drinkers, musicians, players upon musical instruments, and singers. They will love the manual arts, such as painting and other things which are made neatly and without sweepings.[9]

I have ventured to give at considerable length these prognostications regarding the influence of Venus in Taurus, because in any correct interpretation of Chaucer's Wife of Bath it is necessary that one realize what she might have been. Such a fascinating personal appearance and attractive disposition might have been assured her at birth had not fate—or perhaps her creator—decreed that she should sink in the scale by virtue of the malignant influence of the war-planet, Mars, at that time in platic conjunction with Venus in Taurus. At the conclusion of a long discussion of the beauty and charm of one born under the dominion of Venus, Indagine remarks: 'But if Mars mingles his occult influence with hers, he changes all these prognostications into vain words and lies, and into that which is according to his nature.'[10] Let us consider, therefore, the power and nature of Mars.

All the writers on these occult matters whom I have consulted agree with convincing unanimity that Mars, either in his own houses or in those of other planets, is a powerful worker of evil. Porta, in his discussion of Mars in the various zodiacal signs, quotes Haly and Maternus as follows:

> Mars in the third face of Taurus (says Haly) gives a form marvelously foul and ugly, and a repulsive countenance; the native shall be a jester, delighting in merriment, incantations, and vices. If Mars is discovered anywhere in Taurus (says Maternus) the native shall be most loathsome of aspect, given to jesting continually, also greedy and rapacious, rash, reckless, criminal, rejoicing in causing unhappiness.[11]

And Taisnier, adding further harrowing details, is in substantial agreement:

> When Mars is found in the house of Venus (e.g., in Taurus) the native shall be voluptuous and a fornicator, perpetrating wickedness with women of his own blood, becoming guilty of incest, or committing adultery with women whom he has seduced by promises of marriage; he shall suffer damages and loss because of women. If Mars is posited in Taurus particularly, it signifies that all voluptuousness and wickedness shall be combined.[12]

Still, one is delighted to learn that the case of a phlegmatic nature —such as that of the Wife of Bath—is not so desperate as that of the melancholic and the choleric:

> Mars in the nativity of a phlegmatic nature (says Indagine) is evil enough; he produces a native with a mean and violent disposition, strong, adventurous, a great babbler and liar. He burns the hair on the top of the head, makes the face coarse, enlarges the head; the native shall be cruel, casting his eyes aside, exceedingly courageous,

173

a boaster, a traitor, fiery, arrogant, a maker of noises, a pillager, a beater of people, slayer of his father and mother, worthy of being beaten himself, and secretly boresome to his friends. Nevertheless all these characteristics are not so strongly marked in the phlegmatic as in melancholic and choleric natures, because the phlegmatic humour foams and cools the heat.[13]

Thus the power of Mars, situated alone in Taurus or posited at all in the nativities of phlegmatic natures, is exerted for evil; but when he mingles in his influence with that of Venus, the situation is, according to Guido Bonatus and Cardan, indeed deplorable:

He that has Mars in his ascendante shall be exposed to many dangers, and commonly at last receives a great scar in his Face. When Mars is Lord of a Woman's Ascendant, and Venus is posited in it, or Venus is Lady of it, and Mars in it . . . 'tis more than probable that she will Cucold her Husband. When Venus shall be too powerful in a Geniture, and in place of the Infortunes (i.e., in conjunction with Mars, for example), inconveniences are to be feared from unlawful Loves. If in a Woman's nativity Mars shall be under the Sun Beams, she will be apt to play the Harlot with her Servants and mean fellows; but if Venus be there, then she will trade discreetly with nobles and Gallants of Quality.[14]

And William Lilly has it that 'Mars with Venus denote the Wife full of spirit, movable, an ill Housewife, prodigall, and that the native is or will be an Adulterer.'[15] But it is Albohazen Haly who gives the best account of the combined influences of Mars and Venus in good and bad positions:

If Mars is in harmony with Venus and in a good position (says he), they create a native who is in agreement with men, one who is credulous but a deceiver of friends, one who loves a vicious and depraved life. Such a native delights in quiet simplicity and loves to sing and dance. He is a reveler, is transported by love, and has unlawful and sinful relations with the opposite sex; he is sensitive, a mocker and a deceiver, but none the less happy, a deep thinker, a waster, easily angered. But if these planets are in positions opposite to that of which we have spoken (e.g., in conjunction to

Taurus), they make the native of a passionate disposition, desiring to lie with women without any consideration or sense of shame, seeing that he is exceedingly irresponsible in his actions; he is meretricious, a dishonorer, a teller of lies, and a deceiver of friends and others; successful in satisfying his desires, seducing and corrupting good women and virgins, wise in perpetrating frauds and betrayals. He is a perjurer, a scoffer and reviler, a reprobate in habits of thought, busily engaged in conceiving corrupt acts and in the practice of abominable fornication.[16]

So far as the personal appearance of the native is concerned, however, Maternus is of the opinion that:

When Mars participates with Venus in a nativity, he lays aside the utmost ardor of his evil. The person born when Mars is in conjunction with Venus has a complexion pleasingly mixed with white; a face rounded but not too full with cheeks appropriately plump; lovely eyes a little too dark for the greatest beauty but not black enough to be called ugly; a becomingly medium stature; and a body not fat to the point of being obese but, as one might say, semi-fat.[17]

Such a person one might expect the Wife of Bath to be.

Not all the astro-physiognomical material that may aid in the correct interpretation of her constellation has been presented, however, until some explanation has been offered of the mysterious 'prente of seynt Venus seel,' located everywhere about her person, and of 'Martes mark' which is found upon her face and 'also in another privee place.' What is the nature of these 'marks,' and precisely where are they placed? It is a marvellous truth, we are told by the celestial physiognomists,[18] that every human being has printed upon his body, at the hour of conception or perhaps at birth, the 'mark' of at least the ascendent sign and of the dominant star which are supposed to rule his fortunes. These marks are found in those parts of the body that are referred or 'attributed' to the various signs and planets; and whether they are placed before, behind, or to the left or right side depends upon the 'face' of the sign just appearing above the horizon. If there should be another planet in conjunction, moreover, and if the Sun should be in the ascendent, then the native will have an additional set of marks on those parts of the body which correspond to these stars. Thus it comes about that a person may have four marks, each one of which may possibly be duplicated in another place. The mark of the ascendent sign, it must be observed, is usually the highest, that of the Sun lower—if he happens to be rising,—that of the dominant star still lower, and that of the planet in conjunction lowest of all.

For example, the Wife of Bath's horoscope is in Taurus, but Chaucer has unfortunately neglected to inform us as to which face of the sign was in the ascendent at the time of her birth. We may locate, therefore, the mark of this sign somewhere on the neck; but whether it is on the throat, or on the side, or on the nape of the neck cannot be determined. M. Belot says in this connection:

When a person is born under the sign Taurus, he has a mark on the neck; if the first face, which the Arabians call *Adoldaya,* is just rising, the mark is found upon the throat in the form of a small strawberry or of a little red spot something like the foot-print of a cat; this is an evil sign. If the person is born under the second face of the sign, i.e., from ten to twenty degrees, the mark is on one of the two sides of the neck; and if he is born under the third face of the sign, the mark is on the back of the neck, but in this case it is most often in the form of a small bulbous mole.[19]

Le Sievre de Pervchio furnishes additional information and interpretation:

The head of Taurus (from one to ten degrees) dominates in the middle of April; its mark is impressed upon the neck in the form of a red spot, denoting birth in that season. It indicates a person courageous, honest, endowed with a lovable disposition, but given to anger and lasciviousness, having a good color and long hair. . . . The heart of Taurus (from ten to twenty degrees) presides at the end of April and places its mark upon the side of the neck. . . . The tail of Taurus (from twenty to thirty degrees) is powerful at the beginning of May, at which time are born those who have the mark on the back of their neck.[20]

And Rosa Baughan says that 'When Taurus is rising at birth, the native bears a mark in the front of the throat; sometimes in the form of a raspberry or red-colored mole, which mark is always ill in its effects.'[21] Since there is no indication in Chaucer's text of the relation of the Sun to the Wife of Bath's constellation, one may safely conclude that she has escaped being branded on the left arm by that planet.

But, as we have already seen, she is stamped with the print of Venus's seal. If one may credit Le Sievre de Pervchio, 'Venus, when she is discovered in the ascendent, imprints upon the native's left arm a red mark, a sort of scar decorated with a tint of vermillion.'[22] Or according to M. Belot, whose opinion differs slightly from that of Pervchio, 'When Venus is the dominant star in a nativity, her marks are found upon the loins, testicles, thighs, or perhaps upon the neck because Taurus, the first house of Venus rules in that part; the form of these marks may be either bulbous or flat and the color either violet or whitish. They signify nothing but a lascivious nature.'[23] On the whole I am inclined to think that M. Belot is the more trustworthy authority and to accept his location of the mark of Venus, especially so since all astrologers and physiognomists agree in attributing the secret parts of the body to that planet. Nor is that all. The good Wife has Mars's mark somewhere in her face and—because . . . every mark or mole on the face is certainly reduplicated in a corresponding part of the body—also in another 'privee place.' M. Belot says:

If Mars is powerful in a nativity, his marks are found on the right side and most commonly in the front parts of the head [i.e., in the face or somewhere about the forehead, though one cannot be sure as to the exact position], or [he might have said, 'and also'] on the 'little stomach' near the secret parts. These marks are red or purple, most often as large as small roses or drops of wine, moles colored like strawberries or cherries.[24]

It should be quite apparent by this time that Chaucer, the artist, considered it necessary only to make suggestions, in connection with the constellation in question, concerning certain planetary marks, being confident that his educated and cultured— from the medieval point of view—hearers or readers would instantly understand their exact nature, color, shape, size, location, and significance.

III

With the above astrological principles and interpretations in mind, one is practically forced to the conclusion that Chaucer's Wife of Bath is in some measure the living embodiment, both in form and in character, of mingled but still conflicting astral influences. That she herself is aware—and makes capital—of this conflict started within her nature at birth is suggested by her somewhat pitiful lamentation:

> For certes, I am al Venerien
> In felinge, and myn herte is Marcien.
> Venus me yaf my lust, my likerousnesse,
> And Mars yaf me my sturdy hardinesse . . .
> I folwed ay myn inclinacioun
> By vertu of my constellacioun.

Instead of having the naturally beautiful and well-proportioned figure—stately and tall, plump but never stout, graceful, with white skin touched delicately to pink—which might have been hers under the free, beneficient influence of Venus, she is endowed by the Mars-Venus combination with a stockily built, more or less ungraceful, buxom form of medium height. That strength which should have accompanied grace and beauty of body has been distorted into a powerful fecund energy; her large hips indicate excessive virility. In place of the attractive face—round but not too large, with finely chiseled features, resplendent black eyes and delicately arched eyebrows, and with a lovely peachbloom complexion set off by thick, curling hair of a dark shade—which Venus might have given, she has inflicted upon her by the malignancy of Mars a slightly heavy face inclined to fatness, char-

acterized by perhaps coarsened features and certainly by a sus-
piciously red or florid complexion, which indicates that the woman
is immodest, loquacious, and given to drunkenness. Let no such
woman be trusted, say the physiognomists. Her voice, which should
have been sweet, low, and well-modulated, is harsh, strident, and
raised continually, as one might expect, in vulgar jest and in-
delicate banter. Such a voice is especially significant in its betrayal
of the Wife's voluptuous and luxurious nature; one has suspected
for a long time that she knows only too well how to 'laughe and
carpe' in fellowship with the most dissolute rakes among the
pilgrims. It is not surprising, therefore, to find that her physical
characteristics and her disposition correspond in a remarkable way
with the 'Signa mulieris calidae & quae libenter coit' which are
these:

> She reaches maturity at the age of twelve years; has small breasts
> becoming full and hard, and coarse hair. She is bold in speech,
> having a keen, high-pitched voice, proud in mind, red of face,
> erect in carriage, given to drink; she loves to sing, wanders much,
> and delights in adorning herself as much as possible.[25]

And the Love-star might have given her small, sharp teeth, white
as alabaster and evenly set in gums like coral; Mars is perhaps
responsible for the long, spike-like teeth, set far apart with gaps
between, which she possesses. Unfortunately the good Wife is
'gat-tothed,' which interpreted as meaning 'gap-toothed' may signify that she is 'envious, irreverent, luxurious by nature, bold,
deceitful, faithless, and suspicious.'[26]

Not less remarkable than this more or less distortion of the Wife
of Bath's body is the warping of her character which results from
the Venus-Mars conjunction in Taurus. One may still find everywhere traces of the Venerean disposition—never essentially evil
or vulgar, but *inclining* sometimes to be so—intensified or turned
awry or metamorphosed by Martian influence into something resembling a caricature—or even into what is quite the contrary—of
that which she might have been. The children of Venus, as we
have already seen, are naturally of a happy, joyous disposition,
amiable and therefore charming and universally attractive, de-

lighting in the dance and in all forms of innocent amusement, but withal characterized by a gentleness, a refinement, and by a calm dignity which results in a well-developed hatred of brawls and strife of any description. They are religious by nature, just in their dealings with men, leaders of noble lives, and—this is most important—of an artistic nature which expresses itself in an appreciation of song and instrumental music, in a love for delicate and pleasant odors, and which revels in the colors of elegant wearing apparel and in precious jewels. Being tender-hearted, bountiful, and benevolent, they are particularly happy in their social intercourse with people of culture and with those who have a taste for the artistic. Endowed with the warmest and most affectionate hearts, they are lightly prone to violent *amours* with the opposite sex, though it must be observed that their amatory relations need not of necessity lead to vice; they may be pleasure-loving and even voluptuous by inclination without being touched by wantonness, passionate without being sensual or lustful, and full of a consuming and perhaps entirely human desire without a trace of licentiousness. Their nature demands that variety of scene and the spice of exotic life which comes only through travel in foreign countries and through the association with people of unlike customs and manners. The children of Venus are your true aristocrats.

Such a woman the cloth-maker of Bath might have been. But how different! The natural cheerfulness of her disposition resolves itself into a sort of crude and clamorous hilarity, an overflow of superabundant animal and intellectual spirits, which makes of her a *bonne vivante* and a fitting companion for such tavern revelers as the Pardoner and her fourth husband. Her religious instinct has been debased to the extent that she goes to vigils and to preaching for the sole purpose, apparently, of showing her finery and arousing the envy of less fortunate women as she parades to the offering before everybody else; she attends miracle plays and follows the routes taken by devout pilgrims to the shrines of saints in order that she may satisfy an idle curiosity or find another lusty husband, no doubt; her readings—or the passages she most easily remembers having heard read—from the Bible or from St. Jerome are significant texts dealing with marriage and other complex sex-relations. The artistic temperament which should have been hers has been cheapened by the influence of the Warstar, so that she flashily decks herself out in gaudy colors—in scarlet dresses and hose, to say nothing of brand new shoes and silver spurs—and adorns herself on Sundays with coverchiefs weighing ten pounds and on the pilgrimage with a hat as large as a buckler. Even this strikingly overdressed woman shows a certain feeling, all the more pitiful because it is uncultivated or perverted, for the beautiful in dress; she is at least delightfully neat and trim for a middle-class woman of her time. But worst of all, Mars has played havoc with the luxurious impulses—the 'likerousnesse'—which come from her mistress, Venus; she has always had a 'coltes tooth.' Whatever else she may be, in the Prologue to her tale she appears as an unusually healthy and frank female animal, human and sexually attractive, whose dominating idea seems to be the glorification of fleshly delights and the gratification of physical desire. Mars has given her a 'sturdy hardinesse' and a body so full of 'ragerye' that even at the age of forty she is still 'faire and yong and wel bigoon.' She has married five husbands at the church door—besides other 'companye in youthe,' which may mean almost anything— has enjoyed them with varying degrees of animal pleasure, and has laid them to rest after their marital labors were ended. Welcome the sixth; eight would be all too few. With the most brazen and shameless lack of modesty she reveals her exciting experiences abed, omitting neither the feigned appetite which secures for her whatever funds she needs for the decking of her person, nor the passionate love-making —an excellent example of misdirected tenderness—with which she wins the services of her three old husbands. She is not so much a restless wanderer as a gadder about in search of excitement— until her fifth husband puts a stop to her going and her gossiping for a season. And it is Mars who impels her to gain at all costs the dominating power over her husbands and who makes of her a scold, a wrangler, and a striker of blows—worthy of being beaten herself—until she attains her purpose. Truly, whatever one may say of Venus's influence it is turned into a baser order when Mars is discovered in conjunction. So the Wife of Bath appears in the Prologue to her tale: a fair Venerean figure and character imposed upon and oppressed, distorted in some measure and warped, by the power of Mars.

No one must suppose, however, that this worthy woman is entirely depraved or that she is unattractive; after the worst has been said, she still has Venus for her mistress. Everybody knows that, even in the Prologue to her tale, she is pursued by the melancholy conviction that the type of life she has led is not the best possible; her laughing and carping, and perhaps her coarseness are assumed in part as a mask to hide the bitterness which has been forced upon her by an unholy constellation. She knows better, at least, and still has the grace to cry,

Allas! allas! that ever love was sinne.

Consequently, there need be no occasion for surprise when we come to her tale to find that her creator, not only a genius but among the most sympathetic of men, should lift the veil for a moment from the secret places of her nature and should have permitted her to tell a story of the most delicate beauty and grace. It is an artistically woven tale of faery, centering, to be sure, about the Wife's original contention that women should have dominion over their husbands but nonetheless imaginative and free from the slightest touch of vulgarity, and containing a long and nobly expressed sermon on what constitutes true 'gentilesse' of heart and life. So excellent a critic as Ten Brink, not understanding the artistic side of her character and finding something dramatically inappropriate in such sentiments from the lips of a clothweaver, is moved to say: 'The thoroughly sound moral of the long sermon given by the wise old woman, before her metamorphosis, to her young, unwilling husband, comes more from the heart of the poet than from the Wife of Bath.'[27] But it does not seem so to me; both the story and the sermon may be considered as highly characteristic of the unfortunate teller.

Professor Root gives, with a remarkably keen and sympathetic insight into the complexities of the character under discussion, a more or less correct description of—though not the 'key' to—the whole contradictory situation.

I conceive of the Wife of Bath (says he), as endowed originally with strong passions and vivid imagination, with what we are wont to call the poetic temperament. Had she been born in a palace, she might have become your typical heroine of romance, her inevitable lapses from virtue gilded over with the romantic adornments of moonlight serenades and secret trysts. But born an heiress to a weaver's bench, there was no chance for her poetic imaginativeness to develop. Laughed at by others for her fine-spun fancies, she would certainly grow ashamed of them herself. I can believe that her excessive coarseness of speech was originally an affectation which easily became second nature to her. Her strong passions demanded expression; and denied a more poetic gratification, and quite unrestrained by moral character, they express themselves in coarse vulgarity. It is only when called upon to tell a story, to leave the practical every-day world, in which she is forced to live, for the other world of fantasy, that the original imaginativeness of her nature finds opportunity to reveal itself.[28]

Precisely! The key to her character, however, lies in the fact, as I have already indicated, that the fineness and delicacy which achieves expression in the story is but the resurging as it were, of the artistic Venerean impulse, an outcropping of the poetic temperament which somehow has been kept, subconsciously no doubt, pure and untainted from the blasting and warping influence of Mars and circumstance. Or perhaps she has guarded faithfully as a kind of sacred possession this love of the beautiful, which no one about her could understand; it may be that in moments of world-weariness she sought the fairy realm of the imagination given to her by her mistress, and found refuge for a time from the coarseness inflicted upon her by the War-star. The unsatisfied yearning for that gentility and nobility of character which might and should have been hers, but for the power of an evil planet, is pathetic; the struggle which has kept unmarred a bit of her original nature in the midst of sordid conditions of life and in the face of adverse circumstances is heroic. The poet may, after all, have considered her his most tragic figure because—as is certainly the case—she is the most nearly completely human.

How does such a character grow? Any dogmatizing by a layman

upon the workings of an artist's mind in the act of creation is hazardous in the extreme, but speculation is always fascinating and perhaps harmless. It may be conceived by some that Chaucer is here drawing, to the best of his ability, the portrait of an actual middle-class person of his time, whom he has known on intimate terms of association. In that case he has no doubt noted carefully and recorded faithfully the significant speech and actions, the mannerisms and emotional reactions of the woman under observation, and has interpreted these external indications of inward personality in terms of character. The idea is intriguing; but since it is manifestly impossible for even the most cunning artist to penetrate the mystery of another person's individuality, to sound its depths and shallows, and to discover the mixed sources of action and feeling in any given instance, such a process of imaginative interpretation from the outside must inevitably remain largely descriptive, resulting in a character-sketch and not a character-creation. The Wife of Bath is a character-creation. Or, again, most critics hold that the original 'model' for Chaucer's 'portrait' of the cloth-weaver may be found in the figure of an old harridan, La Vielle, taken from the *Roman de la Rose*. Professor W. E. Mead is of the opinion that, though the poet:

> did not attempt to copy the portrait of La Vielle as a whole, he took from her the general suggestions for the outlines of the Wife of Bath. But he modified the figure of La Vielle by making her younger and more vigorous, by giving her as keen an interest in life as she had ever had, by representing her as still ready for matrimony whenever opportunity should offer. Furthermore, Chaucer transformed the somewhat morose and broken-spirited old woman, entirely out of sympathy with life, into a witty and frisky shrew—good-natured in a way, but still a shrew. Where did Chaucer pick up the hint for that?

Quite likely, concludes Professor Mead, he borrows again from the French poem some characteristics of a jealous husband, Le Jaloux, whose scolding is somewhat similar to that indulged in by the Wife of Bath.[29] But granting that Chaucer has borrowed from the *Roman de la Rose* and from other literary sources certain ideas, or outlines, or human qualities, or personal characteristics, as it were, literary scraps and fragments, we are still but little nearer the solution of the problem. A figure consisting merely of a composite of many elements, a mosaic of human qualities and characteristics, is—to use the terms of scholastic philosophy—a monstrosity of 'accidents' without 'substance.' The Wife of Bath is essentially 'substance.'

And finally, the present writer—influenced by the material presented in this chapter—once entertained the perilous theory that Chaucer may have fashioned Dame Alisoun in accordance with astrological principles. Being continually exercised over the problem of foreordination—I have said elsewhere—[30] and apparently believing to some extent in the influence of the stars upon the affairs of men, he has, in the case of the Wife of Bath, assumed the prerogatives and the responsibilities of a creator, setting up carefully a horoscope, producing a human being to be ruled by it, and amusing himself—perhaps like some other Creator—with the inevitable actions and emotions of his living creature. But upon more mature consideration I have concluded that such a theory in application is so mechanical and so simple in its execution that the resultant figure is likely to be little better than a highly colored dummy glavanized into a semblance of activity and emotion by astral influences, and in no sense a complex human being. Under the spell of Chaucer's pen one rests under the illusion that the Wife of Bath is a complex human being. Endowed with passion, reason, memory, and imagination, she is discovered undergoing a succession of human experiences which compass many joys and ills this flesh is heir to, growing old with the passing of time like the rest of us, recalling her youth with a gusto not unmixed with regret and sadness, sending her imagination abroad and forward with that pathetic wistfulness characteristic of those whose pleasures are chiefly material but whose spiritual powers are sufficiently developed to afford glimpses of something better. I do not know how Chaucer has created such a character, but I suspect that the soul and personality of this woman was conceived in the poet's imagination as a complete whole; at least, he alone could understand fully the sources of her contradictory thinking, feeling, and action. And in order to body her forth he has evidently drawn upon a rich store of human materials gleaned here and there from observation, from the imaginative interpretation of the common experiences of life, and from the literary works of other men, assimilating these raw materials by the power of a creative imagination into the personality of the Wife of Bath. In this process of creation the astrological material has played only a relatively small part. But a full interpretation of the horoscope and a consideration of astral influences moving upon the character in question would seem to be necessary for a thorough understanding of the poet's original conception.

NOTES

1. G. L. Kittredge, *Chaucer and His Poetry*, p. 189.

2. *Absolvtissimae Chryomantiae Libri Octo*, In quibus quicquid ad chyromantiae, physiognomiae, & naturalis astrologiae perfectionem spectat, continentur, Coloniae Agrippinae, 1563, p. 496.

3. Philippi Finella, *De metroposcopia*, Antverpiae, 1648, p. 134.

4. Erra Pater (pseud.), *The Book of Knowledge*, Boston, p. 14.

5. Ioannes Baptista Porta, *Coelestis physiognomoniae libri sex*, Neapoli, 1603, p. 116.

6. *Op. cit.*, p. 61.

7. *Op. cit.*, pp. 64–65.

8. Ioannes Fredericus Helvetius, *Amphitheatrum physiognomiae medicum*, Hydelbergi, 1660, pp. 91–95.

9. Iean de Indagine, *Chiromance & Physiognomie* (trans. Antoine de Moulin Masconnois), Lyon, 1549, p. 279.

10. *Op. cit.*, p. 279.

11. *Op. cit.*, p. 147.

12. *Op. cit.*, p. 615.

13. Indagine, *op. cit.*, p. 278.

14. Guido Bonatus, 'Choice Aphorismes of Cardan's Seven Segments,' in *Anima astrologiae, or a Guide for Astrologers* (trans. W. Lilly), London, 1683, pp. 9–33, *passim*.

15. *Christian Astrology*, p. 595.

16. Quoted from Porta, *op. cit.*, Rothomagi, 1560, p. 77.

17. Indagine, *op. cit.*, p. 278.

18. This paragraph is a free translation of the exposition given by M. Belot (*Oeuvres*, Lyon, 1654, pp. 219–221) except that I have omitted his irrelevant illustration which takes up the Sun and certain other planets in conjunction in the sign Aries.

19. *Op. cit.*, p. 221.

20. *Op. cit.*, p. 110.

21. *Op. cit.*, p. 184.

22. *Op. cit.*, p. 107.

23. *Op. cit.*, p. 225.

24. *Op. cit.*, p. 223.

25. On the significance of the Wife's voice, see *PMLA*, xxxvii, p. 45, note 36.

26. For a full discussion of the Wife of Bath's teeth set far apart, see my study in *PMLA*, xxxvii, p. 45, note 38.

27. Ten Brink, *The History of English Literature*, trans. Robinson, ii, 163.

28. R. K. Root, *The Poetry of Chaucer* (first ed.), p. 239.

29. W. E. Mead, 'The Prologue of the Wife of Bath's Tale,' *PMLA*, xvi, 388 ff.

30. 'More About Chaucer's Wife of Bath,' *PMLA*, xxxvii, 51.

GEORGE LYMAN KITTREDGE

Chaucer's Discussion of Marriage

WE are prone to read and study the *Canterbury Tales* as if each tale were an isolated unit and to pay scant attention to what we call the connecting links,—those bits of lively narrative and dialogue that bind the whole together. Yet Chaucer's plan is clear enough. Structurally regarded, the *Canterbury Tales* is a kind of Human Comedy. From this point of view, the Pilgrims are the *dramatis personae*, and their stories are only speeches that are somewhat longer than common, entertaining in and for themselves (to be sure), but primarily significant, in each case, because they illustrate the speaker's character and opinions, or show the relations of the travelers to one another in the progressive action of the Pilgrimage. In other words, we ought not merely to consider the general appropriateness of each tale to the character of the teller: we should also inquire whether the tale is not determined to some extent, by the circumstances,—by the situation at the moment, by something that another Pilgrim has said or done, by the turn of a discussion already under way.

Now and then, to be sure, the point is too obvious to be overlooked, as in the squabble between the Summoner and the Friar and that between the Reeve and the Miller, in the Shipman's intervening to check the Parson, and in the way in which the gentles head off the Pardoner when he is about to tell a ribald anecdote. But despite these inescapable instances, the general principle is too often blinked or ignored. Yet its temperate application should

---

clear up a number of things which are traditionally regarded as difficulties, or as examples of heedlessness on Chaucer's part.

Without attempting to deny or abridge the right to study and criticize each tale in and for itself,—as legend, romance, *exemplum*, fabliau, or what-not,—and without extenuating the results that this method has achieved, let us consider certain tales in their relation to Chaucer's structural plan,—with reference, that is to say, to the Pilgrims who tell them and to the Pilgrimage to which their telling is accidental. We may begin with the story of Griselda.

This is a plain and straightforward piece of edification, and nobody has ever questioned its appropriateness to the Clerk, who, as he says himself, has traveled in Italy and has heard it from the lips of the laureate Petrarch. The Clerk's 'speech,' according to the General Prologue, was 'sowning in moral vertu,' so that this story is precisely the kind of thing which we should expect from his lips. True, we moderns sometimes feel shocked or offended at what we style the immorality of Griselda's unvarying submission. But this feeling is no ground of objection to the appropriateness of the tale to the Clerk. The Middle Ages delighted (as children still delight) in stories that exemplify a single human quality, like valor, or tyranny, or fortitude. In such cases, the settled rule (for which neither Chaucer nor the Clerk was responsible) was to show to what lengths that quality may conceivably go. Hence, in tales of this kind, there can be no question of conflict between duties, no problem as to the point at which excess of goodness becomes evil. It is, then, absurd to censure a fourteenth-century Clerk for telling (or Chaucer for making him tell) a story which exemplifies in this hyperbolical way the virtue of fortitude under affliction. Whether Griselda could have put an end to her woes, or ought to have put an end to them, by refusing to obey her husband's commands is *parum ad rem*. We are to look at her trials as inevitable, and to pity her accordingly, and wonder at her endurance. If we refuse to accept the tale in this spirit, we are ourselves the losers. We miss the pathos because we are aridly intent on discussing an ethical question that has no status in this particular court, however pertinent it may be in the general forum of morals.

Furthermore, in thus focusing attention on the morality or immorality of Griselda's submissiveness, we overlook what the Clerk takes pains to make as clear as possible,—the real lesson that the story is meant to convey,—and thus we do grave injustice to that austere but amiable moralist. The Clerk, a student of 'Aristotle and his philosophye,' knew as well as any of us that every virtue may be conceived as a mean between two extremes. Even the Canon's Yeoman, an ignorant man, was aware of this principle:

> 'That that is overdoon, it wol nat preve
> Aright, as clerkes seyn,—it is a vyce.'

Chaucer had too firm a grasp on his *dramatis personae* to allow the Clerk to leave the true purpose of his parable undefined. 'This story is not told,' says the Clerk in substance, 'to exhort wives to imitate Griselda's humility, for *that* would be beyond the capacity of human nature. It is told in order that every man or woman, in whatever condition of life, may learn fortitude in adversity. For, since a woman once exhibited such endurance under trials inflicted on her by a mortal man, *a fortiori* ought *we* to accept patiently whatever tribulation God may send us. For God is not like Griselda's husband. He does not wantonly experiment with us, out of inhuman scientific curiosity. God *tests* us, as it is reasonable that our Maker should test his handiwork, but he does not *tempt* us. He allows us to be beaten with sharp scourges of adversity, not, like the Marquis Walter, to see if we can stand it, for he knoweth our frame, he remembereth that we are dust: all *his* affliction is for our better grace. Let us live, therefore, in manly endurance of the visitations of Providence.'

And then, at verse 1163, comes that matchless passage in which the Clerk (having explained the *universal* application of his parable,—having provided with scrupulous care against any misinterpretation of its serious purport) turns with gravely satiric courtesy to the Wife of Bath and makes the particular application of the story to her 'life' and 'all her sect.'

Here one may appreciate the vital importance of considering the *Canterbury Tales* as a connected Human Comedy,—of taking into account the Pilgrims in their relations to one another in the great drama to which the several narratives are structurally incidental. For it is precisely at this point that Professor Skeat notes a difficulty. 'From this point to the end,' he remarks, 'is the work of a later period, and in Chaucer's best manner, though unsuited *to the coy Clerk.*' This is as much as to say that, in the remaining stanzas of the Clerk's Tale and in the Envoy, Chaucer has violated dramatic propriety. And, indeed, many readers have detected in these concluding portions Chaucer's own personal revulsion of feeling against the tale that he had suffered the Clerk to tell.

Now the supposed difficulty vanishes as soon as we study vvs. 1163–1212, not as an isolate phenomenon, but in their relation to the great drama of the Canterbury Pilgrimage. It disappears when we consider the lines in what we may call their dramatic context, that is (to be specific), when we inquire what there was in the situation to prompt the Clerk, after emphasizing the serious and universal moral of Griselda's story, to give his tale a special and peculiar application by annexing an ironical tribute to the Wife of Bath, her life, her 'sect,' and her principles. To answer this question we must go back to the Wife of Bath's Prologue.

The Wife of Bath's Prologue begins a Group in the *Canterbury Tales,* or, as one may say, a new act in the drama. It is not connected with anything that precedes. Let us trace the action from this point down to the moment when the Clerk turns upon the Wife with his satirical compliments.

The Wife has expounded her views at great length and with all imaginable zest. Virginity, which the Church glorifies, is not required of us. Our bodies are given us to use. Let saints be continent if they will. She has no wish to emulate them. Nor does she accept the doctrine that a widow or a widower must not marry again. Where is bigamy forbidden in the Bible, or octogamy either? She has warmed both hands before the fire of life, and she exults in her recollection of her fleshly delights.

True, she is willing to admit, for convention's sake, that chastity is the ideal state. But it is not *her* ideal. On the contrary, her admission is only for appearances. In her heart she despises virginity. Her contempt for it is thinly veiled, or rather, not veiled at all. Her discourse is marked by frank and almost obstreperous animalism. Her whole attitude is that of scornful, though good-humored, repudiation of what the Church teaches in that regard.

Nor is the Wife content with this single heresy. She maintains also that wives should rule their husbands, and she enforces this doctrine by an account of her own life, and further illustrates it by her tale of the knight of King Arthur who learned that

> Wommen desiren to have sovereyntee
> As wel over hir housbond as hir love,
> And for to been in maistrie him above,

and who accepted the lesson as sound doctrine. Then, at the end of her discourse, she sums up in no uncertain words:

> And Iesu Crist us sende
> Housbandes meke, yonge, and fresshe abedde,
> And grace to overbyde hem that we wedde;
> And eek I preye Iesu shorte her lyves
> That wol nat be governed by her wyves.

Now the Wife of Bath is not *bombinans in vacuo*. She addresses her heresies not to *us* or to the world at large, but to her fellow-pilgrims. Chaucer has made this point perfectly clear. The words of the Wife were of a kind to provoke comment,—and we have the comment. The Pardoner interrupts her with praise of her noble preaching:

> 'Now, dame,' quod he, 'by God and by seint Iohn,
> Ye been a noble prechour in this cas!'

The adjective is not accidental. The Pardoner was a judge of good preaching: the General Prologue describes him as 'a noble ecclesiaste' and he shows his ability in his own sermon on Covetousness. Furthermore, it is the Friar's comment on the Wife's preamble that provokes the offensive words of the Summoner, and that becomes thereby the occasion for the two tales that immediately follow in the series. It is manifest, then, that Chaucer meant us to imagine the *dramatis personae* as taking a lively interest in whatever the Wife says. This being so, we ought to inquire what effect her Prologue and Tale would have upon the Clerk.

Of course the Clerk was scandalized. He was unworldly and an ascetic,—he 'looked holwe and therto sobrely.' Moral virtue was his special study. He had embraced the celibate life. He was grave, devout, and unflinchingly orthodox. And now he was confronted by the lust of the flesh and the pride of life in the person of a woman who flouted chastity and exulted that she had 'had her world as in her time.' Nor was this all. The woman was an heresiarch, or at best a schismatic. She set up, and aimed to establish, a new and dangerous sect, whose principle was that the wife should rule the husband. The Clerk kept silence for the moment. Indeed, he had no chance to utter his sentiments, unless he interrupted,—something not to be expected of his quiet ('coy') and sober temperament. But it is not to be imagined that his thoughts were idle. He could be trusted to speak to the purpose whenever his opportunity should come.

Now the substance of the Wife's false doctrines was not the only thing that must have roused the Clerk to protesting answer. The very manner of her discourse was a direct challenge to him. She had garnished her sermon with scraps of Holy Writ and rags and tatters of erudition, caught up, we may infer, from her last husband. Thus she had put herself into open competition with the guild of scholars and theologians, to which the Clerk belonged. Further, with her eye manifestly upon this sedate philosopher, she had taken pains to gird at him and his fellows. At first she pretends to be modest and apologetic,—'so that the clerkes be nat with me wrothe,'—but later she abandons all pretense and makes an open attack:

'For trusteth wel, it is an impossible
That any clerk wol speken good of wyves,
But-if it be of holy seintes lyves,
Ne of noon other womman never the mo. . . .

The clerk, whan he is old, and may noght do
Of Venus werkes worth his olde sho,
Than sit he doun, and writ in his dotage
That wommen can nat kepe his mariage.'

And there was more still that the Wife made our Clerk endure. Her fifth husband was, like him, a 'clerk of Oxenford'—surely this is no accidental coincidence on Chaucer's part. He had abandoned his studies ('had left scole'), and had given up all thought of taking priest's orders. The Wife narrates, with uncommon zest, how she intrigued with him, and cajoled him, and married him (though he was twenty and she was forty), and how finally she made him utterly subservient to her will,—how she got 'by maistrye al the soveraynetee.' This was gall and wormwood to our Clerk. The Wife not only trampled on his principles in her theory and practice, but she pointed her attack by describing how she had subdued to her heretical sect a clerk of Oxenford, an alumnus of our Clerk's own university. The Wife's discourse is not malicious. She is too jovial to be ill-natured, and she protests that she speaks in jest. But it none the less embodies a rude personal assault upon the Clerk, whose quiet mien and habitual reticence made him seem a safe person to attack. She had done her best to make the Clerk ridiculous. He saw it; the company saw it. He kept silent, biding his time.

All this is not speculation. It is nothing but straightforward interpretation of the text in the light of the circumstances and the situation. We can reject it only by insisting on the manifest absurdity (shown to be such in every headlink and endlink) that Chaucer did not visualize the Pilgrims whom he had been at such pains to describe in the Prologue, and that he never regarded them as associating, as looking at each other and thinking of each other, as becoming better and better acquainted as they jogged along the Canterbury road.

Chaucer might have given the Clerk a chance to reply to the Wife immediately. But he was too good an artist. The drama of the Pilgrimage is too natural and unforced in its development under the master's hand to admit of anything so frigidly schematic. The very liveliness with which he conceived his individual *dramatis personae* forbade. The Pilgrims were interested in the Wife's harangue, but it was for the talkative members of the company to thrust themselves forward. The Pardoner had already interrupted her with humorous comments before she was fully under way and had exhorted her to continue her account of the 'praktike' of marriage. The Friar, we may be confident, was on good terms with her before she began; she was one of those 'worthy wommen of the toun' whom he especially cultivated. He, too, could not refrain from comment:

> The Frere lough, whan he had herd al this:
> 'Now, dame,' quod he, 'so have I ioye or blis,
> This is a long preamble of a tale!'

The Summoner reproved him, in words that show not only his professional enmity but also the amusement that the Pilgrims in general were deriving from the Wife's disclosures. They quarreled, and each threatened to tell a story at the other's expense. Then the Host intervened roughly, calling for silence and bidding the Wife go ahead with her story. She assented, but not without a word of good-humored, though ironical, deference to the Friar:

> 'Al redy, sir,' quod she, 'right as yow lest,
> If I have license of this worthy Frere.'

And, at the very beginning of her tale, she took humorous vengeance for his interruption in a characteristic bit of satire at the expense of 'limitours and other holy freres.' This passage, we note, has nothing whatever to do with her tale. It is a side-remark in which she is talking at the Friar, precisely as she has talked at the Clerk in her prologue.

The quarrel between the Summoner and the Friar was in abeyance until the Wife finished her tale. They let her end her story and proclaim her moral in peace,—the same heretical doctrine that we have already noted, that the wife should be the head of the house. Then the Friar spoke, and his words are very much to our present purpose. He adverts in significant terms both to the subject and to the manner of the Wife's discourse,—a discourse, we should observe, that was in effect a doctrinal sermon illustrated (as the fashion of preachers was) by a pertinent *exemplum*:

> 'Ye have here touched, al-so moot I thee,
> In scole-matere great difficultee.'

She has handled a hard subject that properly belongs to scholars.
She has quoted authorities, too, like a clerk. Such things, he says,
are best left to ecclesiastics:

> 'But, dame, here as we ryden by the weye,
> Us nedeth nat to speken but of game,
> And lete auctoritees, on Goddes name,
> To preching and to scole eek of clergye.'

This, to be sure, is but a device to 'conveyen his matere,'—to lead
up to his proposal to 'telle a game' about a summoner. But it serves
to recall our minds to the Wife's usurpation of clerkly functions.
If we think of the Clerk at all at this point (and assuredly Chaucer
had not forgotten him), we must feel that here is another prompt-
ing (undesigned though it be on the Friar's part) to take up the
subject which the Wife has (in the Clerk's eyes) so shockingly
maltreated.

Then follows the comic interlude of the Friar and the Summoner,
in the course of which we may perhaps lose sight of the serious
subject which the Wife had set abroach,—the status of husband
and wife in the marriage relation. But Chaucer did not lose sight
of it. It was a part of his design that the Host should call on the
Clerk for the first story of the next day.

This is the opportunity for which the Clerk has been waiting.
He has not said a word in reply to the Wife's heresies or to her
personal attack on him and his order. Seemingly she has triumphed.
The subject has apparently been dismissed with the Friar's words
about leaving such matters to sermons and to school debates. The
Host, indeed, has no idea that the Clerk proposes to revive the
discussion; he does not even think of the Wife in calling upon the
representative of that order which has fared so ill at her hands.

> 'Sir clerk of Oxenford,' our hoste sayde,
> 'Ye ryde as coy and stille as doth a mayde
> Were newe spoused, sitting at the bord;
> This day ne herd I of your tonge a word.
> I trowe ye studie about som sophyme.'

Even here there is a suggestion (casual, to be sure, and, so far as the Host is concerned, quite unintentional) of *marriage*, the subject which is occupying the Clerk's mind. For the Host is mistaken. The Clerk's abstraction is only apparent. He is not pondering syllogisms; he is biding his time.

'Tell us a tale,' the unconscious Host goes on, 'but don't preach us a Lenten sermon—tell us som mery thing of aventures.' 'Gladly,' replies the demure scholar. 'I will tell you a story that a worthy *clerk* once told me at Padua—Francis Petrarch, God rest his soul!'

At this word *clerk*, pronounced with grave and inscrutable emphasis, the Wife of Bath must have pricked up her ears. But she has no inkling of what is in store, nor is the Clerk in any hurry to enlighten her. He opens with tantalizing deliberation, and it is not until he has spoken more than sixty lines that he mentions marriage. 'The Marquis Walter,' says the Clerk, 'lived only for the present and lived for pleasure only'—

> 'As for to hauke and hunte on every syde,—
> Wel ny al othere cures leet he slyde;
> And eek he nolde, and that was worst of alle,
> Wedde no wyf, for noght that may bifalle.'

These words may or may not have appeared significant to the company at large. To the Wife of Bath, at all events, they must have sounded interesting. And when, in a few moments, the Clerk made Walter's subjects speak of 'soveraynetee,' the least alert of the Pilgrims can hardly have missed the point:

> 'Boweth your nekke under that blisful yok
> Of soveraynetee, noght of servyse,
> Which that men clepeth spousialle or wedlock.'

'Sovereignty' had been the Wife's own word:

> 'And whan that I hadde geten unto me
> By maistrie al the soveraynetee';

> 'Wommen desyren to have soveryntee
> As wel over his housband as hir love,
> And for to been in maistrie him above.'

Clearly the Clerk is catching up the subject proposed by the Wife. The discussion is under way again.

Yet despite the cheerful view that Walter's subjects take of the marriage yoke, it is by no means yet clear to the Wife of Bath and the other Pilgrims what the Clerk is driving at. For he soon makes Walter declare that 'liberty is seldom found in marriage,' and that if he weds a wife, he must exchange freedom for servitude. Indeed, it is not until vvs. 351–57 are reached that Walter reveals himself as a man who is determined to rule his wife absolutely. From that point to the end there is no room for doubt in any Pilgrim's mind: *the Clerk is answering the Wife of Bath;* he is telling of a woman whose principles in marriage were the antithesis of hers; he is reasserting the orthodox view in opposition to the heresy which she had expounded with such zest and with so many flings and jeers at the clerkly profession and character.

What is the tale of Griselda? Several things, no doubt—an old *märchen*, an *exemplum*, a *novella*, what you will. Our present concern, however, is primarily with the question what it seemed to be to the Canterbury Pilgrims, told as it was by an individual Clerk of Oxford at a particular moment and under the special circumstances. The answer is plain. To them it was a retort (indirect, impersonal, masterly) to the Wife of Bath's heretical doctrine that the woman should be the head of the man. It told them of a wife who had no such views,—who promised ungrudging obedience and kept her vow. The Wife of Bath had railed at her husbands and badgered them and cajoled them: Griselda never lost her patience or her serenity. On its face, then, the tale appeared to the Pilgrims to be a dignified and scholarly narrative, derived from a great Italian clerk who was dead, and now utilized by their fellow-pilgrim, the Clerk of Oxford, to demolish the heretical structure so boisterously reared by the Wife of Bath in her prologue and her tale.

But Chaucer's Clerk was a logician—'unto logik hadde he longe ygo.' He knew perfectly well that the real moral of his story was not that which his hearers would gather. He was aware that Griselda was no model for literal imitation by ordinary womankind. If so taken, his tale proved too much; it reduced his argument *ad absurdum.* If he let it go at that, he was playing into his opponent's hands. Besides, he was a conscientious man. He could not misrepresent the lesson which Petrarch had meant to teach and had so clearly expressed,—the lesson of submissive fortitude under tribulation sent by God. Hence he does not fail to explain this moral fully and in unmistakable terms, and to refer distinctly to Petrarch as authority for it:

> And herkeneth what this auctor seith therefore.

> This is seyd, nat for that wyves sholde
> Folwen Grisolde as in humilitee,
> For it were importable, though they wolde;
> But that for every wight, in his degree,
> Sholde be constant in adversitee
> As was Grisilde; therfor Petrark wryteth
> This storie, which with heigh style he endyteth.

> For, sith a womman was so pacient
> Un-to a mortal man, wel more us ogthe
> Receyven al in gree that God us sent;
> For greet skile is, he preve that he wroghte.
> But he no tempteth no man that he boghte,
> As seith sent Iame, if ye his pistel rede;
> He preveth folk al day, it is no drede,

> And suffreth us, as for our exercyse,
> With sharpe scourges of adversitee
> Ful often to be bete in sondry wyse;
> Nat for to knowe our wil, for certes he,
> Er we were born, knew al our freletee;
> And for our beste is al his governaunce:
> Lat us than live in vertuous suffrance.

Yet the Clerk has no idea of failing to make his point against the Wife of Bath. And so, when the tale is finished and the proper Petrarchan moral has been duly elaborated, he turns to the Wife (whom he has thus far sedulously refrained from addressing) and distinctly applies the material to the purpose of an ironical answer, of crushing force, to her whole heresy. There is nothing inappropriate to his character in this procedure. Quite the contrary. Clerks were always satirizing women—the Wife had said so herself—and this particular Clerk had, of course, no scruples against using the powerful weapon of irony in the service of religion and 'moral vertu.' In this instance, the satire is peculiarly poignant for two reasons: first, because it comes with all the suddenness of a complete change of tone (from high seriousness to biting irony, and from the impersonal to the personal); and secondly, because in the tale which he has told, the Clerk had incidentally refuted a false statement of the Wife's, to the effect that

> 'It is an impossible
> That any clerk wol speke good of wyves,
> But if it be of holy seintes lyves,
> No of noon other womman never the mo.'

Clerks *can* 'speak well' of women (as our Clerk has shown), and when women deserve it; and he now proceeds to show that they can likewise speak well (with biting irony) of women who do *not* deserve it—such women as the Wife of Bath and all her sect of domestic revolutionists.

It now appears that the form and spirit of the conclusion and the Envoy are not only appropriate to clerks in general, but peculiarly and exquisitely appropriate to this particular clerk under these particular circumstances and with this particular task in hand,—the duty of defending the orthodox view of the relations between husband and wife against the heretical opinions of the Wife of Bath: 'One word in conclusion, gentlemen. There are few Griseldas now-a-days. Most women will break before they will bend. Our companion, the Wife of Bath, is an example, as she has told us herself. Therefore, though I cannot sing, I will recite a song in honor, not of Griselda (as you might perhaps expect), but of the Wife of Bath, of the sect of which she aspires to be a doctor, and of the life which she exemplifies in practice—

> 'For the wyves love of Bathe,
> Whos lif and al hir secte God mayntene
> In high maistrye, and elles were it scathe.'

Her *way of life*—she had set it forth with incomparable zest. Her *sect*—she was an heresiarch or at least a schismatic. The terms are not accidental: they are chosen with all the discrimination that befits a scholar and a rhetorician. They refer us back (as definitely as the words 'Wife of Bath' themselves) to that prologue in which the Wife had stood forth as an opponent of the orthodox view of subordination in marriage, as the upholder of an heretical doctrine, and as the exultant practicer of what she preached.

And then comes the Clerk's Envoy, the song that he recites in honor of the Wife and all her sect, with its polished lines, its ingenious rhyming, and its utter felicity of scholarly diction. Nothing could be more in character. To whom in all the world could such a masterpiece of rhetoric be appropriate if not to the Clerk of Oxenford? It is a mock encomium, a sustained ironical commendation of what the Wife has taught.

'O noble wives, let no clerk ever have occasion to write such a story of you as Petrarch once told me about Griselda. Follow your great leader, the Wife of Bath. Rule your husbands, as she did; rail at them, as she did; make them jealous, as she did; exert yourselves to get lovers, as she did. And all this you must do whether you are fair or foul [with manifest allusion to the problem of beauty of ugliness presented in the Wife's story]. Do this, I say, and you will fulfil the precepts that she has set forth and achieve the great end which she has proclaimed as the object of marriage: that is, *you will make your husbands miserable, as she did!*'

> 'Be ay of chere as light as leef on linde,
> And let him care and wepe and wringe and waille!'

And the Merchant (hitherto silent, but not from inattention) catches up the closing words in a gust of bitter passion:

> 'Weping and wayling, care and other sorwe
> *I* know ynough on even and amorwe.'
> Quod the Merchant, 'and so don othere mo
> That wedded ben.'

The Clerk's Envoy, then, is not only appropriate to his character and to the situation: it has also a marked dynamic value. For it is this ironical tribute to the Wife of Bath and her dogmas that, with complete dramatic inevitability, calls out the Merchant's *cri de coeur*. The Merchant has no thought of telling a tale at this moment. He is a stately and imposing person in his degree, by no means prone (so the Prologue informs us) to expose any holes there may be in his coat. But he is suffering a kind of emotional crisis. The poignant irony of the Clerk, following hard upon the moving story of a patient and devoted wife, is too much for him. He has just passed through his honeymoon (but two months wed!) and he has sought a respite from his thraldom under color of a pilgrimage to St. Thomas.

> 'I have a wyf, the worste that may be!'

She would be an overmatch for the devil himself. He need not specify her evil traits: she is bad in every respect.

> 'There is a long and large difference
> Bitwix Grisildis grete pacience
> And of my wyf the passing crueltee.'

The Host, as ever, is on the alert. He scents a good story:

> 'Sin ye so muchel knowen of that art,
> Ful hertely I pray yow telle us part.'

The Merchant agrees, as in duty bound, for all the Pilgrims take care never to oppose the Host, lest he exact the heavy forfeit established as the penalty for rebellion. But he declines to relate his own experiences, thus leaving us to infer, if we choose,—for nowhere is Chaucer's artistic reticence more effective,—that his bride has proved false to him, like the wife of the worthy Knight of Lombardy.

And so the discussion of marriage is once more in full swing. The Wife of Bath, without intending it, has opened a debate in which the Pilgrims have become so absorbed that they will not leave it till the subject is 'bolted to the bran.'

The Merchant's Tale presents very noteworthy features, and has been much canvassed, though never (it seems) with due attention to its plain significance in the Human Comedy of the Canterbury Tales. In substance, it is nothing but a tale of bawdry, one of the most familiar of its class. There is nothing novel about it except its setting, but that is sufficiently remarkable. Compare the tale with any other version of the Pear-Tree Story,—their name is legion,—and its true significance comes out in striking fashion. The simple fabliau devised by its first author merely to make those laugh whose lungs are tickle o' the sere, is so expanded and overlaid with savage satire that it becomes a complete disquisition of marriage from the only point of view which is possible for the disenchanted Merchant. Thus considered, the cynicism of the Merchant's Tale is seen to be in no way surprising, and (to answer another kind of comment which this piece has evoked) in no sense expressive of Chaucer's own sentiments, or even of Chaucer's momentary mood. The cynicism is the Merchant's. It is no more Chaucer's than Iago's cynicism about love is Shakespeare's.

In a word, the tale is the perfect expression of the Merchant's angry disgust at his own evil fate and at his folly in bringing that fate upon himself. Thus, its very lack of restraint—the savagery of the whole, which has revolted so many readers—is dramatically inevitable. The Merchant has schooled himself to his debts and his troubles. He is professionally adept at putting a good face on matters, as every clever business man must be. But when once the barrier is broken, reticence is at an end. His disappointment is too fresh, his disillusion has been too abrupt, for him to measure his words. He speaks in a frenzy of contempt and hatred. The hatred is for women; the contempt is for himself and all other fools who will not take warning by example. For we should not forget that the satire is aimed at January rather than at May. That egotistical old dotard is less excusable than his young wife, and meets with less mercy at the Merchant's hands.

That the Merchant begins with an encomium on marriage which is one of the most amazing instances of sustained irony in all literature, is not to be wondered at. In the first place, he is ironical because the Clerk has been ironical. Here the connection is remarkably close. The Merchant has fairly snatched the words out of the Clerk's mouth ('And lat him care and wepe and wringe and waille'—'Weping and wayling, care and other sorwe'), and his mock encomium on the wedded state is a sequel to the Clerk's mock encomium on the Wife of Bath's life and all her sect. The spirit is different, but that is quite proper. For the Clerk's satire is the irony of a logician and a moral philosopher, the irony of the intellect and the ethical sense: the Merchant's is the irony of a mere man, it is the irony of passion and personal experience. The Clerk is a theorist,—he looks at the subject from a point of philosophical detachment. The Merchant is an egotist,—he feels himself to be the dupe whose folly he depicts. We may infer, if we like, that he was a man in middle age and that he had married a young wife.

There is plenty of evidence that the Merchant has been an attentive listener. One detects, for instance, a certain similarity between January and the Marquis Walter (different as they are) in that they have both shown themselves disinclined to marriage. Then again, the assertion that a wife is never weary of attending a sick husband—

'She nis nat wery him to love and serve,
Thogh that he lye bedrede til he sterve'—

must have reminded the Pilgrims of poor Thomas, in the Summoner's Tale, whose wife's complaints to her spiritual visitor had precipitated so tremendous a sermon. But such things are trifles compared with the attention which the Merchant devotes to the Wife of Bath.

So far, in this act of Chaucer's Human Comedy, we have found that the Wife of Bath is, in a very real sense, the dominant figure. She has dictated the theme and inspired or instigated the actors; and she has always been at or near the center of the stage. It was a quarrel over her prologue that elicited the tale of the Friar and that of the Summoner. It was she who caused the Clerk to tell of Griselda—and the Clerk satirizes her in his Envoy. 'The art' of which the Host begs the Merchant to tell is *her* art, the art of marriage on which she has discoursed so learnedly. That the Merchant, therefore, should allude to her, quote her words, and finally mention her in plain terms is precisely what was to be expected.

The order and method of these approaches on the Merchant's part are exquisitely natural and dramatic. First there are touches, more or less palpable, when he describes the harmony of wedded life in terms so different from the Wife's account of what her husbands had to endure. Then—after a little—comes a plain enough allusion (put into January's mouth) to the Wife's character, to her frequent marriages, and to her inclination to marry again, old as she is:

> 'And eek thise olde widwes, God it wot,
> They conne so muchel craft on Wades boot,
> So muchel broken harm, whan that hem leste,
> That with hem sholde I never live in reste!
> For sondry scoles maken sotil clerkis:
> Wommen of many scoles half a clerk is.'

Surely the Wife of Bath was a woman of many schools, and her emulation of clerkly discussion had already been commented on by the Pardoner and the Friar. Next, the Merchant lets Justinus quote some of the Wife's very words—though without naming her: 'God may apply the trials of marriage, my dear January, to your salvation. Your wife may make you go straight to heaven without passing through purgatory.'

> 'Paraunter she may be your purgatorie!
> She may be Goddes mene, and Goddes whippe;
> Than shal your soule up to hevene skippe
> Swifter than doth an arwe out of the bowe.'

This is merely an adaptation of the Wife of Bath's own language in speaking of her fourth husband:

> 'By God, in erthe I was his purgatorie,
> For which I hope his soule be in glorie.'

Compare also another phrase of hers, which Justinus echoes: 'Myself have been the whippe.' And finally, when all the Pilgrims are quite prepared for such a thing, there is a frank citation of the Wife of Bath by name, with a reference to her exposition of marriage:

'My tale is doon:—for my wit is thinne.
Beth not agast herof, my brother dere.
But lat us waden out of this matere:
The Wyf of Bathe, if ye han understonde,
Of marriage, which we have on honde,
Declared hath ful wel in litel space.
Fareth now wel, God have yow in his grace.'

Are the italicized lines a part of the speech of Justinus, or are they interpolated by the Merchant, in his own person, in order to shorten Justinus' harangue? Here is Professor Skeat's comment: 'These four parenthetical lines interrupt the story rather awkwardly. They obviously belong to the narrator, the Merchant, as it is out of the question that Justinus had heard of the Wife of Bath. Perhaps it is an oversight.' Now it makes no difference whether we assign these lines to Justinus or to the Merchant, for Justinus, as we have seen, has immediately before quoted the Wife's very words, and he may as well mention her as repeat her language. Either way, the lines are exquisitely in place. *Chaucer* is not speaking, and there is no violation of dramatic propriety on *his* part. It is not Chaucer who is telling the story. It is the Merchant. And the Merchant is telling it as a part of the discussion which the Wife has started. It is dramatically proper, then, that the Merchant should quote the Wife of Bath and that he should refer to her. And it is equally proper, from the dramatic point of view, for Chaucer to let the Merchant make Justinus mention the Wife. In that case it is the Merchant—not *Chaucer*—who chooses to have one of his characters fall out of his part for a moment and make a 'local allusion.' Chaucer is responsible for making the *Merchant* speak in character; the Merchant, in his turn, is responsible for *Justinus*. That the Merchant should put into the mouth of Justinus a remark that Justinus could never have made is, then, not a slip on Chaucer's part. On the contrary, it is a first-rate dramatic touch, for it is precisely what the Merchant might well have done under the circumstances.

Nor should we forget the exquisitely comical discussion between Pluto and Proserpina which the Merchant has introduced near the end of his story. This dialogue is a flagrant violation of dramatic propriety—not on Chaucer's part, however, but on the Merchant's. And therein consists a portion of its merit. For the Merchant is so eager to make his point that he rises superior to all artistic rules. He is bent, not on giving utterance to a masterpiece of narrative construction, but on enforcing his lesson in every possible way. And Chaucer is equally bent on making him do it. Hence the Queen of the Lower World is brought in, discoursing in terms that befit the Wife of Bath (the presiding genius of this part of the *Canterbury Tales*), and echoing some of her very doctrines. And note that Pluto (who is as fond of citing authorities as the Wife's last husband) yields the palm of the discussion to Proserpine. This, too, was the experience of the Wife's husbands. The tone and manner of the whole debate between Pluto and his queen are wildly absurd if regarded from the point of view of gods and goddesses, but in that very incongruity resides their dramatic propriety. What we have is not Pluto and Proserpine arguing with each other, but the Wife of Bath and one of her husbands attired for the nonce by the cynical Merchant in the external resemblance of King Pluto and his dame.

The end of the Merchant's Tale does not bring the Marriage Chapter of the *Canterbury Tales* to a conclusion. As the Merchant had commented on the Clerk's Tale by speaking of his own wife, thus continuing the subject which the Wife had begun, so the Host comments on the Merchant's story by making a similar application:

> 'Ey, Goddes mercy,' seyde our Hoste tho,
> 'Now such a wyf I pray God kepe me fro!'

'See how women deceive us poor men, as the Merchant has shown us. However, *my* wife is true as any steel; but she is a shrew, and has plenty of other faults.' And just as the Merchant had referred expressly to the Wife of Bath, so also does the Host refer to her expressly: 'But I must not talk of these things. If I should, it would be told to her by some of this company. I need not say by whom, 'sin wommen connen outen swich chaffare!' Of course the Host points this remark by looking at the Wife of Bath. There are but three women in the company. Neither the highborn and dainty Prioress nor the pious nun who accompanies her is likely to gossip with Harry Baily's spouse. It is the Wife, a woman of the Hostess's own rank and temper, who will tattle when the party returns to the Tabard. And so we find the Wife of Bath still in the foreground, as she has been, in one way or another, for several thousand lines.

But now the Host thinks his companions have surely had enough of marriage. It is time they heard something of love, and with this in view he turns abruptly to the Squire, whom all the Pilgrims have come to know as 'a lovyer and a lusty bachiller.'

> 'Squier, com neer, if it your wille be,
> And sey somewhat of *love;* for certes ye
> Connen theron as muche as any man.'

The significance of the emphasis on *love,* which is inevitable if the address to the Squire is read (as it should be) continuously with the Host's comments on marriage, is by no means accidental.

There is no psychology about the Squire's Tale,—no moral or social or matrimonial theorizing. It is pure romance, in the mediaeval sense. The Host understood the charm of variety. He did not mean to let the discussion drain itself to the dregs.

But Chaucer's plan in this Act is not yet finished. There is still something lacking to a full discussion of the relations between husband and wife. We have had the wife who dominates her husband; the husband who dominates his wife; the young wife who befools her dotard January; the chaste wife who is a scold and stirs up strife. Each of these illustrates a different kind of marriage, —but there is left untouched, so far, the ideal relation, that in which love continues and neither party to the contract strives for the mastery. Let this be set forth, and the series of views of wedded life begun by the Wife of Bath will be rounded off; the Marriage Act of the Human Comedy will be concluded. The Pilgrims may not be thinking of this; but there is at least *one* of them (as the sequel shows) who has the idea in his head. And who is he? The only pilgrims who have not yet already told their tales are the yeoman, two priests, the five tradesmen (haberdasher, carpenter, weaver, dyer, and tapicer), the parson, the plowman, the manciple, and the franklin. Of all these there is but one to whom a tale illustrating the ideal would not be inappropriate—the Franklin. To him, then, must Chaucer assign it, or leave the debate unfinished.

At this point, the dramatic action and interplay of characters are beyond all praise. The Franklin is not brought forward in formal fashion to address the company. His summons is incidental to the dialogue. No sooner has the Squire ended his chivalric romance, than the Franklin begins to compliment him:

> 'In feyth, squier, thou hast thee well yquit
> And gentilly. . . .'

'You have acquitted yourself well and *like a gentleman!*' *Gentilesse*, then, is what has most impressed the Franklin in the tale that he has just heard. And the reason for his enthusiasm soon appears. He is, as we know, a rich freeholder, often sheriff in his county. Socially, he is not quite within the pale of the gentry, but he is the kind of man that may hope to found a family, the kind of man from whose ranks the English nobility has been constantly recruited. And that such is his ambition comes out naïvely and with a certain pathos in what he goes on to say: 'I wish my son were like you.' It is the contrast between the Squire and his own son, in whom his hopes are centered, that has led the Franklin's thoughts to *gentilesse*, a subject which is ever in his mind.

But the Host interrupts him rudely: 'Straw for your gentilesse! It is your turn to entertain the company':

> 'Telle on thy tale withouten wordes mo!'

The Franklin is, of course, very polite in his reply to this rough and unexpected command. Like the others, he is on his guard against opposing the Host and incurring the forfeit.

Here, then, as in the case of the Merchant, the Host has taken advantage of a spontaneous remark on some Pilgrim's part to demand a story. Yet the details of the action are quite different. On the previous occasion, the Merchant is requested to go on with an account of his marriage, since he has already begun to talk about it; and, though he declines to speak further of his own troubles, he does continue to discuss and illustrate wedlock from his own point of view. In the present instance, on the contrary, the Host repudiates the topic of *gentilesse*, about which the Franklin is discoursing to the Squire. He bids him drop the subject and tell a story. The Franklin pretends to be compliant, but after all, he has his own way. Indeed, he takes delicate vengeance on the Host by telling a tale which thrice exemplifies *gentilesse*—on the part of a knight, a squire, and a clerk. Thus he finishes his interrupted compliment to the Squire, and incidentally honors two other Pilgrims who have seemed to him to possess the quality that he values so highly. He proves, too, both that *gentilesse* is an entertaining topic and that it is not (as the Host has roughly intimated) a theme which he, the Franklin, is ill-equipped to handle.

For the Franklin's Tale is a gentleman's story, and he tells it like a gentleman. It is derived, he tells us, from 'thise olde *gentil* Britons.' Dorigen lauds Arveragus' *gentilesse* toward her in refusing to insist on soveraynetee in marriage. Aurelius is deeply impressed by the knight's *gentilesse* in allowing the lady to keep her word, and emulates it by releasing her. And finally, the clerk releases Aurelius, from the same motive of generous emulation.

Thus it appears that the dramatic impulse to the telling of the Franklin's Tale is to be found in the relations among the Pilgrims and in the effect that they have upon each other,—in other words, in the circumstances, the situation, and the interplay of character.

It has sometimes been thought that the story, either in subject or in style, is too fine for the Franklin to tell. But this objection Chaucer foresaw and forestalled. The question is not whether this tale, thus told, would be appropriate to a typical or 'average' fourteenth-century franklin. The question is whether it is appropriate to this particular Franklin, under these particular circumstances, and at this particular juncture. And to this question there can be but one answer. Chaucer's Franklin is an individual, not a mere type-specimen. He is rich, ambitious socially, and profoundly interested in the matter of *gentilesse* for personal and family reasons. He is trying to bring up his son as a gentleman, and his position as 'St. Julian in his country' has brought him into intimate association with first-rate models. He has, under the special circumstances, every motive to tell a gentleman's story and tell it like a gentleman. He is speaking under the immediate influence of his admiration for the Squire and of his sense of the inferiority of his own son. If we choose to conceive the Franklin as a mediaeval Squire Western and then to allege that he could not possibly have told such a story, we are making the difficulty for ourselves. We are considering—not Chaucer's Franklin (whose character is to be inferred not merely from the description in the General Prologue but from all the other evidence that the poet provides)—not Chaucer's Franklin, but somebody quite different, somebody for whom Chaucer has no kind of responsibility.

In considering the immediate occasion of the Franklin's Tale, we have lost sight for a moment of the Wife of Bath. But she was not absent from the mind of the Franklin. The proper subject of his tale, as we have seen, is *gentilesse*. Now that (as well as marriage) was a subject on which the Wife of Bath had descanted at some length. Her views are contained in the famous harangue delivered by the lady to her husband on the wedding night: 'But for ye speken of swich gentilesse,' etc. Many readers have perceived that this portentous curtain-lecture clogs the story, and some have perhaps wished it away, good as it is in itself. For it certainly seems to be out of place on the lips of the *fée*. But its insertion is (as usual in such cases) exquisitely appropriate to the teller of the tale, the Wife of Bath, who cannot help dilating on subjects which interest her, and who has had the advantage of learned society in the person of her fifth husband. Perhaps no *fée* would have talked thus to her knightly bridegroom on such an occasion; but it is quite in character for the Wife of Bath to use the *fée* (or anybody else) as a mouthpiece for her own ideas, as the Merchant had used Proserpine to point his satire. Thus the references to Dante, Valerius, Seneca, Boethius, and Juvenal—so deliciously absurd on the lips of a *fée* of King Arthur's time—are perfectly in place when we remember who it is that is reporting the monologue. The Wife was a citer of authorities—she makes the *fée* cite authorities. How comical this is the Wife did not know, but Chaucer knew, and if we think he did not, it is our own fault for not observing how dramatic in spirit is the *Canterbury Tales.*

A considerable passage in the curtain-lecture is given to the proposition that 'swich gentilesse as is descended out of old richesse' is of no value: 'Swich arrogance is not worth an hen.' These sentiments the Franklin echoes:

> 'Fy on possessioun
> But-if a man be vertuous withall!'

But, whether or not the Wife's digression on *gentilesse* is lingering in the Franklin's mind (as I am sure it is), one thing is perfectly clear: the Franklin's utterances on marriage are spoken under the influence of the discussion which the Wife has precipitated. In other words, though everybody else imagines that the subject has been finally dismissed by the Host when he calls on the Squire for a tale of *love,* it has no more been dismissed in fact than when the Friar attempted to dismiss it at the beginning of his tale. For the Franklin has views, and he means to set them forth. He possesses, as he thinks, the true solution of the whole difficult problem. And that solution he embodies in his tale of *gentilesse.*

The introductory part of the Franklin's Tale sets forth a theory of the marriage relation quite different from anything that has so far emerged in the debate. And this theory the Franklin arrives at by taking into consideration both *love* (which, as we remember, was the subject that the Host had bidden the Squire treat of) and *gentilesse* (which is to be the subject of his own story).

Arveragus had of course been obedient to his lady during the period of courtship, for obedience was well understood to be the duty of a lover. Finally, she consented to marry him—

> To take him for hir houbonde and hir lord,
> Of swich lordshipe as men han over her wyves.

Marriage, then, according to the orthodox doctrine (as held by Walter and Griselda) was to change Arveragus from the lady's servant to her master. But Arveragus was an enlightened and chivalric gentleman, and he promised the lady he would never assert his marital authority, but would content himself with the mere name of sovereignty, continuing to be her servant and lover as before. This he did because he thought it would ensure the happiness of their wedded life.

But, just as Arveragus was no disciple of the Marquis Walter, so Dorigen was not a member of the sect of the Wife of Bath. She promised her husband obedience and fidelity in return for his gentilesse in renouncing his sovereign rights. This, then, is the Franklin's solution of the whole puzzle of matrimony, and it is a solution that depends upon love and *gentilesse* on both sides. But he is not content to leave the matter in this purely objective condition. He is determined that there shall be no misapprehension in the mind of any Pilgrim as to his purpose. He wishes to make it perfectly clear that he is definitely and formally offering this theory as the only satisfactory basis of happy married life. And he accordingly comments on the relations between the married lovers with fulness, and with manifest reference to certain things that the previous debaters have said.

The arrangement, he tells the Pilgrims, resulted in 'quiet and rest' for both Arveragus and Dorigen. And, he adds, it is the only arrangement which will ever enable two persons to live together in love and amity. Friends must 'obey each other if they wish to hold company long.' Hence it was that this wise knight promised his wife 'suffraunce' and that she promised him never to abuse his goodness. The result, the Franklin adds, was all that could be desired. The knight lived 'in blisse and in solas.' And then the Franklin adds an encomium on the happiness of true marriage:

> 'Who coulde telle, but he had wedded be,
> The ioye, the ese, and the prosperitee
> That is bitwixe an housbonde and his wyf?'

This encomium echoes the language of the Merchant:

> 'A wyf! a Seinte Marie! *benedicte!*
> How mighte a man han any adversitee
> That hath a wyf? Certes, I can nat seye!
> The blisse which that is bitwixe hem tweye
> Ther may no tonge telle or herte thinke.'

The Franklin's praise of marriage is sincere; the Merchant's had been savagely ironical. The Franklin, we observe, is answering the Merchant, and he answers him in the most effective way—by repeating his very words.

And just as in the Merchant's Tale we noted that the Merchant has enormously expanded the simple *fabliau* that he had to tell, inserting all manner of observations on marriage which are found in no other version of the Pear-Tree story, so also we find that the Franklin's exposition of the ideal marriage relation (including the pact between Arveragus and Dorigen) is all his own, occurring in none of the versions that precede Chaucer. These facts are of the very last significance. No argument is necessary to enforce their meaning.

It is hardly worth while to indicate the close connection between this and that detail of the Franklin's exposition and certain points that have come out in the discussion as conducted by his predecessors in the debate. His repudiation of the Wife of Bath's doctrine that men should be 'governed by their wives' is express, as well as his rejection of the opposite theory. Neither party should lose his liberty; neither the husband nor the wife should be a thrall. Patience (which clerks celebrate as a high virtue) should be mutual, not, as in the Clerk's Tale, all on one side. The husband is to be both servant and lord—servant in love and lord in marriage. Such servitude is true lordship. Here there is a manifest allusion to the words of Walter's subjects in the Clerk's Tale:

> That blisful yok
> Of sovereynetee, noght of servyse;

as well as to Walter's rejoinder:

> 'I me reioysed of my libertee,
> That selde tyme is founde in mariage;
> Ther I was free, I moot been in servage.'

It was the regular theory of the Middle Ages that the highest type of chivalric love was incompatible with marriage, since marriage brings in mastery, and mastery and love cannot abide together. This view the Franklin boldly challenges. Love *can* be consistent with marriage, he declares. Indeed, without love (and perfect *gentle* love) marriage is sure to be a failure. The difficulty about mastery vanishes when mutual love and forbearance are made the guiding principles of the relation between husband and wife.

The soundness of the Franklin's theory, he declares, is proved by his tale. For the marriage of Arveragus and Dorigen was a brilliant success. Thus the whole debate has been brought to a satisfactory conclusion, and the Marriage Act of the Human Comedy ends with the conclusion of the Franklin's Tale.

Those readers who are eager to know what Chaucer thought about marriage may feel reasonably content with the inference that may be drawn from his procedure. The Marriage Group of Tales begins with the Wife of Bath's Prologue and ends with the Franklin's Tale. There is no connection between the Wife's Prologue and the group of stories that precedes: there is no connection between the Franklin's Tale and the group that follows. Within the Marriage Group, on the contrary, there is close connection throughout. That act is a finished act. It begins and ends an elaborate debate. We need not hesitate, therefore, to accept the solution which the Franklin offers as that which Geoffrey Chaucer the man accepted for his own part. Certainly it is a solution that does him infinite credit. A better has never been devised or imagined.

HENRY BARRETT HINCKLEY

The Debate on Marriage in *The Canterbury Tales*

SCHOLARS have always recognized that there is a large degree of appropriateness in the assignment of the various *Canterbury Tales* to their respective tellers, and in a few cases an appropriateness also to the situation. Recently there have been determined efforts to extend the application of these principles as far as possible. Conspicuous among these is the position asserted with great emphasis and confidence by Professor Kittredge,[1] who would have us believe that Groups D, E, and F of the *Canterbury Tales* constitute a 'complete and highly finished' 'act' in Chaucer's 'Human Comedy'; that the *Wife's Prologue* is a fling at the Clerk; that this gentleman finds it 'gall and wormwood' and in his *Tale* and *Envoy* makes a deliberate and a studied reply; that during the *Merchant's Tale* the Wife is 'still in the foreground,' and even 'holds the centre of the stage'; and that the Franklin, by a process that is 'manifestly deliberate,' carries the debate to 'a triumphant conclusion by solving the problem.'

The facts on which this theory is supposed to rest may be summarized as follows: The Wife commends matrimony; she asserts the sovereignty of wife over husband; she gives several flings at the ill-natured remarks that clerks have made about women, and mentions that her own fifth husband was a clerk of Oxford; she

---

Reprinted, by permission, from *PMLA*, XXXII (1917), 292-305.

tells the story of a husband who had his own wish simply by letting his wife have hers; and she gives a discourse on 'gentillesse.' Chaucer's Clerk of Oxford tells the story, after the clerk Petrarch, of an exceedingly submissive wife, whose virtues he commends, and in conclusion he recites an ironical poem bidding wives make their husbands miserable. The Merchant declares that this is just what his wife has done to him, and he tells the story of a wife who, when caught in the very act of adultery, succeeded in making her husband believe that she was devotedly faithful to him. This *Tale* incorporates a debate on marriage between Placebo and Justinus, the friends of the wronged husband, and another as to the worth of women between Pluto and Proserpine. The Merchant also echoes the language of the Wife of Bath, and once explicitly refers to her in the following terms:

> But lat us waden out of this mateere.
> The Wyf of Bath, if ye han understonde,
> Of mariage which ye have on honde,
> Declared hath ful wel in litel space.

When the Merchant has finished, Our Host remarks that he, too, could say something of personal domestic troubles, but he cannot trust the discretion of the ladies present. The Franklin tells the story of a married couple who practiced mutual sovereignty and subjection, a story which he introduces with a discourse on 'gentillesse,' wherein he mentions the praise which clerks have bestowed upon the virtue of patience. Last of all, Professor Lowes has shown that the *Wife's Prologue* and the *Merchant's Tale* both indisputably borrow ideas from the *Miroir de Mariage* of Eustache Deschamps.

The order and date of the *Tales* in question receive no discussion from Professor Kittredge, who argues thruout as if all these *Tales* were written after the *Canterbury Tales* had been planned, and as if they were intended to stand in order as in the *Oxford Chaucer*. For the sake of simplicity I shall make the same assumption as to the dates of composition, except that I must register a doubt whether the *Clerk's Tale* was not written much earlier than 1384 and the Clerk's *Envoy* later, possibly much later, than his *Tale*. As to the order in which the *Tales* should stand, the eight manuscripts printed by Dr. Furnivall all give the parts of Group D in the same order. And there is no doubt that the *Tales* of Clerk and Merchant, both of which refer to the Wife of Bath, should come later than D. As to the position of Group F there is room for serious doubt. It might precede D and E, it might come between them, or it might follow them. If we were bound to co-ordinate F with D and E, we should do well to put F before D. Then the sorrows of Dorigen, which are exquisitely portrayed, would naturally lead the Wife 'to speke of wo that is in mariage'; and the Wife's discourse on 'gentillesse,' which she declares to be independent of birth or fortune, is better fitted by its more argumentative tone to follow than to precede the sermon of the Franklin, who clearly believes that 'gentillesse' is not unconnected with birth and station, but who assumes rather than asserts this position. But let us turn to the sequence of Wife and Clerk, as to the nature of which I believe Professor Kittredge to be seriously in error.

Between Wife and Clerk come the *Tales* of Friar and Summoner. These rascals begin to quarrel just before the Wife begins her *Tale*. The Summoner declares that before the company reaches Sittingbourne he will tell a story or two at the expense of the Friar. When the Summoner has finished his *Tale* he has amply fulfilled his threat, and he announces that the Pilgrims have almost come to town. That Our Host, in introducing the Clerk, makes absolutely no reference or allusion either to Sittingbourne or to the Summoner is strong presumptive evidence that Chaucer did not intend the *Clerk's Tale* immediately to follow the Summoner's. Let us remember that there were to have been upwards of a hundred and twenty Tales in all. Group D ends abruptly, and this is in itself no slight argument that the *Clerk's Tale* was not intended to answer the Wife of Bath.

Professor Kittredge treats the *Wife's Prolog* and *Tale* as a polemic on matrimony. It is easy to believe with him and Professor Lounsbury that in her heart she despises celibacy,[2] yet formally, at least, she is in accord with Saint Paul; and I find her far less bent on heresy and schism than on looking for a sixth husband. It would be an exaggeration to call her garrulous and frequently naïve discourse a marriage advertizement. Yet it strongly partakes of that nature. She begins by arguing that there is no reason why she should not take a sixth husband. She states her terms and conditions; she gives her history; she quotes the testimony of five husbands as to the satisfaction she has given. She announces that she is ready for a sixth. The rough story of her bullying her husbands seems later to impress her as likely to frighten the game, and accordingly toward the end of her *Prolog* and all through her *Tale* she assumes a more assuring tone. 'Women are as gentle as lambs, and a child can lead them if you only let them have their way.' That is the moral of her *Tale*. Finally she gives us a long discourse on 'gentillesse,' a discourse which experience has perhaps taught her to be a good decoy when hunting for husbands.

This interpretation has at least the merit of covering, not too closely, the whole of her harangue, both *Prolog* and *Tale,* and giving to them a certain much needed unity. Her defence of matrimony is of surpassing interest. In the words of Professor Lounsbury 'it embodies the protest of human nature' against monkish doctrine. But this is a mere detail of her talk. Her flings at clerks and the bitter things they have said about women are equally a detail, overwhelmed in the flood of her volubility. If her fifth husband was a clerk of Oxford, so too was the rascally hero of the *Miller's Tale*. If Chaucer had intended his own Clerk of Oxford to be sensitive, this should have been made absolutely clear in one or both cases.

It is not enough to say, with Professor Kittredge, that the *Clerk's Tale* 'contains no personal allusions.' Until we reach the casual reference to 'the Wyves love of Bath' the *Clerk's Tale* is absolutely and demonstrably unco-ordinated with the Wife of Bath. On three points the Clerk is essentially in agreement with the Wife. He believes in marriage; he asserts that the character of the child is not determined by its parentage; and he expressly declares that, whatever clerks may say to the contrary, women surpass men in humility and in loyalty:

> Men speke of Job, and moost for his humblesse,
> As clerkes, whan hem list, konne wel endite,
> Namely of men, but as in soothfastnesse,
> Thogh clerkes preise wommen but a lite,

Ther kan no man in humblesse hym acquite
As wommen kan, ne kan been half so trewe
As wommen been, but it be falle of newe.

If there were the slightest co-ordination, up to this point, between
the *Tales* of Clerk and Wife, we should certainly have found here
an allusion, or more than an allusion, to the Wife of Bath, whose
want of 'humblesse' I need only mention, and whose loyalty was
not of such a nature as to prevent her from engaging a fifth husband before her fourth was dead. The grave and gentle irony of
the words 'but it be falle of newe' is inadequate to serve as an
allusion. It serves rather to mark how utterly oblivious of the Wife
of Bath are both Chaucer and the Clerk when this point is reached.
But we may go further. It is not even Griselda's position as a
wife that is intended to interest us. The moral of her story has
nothing to do with matrimony. It may be a mere coincidence that
the four *Canterbury Tales* which are written in rime royal are all
of them religious, but there can be no doubt that the sentiment of
the *Clerk's Tale* is profoundly so. We are even reminded that in
the humble circumstances of her birth, Griselda resembled Christ
himself:

But hye God som tyme senden kan
His Grace into a litel oxe stalle.

On different occasions both Griselda and her father imitate or
employ the language of Job. In her own eyes, Griselda is always
first and foremost, not a wife, but a serf. And when Chaucer or the
Clerk, whichever you will, has solemnly insinuated that the
patience of Griselda surpassed that of Job himself, we are the more
prepared for the explanation that her *Tale* is intended to typify
the submission of the true Christian to God. It is this religious
significance which commended the story to Petrarch and to some
of his contemporaries, and which still renders it to some modern
readers a beautiful and a touching thing.
Boccaccio, however, had ignored the religious and allegorical
possibilities of the story. With downright common sense he called
the conduct of the Marquis 'a piece of sheer stupidity,' *una matta*

bestialità; and Sercambi, who, despite his protestations, followed Boccaccio, called the nobleman 'a fool,' *uno matto.* Chaucer, in his heart of hearts, was very clearly of the same opinion. Accordingly the English poet wrote a little poem, sparkling with brilliant and airy mockery, and bidding wives be as unlike Griselda as possible. Nowhere does this little poem mention the Wife of Bath, nor echo her language. It is difficult to believe that it was originally intended to caricature her. The problem was how to get it into the mouth of Chaucer's Clerk, a serious and edifying young man, who loved Aristotle more than 'robes riche or fithele or gay sautrye'; and who, in response to a request for 'som mery thyng of aventures,' had given the company a *Tale* that is anything but merry. It occurred to Chaucer that the Clerk might explain that he wishes to 'stinte of ernestful matere,' and recite, 'for the Wyves love of Bath,' a poem which is thus made incidentally to caricature to some extent the lady of Bath while it mainly satirizes the story of Griselda. The real co-ordination between the *Tales* of Wife and Clerk is thus reduced to the three verses:

> For which heere, for the Wyves love of Bathe,—
> Whos lyf and al hire secte God maynteyne
> In heigh maistrie, and elles were it scathe.

That this and the following *Envoy* are later additions to the original *Tale* is rendered a yet more probable conclusion by the fact that four of the best manuscripts, including the two very best of all, preserve at the end of the *Envoy* what appears to have been the ending of the *Tale* before the *Envoy* was written.

I find no evidence for Professor Kittredge's assertion that the Clerk was rigidly orthodox, or that he was especially interested in celibacy. Theology is not mentioned as one of his studies. He exhibits not the slightest interest in ecclesiastical discipline. The extremely high respect which he expresses for women marks him as a man of distinctly amiable virtues. Furthermore, he is a man of travel as well as of study. By Petrarch he has been treated with distinguished consideration, and obviously he shows an innocent vanity in introducing the company to his illustrious friend. To suppose that he finds 'gall and wormwood' in the words of the Wife

of Bath, and after long dissembling, attacks her with 'smiling ur-
banity' and 'in mordant irony' is to suppose things hardly consistent
one with another, to miss the airy lightness of the *Envoy*—which
is perfectly good-humored—and gratuitously to degrade the Clerk.

But the *Envoy* is undoubtedly made the means of introducing
the *Merchant's Tale*. The Merchant has no feeling for the religious
significance of the *Clerk's Tale*. Like the *Envoy*, he thinks of the
story of Griselda only as a story of married life, and he has little
faith in women who seem meek and patient like Griselda. In a
sense, therefore, he takes issue with the Clerk, and to this extent
Group E gives us a debate. But by no means does it follow that
the Wife of Bath holds 'the centre of the stage,' or even that she is
'in the foreground.' Rather does all literary perspective disappear.

For in spite of brilliant details, the *Merchant's Tale* is very
inartistically told. It is nearly as much out of character for the
Merchant as the Clerk's *Envoy* is for the Clerk. For though the Merchant, in his *Headlink*, begins with words of great bitterness about
women, the misogyny of his *Tale* itself is not consistently maintained. The tyrannous jealousy of January, the husband, is depicted in terms that transfer a large share of our sympathy to May,
the young wife, whose error, we are naïvely assured, is only that
she took compassion on a handsome young man who was languish-
ing for love of her. A long eulogy of matrimony loses not a little of
its intended effect of irony because the irony is long sustained without being obvious. A passage repeating the language and ideas of
the Wife of Bath leads us to expect that May, the wife, is going
to play the bully, whereas she skillfully maintains, everywhere,
the outward appearance of a submissive and a devoted wife. The
reference to the Wife of Bath is so introduced that there is serious
doubt who is speaking *in propria persona*, Chaucer, The Merchant,
or Justinus the friend of January. It is made almost the most striking lapse from dramatic propriety in the entire *Canterbury Tales*.
It is introduced indolently and pedantically, as if to save time and
labor, rather than to co-ordinate the *Tale* with the Wife of Bath.
And to whatever degree the Merchant repeats ideas from the *Wife's
Prolog* he does not take issue with her. So far from keeping the
Wife of Bath 'in the foreground,' or in 'the centre of the stage,' the

Merchant's Tale serves rather to show that, for the moment, there is neither foreground nor center to hold. Literary perspective, in fact, disappears.

The *Franklin's Tale* is very beautifully co-ordinated with the Squire's. The story of the 'faucoun peregrine' is expressive of great sensibility and compassion, far more so than the Wife's discourse on 'gentillesse,' which is distinctly argumentative. Not only does the Squire actually use the words *gentil, gentillesse,* some nine or ten times, but he is telling a tale of courtly love and tender sensibility. Surely there is every reason to suppose that the Franklin is entirely candid when he appears to take his cue from the Squire, even for his introductory discourse on 'gentillesse.' For in fact, the *Franklin's Tale* is barely if at all co-ordinated with anything that precedes the Squire's. The mere mention of sovereignty and service hardly reminds us of the Wife of Bath; neither does the mention of the praise which clerks have given to patience inevitably recall the Clerk of Oxford. And there is absolutely nothing that has as yet been tortured into a reference or allusion by the Franklin to the Merchant.

On the other hand the Franklin is in a number of ways co-ordinated with the Squire, and if some of these are subtle or even fortuitous, others are deliberate and unmistakable, and the import of the whole is not open to a doubt. Whichever of the four chief characters of the *Franklin's Tale* may appear to us the most generous, there is no doubt that Aurelius and Dorigen are the most prominent. And Aurelius, as Professor Kittredge ingeniously points out, is a young squire with just such graces and accomplishments as Chaucer's pilgrim Squire possesses, and as the Franklin wishes his own son to acquire. The story of Aurelius is now used as a compliment to the pilgrim Squire, and indirectly to his father, the pilgrim Knight. On previous occasions we may believe, if we will, that Aurelius has been held up as an example to the Franklin's graceless son. Hence the heart-felt eloquence of the beautiful little discourse on mutual subjection and forbearance.

Nor does this exhaust the exquisite adjustment of the *Franklin's Tale* alike to the character of the teller and to the situation. Whether by accident, by instinct, or by design, the Franklin chooses the very happiest moment and method to introduce himself to the attention of his social superiors. I find it difficult to believe that he is at the same time thinking of the Wife of Bath.

The Franklin confesses with regret that he has never studied Marcus Tullius Cicero, a name whose luster Petrarch had recently renewed. But Chaucer seems at least to have heard of Cicero's treatise on 'gentillesse,' the *De Amicitia*, though he may have confused it with the *De Beneficiis* of Seneca when he bade Scogan 'thenke on Tullius Kyndenesse.' If we may take the beautiful discourse on mutual forbearance and subjection as an attempt on the part of Chaucer or the Franklin to give us a medieval *De Amicitia*, the Franklin's reference to Cicero is explained. And, indeed, I know of no reason why we should not so understand the Franklin's sermon, even though the Franklin emphasizes Christian and medieval virtues, and includes and even emphasizes marriage as a form of friendship.

Certainly it is a mistake to regard the Franklin's sermon as primarily concerned with matrimony. There is a long passage of twenty-six lines in which women, love, and friendship are mentioned, but never marriage. Dorigen and Aurelius are unmarried one to another. The Franklin is obviously interested in the Squire, in his own son and in 'gentillesse.' He does not mention his own wife, nor does he evince any pre-occupation with matrimony. And certainly he cannot be said to bring a debate on matrimony to a 'triumphant conclusion' so long as his *Tale* is followed in any degree of proximity by the *Second Nun's Tale* of the unconsummated marriage of Saint Cecilia, which might easily be drawn into the debate by just such processes of reasoning as those by which the debate itself has been constructed.

It is not the least defect of Professor Kittredge's interpretation of Groups D, E, and F that he makes the Clerk and the Franklin surprize the reader by entering the debate quite as truly—or as hypothetically—as they surprize the Canterbury Pilgrims. An author or a playwright may surprize his characters as much as he pleases, but the moment he begins to surprize the reader or the spectator he begins to destroy the literary or dramatic illusion which it is his business to create. But this subject has been so competently treated by such writers as Messrs. William Archer and Brander Matthews that I gladly excuse myself from discussing it further, and I summarize my conclusions as follows:

The debate on, or discussion of, matrimony, amounts to this: Both Wife and Merchant discuss matrimony, deliberately, formally, and fully, but without taking issue one with another; and the Merchant takes issue with the Clerk, not so much as to matrimony as concerning the sincerity and virtue of women. The Merchant also incorporates in his *Tale* two debates, one on matrimony, the other as to the worth of women.

On the other hand the *Wife's Prolog* and *Tale* find their most unifying theme neither in heresy, in schism, nor even in polemic, but in the Wife's practical search for a sixth husband. The Clerk is interested in matrimony merely because it typifies the Christian life. His *Tale* is demonstrably unco-ordinated with the Wife's talk until we reach a casual allusion to the Wife at the very end. The Clerk's *Envoy* was originally written to satirize the story of Griselda, and not to caricature the Wife of Bath. It is not in character for the Clerk. The *Merchant's Tale* is out of character for the teller, and mentions the Wife of Bath in such a way as to destroy literary perspective rather than to place the Wife in a foreground or center. The position of Group F with reference to D and E is uncertain. If it had to be related to D—which it does not—we should do well to place F before D rather than after E. The Franklin evinces no interest in any individual pilgrims except Our Host, the Squire, and possibly by implication the Knight. He discusses marriage only as a form of friendship. His *Tale* cannot be said to terminate any discussion of marriage so long as it is followed in any degree of proximity by the *Second Nun's Tale*. In fact, Groups D, E, and F, taken in their entirety, are far from constituting a 'complete and highly finished' 'act' in 'Chaucer's Human Comedy.'

NOTES

1. *Chaucer's Discussion of Marriage, in Modern Philology*, IX, pp. 436–467 (April, 1912); *Chaucer and his Poetry* (Harvard University Press, 1915), pp. 185–210.

2. Kittredge, *Chaucer and His Poetry*, p. 186. Lounsbury, *Studies in Chaucer*, vol. II, p. 526.

JAMES SLEDD

The Clerk's Tale: The Monsters and The Critics

IN THE study of the *Clerk's Tale*, the chief problems have been taken to be the morality and probability of character and action. The Marquis Walter marries the peasant girl Griselda, after first exacting from her a promise of complete obedience. Griselda becomes the perfect wife and lady, but Walter determines to test her patience and obedience and proceeds to do so most severely. He takes her two children from her in their infancy, ostensibly to murder them, actually to have them tenderly but secretly reared. Griselda surrenders the children, patiently and obediently. After some years, Walter pretends that he will put away his wife and take another, and sends Griselda back to her peasant's cottage. Patiently and obediently, she goes, but she is not left in peace for long. Walter summons her again to the palace, to receive his new wife and the wedding guests. Griselda is all patience and obedience, ready and skilful to do her master's will. As a final test, she is publicly called upon to praise the bride, and when her patience and obedience bend but do not break, the Marquis drops his pretenses and takes her again into his loving arms. The pretended bride is Griselda's long-lost daughter, the bride's brother her little son; and they all live happily ever after.

From the beginning, as Petrarch, who was one of Chaucer's sources, directly tells us,[1] and as Chaucer makes equally clear in his somewhat different way, two very different effects have been produced by this sad story. Some readers have been moved to compassion and wonder, others to contempt and disbelief; and for some generations now, the contemptuous and the skeptical have outnumbered the compassionate admirers. The fact remains that Boccaccio, Petrarch, Chaucer, and dozens of others have found

Reprinted, by permission, from *Modern Philology*, LI (1953), 73-82. Copyright, 1953, by The University of Chicago.

the story worth telling, and that countless readers have found it worth reading. Walter and Griselda, either or both, may be desperately wicked, and their actions improbable or impossible; but Chaucer's telling of their story cannot be abruptly dismissed as an unfortunate episode in an otherwise commendable poetic career. I think one can say without undue solemnity that the *Clerk's Tale* deserves and demands consideration, not as a monument to a departed taste, but as a tale whose admittedly limited values still can be perceived, though perhaps not deeply felt; and it is part of my thesis in this moderately solemn paper that in the present century the tale has suffered because outstanding scholars have too hastily condemned it.

The first of the representative studies to which I shall refer was both witty in itself and the cause of wit in other men: Kittredge's famous article entitled 'Chaucer's Discussion of Marriage,' which appeared some forty years ago. To the more moderate statements in that article, most students have given full assent, whether they have been interested in the tales as tales or as dramatic speeches; and a certain exaggeration of the dramatic aspects is due simply to the fact that Kittredge was writing to redress a balance. In Kittredge's view, the study and criticism of 'each tale in and for itself' was perfectly proper, though much had been lost because the tales were read *only* as isolated units. He was at his most persuasive in showing the extent of that loss. As a result, Chaucerians have since rather generally accepted even his extreme statement that structurally, the tales which the pilgrims tell 'are only speeches that are somewhat longer than common, entertaining in and for themselves (to be sure), but primarily significant, in each case, because they illustrate the speaker's character and opinions, or show the relations of the travelers to one another in the progressive action of the Pilgrimage.' Here Kittredge claims a good deal more than one need claim in order to maintain the theory of a Marriage Group, as various scholars have maintained it, before and after 1912; for one can do full justice to the dramatic element in the *Tales* without slighting them as narratives.

The consequences of the Kittredge version of the theory, even when allowance is made for rhetorical overstatements, are rather striking. For him, one of the finished acts of 'Chaucer's Human Comedy . . . begins with the Wife of Bath's Prologue and ends with the Tale of the Franklin,' thus including the *Clerk's Tale* as its fourth large unit. The 'subject' of this finished act 'is Marriage, which is discussed from several points of view, as the most important problem in organized society. The solution of the problem brings the act to an end' when the Franklin summarizes the whole debate and presents his and Chaucer's doctrine of forbearance and equality in Christian marriage—'a definitive conclusion which we are to accept as a perfect rule of faith and practice.' In short, the Marriage Group is not only dramatic; it is a problem play. Presumably, then, one's ultimate judgment on the Group would be rhetorical or moral or sociological; but since Chaucer presents his doctrine of marriage dramatically, and since the speeches in the drama are tales which the speakers use for their own rhetorical purposes, this ultimate judgment would rest on an intricate series of earlier judgments, rhetorical, moral, sociological, and poetic as well. The student who accepts a Marriage Group must develop elaborate critical machinery in order to deal with it, in its parts and as a whole; but such subtlety has not marked discussions of the *Clerk's Tale*.

The hidden complexity of Kittredge's theory is no objection to it, though one might wish that so simple a doctrine of marriage had not demanded so much maneuvering for its expression; but the consequences of his exaggeration of his basic contention are more serious. Despite some eminently sound remarks on the *Clerk's Tale* as a tale, Kittredge in his article leaves the impression that he could not quite stomach that monster Walter and his monstrous wife. The story as story is treated as infinitely less important than the story as a dramatic speech expressing one of the opposed views of marriage, so that followers of Kittredge have every inducement to discuss the drama and every excuse for ignoring the tale. That is a dangerous predicament, as Professor Malone has shown,[2] for it follows either that Chaucer shared the taste of his age—a perverted taste—or that he deliberately told a bad story in order to make a good drama. Even more unfortunately, the drama itself becomes hard to defend, since the neglect of the story forces gay conjecture, the discovery, if not the invention, of something to take the story's place. A moderate statement of the theory of a Marriage Group imposes no necessity for such conjecture; but unless one states his theory with circumspection, he will find himself neglecting the tales which Chaucer did write, inventing dramatic episodes which Chaucer did not write, and yet exposing Chaucer, when all is said, as a botcher who could not make his own intentions clear. For a solution, therefore, of the problems of morality and probability in the *Clerk's Tale*, considered as a tale, the student cannot go to Kittredge, whose tactics are really to submerge the narrative problems in the problems of the drama.

Like so much else of the best Chaucerian scholarship, the next two studies which I shall consider were partly inspired by a remark of Kittredge. I mean Professor Griffith's book on the origin of the Griselda story, and the article by Mr. W. A. Cate on the same topic.[3] For Griffith and Cate, the assumption of the standards of realistic fiction makes possible the initial assertion that the story is peculiar, contradictory, and irrational. Readers have not always been affected in this way, for the frankly marvelous has not always been in disrepute; but Mr. Griffith's Griselda and Mr. Cate's Griselda is no longer the saintly heroine of a piteous, marvelous, and gracious tale. She and her story have undergone a sea-change into something illogical, incoherent, and incomprehensible, and not all the praise which Griffith and Cate give to various tellers of the story can hide their conviction that there is something radically wrong with it.

Beginning, then, with this conviction, they seek an explanation of the improbabilities which Boccaccio, Petrarch, and Chaucer all tolerated; and essentially, Griffith and Cate agree in the explanation which they find. Griffith, said Cate, 'is . . . entirely correct in his belief that the Griselda novella represents a literary treatment of a highly rationalized sub-group . . . the "Patience Group" of Cupid and Psyche folktales . . . , and . . . Gualtieri's domineering, illogical, and ill-motivated actions are caused by—and are an expression of—his otherworld nature.' Griselda is the mortal wife of an other-world lover, and only when this fact is understood can the problems of her story be resolved.

No one could question this statement of the origin of the Griselda story. One *can* ask exactly what follows from it, and what does not. It has not been made clear to me that the story is so thoroughly improbable as Griffith and Cate seem to believe, or that to understand Chaucer's version one must keep looking over one's shoulder at a folk tale of which Chaucer knew nothing. The misconception which I am getting at only creeps round the edges of the studies by Griffith and Cate, but in some of the reviews of their work it stands out in clear daylight, as naked as Walter's bride. In the words of one review, 'There is no doubt that Griffith's theory does succeed in explaining much in Boccaccio's and Chaucer's stories that has hitherto seemed peculiar and even repulsive.'[4] Transferring the epithets, I would call this judgment peculiar, repulsive, and unfair to an excellent book, in which some admirable things are said about Boccaccio's story. The judgment is unfair because, by claiming too much, it brings suspicion on a genuine accomplishment, and it is repulsive because its consequences are bad criticism and hence bad history. A knowledge of literary origins may sharpen our appreciation of narrative success and show us the causes of narrative failure, but it is a means to interpretation, not a substitute for it; and until the literary versions of the Griselda story have been interpreted independently and in their own terms, we cannot even compare them accurately with the folk tale from which they sprang. Griselda and Walter are the grandchildren of monsters; their own condition must be determined by a separate inquiry.

The fourth and last study which I shall examine tells us much more about the *Clerk's Tale* itself than any of the other three, from which it differs in its scope and in its purpose. In his notable book, *The Literary Relationships of Chaucer's 'Clerkes Tale,'*[5] Professor Severs set himself an ambitious task: 'to determine precisely the poet's sources for his tale of Griseldis; to establish satisfactory texts of the sources; and to examine the poet's treatment of them.' I shall say nothing of his careful study of the manuscripts and texts of Chaucer's immediate sources, Petrarch's Latin and an anonymous version in French prose. In fact, I am concerned only with Severs' first and fourth chapters, much less than one-half of a work whose solid merit has been generally recognized. In these chapters, perhaps because Chaucer followed his sources closely and 'made no changes in the sequence of events which he found' there, Severs accepts, without structural analysis of the story, the conclusion of Griffith and Cate. 'There are present,' he says, 'in the tale of Griselda certain vestigial relics of the pre-literary form—elements which, either illogical or impertinent in the literary versions, become fully comprehensible only when we realize that they are traces of the primitive folk tale.' This conclusion he supports by a rather terrifying list of illogicalities and impertinences, in which it is taken for granted that what was originally magical in the Griselda story 'has become monstrous.'[6]

A difficulty arises when it turns out that Chaucer, in Severs' account, did nothing to make the story less absurd. On the other hand, his 'chief contribution seems to have been a heightening and intensification of the contrasts' which the story offered, so that Walter becomes 'more unfeeling' and Griselda 'more submissive.' 'The essential qualities of character and setting' were thus 'brought into more vivid contrast,' and 'the successive situations [were] developed into a more effective, more arresting plot.' It is hard to see how an already absurd plot could be made more effective by heightening its absurdity, but the key to the argument, if I follow it at all, seems to lie partly in Severs' method and partly in the term 'contrast.' Since Chaucer did not change 'the sequence of events,' Severs compares the *Clerk's Tale* with its sources, not structurally, but passage by passage, phrase by phrase. If isolated passages in Chaucer seem somehow better than the corresponding passages in his sources, and if the diction of his English poetry seems somehow more effective than the diction of the French and Latin prose on which it was based, then one is tempted to conclude that Chaucer achieved an 'almost magical transformation.' The only theoretical basis which I can imagine for such reasoning would be a concept of a good narrative poem as a series of episodes strung together in defiance of probability, but full of vivid contrasts and described in 'vivid, connotative terms'; and I am driven to conclude, with all respect, that it is some such notion which Severs asks us to entertain.

What now emerges from this brief survey of scholarship? Chiefly the fact that the problems of morality and probability which the *Clerk's Tale* poses have been treated, in the best and most representative studies, as insoluble within the tale. Kittredge would submerge them in the problems of the Marriage Group; Griffith and Cate would display their origin in the Cupid and Psyche tales; Severs would recognize them and display their origin still more fully, but tacitly dismiss them as inessential. If the *Clerk's Tale* merits the amount of attention which has already been devoted to it, surely it deserves more direct treatment of these central issues.

The moral question is not just one question, but two at least. In one of its forms, it is the question why alleged cruelty and criminal stupidity are represented either without proper abhorrence, or even with the praise that should be reserved for virtue; we are asked, it is said, to tolerate an intolerable tyrant, and to admire a dolt. In another form, the moral question is whether the *Clerk's Tale* offers us *sentence* or *solas*, whether it is a sermon or a story or both together; our answer here will affect the standards of judgment which we apply to the tale. Its early tellers, Petrarch and Chaucer included, have of course invited a moral judgment. The adventures of Patient Grizel have been variously used to teach submission to the will of God, or female virtue as a means to get rich husbands; and no one would deny the currency, in medieval and modern times, of the belief that poetry is an accessory to moral philosophy. On the other hand, there is abundant evidence, from Petrarch's first two readers onward, that the story was valued 'in and for itself,' and if one grants the possibility of less limited readings, one may justly maintain that a simple narrative analysis is at least an indispensable first step. I shall therefore say little, and that little in my conclusion, about the second form of the moral question, and proceed at once to the first, which Lounsbury raises somewhat crudely, but typically and with his usual vigor.

According to Lounsbury, the events of the Griselda story, 'while susceptible of poetic treatment, are in no way consonant with the truth of life,' and its 'central idea . . . is . . . too revolting . . . for any skill in description to make it palatable. Griselda does not even exhibit the degree of sensibility which exists in the females of the brute creation. Her patience outrages every instinct of maternity, and the respect which men pay to that quality in woman,' so that 'the modern man, and still more the modern woman, . . . is much disposed to give it the name of weak-spirited, and even despicable.'[7] She is a ninny, Walter a brute, and the conduct of both as preposterous as it is unreal.

If one makes the necessary assumptions, all this, and more, is undoubtedly true. It is not only Griselda's children, whose sex life will be ruined by their childhood experiences, that one has, to worry about. There is also, to take but one example, the reputation of the Pope, whose counterfeit letters are made the excuse for the pretended divorce. Once it is assumed that the fictions of the fourteenth century may be equated with realities half a millennium later, and that every medieval story must have a 'central idea' acceptable to the 'modern woman,' the irrelevant inferences which a tolerably agile mind can draw are unlimited; the *Clerk's Tale* can be made to look as silly as the assumptions on which the moralist condemns it.

Lounsbury himself was unwilling to go so far, and his own qualifications take much of the sting out of his charges, which indeed are very simply answered. If a storyteller is to get under way at all, he must take for granted some principles of moral judgment, principles which he might be quite unwilling to accept or advocate in real life or which he might hope to transform and transcend in the very work in which initially he assumed them. For the purposes of the *Clerk's Tale,* wifely obedience to husband, lord, and benefactor is explicitly set up as a good, and in accordance with the medieval tradition of exalting a single virtue in its essence, other signs of Griselda's goodness are not much needed. In fact, more highly detailed and less objective representation, as surely as ill-judged humor, might have wrecked this secular saint's legend, in which extreme cruelty and extreme long-suffering had to be pictured without arousing disgust for brutality or contempt for the absurd. Medieval readers were less troubled by Griselda's obedience than we are, as anyone can see who looks into their treatises on female duty; but my argument is not that in any world of reality, medieval or modern, Griselda would be looked upon with favor. When one brings the world of fiction and the world of reality too abruptly into contact, both worlds are distorted; the Clerk's 'Envoy' makes capital of the distortion. Instead, my argument is that Griselda is represented as supremely good, by signs which medieval readers of her story could not take *except* as signs of goodness, and we have no more right to take them as signs of badness than we have to mistranslate Middle English. Griselda's superhuman endurance arouses wonder, her unmerited sufferings provoke compassion; to the production of this effect, the judgment that she is good is an essential preliminary; but the presuppositions of a poem are not to be confused with the text of a sermon. We need not write a history of medieval taste, therefore, to discover the narrative values of the *Clerk's Tale*, which other means make clear enough; and though the remoteness of the tale's presuppositions may prevent us from realizing those values fully, our difficulty will be lessened if we remember that Chaucer does not invite us, but ultimately forbids us, to apply the rules of his fictional world outside his fiction.

What values *other* than narrative values we may discover is a question which can best be dealt with, as I have suggested, when the narrative has been more fully explored; the pious reflections of Petrarch and others may grow naturally out of the story, but the story cannot be evolved from the pious reflections. What I shall say of the repeated objection to its improbability is hardly more novel than the objection itself, and I shall not be foolish enough to claim that in the *Clerk's Tale* all problems are happily solved. A number of defects, as the folklorists have well shown, were inherent in the material; for to the extent that Walter and Griselda are represented as human and subject to the known limitations of fourteenth-century humanity, the original motivation of the folk tale must somehow be replaced. What the folklorists have not shown so well is the method by which and the extent to which that replacement was accomplished in the literary versions, where at least a partially successful effort was made to transform the generally improbable into the specifically probable. The difficulty of the task now seems disproportionate to the modest reward which the best solution offered. To destroy the extremes in the Griselda story would be to destroy its effect, but a wrong treatment could make those same extremes either ludicrous or sickening. The behavior of Walter and Griselda had to be prepared for by the quiet establishment of initial premises from which that behavior might follow, and their actions had then to be narrated with the kind and amount of detail which would make them moving, not revolting or grotesque. Thus the first two parts of the *Clerk's Tale* present the characters of Walter and Griselda and relate them one to the other in such a way that when later the element of the marvelous is introduced, we are receptive to it. The marvelous is then frankly depicted as marvelous, with reassuring remarks thrown in by the narrator at peculiarly difficult points, so that, having accepted the first two parts of the story, we are brought, not unwillingly, to accept what follows. Chaucer proceeds, as Severs has indicated, to make all he can of some situations; but he does not push Walter's cruelty beyond the limits of humanity, and Griselda's rather stylized grief is neither agonizing nor insipid. In this way, when the folk tale has passed under three pairs of skilful hands, it has been transformed as successfully as it could be; its monsters remain rare birds, but no longer monstrous.

Part I of the tale, to be specific, is devoted entirely to Walter; he must be the best possible man who could be capable of so cruelly testing his wife. He is represented, therefore, as young, strong, courteous, honorable, and intelligent, a capable ruler who could make himself both loved and feared by his subjects and who could be moved by considerations of the common good; but he is not without less admirable qualities, notably self-indulgence and devotion to his present pleasure. In his exchange of speeches with his subjects when they entreat him to marry and promise to provide him with a noble bride, he is the traditional skeptic, fearful that in marriage he will lose his liberty; and he grounds his insistence that he will choose his own wife on blunt distrust of heredity as well as on faith in God. His fear of marriage motivates his later demand upon Griselda for a premarital oath of complete obedience, and his distrust of heredity prepares for his choice of a peasant.[8] In Part II it will appear that he has already decided, if ever he should marry, to marry Griselda, whose goodness he has had the sense to recognize; but with typical self-will and secretiveness, he conceals this decision until the day of the wedding. To his subjects, he says nothing of his choice; but he charges them, on their lives, that they will reverence whatever wife he takes, and he demands a vow that against his choice they will never complain. If he can demand and get such obedience from his chief subjects, it is hardly improbable that he will demand and get it from his poorest peasants; and if he marries a peasant, his attendant lords will certainly expect behavior which will try their patience.

No such complexities are needed in the characterization of Griselda. She is poor, but beautiful and good, and she draws her strength not only from hardship and her long self-sacrifice in caring for her father. Even before her introduction into the story is signalized by the announcement of her excellent virtue, we are carefully reminded that God can send His grace into the very stalls of oxen; and since marriage has been suggested to Walter and accepted by him for the common good, we know that Griselda will be enabled, in so important a matter, to keep her oath of obedience to her benefactor, lord, and husband. By the introduction of Christian assumptions, the initial framework of largely secular values and probabilities is thus gradually extended. If the prototype of Walter had superhuman power in the folk tale, the Griselda of Chaucer's version enjoys the grace of God; and at her marriage, the power of divinely favored virtue is immediately manifested. Griselda is transformed from the good and beautiful peasant girl to the still more lovely, virtuous, and capable lady, the perfect mistress of her household, and noted for her skill in public affairs. The story may now proceed with the old marvels of the folk tale; but they have been placed on a new foundation, and they have been rendered available (it might be further argued) as the bearers of a new significance.

With Part III, the testing begins, and from this point, as I have said, the marvelous is frankly but not carelessly accepted. The narrator assumes a disarming role, with his direct condemnation of Walter's cruelty but his simple assertion that such things can be; for

wedded men ne knowe no mesure,
Whan that they fynde a pacient creature.

236

Chaucer can hardly be blamed, it might be said in passing, if his attempt to expand the limits of human nature by poetic fiat has misled some of his readers to defend him by asserting that the world of the *Clerk's Tale* is the real world and that there have, too, been men like Walter and women like Griselda. Wiser readers have noted that Griselda's strength, in the world which Chaucer and the others created for her, is made believable by repeated scriptural echoes that remind us of its source. These echoes are heard, for example, in Griselda's farewell to her daughter and in her words to Walter at their separation:

'Naked out of my fadres hous,' quod she,
'I cam, and naked moot I turne agayn.'

God's grace, our knowledge of Walter's secret pity and repentance, and the narrator's broad hints that all may yet be well, combine to take the edge off Griselda's sufferings and to assure us that Walter is not so ruthless as she might believe; and as the carefully ordered tests grow more severe, the reassurances become more obvious. Griselda is tested first by the loss of her daughter and then of her more precious man-child, only less dear to her than her tormentor: but the scene in which the boy is taken from her is deliberately left undeveloped; we are promptly told, quite bluntly, that 'al fil for the beste'; and if Griselda thinks her children dead, we know that they are safely cared for. More concentrated suffering is imposed on Griselda by her dismissal, by the summons to welcome her successor, and last by the order to praise the second bride; yet we really cannot worry too much about the children, or Griselda, or the Pope himself, for even before the dismissal, the grand restoration is already being prepared. Whatever other merits the *Clerk's Tale* may have, it does not operate through variety or surprise. Chaucer takes every opportunity for pathos, but comfortable pathos; and he hurries over those parts of the story, such as the twelve long years of Griselda's separation from her children, which any but a summary and objective treatment would make too painful. Gross sentimentality would indeed be a more likely charge against the *Clerk's Tale* than that of improbability, which takes a last blow from Walter's words at the reconciliation: ' "This is ynogh, Grisilde myn," quod he,' precisely as he had received her promise of obedience before the marriage; and the repetition of the line seems to suggest again that the story is all of a piece.

It is far from a perfect tale, as I would be the last to deny. If sentimentality is one likely charge against it, plain dulness is another, for interesting complications—Grisilde answerde and seyde, 'Stynt thy clappe!'—interesting complications cannot be expected from a story how the marvelous patience of a pious wife converts a husband from cruel suspicion to the ultimate conviction that she is really what she seems. Through it all, Griselda must remain immutable, and Walter's activity consists solely in teasing her and wondering how she stands it. Chaucer does his best to make Griselda a convincingly human embodiment of patience and Christian humility, and he makes the most of her big situations without allowing them to become grotesquely painful; but I do not wish that the *Clerk's Tale* were longer.

I will, however, risk one word more in its defense. Dulness and sentimentality are perhaps harsh terms for a tale which rather neatly evades the blunt opposition of mere sermon to mere story, and the Clerk's is such a tale. Whatever one thinks about the categories of the didactic and the mimetic or about the idea of medieval poetry as one vast composite denunciation of cupidity, the simple narrative analysis which I have attempted must somewhere be made; yet the Clerk's *moralitee* is too obvious to be ignored, and need not be received with embarrassed silence. Briefly and tentatively, I should say that what is put into the story in one form is extracted from it in another, and that this is the answer to the second of my 'moral questions.' Standards of conduct are assumed in order that the story may have its proper effect of compassionate wonder; they are raised to a higher level when the story is given its moral application. Similarly, divine grace and the transcendent goodness of Griselda, which help to make her ultimate triumph probable, are made the bases of the argument for Christian submission to the will of God. In this way, the effectiveness of the story becomes the source of power in the exemplum, and the presuppositions of the poem, though distinct from the text of the sermon, are integrated with it.

The discovery, if not the invention, of a higher integration stretches the limits of moderate solemnity. It has been suggested that Chaucer himself had some reservations about his story, and one might guess that his attitude toward it was somewhat mixed. At any rate, he was willing to risk the experiment, in the 'Envoy,' of clashing his world of fiction against reality. The experiment worked. He still gets his laugh, and by laughing himself he managed to keep the best of both worlds. Perhaps the lesson for us, if I may be allowed a moral and an envoy of my own, is that our critical methods have sometimes been too simple even for the *Clerk's Tale*. It is a fairly straightforward, middling kind of yarn, but oversimple assumptions have led to its unjust condemnation as flatly bad; and these thoughtless assumptions, for example the confusion of fiction with reality, may cause more serious misjudgments of better pieces.

I will take a single instance. If the pilgrimage is dated April, 1387, then the Squire, who was twenty years old, was conceived in July, 1366. At that time the Knight was in the Middle East. I once drew the consequences of these facts and submitted my parody to a learned journal. The editors returned it, not because it wasn't funny, as perhaps it wasn't, but because it was, they said, too 'speculative.'

I would have called it an illegitimate inference.

NOTES

1. Cf. A. S. Cook, 'The First Two Readers of Petrarch's Tale of Griselda,' *MP*, xv (1918), 633–43.

2. Kemp Malone, *Chapters on Chaucer* (Baltimore, 1951), pp. 210 ff., 222 ff.

3. D. D. Griffith, *The Origin of the Griselda Story* (Seattle, 1931); W. A. Cate, 'The Problem of the Origin of the Griselda Story,' *SP*, xxix (1932), 389–405.

4. *Year's Work in English Studies*, xii (1931), 91.

5. J. Burke Severs, *The Literary Relationships of Chaucer's 'Clerkes Tale'* (New Haven, 1942).

6. Since this assumption is almost universally made, I take a convenient phrasing of it from Nevill Coghill, *The Poet Chaucer* (London, 1949), p. 140.

7. Thomas R. Lounsbury, *Studies in Chaucer* (New York, 1892), iii, 340 ff.

8. Walther Küchler, 'Über Herkunft und Sinn von Boccaccios Griselda-Novelle,' *Die neueren Sprachen*, xxxiii (1925), 250 f.

C. HUGH HOLMAN

Courtly Love in the Merchant's and the Franklin's Tales

THAT Chaucer's Merchant's Tale and Franklin's Tale have structural similarities has often been pointed out,[1] and their similarities have usually been explained by George Lyman Kittredge's provocative theory that certain of the *Canterbury Tales* fall into a 'marriage group.' However, the marriage group is unproved speculation,[2] is not essential to a comprehension or appreciation of the dramatic quality of the *Canterbury Tales*,[3] and in the instance of the Merchant's and the Franklin's tales has tended to obscure the true nature of their similarities and the significance of their differences. There is no need either to accept or reject Professor Kittredge's theory in examining these stories; it is necessary, however, to prevent the concept of the marriage group from so clouding the tales themselves that we fail to see what actually is in them. It is my belief that these two stories may be rewardingly examined in terms of the medieval concept of courtly love, and this essay is an attempt to show that their numerous parallels and their significant structural differences are closely allied to the conventions of courtly love.

The similarities between the two tales are almost too self-evident to need enumeration. In each are three main characters: a husband-knight, his wife, and a squire who is the would-be lover of the wife. In each the squire, wasting away for love of his lady, makes known his passionate desires. In each the husband is tem-

Reprinted, by permission, from *ELH, A Journal of English Literary History*, XVIII (1951), 241-52.

porarily removed from the scene: in the Merchant's Tale by his blindness, in the Franklin's by his absence in England. In each a major crisis hinges on supernatural happenings: in the Merchant's Tale on the intervention of Pluto and Proserpine, in the Franklin's on the magical labors of the clerk of Orleans. In each a garden plays an important part as the intended place of rendezvous. In each the wife is finally restored to her husband, and the reader is left with the feeling that nothing deeply significant has happened to change the fundamental relationships that existed among the characters before the crises. No sooner has the initial situation of his story been sketched than the Merchant begins a long celebration of the joys and felicities of marriage. It is so excellent a paean that it would probably be regarded as one of Chaucer's most profound statements on marriage were it not embedded in a story of such dark cynicism as the Merchant's. At the same place in the Franklin's Tale an almost equally excellent section is devoted to the bases of married felicity. Here the obvious similarities between the stories end, and in other respects they seem, on the surface, to be completely different. The Franklin's is one of the gentlest, most gracious, smiling tales ever spoken with unhumorous dignity, and the Merchant's one of the most savagely obscene, angrily embittered, pessimistic, and unsmiling tales in our language.

But if these two stories are considered in the light of courtly love, their parallels do not stop here; for the tales, although violently dissimilar, become recto and verso of the same page representing complementary aspects of Chaucer's portrayal of courtly love. Whether they are or are not in the schema of a marriage debate, both certainly are concerned with people caught in the conflict between the demands of matrimony and the courts of love. In the Merchant's Tale the people are a collection of lost souls who would destroy any institution no matter how excellent; in the Franklin's Tale they are people of such excellence and high good sense that they would make a worthy existence under almost any institution. Yet, despite this implied judgment of individual character and conduct, the structural patterns of the tales suggest a criticism of courtly love conventions.[4]

In English there has been perhaps no poet who served the Venus of courtly love with finer musical accompaniment than the Geoffrey Chaucer of the French period. As C. S. Lewis says, Chaucer was a poet of 'dream and allegory, of love-romance and erotic debate, of high style and profitable doctrine' to his fourteenth century audience.[5] That Chaucer actually knew Andreas Capellanus' *De Amore*, the codification of the religion of courtly love, is doubtful. But his early models, Machaut, Froissart, Deschamps, and *Le Roman de la Rose* had given graceful and sophisticated expression to the system that Marie de France's chaplain had expounded, and, as Karl Young has pointed out, Andreas's doctrines were widely known and pervasively influential in fourteenth century England, and certainly affected Chaucer.[6] *Troilus and Criseyde* is at once the apex of that portion of Chaucer's career in which courtly love was a major theme and his first strong questioning of the moral worthiness of its system of values.[7] It comes as the last, full-throated song of a man taking leave of his youth, an expression of what the Knight in the *Tales* might well have felt when his days as 'A lovyere and a lusty bacheler' had to yield to the sterner voice of 'his lordes werre.' The Chaucer who wrote it was not the same man who later wrote the *Canterbury Tales*, in the sense that the Squire is not yet the Knight, but the change was gradual, and epilogue of *Troilus* adumbrates the knight's holy wars.

The breath of a wholesome reality blows across Chaucer's pilgrims when they gather at the Tabard. The world in which they move is not the isolated garden of love where the rose of romance is to be plucked according to the rules of a misread Ovid; in fact, the garden may have become for Geoffrey the Pilgrim in some ways similar to that equally attractive garden which January maintains in order to distort some of the strength and joy of the world into weakness and lust. C. S. Lewis has argued that courtly love is no longer a force in Chaucer's writing in the period of the *Canterbury Tales*. However, Chaucer's continued use of the techniques and subjects of his earlier work, changed though his viewpoint concerning them may be, is quite evident; and we should naturally expect to find the courtly love system for which he was a spokesman in his French period playing some part in his later works. Courtly love conventions appear in the Wife of Bath's Tale,[8] in the Miller's Tale, with its husband, wife, and squire, and in the Merchant's and the Franklin's tales, as well as the Knight's Tale. The older subjects are not abandoned; they have merely been altered. The eternal enigma of man and woman is still paramount in Chaucer's mind, coloring almost everything he touches. But his concern now is more with that aspect of human love which Boethius considered 'an integral part of the universal love without which the whole created world cannot exist,'[9] than with courtly love which the religion of his day considered 'idealized extramarital sensuality.'[10] The question is from what point of view Chaucer looks at Andreas' doctrines; I believe that the employment he gave courtly love conventions in the Merchant's and the Franklin's tales indicates a criticism of and some distaste for courtly love.

Margaret Schlauch finds that the situation in the Merchant's dark story of deceit, lust, and vileness is 'like a perfectly serious thirteenth century French romance,' and believes that 'the plot makes fun of the general tenets of the code of *amour courtois*.' A comparison of the events of the Merchant's Tale with Andreas' code bears out her conclusion.

May is not in love with her husband; this is in keeping with courtly love conventions. Andreas teaches, 'One cannot love one's own wife but must love the wife of some other man.'[11] Damien, the love-sick squire has been criticized as lacking interest or sympathy, but this feeling comes from the fact that Damien is so perfect an illustration of the courtly love lover that he loses individuality because of the conventional nature of all his reactions. Andreas tells us, in his Rules of Love, 'Every lover regularly turns pale in the presence of his beloved. When a lover suddenly catches sight of his beloved his heart palpitates. . . . He whom the thought of love vexes eats and sleeps very little. . . . A true lover is constantly and without intermission possessed by the thought of his beloved.'[12] Of Damien Chaucer says:

> And ful of joye and blisse is every man,—
> Al but a squyer, highte Damyan,
> Which carf biforn the knyght ful many a day.
> He was so ravysshed on his lady May

That for the verray peyne he was ny wood.
Almoost he swelte and swowned ther he stood,
So soore hath Venus hurt hym with hire brond.

This sike Damyan in Venus fyr
So brenneth that he dyeth for desyr,
For which he putte his lyf in aventure.

In courtly love, complaints and lays were a manner of communication between lovers, and

But prively a penner gan he borwe,
And in a lettre wroot he al his sorwe,
In manere of a compleynt or a lay,
Unto his faire, fresshe lady May.

In courtly love convention, the life of the lover is in danger, secrecy
is essential, and the pity and generosity of the beloved are prime
virtues. Damien pleads to May:

'Mercy! and that ye nat discovere me . . .'

May's response to Damien's 'lay' is conventional:

But sooth is this, how that this fresshe May
Hath take swich impression that day,
For pitee of this sike Damyan,
That from hire herte she ne dryve kan
The remembrance for to doon hym ese.

Heere may ye se how excellent franchise
In wommen is, whan they hem narwe avyse.
Som tyrant is, as ther be many oon,
That hath an herte as hard as any stoon,
Which wolde han lat hym sterven in the place
Wel rather than han graunted hym hire grace;
And hem rejoysen in hire crueel pryde,
And rekke nat to been an homycide.

In the conventions of courtly love, the lover, on being looked upon
with favor by his lady, is ennobled and acquires great virtues. On
learning that he has his lady's favor,

> Up riseth Damyan the nexte morwe;
> Al passed was his siknesse and his sorwe.
> He kembeth hym, he proyneth hym and pyketh,
> He dooth al that his lady lust and lyketh;
> ... He is so plesant unto every man
> (For craft is al, whoso that do it kan)
> That every wight is fayn to speke hym good;
> And fully in his lady grace he stood.

Andreas instructs, 'Every attempt of a lover tends toward the enjoyment of the embraces of her whom he loves';[13] the whole aim of the plot in this story is adultery. The morality involved is that of the courts of love. May was bored with January, but to the courts of love, marriage was the institution of boredom. Damien was betraying the trust and friendship of his lord, but what is true of him is true to a greater degree of Lancelot. A blind husband is made a dupe, a foolish, goatish cockold; but the very aim of courtly love was to blind all husbands and make them dupes.

And Chaucer's language and imagery underscored the point. Not only was it Venus who kindled the fire that laid Damien waste; Chaucer says of the garden of January:

> For, out of doute, I verraily suppose
> That he that wroot the Romance of the Rose
> Ne koude of it the beautee wel devyse;
> Ne Priapus ne myghte nat suffise,
> Though he be god of gardyns, for to telle
> The beautee of the gardyn and the welle.

A little later he writes:

> O noble Ovyde, ful sooth seystou, God woot,
> What sleighte is it, thogh it be long and hoot,
> That Love nyl fynde it out in some manere?

The poem is written with the glitter and polish of French sophistication. May is described as a court lady:

> Hir fresshe beautee and hir age tendre,
> Hir myddel smal, hire armes longe and sklendre,

Hir wise governaunce, hir gentillesse,
Hir wommanly berynge, and hire sadnesse.

. . . she was lyk the brighte morwe of May,
Fulfild of alle beautee and plesaunce.

Orpheus, Amphion, Theodamus, Bacchus, 'laughing Venus,' Paris,
Helen, Pyramus and Thisbe—all add their luster to the telling. The
garden glows like a gem. Night descends with a richness of poetic
diction. The marriage feast glitters and pulses. The rapturous
Troilus never celebrated his Criseyde with more real beauty than
January's paraphrase of the Song of Songs. This is rich poetry of
the finest order, and yet it serves to illuminate a dark, cynical, and
unlovely tale. Certainly there is irony here, and it is irony subject
to another interpretation than that resulting from the Merchant's
bitterness about his own marriage.[14] Miss Schlauch's comment
seems justified: 'It is not only the characters whom Chaucer is
willing to condemn as individuals, but in part also their code.'[15]

That courtly love plays a large part in the Franklin's Tale is not
seriously disputed. The story opens with an account of the wooing
of Dorigen by Arveragus, which seems superficial in the courtly
love tradition in speaking of Arveragus' 'wo, his peyne, and his distresse,' but it culminates in marriage; as opposed to courtly love
which teaches that 'One cannot love one's own wife, but must love
the wife of some other man.'[16] Among their mutual agreements,
Dorigen and Arveragus abandon 'maistrie,' that bone of contention
in court of love disputes. And the poet applauds their wisdom in
abandoning both courtly love and 'maistrie':

> Who koude telle, but he hadde wedded be,
> The joye, the ese, and the prosperitee
> That is bitwixe an housbonde and his wyf?

a sentiment utterly at variance with the idea that ideal love is
extramarital. Into this happy relationship, as into the marriage of
January and May, is introduced a model courtly lover, Aurelius,
who is so similar in actions and motives to Damien that the feeling
that they are radically different characters comes from the fact that
Aurelius (unhappily from his viewpoint) is given an opportunity

to be generous and Damien is confronted with no such dilemma. We are told more about Aurelius than we are about Damien, but nothing about either that is in conflict with the other's character. Aurelius is a 'lusty squier, servant to Venus'; he loves Dorigen but dares not speak his love, 'save in his songes'; he made 'layes, Songes, compleintes, roundels, virelayes'; he

> But langwissheth as a furye dooth in helle;
> And dye he moste, he seyde, as dide Ekko
> For Narcisus, that dorste nat telle hir wo.

He bega Dorigen to

> 'Have mercy, sweete, or ye wol do me deye!'

Presented with a seemingly impossible task to perform,

> He to his hous is goon with sorweful herte.
> He seeth he may not fro his deeth asterte;
> Hym semed that he felte his herte colde.

> In langour and in torment furyus
> Two yeer and moore lay wrecche Aurelyus,
> Er any foot he myghte on erthe gon.

He prays to Phoebus and to Lady Venus; and does, in short, all that we should have expected Damien to do had May been less eager to receive his embraces.[17] And it is delightful irony that allows the worry about his lady-love of the 'wrecche Aurelyus' to change to worry about money after the climax of the story.

In Dorigen, however, we have a sharp contrast to that 'Pitee' and 'excellent franchise' which courtly love demanded and which May so gayly yielded. Dorigen's answer to Aurelius is utter treason to the religion of love:

> 'By thilke God that yaf me soule and lyf,
> Ne shal I nevere been untrewe wyf
> In word ne werk, as fer as I have wit;
> I wot been his to whom that I am knyt.'

We can imagine the ladies of a court of love reading such a reply with incredulous eyes and declaring, 'How plebian! *If* she means it!' But the intensity of her sorrow proves that she does mean it. And Arveragus, the depth of whose love we do not question, behaves in a manner foreign to the doctrines of courtly love. In his Rules of Love, Andreas declares, 'A man in love is always apprehensive. . . . Real jealousy always increases the feeling of love. . . . A slight presumption causes a lover to suspect his be-loved.'[18] Yet, on returning to his wife after a long absence,

> No thyng list hym to been ymaginatyf,
> If any wight hadde spoke, whil he was oute,
> To hire of love; he hadde of it no doute.
> He noght entendeth to no swich mateere.

Early in the story Chaucer enlists our sympathies *against* the courtly lover and *for* the preservation of the institution which courtly love attacked—marriage. The hero is the husband, the heroine the wife, the triumph that of conjugal love. How complete a reversal of the system of courtly love! And in contrast to the telling of the Merchant's Tale, the Franklin's is written with relative simplicity and quiet dignity. Although the Franklin is not altogether true to his promise not to use colors of rhetoric, the story he tells is far freer from rhetorical extravagance than the Merchant's Tale.

Thus it appears that the conventions of courtly love form the basic structural patterns for the Merchant's Tale and the Franklin's Tale. Each is a 'triangle' story of husband, wife, and lover, in which the lover, following the conventions of courtly love, attempts to persuade the wife to be unfaithful to her husband. The young squires in each are startlingly similar characters, both following the behavior patterns that courtly love assigned them. The wives differ in that Dorigen rejects as base the rôle courtly love assigns her while May accepts that rôle with pleasure. Although Chaucer treats May with some sympathy, it is clear that he regards Dorigen's decision as right. The husbands differ most; Arveragus is a perfect husband-lover, bound to his wife by strong and enduring bonds, one of the principal of which is trust. January is a perversion of marriage, whose motives are sensual and who converts what his era considered a venial sin into a deadly one. It is this difference between the wives, that determines the divergent directions of the plots. Those who make of marriage something noble and splendid achieve enviable happiness, while those who seek pleasure in the pattern of lust or of courtly love finally achieve a will-o-the-wisp, a false felicity that rests on illusion.

The two stories mutually enrich each other, and that enrichment is the result of their parallel structure. Either consciously or unconsciously, in the Merchant's Tale and the Franklin's Tale, Chaucer employed courtly love conventions to comment on what men and women make of institutions. The framework of these two tales is in the pattern of Andreas' Rules of Love, yet the stories are recto and verso of the same richly embellished sheet on which the poet has written his faith that human dignity and sincere love create the true beauty, grace, and charm of life.

NOTES

1. See, for example, Howard Rollin Patch, *On Rereading Chaucer* (Cambridge, Mass., 1939), pp. 220, 226; Marchette Chute, *Geoffrey Chaucer of England* (New York, 1946), p. 289; J. S. P. Tatlock, 'Chaucer's Merchant's Tale,' *MP*, xxxiii (1936), 367–381.

2. See Clifford P. Lyons, 'The Marriage Debate in the *Canterbury Tales*,' *ELH*, ii (November, 1935), 252–262, where, after an examination of the Prologue and the links in an attempt to find direct reference to a 'marriage debate,' Lyons concludes. 'A survey of the comments of the Host and narrators in the links reveals little justification for believing that the ideas on marriage in the tales are dramatized as a debate among the Pilgrims.'

3. To recognize that Chaucer was an excellent dramatic artist makes it impossible to overlook the profound verbal bombshell which the Wife of Bath released among the pilgrims. But recognition of this dramatic quality can be accepted without implying that the reactions provoked by such an intellectual disturbance as that which the Wife's Prologue must have produced would result in a series of formulated discourses on matrimony, even though the frank expression of the Wife would certainly turn the thoughts of the pilgrims to issues of men and women. That Chaucer was aware of the associative nature of the wanderings of the human mind is demonstrated by even so early a poem as *The Book of the Duchess*.

4. Margaret Schlauch, in 'Chaucer's "Merchant's Tale" and Courtly Love,' *ELH*, iv (1937), 201–212, examines the story as a satire on the whole system of feudal love, but does not consider its relationship to the Franklin's Tale.

5. *The Allegory of Love: A Study in Medieval Tradition* (Oxford, 1936), p. 161.

6. 'Chaucer's Renunciation of Love in *Troilus*,' *MLN*, xl (1925), 270–276.

7. Although Chaucer's magnificently successful employment of the courtly love traditions in *Troilus and Criseyde* justifies classification of that poem as his supreme accomplishment with courtly love material, it should be noted that the final effect, unless the epilogue is ignored, is that of a rejection of the convention. George R. Coffman, in 'Some Recent Trends in English Literary Scholarship,' *SP*, xxxv (1938), 514, maintains that 'Chaucer was more than a mile post along the highway that led to Spenser. Essentially, where courtly love is involved, he finally emerges to condemn the code or to advocate married love.'

8. George R. Coffman, in 'Chaucer and Courtly Love Once More—"The Wife of Bath's Tale," ' *Speculum*, xx (1945), 43–50, finds evidence that the courts of love were a basis for the Wife's story, and says, 'Ten Brink's statement that Chaucer wrote in the Indian summer of chivalry applies with equal emphasis to the literary convention of courtly love. And he is, in "The Wife of Bath's Tale," I believe, the Meredithian Comic Spirit presenting and observing its incongruities.'

9. Eugene Edward Slaughter, *Love and the Virtues and Vices in Chaucer* (Vanderbilt, 1946), p. 11.

10. *Ibid.*, pp. 16–17.

11. 'Introduction,' Andreas Capellanus, *The Art of Courtly Love*, trans. and ed. by John Jay Parry (New York, 1941), p. 6.

12. *Art of Courtly Love*, pp. 185–186.

13. *Art of Courtly Love*, p. 30.

14. Albert C. Baugh, in 'The Original Teller of the Merchant's Tale.' *MP*, xxxv (1937), 15–26, has advanced the theory that the Merchant's Tale was intended for the Friar originally. J. M. Manly (ed.), *The Canterbury Tales* (New York, 1928), p. 624, has pointed out the possibility of the story's being assigned originally to a member of a religious order, possibly the Monk. From the mouths of either, the story would lack the personal bitterness that we now read into it, but none of the elements which have been indicated as attacks on courtly love would be changed.

15. 'Chaucer's "Merchant's Tale" and Courtly Love,' p. 206.

16. Andreas, *Art of Courtly Love*, p. 6.

17. J. L. Lowes, in 'The Franklin's Tale, the Teseide, and the Filocolo,' *MP*, xv (1918), 689–728, suggests that 'In that part of Chaucer's narrative which deals with Aurelius' unrevealed love for Dorigen, Chaucer is drawing upon Boccaccio's account, in the fourth book of the *Teseide*, of Arcita's unspoken passion for Emilia.' This further links the action of the 'lusty squier' with the accepted tradition of courtly love.

18. *Art of Courtly Love*, pp. 185–186.

CHARLES A. OWEN, Jr.

The Crucial Passages in Five of *The Canter-*
bury Tales: A Study in Irony and Symbol

CHAUCER's art in the *Canterbury Tales* projects a complex world.
To the dramatic pose of simplicity already adopted by Chaucer in
many of his narrative poems is added the complication of a group
of observed narrators. The intrinsic value of each of the tales is not
its final one. Behind the artificial world created in the tale are the
conscious purposes of the narrator and the self-revelation, involuntary and often unconscious, involved in all artistic effort. The
simplest of the plots in the *Canterbury Tales* is that of the frame.
It makes the same demand of each character involved, that he ride
in the company of the others to Canterbury and back and partici-
pate in the creative activity of the tale-telling. Each character projects his tale, the limited vision it embodies, and his limiting
personality into the world of the pilgrimage. The plot is simple but
dynamic. For each vision has the potentiality of bringing into new
focus those that preceded and of influencing those that will follow.
The possibilities are soon unlimited. They lead to a richness that
defies final analysis but finds its most concentrated expression in
passages that at once embody and expose the limited vision of
created character and creating narrator. These passages foreshadow in the unwitting speech or opinion of a character the outcome of the plot and help to create symbolic values that give the

Reprinted, by permission, from *The Journal of English and Germanic Philology*, LII (1953), 294-311.

narrative an added and unifying dimension. They are in a sense symbolic of the whole work: in the contrast between what *is* and what men see—of themselves and of others—lies Chaucer's deepest vein of comedy.

Passages that foreshadow the outcome in the unwitting speech of a character are fairly numerous in the *Canterbury Tales,* but I have found only five that perform also a symbolic and unifying function. These five passages occur in five of the most important tales. It will be the purpose of this paper to analyze the five passages and to explore the multiple meanings, both within the tales and in the world of the pilgrimage, which they epitomize.

I

One of the clearest of the symbolic passages is the speech in the *Franklin's Tale,* where Dorigen softens her refusal to Aurelius and at the same time expresses her love for her husband:

> But after that in pley thus seyde she:
> 'Aurelie,' quod she, 'by heighe God above,
> Yet wolde I graunte you to been youre love,
> Syn I yow se so pitously complayne,
> Looke what day that endelong Britayne
> Ye remoeve alle the rokkes, stoon by stoon,
> That they ne lette ship ne boot to goon.
> I seye, whan ye han maad the coost so clene
> Of rokkes that there nys no stoon ysene,
> Thanne wol I love yow best of any man,
> Have heer my trouthe, in al that evere I kan.'

This speech of Dorigen provides the final element necessary to the plot. The happy marriage, the temporary absence of Arveragus, the enduring love of Aurelius, have all been presented. The wife's rash promise is the catalytic element that sets the others to reacting.

But because of the view we have had of Dorigen's grief, in which the rocks played so menacing a part, the rash promise is at the same time an expression of Dorigen's love for her husband. Her mention of the rocks tells us even more certainly than her refusal that she is entirely devoted to her husband. This speech introduces for the first time in the tale the contrast, extremely important later, between the appearance of things and the reality. On the surface the speech is an agreement under certain conditions to commit adultery. Beneath the surface it is an expression of conjugal loyalty.

In fact Dorigen has endeavored without realizing it to transform the symbolic meaning of the rocks. Up to this point they have represented to her the menace of natural forces to her husband's life. Hereafter their permanence is a guarantee of her enduring love for her husband. The rocks occur to her not only because her husband's life is in danger from them but because their immutability is like her love. She has seen beyond the menacing appearance of the rocks and has invoked the symbolic value of their endurance at the same time that she has finally accepted their reality.

The changed significance of the rocks is emphasized in several ways by Chaucer. Before her rash promise Dorigen questions on grounds of reason the purpose of the rocks in God's world and prays

> 'But wolde God that alle thise rokkes blake
> Were sonken into helle for his sake!
> Thise rokkes sleen myn herte for the feere.'

After her promise to Aurelius it is his turn to pray for the removal of the rocks. Instead of Eterne God, he addresses Apollo, and asks him to persuade his sister Lucina to cause a two-year flood tide high enough to cover the rocks with five fathoms, or, if this is not feasible,

> 'Prey hire to synken every rok adoun
> Into hir owene dirke regioun
> Under the ground, ther Pluto dwelleth inne,
> Or nevere mo shal I my lady wynne.'

The parallelism of the prayers emphasizes the transformation of the symbol. The removal of the rocks is now the menace to the marriage. In both the prayers the desire to see the rocks removed is a sign of weakness, of unwillingness to accept the real world.

Dorigen transcends her weakness when she accepts the permanence of the rocks. Aurelius transcends his weakness when he recognizes the quality of Dorigen's and Arveragus's love as superior to his own passion.

The rocks play an important part in the contrast between appearance and reality. There is never any question of doing away with the rocks: Aurelius's brother doesn't expect to achieve that when he proposes the trip to Orleans, nor can the magician do more than make them *seem* to vanish.

> But thurgh his magik, for a wyke or tweye,
> It semed that alle the rokkes were aweye.

Aurelius responds at first to the appearance of things.

> he knew that ther was noon obstacle,
> That voyded were thise rokkes everychon.

But gradually he finds that the obstacles are still there. He himself makes no demand of Dorigen but merely reminds her of her promise. And when he hears of Arveragus's 'gentillesse' and sees Dorigen's distress, he gallantly releases her. The real obstacles, like the rocks, only seem to have vanished. They are the honor, the decency, the gentility of all the people involved, and the true love of Dorigen and Arveragus for one another.

Dorigen's rash promise also functions in the tale in a way not intended by the Franklin. In addition to its other meanings it is an expression of 'gentillesse' in its superficial sense. Dorigen tempers her absolute refusal in a way that makes it sound courteous, though in her heart she knows of the removal of the rocks,

> 'It is agayns the proces of nature.'

Even while accepting the natural order, she is shirking a part of her duty in the moral. That the rocks play so great a part in the thought and fate of this soft-hearted woman is a further irony. When faced at the end with the disappearance of the rocks and the necessity of keeping her promise, she will propose to herself suicide but allow her purpose to disintegrate as she calls to mind the sad fate of women who firmly carried out such a purpose.[1] Arveragus alone displays a firmness to which the rocks have relevance. His temporary absence makes possible the rash promise and his decision at the crisis forces Aurelius to see the 'obstacles' that have only seemed to vanish. The superficial gentility of Dorigen's promise foreshadows and contrasts with the gentility of the ending, and the tale becomes a criticism of some aspects of gentility, more subtle than the Host's in the prologue to the tale and more justified.

The Franklin presents in his tale an ideal of marriage and of 'gentillesse,' and manages at the same time to compliment the Knight, the Squire, and the Clerk. But his story is, without his realizing it, a critique of 'gentillesse,' for it is Dorigen's courteous softening of her refusal that makes the exhibition of gentility at the end necessary. The rocks which suggest the enduring value of gentility also suggest the distinctions which the Franklin in his easy acceptance of the good things of life fails to make.

II

The crucial passage in the *Merchant's Tale* [2] comes in the middle of the epithalamion and sends echoes and reverberations through the two consultations and the marriage to a crowning climax in the garden scene at the end. The Merchant is showing us January's reasons for wanting to marry:

> Mariage is a ful greet sacrement.
> He which that hath no wyf, I holde him shent;
> He lyveth helplees and al desolat,—
> I speke of folk in seculer estaat.
> And herke why, I sey nat this for noght,
> That womman is for mannes helpe ywroght.
> The hye God, whan he hadde Adam maked,
> And saugh him al allone, bely-naked,
> God of his grete goodnesse seyde than,
> 'Lat us now make an helpe unto this man
> Lyk to hymself'; and thanne he made him Eve.
> Heere may ye se, and heerby may ye preve,
> That wyf is mannes helpe, and his confort,
> His paradys terrestre, and his disport.

So buxom and so vertuous is she
They moste nedes lyve in unitee.
O flessh they been, and o flessh, as I gesse
Hath but oon herte, in wele and in distresse.

The concept of marriage as an earthly paradise has come to January late but with the blinding light of revelation: it has taken complete possession of his mind. The cautious habits and the short-sighted shrewdness of old age will be called on to support rather than examine this new vision. As in his judicious exclusion of the clergy and his appeal to example, he will use the forms of wisdom but not its substance. Marriage will carry all before it because it promises to combine the self-indulgence he has practised all his life with two things that old age makes vital to him for the first time—help for his physical weakness and the salvation of his soul. His lust for pleasure and his desire for salvation combine in the first consultation scene to blind him to the danger inherent in taking a young wife. The only danger he can foresee by the time he has chosen the girl and called his friends together the second time is so much felicity in marriage as to ruin his chance of a blissful after-life.

Besides epitomizing the precise and willful blindness of his attitude toward marriage, the passage foreshadows many of the details of his fate. The helpfulness that he anticipates in a wife will serve May as excuse for being in Damian's arms in the pear tree, and it will take the form before his very eyes of a nakedness similar to Adam's, her smock upon her breast. But as he sees in Adam's story a proof of marital bliss, so he will see in the pear tree only what his wife wants him to, an example of her care for his welfare. The 'unitee' and 'o flessh' receive an ironical fulfillment in the blind old man's constant clutch on his buxom and perforce virtuous May, and an additional twist in the line from his invitation to the garden,

'No spot of thee ne knew I al my lyf,'

where the irony of the contrast between his ugly passion and the romantic imagery and sacred associations of the Song of Songs (which is Solomon's!) matches the irony of his being as unconscious of the physical spot he is even then touching as he will later be of the moral spot—adultery—when he is looking at it with miraculously unblinded eyes.

The controlling images in the poem, however, are the linked ones of the garden, the blindness, and the tree. They are linked for the first time in this passage. 'Heere may ye se,' says the Merchant for January. But you can see in the story of Adam and Eve that a wife is man's earthly paradise, only if you are blind to the tree of the knowledge of good and evil and the forbidden fruit. As January is blind in the Garden of Eden, so is he blind in the paradise of his wife's arms:

> 'A man may do no synne with his wyf,
> Ne hurte hymselven with his owene knyf.'

Adam and Eve and the first sin link up in these fatuous lines with Damian,

> Which carf biforn the knyght ful many a day

and the sin soon to be committed in January's private paradise. The garden that January builds is the consummation of his folly and the symbol of his marriage. Its beauty is May, and the stone wall with which it is 'enclosed al aboute' is the jealous precautions of the blind January as well as the inescapable unpleasantness of his lovemaking. There is no stone of tyranny in May's nature, and in fact we find her pliancy which January expected to be like warm wax taking a ready impression from Damian's wooing. The silver key to the garden which is January's alone is his privilege as husband, but from the warm wax of May's nature a suitable replica is provided for Damian—his privilege as lover. The blindness is the physical counterpart of the ignorance of marriage and of women that January has shown all along. It prevents him to the end from seeing the tree in the garden and the knowledge of evil which it represents. And the regaining of his sight wipes out even the alertness to danger which accompanied the blindness.

The tree plays a further and more striking part in the tale. January fails to see it in the Garden of Eden, but brings it in as an image of his own virility in the first consultation with his friends:

'Though I be hoor, I fare as dooth a tree
That blosmeth er that fruyt ywoxen bee
And blosmy tree nys neither drye ne deed.
I feele me nowhere hoor but on myn heed;
Myn herte and alle my lymes been as grene
As laurer thurgh the yeer is for to sene.'

The image bears fruit in the final part of the story. In January's private paradise, his arms around the trunk of the pear tree, he serves his wife as stepping stone to the forbidden fruit of adultery. At the same time he becomes the symbol of his folly, cuckolded in the branches which spring from his head as horns.

The imagery of growth has structural significance. The story is essentially the growth of an idea to complete fulfillment. Starting in the mind of January, a germ with all that develops already implicit, it attains in each part of the story a new mode of actualization—first verbal expression in general terms; then the fixing of the dream to a specific woman; then the literal fulfillment. At each stage January's blindness to his own folly achieves some new fatuity linked to the imagery in which he first clothed his 'vision.' But the story does not stop with a single literal fulfillment. Through Proserpina's vow it suggests repetition through the ages. And it creates in the literal world the symbolic fulfillment of the idea. The garden and the blindness, in January's mind from the beginning, are now fully materialized. No miracle can make him see the tree as horns growing from his head, nor make him see the adultery committed before his very eyes.

The Merchant has taken care to tell us that this tale is not autobiographical:

'of myn owene soore,
For soory herte, I telle may namoore.'

Moved by the ironical moral of the *Clerk's Tale,* he will join the discussion opened by the Wyf of Bath and present directly a male view of marriage. The Wife and her theories are clearly in his mind for he commits the anachronism of having Justinus refer to her in the tale. His real intentions in telling the story are clear from two passages. In the prologue he says,

> 'We wedded men lyven in sorwe and care. . . .
> As for the moore part, I say nat alle.'

And in the tale itself, speaking of Argus,

> Yet was he blent, and, God woot, so been mo,
> That wenen wisly that it be nat so.
> Passe over is an ese, I sey namoore.

For the Merchant January is the type of that *rara avis*—the happily married man: Not all married men are miserable; some are blind.

The Merchant participates in the blindness of his creature January in not realizing the extent to which he is talking of his own sore in the tale. His imperceptiveness extends even to thinking that he can disguise the vulgarity of his tale in circumlocution. The circumlocutions in fact call attention to the vulgarity, just as January's blissful ignorance contrasts with but does not conceal the Merchant's disillusionment. The creator of January is evidently a converted idealist, and the bitterness of his cynicism is the measure of his former folly. He can be so penetrating in exposing January's reasons for marriage because he is really looking at his own from beyond the gulf of two shattering months of marital experience. The cynical egoist looks at the delusions of an idealistic egoist and cannot see that his bitterness betrays him.

III

The *Wife of Bath's Tale* is ostensibly a two-part exposition of the Wife's thesis that marriages are happy only when the woman is the master. The crucial passage occurs when the 'olde wyf' at the juncture of the two parts reiterates in stronger terms her demand that the knight marry her:

> 'Nay thanne,' quod she, 'I shrewe us bothe two!
> For thogh that I be foul, and oold, and poore,
> I nolde for al the metal, ne for oore,
> That under erthe is grave, or lith above,
> But if thy wyf I were, and eek thy love.'

The old woman's demand is not only the conclusion of the quest plot, the price the knight pays for his life, but it is also the point of departure for the husband's dilemma. The woman must first secure her man before she can offer him her alternatives. The Wife of Bath's story passes with this speech from its public to its private demonstration of the thesis. The world-wide scene of the quest dwindles to the marriage-bed of the dilemma. We pass from generally accepted theory to the practice of one woman in achieving first sovereignty then happiness in her marriage.

But the husband's dilemma and the Wife of Bath's thesis are merely the surface of the story. The old woman has already demanded that the knight marry her. In her reiteration she reveals her real desire. She wants not just a husband but a husband's love. The phrase 'and eek thy love' brought here into conjunction with the woman's ugliness, age, and poverty suggests that the real dilemma in the second part of the story is the wife's rather than the husband's; it foreshadows the necessity for miracle at the end and reveals for the story a second and more valid theme, operating on the instinctive level beneath the Wife's and her heroine's theories—the quest for love.

On this level the tale as a whole progresses from rape to marriage to love with each of the three crises of the story presenting a common pattern. In each there is a problem, a theoretical solution, and a modification of theory in practice. At the beginning of the story the knight's crime of rape is to be punished by death until the ladies intervene and send him off in quest of crucial information about women. The second problem, what women most desire, is solved theoretically by the answer the knight gives the court. But it is clear from the 'olde wyf's' demand that in practice one woman wants not sovereignty over husband and lover, but merely a husband and his love. The final problem is the obtaining of the husband's love, theoretically solved when he leaves the choice in his dilemma and thus the sovereignty to his wife. Actually the wife attains the knight's love by magically slipping between the horns of the dilemma and giving him exactly what he wants. The happy married life that results differs markedly from the blueprint of the Wife's thesis:

> And she obeyed hym in every thyng
> That myghte doon hym plesance or likyng.

The Wife of Bath had good reason to tell the story she did. It provided what she considered a good demonstration of her theory. It gave her an opportunity of discussing a number of the questions close to her heart such as the true meaning of 'gentillesse,' and of parodying Arthurian romance with its unrealistic notions of life and love. It had the further appeal of an imaginative wish-fulfillment, for it presented an old woman who gained a young husband and magically changed herself into everything he could desire in a wife. As a story of the quest for love it was the artistic counterpart of her life.

In its continuing contrast between theory and practice the tale repeats the unconscious revelation of the Wife's prologue. For her theory of marriage and her own practise have been worlds apart. In her first three marriages she did maintain her sovereignty, but the marriages were not happy. No doubt the Wife enjoyed the cowed submission she so cleverly exacted from her old dotards. But she is forced to admit,

> And yet in bacon hadde I nevere delit.

The fourth husband with his paramour aroused her jealousy and, to her satisfaction, became jealous in his turn. The Wife of Bath took refuge in travel, and the marriage was little more than nominal. Only with the fifth, her clerk of Oxenford, did she find happiness. Jankyn she cannot name without a blessing. But in the fifth marriage the relationship of the first three was simply reversed. This time she was twice his age and forced to sign over her property before the ceremony. Like the old woman in her tale she had to win his love. At the same time, she would have us believe, she won the upper hand in the marriage. That the triumph, like that of the heroine in her tale, is nominal her own words confess:

> After that day we hadden never debaat.
> God helpe me so, I was to him as kynde
> As any wyf from Denmark unto Ynde,
> And also trewe, and so was he to me.

261

We have further proof of the clerk's influence over her in the stress she puts on authorities in her discussions, on the clear memory she has for the stories in the book she made him burn, and in the strange distortion she makes of the Midas story in her tale. Jankyn left his mark on more than her 'ribbes,' more than her hearing.

The Wife of Bath enjoyed theory on one level and life on another. Her enjoyment of both was intense and convincing, so much so that most critics and readers have appreciated her gusto without noticing the contrast between her theory and practice in both prologue and tale.

IV

In the *Pardoner's Tale*[3] the crucial passage occurs at the point where the revelers find the pile of gold under the tree:

No lenger thanne after Deeth they soughte.

On the primary level of the reveler's limited vision the wealth has driven all thought of their search for Death from their minds. They now think of the pleasures the gold will buy them and plan how to get it home safely. At the same time the statement foreshadows their end. They no longer seek Death because they have found him.

The single line marks a fundamental division in the tale. On the one hand is the drunken search for Death, marked by an unwonted and a deluded altruism. They are sworn brothers. They will slay Death. Drink has given them a mission, stature, pride, contempt for others. The gold has both a sobering and a deflating effect. It brings them back to the real world from their illusions of brotherhood and of slaying Death. Yet their drunken intentions were closer to the final outcome than their sober planning and counterplanning to secure the treasure. The gold has brought them back to their narrow world. It both focuses and limits their vision. These two sections of the tale, as we shall see later, have a symbolic value for the Pardoner.

But first we must explore the complex set of meanings in the tale as a whole. What happens to the gold in the story happens to the story itself. Its value is determined by the human motives focused upon it. In itself it may be an effective warning against cupidity, showing how greed turns gold into death. But as a part of the sermon habitually delivered by the Pardoner to the 'lewed peple' it is at the same time the instrument of the Pardoner's greed. And as a part of the confession made to the other pilgrims it is the expression of the Pardoner's vanity. The pilgrimage gives him the opportunity to display to an intelligent audience the full measure of his cleverness and cynicism. He hopes so to dazzle and shock them that they will fail to see the motive that drives him to the compensation of hypocrisy and greed.

The Pardoner's physical disability has isolated him from some of the normal satisfactions in life. In revenge he has rejected the professed morality of other people and uses it against them to attain the power and comfort that wealth brings. His income is thus a symbol of his victory over physical inadequacy and of his superiority over the normal and stupid louts who are his victims. But the victory is not one that he can fully reveal in his daily life. Here, before the pilgrims, stimulated by the intelligence of his audience and with neither the necessity nor the possibility of assuming his customary role, he can for once reveal the extent of his success, impress his companions with the amount of his income, and shock them with the cynicism that makes it all possible. He seeks at the same time to conceal the emptiness and isolation of his life by reference to the comforts and gaieties he enjoys:

> 'I wol have moneie, wolle, chese, and whete. . . .
> Nay, I wol drynke licour of the vyne,
> And have a joly wenche in every toun.'

The task he has set himself in his confession is as wild and deluded as the drunken revelers' quest in the first part of the tale. Like the quest it has a wider range than his customary hypocrisy and is nearer the ultimate truth. But hypocrisy is his normal and sober world, and like the revelers' vision in the second part of the tale it is narrow and limited. The presumption of the pilgrim and the hypocrisy of the 'noble ecclesiaste' both end in isolation. The Pardoner has also found death without recognizing it. His life is an exemplum of the futility of cynicism. And in the world of the pilgrimage, where we see the Pardoner but he cannot see himself, the crucial passage again functions.

V

The crucial passage in the *Nun's Priest's Tale*[4] is not so obviously a foreshadowing of the plot as in the other instances. It comes at the juncture between the discussion of dreams and the action of the near-fatal third of May. Chauntecleer is speaking:

'Now let us speke of myrthe, and stynte al this.
Madame Pertelote, so have I blis,
Of o thyng God hath sent me large grace;
For whan I se the beautee of youre face,
Ye been so scarlet reed aboute youre yen,
It maketh al my drede for to dyen;
For al so siker as *In principio*,
Mulier est hominis confusio—
Madame, the sentence of this Latyn is,
"Womman is mannes joye and al his blis."
For whan I feele a-nyght your softe syde,
Al be it that I may nat on yow ryde,
For that oure perche is maad so narwe, allas!
I am so ful of joye and of solas,
That I diffye bothe sweven and dreem.'

Here the ultimate victim employs the same technique in his deception of his wife as is later to be used by the fox on him—deceitful flattery. Behind the fair words of his translation, designed to smooth the ruffled feathers of Pertelote, whose laxatives have just been scorned, lurks the malicious dig of the Latin. The cock will later be 'hoist with his own petard,'

As man that koude his traysoun nat espie
So was he ravysshed with his flaterie

Furthermore the cock is delighted with the sound of his own voice. In the long discourse on dreams, of which this is the conclusion, he has displayed the smug assurance of the born raconteur. And it is a moot point here whether his wife's beauty or his own cleverly barbed praise of it most attracts him. The cock is indeed ready to believe that other people admire his voice.

This speech of Chauntecleer brings out the pedantry implicit from the beginning in his actions. He alone can witness and appreciate the victory he has won over his wife. The victory is a pedant's triumph and contrasts strikingly with the one the fox later wins over him, which calls forth a universal clamor.

The cock's vast learning has furthermore contributed to the easy fatalism he has fallen into as a result of his learned rebuttal on dreams. The original dream was clearly a warning dream. The beast in it, which with all his learning the cock can describe but cannot recognize as his natural enemy the fox,

> 'wolde han maad areest
> Upon my body, and wolde han had me deed.'

But in the examples which he uses to refute his wife's skepticism people either fail to heed the warning or they have no chance of evading the fate foretold in their dreams. The cock in effect wins the argument and forgets the dream that occasioned it. His pedantry has led him into a smug fatalism that contemplates his own coming 'adversitee' as merely the concluding proof of the truth of dreams. No effort is called for—only the pursuit of what the soon-to-be-shipwrecked victim in one of the dreams called 'my thynges' and the assumption of the courageous pose which Pertelote recommended and which his prowess makes ridiculous.

The cock, warned by dream and instinct against the fox and prepared by his own deft use of flattery against the technique the fox is to use, unwittingly gives himself a further warning, which he is either not learned enough or too pedantic to apply. Just as truly as the words of St. John's Gospel, woman is man's confusion, he tells his wife in Latin. But the words from the Gospel are *In principio,* in the beginning; and in the beginning Eve was Adam's confusion. So far is he from heeding the warning that the passage which contains it is full of the uxorious passion usually attributed to Adam. The cock's appreciation of his wife's charms diverts him from further thought of his own danger. Here in effect is another

Adam, succumbing to the attractions of his wife when he should be using his reason. The Adam-and-Eve parallel, thus suggested for the cock-and-hen story, contributes to the mock heroics.

The passage is rich in other contributions to the mock heroic effect. It unites the language of exalted human passion with details of hen anatomy and barnyard architecture. The exalted language and the deflating details give the passage a quality that is typical of the whole poem. The courtly behavior and refined pretensions of Chauntecleer are constantly betrayed by the ludicrous activities and ignoble motives contingent upon chicken nature. The suggestion is clear: Objectively viewed, human pride and vanity are similarly betrayed. Only the simple life with frank acceptance of the necessities and limitations of the human lot, as exemplified by the widow and her menage, can have real dignity.

The contrast between Chauntecleer and his owner has a dramatic value in the Canterbury Tales. The Host in calling on the Prioress a little earlier addressed her in terms of the most exaggerated respect. Her Priest, however, he addresses with peremptory intimacy, making game of his poverty. When we remember the Prioress's pains

> to countrefete cheere
> Of court, and to been estatlich of manere,
> And to ben holden digne of reverence,

we can glimpse a guarded purpose. The sexes of the characters in the tale are reversed, as is also the ownership, but the essential relationship between poverty and wealth, between simplicity and pretension is there. The drama is carried a step further when the Priest falls into overt criticism of women. This he does at the expense of the complexity of his tale. The advice of his wife is, as we have seen, a minor detail in the cock's decision. But it is a theme that the Priest attacks with evident relish. He brings himself up sharp with the thought of whom he might be offending, then returns to the attack indirectly by referring his listeners to the 'auctors,' and finally tries to ascribe the whole thing to the cock:

> 'Thise ben the cokkes wordes, and nat myne;
> I kan noon harm of no womman divyne.'

266

The inner conflict of the misogynist employed by a woman has come for a moment to the surface; then it is pushed back behind the artifice of the story, where it has been operating secretly all along. The Host's reaction to the story has thus a double irony. Not only has he failed to see the point, but he imagines the Priest, if he were only a layman, a prodigious treader of hens!

The pedantry, ridiculed in the portrait of Chauntecleer, is also attacked by the Nun's Priest in his criticism of the rhetoricians. The satire is most highly comic when Friday and Master Gaufred are brought in at the climax of the story, and Venus is reproached for not protecting her devotoo on her day, when it was her influence that was partly responsible for Chauntecleer's plight. It is possible, however, to ridicule a thing and be guilty of it on occasion oneself. This trap the Nun's Priest falls into at least once when he gets himself involved in a discussion of free will and God's fore-knowledge—as a result of elaborating too far on a mock heroic color. Like Chauntecleer he is for a moment hoist with his own petard. And in struggling to get back to his tale, he suddenly finds himself involved in the criticism of women. Pedantry which leads to a criticism of women recalls the crucial passage and the cock's gibe, 'In principio,/Mulier est hominis confusio.' The Priest in fact makes the same charge:

> Wommanes conseil broghte us first to wo,
> And made Adam fro Paradys to go,
> Ther as he was ful myrie and wel at ese.

Whatever the cause for the Priest's misogyny (it may well be a combination of intellectual contempt and involuntary attraction), there is no mistaking the animus with which he follows his hero's lead in attributing man's ills to woman. This blanket condemnation of women is a very different thing from his implied criticism of the Prioress's pretensions. In his better moments he knows, as his por-trait of Chauntecleer indicates, the real significance of Adam and Eve for mankind. Hominis confusio is man's own frailty. That the Priest lashes out at women as his stupid cock had done measures the strength of his feelings. In a sense these are the cock's words, and the Priest's recognition of their unworthiness enables him to recover his composure and his story.

On the primary level then the *Nun's Priest's Tale* is a brilliant and complex exposure of vanity, self-esteem, and self-indulgence through the mock heroic treatment of a beast fable. On the secondary level, the Nun's Priest joins the discussions of the Pilgrims on poverty (Man of Law and Wife of Bath), women's advice (Merchant), rhetoric (Host and Squire), and marriage. He is also presenting in the contrast between the widow and Chauntecleer a veiled comment on his position vis-à-vis the Prioress. Finally, on the level of involuntary revelation, he falls into the pedantry that he is ridiculing and uncovers for a moment in his confusion the feelings of a misogynist dependent on a woman. In this moment there is revealed a second conflict, the conflict between the artist, building with the materials of his art a world where his feelings achieve symbolic and universal expression, and the man, expressing his feelings directly.

CONCLUSION

The symbols which Chaucer employed are unobtrusive; they fit in their contexts of sentimental romance or crude realism without 'shake or bind.' Nothing in the tale forces them to the symbolic level. Yet the consistency with which the rocks are developed in the *Franklin's Tale* gives the obvious charm of the story a focused integrity which can be felt even when not clearly analyzed. The linked images of garden, tree, and blindness of the *Merchant's Tale* add to the bitter unity of tone an underlying unity of action: the seed of January's folly grows from the fertile soil of his figurative blindness into the successive realizations of word, fixed purpose, and deed, until it attains full maturity in the garden, the blindness, and the tree-born fruit of adultery, with the head that conceived realistically behorned.

The focus and additional dimension which symbol and image provide in the tales are also attained by the contrast or ambiguity of the narrative elements involved. The intentional pattern of the

Wife of Bath's Tale and the zest with which she tells it lose none of their literal value when we see the ambiguity of the elements she uses to prove her thesis. The nature of love and marriage resists the warping efforts of her dogged feminism and provides the counterpoint of a contrasting and more valid pattern. The quest for love which dominated her life dominates her tale. The greed in which the Pardoner has taken refuge creates the skillful weapon of his tale. With one edge he cynically dupes peasants; with the other he seeks to shock the pilgrims into a recognition of his importance. For the deluded vanity of the second purpose as well as the hypocrisy of the first, the two parts of his tale present analogies; at the very center the symbol of gold as unrecognized death reveals the futile emptiness of both efforts. The concealed purpose of the Nun's Priest finds urbane expression in the contrast between the simple dignity of the people and the ostentation of the chickens in his tale. But a momentary lapse into the pedantry he is mocking in Chauntecleer confuses him and he breaks through the artifice of beast fable to direct expression of his purpose. The artistic expression, where *hominis confusio* is man's own foolish presumption, forms an ironic background for the priest's lapse into an indiscriminate and direct antifeminism.

Chaucer, unlike the Nun's Priest, never expresses his intention directly. Present himself on the pilgrimage and in the occasional asides to the audience, he pictures himself as the simple reporter of experience, not responsible because unable to judge the questions of morals and propriety raised by the tales. Only in his own experience as narrator does the mask become penetrable, and then not to the pilgrims, his imaginary audience, who acquiesce in the Host's misunderstanding and crude estimate of *Sir Thopas* and get for their reward the prosy and long-winded idealism of the *Melibeus*. There is implied in the episode, as in the Man of Law's wrong-headed praise while cudgeling his brains for a tale, a comment on the popular taste and on Chaucer's relation to his real audience. Chaucer did not expect to be understood fully by all his readers. Certain of his effects depend on a knowledge which few of them could have. Others, like the crucial passages that have just been analyzed, are the subtle elaborations by the artist of a design already present. They suggest a personal standard and private satisfaction in his art.

But the simplicity adopted as a mask in the tales is not entirely ironical. It is a token for the deeper simplicity that receives impressions freely and refuses to interpose the eager evaluations, artistic and moral, that prevent full recognition. This deeper simplicity reflects faithfully the paradoxes of personality, the contradictions of experience. It becomes through its forbearance a rare and delicate instrument for evaluation and judgment, and presents a total vision not to be fully appreciated from the mental and spiritual posture of the Host, nor from that of the *homme moyen du moyen âge,* whom Chaucer could not only entertain but also see beyond.

NOTES

1. See James Sledd, 'Dorigen's Complaint,' *MP,* xLv (1947), 36 ff.

2. In this analysis I am indebted to G. G. Sedgewick, 'Structure of the *Merchant's Tale,' UTQ,* xvii (1947–48), 337 ff.

3. I am indebted in this analysis to Curry, *Chaucer and the Medieval Sciences,* 54 ff., and G. G. Sedgewick, 'The Progress of Chaucer's Pardoner, 1880–1940,' *MLQ,* i (1940), 431 ff.

4. I am indebted in this analysis to J. B. Severs, 'Chaucer's Originality in the *Nun's Priest's Tale,' SP,* xLiii (1946), 22 ff.

BERTRAND H. BRONSON

The Book of The Duchess Re-opened

It has been generally agreed that there are glaring faults in Chaucer's elegy for Blanche and that, in spite of occasional beauties, the 'prentice hand is but too apparent. Critics have found the poem tedious, disconnected, and ill-proportioned, languid in its beginning and abrupt in its conclusion, frequently lapsing in taste and in meter, deficient both in humor and in self-fulfilment. Coulton's verdict—'obviously immature and unequal, but full of delightful passages'—would seem, judging by the printed comment, to be that of most sympathetic readers; though many have emphasized the negative rather than the positive half of the judgment. Because I believe that much of the disparagement has arisen from misunderstanding, I invite reconsideration of a work of art that has been rated a good deal lower than it deserves. It may be that characteristic values inherent in the more archaic of Chaucer's writings will reassert themselves in the course of our scrutiny. There have been signs latterly that a truer appreciation is in the making, as in the comments of Wolfgang Clemen and James R. Kreuzer,[1] and to this impulse I wish to add what force I may. Generally, however, the older critical impatience yet prevails.

What has proved the chief stumbling-block 'comes up for emphatic restatement in J. S. P. Tatlock's recent posthumous book, *The Mind and Art of Chaucer* (Syracuse, 1950). 'Indifference to human reality,' Tatlock declares,

---

Reprinted, by permission, from *PMLA*, LXVII (1952), 863-81.

is most marked of all in the dreamer (who is in no sense Chaucer himself). Informed by the overheard soliloquy that the lover's grief is due to his lady's death, to say nothing of his garments of mourning and the loving reminiscence all through his prolonged monologue, at the end the dreamer is astounded to learn that she is dead. Perhaps such forgetfulness is dreamlike. . . . But no explanation of the dreamer's state of mind . . . will persuade most moderns, still less a medieval if he thought about it, to accept the contradiction without question. It is entirely unlike Chaucer's later way . . . here he makes a really inexplicable blur . . . why he should so bluntly at the beginning tell us that the lady is dead, though at the end he is to ignore this, who can say? (p. 30)

There is, I believe, a satisfactory answer to this question, in both its parts, and it will be our main business in the ensuing discussion to find it. It would be true to say that we are bluntly informed because it is important for us to know at once, as the dreamer knows at once, that the lady is dead; because the poem as a whole grows and exfoliates from that central fact, which provides at once the principle of its artistic development, the pivot around which the dialogue revolves, the key to character, and the visible dark that underlies the courtly surface-tissue and gives it poignancy—'bright metal on a sullen ground.' But so summary an answer is *ignotum per ignotius*. We shall have to explore the poem before it can be truly understood.

Kittredge's solution to the immediate problem has long been familiar. In that classic and brilliant lecture on *The Book of the Duchess,* Kittredge anticipates Tatlock's view that the Dreamer is not Chaucer:

He is a purely imaginary figure to whom certain purely imaginary things happen, in a purely imaginary dream. He is as much a part of the fiction . . . as the Merchant or the Pardoner or the Host is a part of the fiction in the Canterbury Tales . . . . The mental attitude of the Dreamer is that of childlike wonder. He understands nothing, not even the meaning of his dream . . . . He wonders what makes the knight so sad; and when the knight tries to tell him, he still wonders, and still questions. Hints and half-truths and figures of speech are lost upon him. . . . This . . . is not Geoffrey Chaucer, the humorist and man of the world. He is a creature of the imagination, and his childlikeness is part of his dramatic character. [Moreover,] the Dreamer is not merely artless by nature; he is dulled, and almost stupified, by long suffering.

Kittredge then, with what appears a strange *volte face*, adds a further page of characterization that can hardly be reconciled with the foregoing, however corrective. 'But what,' he asks:

> is he really deaf and blind to what he hears and sees? By no means! Artless he is, and unsuspicious, and dull with sorrow and lack of sleep; but the dirge is too clear for even him to misunderstand . . . . The Dreamer knows perfectly well that the lady is dead . . . . With instinctive delicacy . . . he suppresses this knowledge [from a desire] to afford the knight the only help in his power—the comfort of pouring his sad story into compassionate ears.[2]

There seems to be a double exposure here. We are first presented with a simpleton who cannot understand anything but the most obvious statements of fact, a childlike dullard stupefied with sorrow and sleeplessness; and then we are asked to incorporate with this conception another character who knows the facts, understands what he hears and sees, and puts his knowledge to use with tact and diplomacy, with the kindly purpose of enabling the stranger to ease his heart. If Chaucer drew this psychological paradox, he would seem to be guilty of that 'inexplicable blur' of which Tatlock complains; or worse, perhaps, of drawing a character with too little inner consistency to compel our belief. But since the Dreamer is the most complex of all the persons depicted, we shall approach him with more assurance when we have considered the simpler characters in the poem.

It is customary to identify the Man in Black as John of Gaunt and the lady whom he describes, as Blanche the Duchess of Lancaster. In these identifications we have, of course, the support of Chaucer's own title, 'The Death of Blanche the Duchess,' in the Prologue to the Legend of Good Women, as well as Shirley's subsequent asseveration. But not all of us stop to consider how far such ascriptions are to be carried, or what precisely is implied by them.

Most readers would willingly allow that Chaucer was not engaged upon the painting of realistic portraits of these persons, such as he was later to render of some of the Canterbury pilgrims. The Man in Black and his lady, it would be admitted, are idealizations appropriate to their context in the poem: they are images in a dream. They are distanced from reality, and depicted in conventionalized attitudes, like figures in a medieval tapestry. They are drawn against the formalized landscape of the dream-vision, and stand forth as ideal courtly lovers. No one among Chaucer's contemporaries would have looked for a photographic realism, or have expected, or even tolerated, an accurate correspondence of the pictures and the life. They welcomed and were well acquainted with the conventions of the genre. When an eighteenth-century poet composed an elegy on Addison's death, he gave it the form of a pastoral dialogue between Pope and Steele, in which 'Richy' recalls to 'Sandy' in the following terms the benefit enjoyed by the reading public from 'Adie's' papers on the *Paradise Lost:*

> Mony a time, beneath the auld birk-tree,
> What's bonny in that sang he loot me see.
> The lasses aft flung down their rakes and pails,
> And held their tongues, O strange! to hear his tales.[3]

Ramsay's audience, we surmise, was not greatly disturbed by this poetic refraction of literal truth. Given a sufficient clue in the names, they took pleasure in the ingenuity of the poet's translation of recent event into the conventions of pathetic pastoral. Similarly, it is to be supposed, Chaucer's audience received the description of Blanche's acceptance of Gaunt, couched in the conventional terms of courtly love. Says the knight:

> she wel understod
> That I ne wilned thyng but god,
> And worship, and to kepe hir name
> Over alle thyng, and drede hir shame,
> And was so besy hyr to serve;

And pitee were I shulde sterve,
Syth that I wilned noon harm, ywis.
So whan my lady knew al this,
My lady yaf me al hooly
The noble yifte of hir mercy . . .

The self-portrait of the lover, from first to last, is the very image of
the same ideal. Years before his affection found its saint, he paid
tributary homage to Love as his rightful lord and devoutly prayed
for grace to become one of Love's elect. 'I ches love to my firste
craft'—owing to native disposition. His time as novice is finally
recognized with favor by the god, 'that had wel herd my boone,'
and he is granted sight of the nonpareil of women. The sequel is
equally orthodox. He worships long without daring to speak. He
composes love-songs and sings them, 'for to kepe me fro ydelnesse.'
He is reduced to desperation by the conflict between fear and desire. At last, like Troilus, he utters his stumbling entreaty for
'mercy,' swearing to be steadfast and true, to love his lady ever
'freshly newe,' to save her worship, and have no other ladies before
her. She at once returns him a categorical No, having none assurance of this stable humility. He mourns and suffers full many a
day. In due course—'another year'—he makes a second appeal. She
is now convinced of his steadfastness and accepts him for her
servant, giving him a ring. He is like a man raised from death to
life. Henceforth she takes him under her rule and they live for
many a year in perfect accord and felicity. It is part of the idealiza-
tion that, although he worshipped Love long ere they met, worshipped his lady long ere she accepted him, and lived long in
unspeakable happiness thereafter, he is still in the Spring of life
when the Dreamer meets him. He looks about twenty-four, his
face just beginning to show a beard.[4] He is adept in the fash-
ionably sophisticated language of paradox and metaphor—

In travayle ys myn ydelnesse
And eke my reste; my wele is woo . . .
My pees, in pledynge and in werre.

It is quite irrelevant that Gaunt married Blanche at the age of nineteen, and lost her in the Plague when he was twenty-nine; that he had spent great part of those ten years away from home and was abroad (with Chaucer) at the time of her death. In the poem, the knight is not identified, even covertly, as Gaunt until the punning allusion to his place of residence, fifteen lines from the end, unless through the name of the lady, which he reveals in figurative gloss. Despite the commentators, there is in the poem no overt suggestion that the knight is describing wedded love. The question does not and should not arise—unless we choose to read the gift of a ring as that of a wedding-ring: but we may recall that Troilus and Criseyde 'entrechaungeden hire rynges' at their first embracing, where, incidentally, Criseyde's charms are detailed in a catalogue warmer, but closely paralleling the one enumerated by the black knight. Within the terms of courtly love it would have been incongruous to mention marriage; and Gaunt would hardly have been complimented by the suggestion that as husband he was governed by his wife:

> In al my yowthe, in al chaunce,
> She took me in hir governaunce.

Similarly, the lady herself, as seen through her servant's eyes, is a paradigm of feminine excellence. From his ecstatic description we learn that she was the embodiment of goodness, truth, fair dealing, charming demeanor, and perfect physical beauty. James Russell Lowell found the portrait as fresh as the first violets gathered in the dew of a spring morning; and certainly it keeps a vernal fragrance, in spite of scholarly research which has shown it to be a florilegium of passages culled from French love-poetry. If Chaucer's audience were able to recognize the borrowings, they would not have been displeased that the garland was woven of blossoms transported from the courtly gardens of sweet France. That would for them have increased its rarity and enhanced its perfume. Not every woman received a tribute so far-sought and precious. We today are so used to equating realism and sincerity that we instinctively devaluate the forms, however exquisite, 'of hammered gold and gold enamelling,' which belong to an earlier and more studied artifice. We are, moreover, so conditioned to the notion—surely a symptom of the modern critical bias—that Chaucer's artistic progress is gauged inversely by the degree of his dependence on established medieval convention that we lack tongues to praise his mastery of that earlier idiom except as it departs from the norm.

Hence we notice signs of verisimilitude in the lover's meandering course of reminiscent eulogy, in the disordered sequence of thought giving rise to impulsive little bursts of ecstasy over one aspect and then another of his lady's merits, and returning upon itself again. But we should also bear in mind that the poet was working within a tradition and keeping a constant eye on the most esteemed models, and that he expected to be judged by the delicacy with which he composed his appliqué into a fresh design. The garment of praise is like his own Squire's habit, 'embrouded as it were a mede.' It has the crowded abundance of detail—and sometimes the irrelevance—that strikes us often in medieval textiles:

> I wolde thoo
> Have loved best my lady free,
> Thogh I had had al the beaute
> That ever had Alcipyades,
> And al the strengthe of Ercules,
> And thereto had the worthynesse
> Of Alysaunder, and al the rychesse
> That ever was in Babiloyne,
> In Cartage, or in Macedoyne,
> Or in Rome, or in Nynyve,—

or was as brave as Hector or as wise as Minerva; because she was as good as Penelope or as Lucrece, although she resembled neither one of them and was in fact unique—'she only queen of love and beauty.'

Coming now to the Dreamer, we confront a problem of far greater complexity. To be truly defined, he must be studied not in isolation but in several different contexts and relationships: as a person outside and inside the dream; in association with the grieving knight of his dream; as he relates to the poet who drew him;

and as he bears upon the human connections between Chaucer and John of Gaunt. It will be easiest to consider these aspects of the character one by one.

First, then, for the person who speaks to us directly as narrator throughout the poem. We meet him, first, engulfed in brooding melancholy, sleepless with 'sorwful ymagynacioun.' It is, we notice, his present condition that he is describing, not a state of mind from which he has fortunately escaped. He has suffered thus, he tells us, for as long as eight years, and has no prospect of recovery. The strange dream that he experienced recently, and that he intends to describe, was only an interruption. The dream is thus framed by, or suspended in, the Dreamer's own melancholy, into which he must be understood to have lapsed again upon awaking. He is resigned and passive about his condition, lost in a gentle wonder that he still lives, but not actively seeking death. It is only natural that his attention should have been caught by the plight of another star-crossed lover, when he happened upon it in a book he had chosen with which to while away the sleepless hours. The story concerned the grief of a queen, Alcyone, whose husband was lost at sea, and who could recover no word of his fate, nor get respite from her longing. The Dreamer's heart went out to her in pity, for he found his own sorrow imaged in hers.

Chaucer has been censured for not finding a closer parallel to John of Gaunt's bereavement. The tale of Ceyx and Alcyone, as he tells it, stresses the wife's grief, not the love of a husband bereft. The poet knew better than to set out the accounts, *seriatim*, of three lorn males. Alcyone breaks the sequence without disturbing the mood. She and the Dreamer are akin in their protracted love-longing, and she and the knight are at one in their grief. Deprivation unites us all, men and women, knights and queens. Unvarying repetition is not needed to drive home this truth.

When we look closely at the narrator—the 'I' inside the poem—it is surprising how little countenance he gives to the view of him that has come to be generally accepted since Kittredge's essay, of a simple-minded man, incapable of mature observation or intelligent response to experience. No doubt it is perilous to assert, where so much depends on the tone of voice, that after five hundred years we can always detect the nuances originally intended. It is at least clear that the narrator is by no means devoid of humor, and also that his sense of humor includes himself. It is not a very childlike person who can take so objective a view of his own predicament that, even while he poignantly feels it, he can both refer to it and refuse to dwell on it, with the civility and lack of overemphasis here displayed. It might be Pandarus himself who is speaking. Eight years is a long time to suffer for love:

> And yet my boote is never the ner;
> For there is physicien but oon
> That may me hele; but that is don.
> Passe we over untill eft;
> That wil not be mot nede be left.

He will talk of his sleeplessness: that, after all, is what leads him of his proper subject. But as to what causes that condition, the less said—short of downright rudeness—the better. A glancing, good-humored allusion is sufficient: who would wish to harp on his own chronic illnesses?

Obviously, too, the narrator can repeat a story with verve; witness the visit of Juno's messenger to the gods of slumber, 'who slept and did no other work.' The comic aspects of the episode are by no means lost upon him:

> 'Awake!' quod he, 'who ys lyth there?'
> And blew his horn ryght in here eere,
> And cried 'Awaketh!' wonder hye.
> This god of slep with hys oon ye
> Cast up, axed, 'Who clepeth ther?'
> 'Hyt am I,' quod this messager.

Here is no lack of lively and humorous awareness. Soon after, he declares—'in my game'—that, rather than die for lack of sleep, he would give that same Morpheus, or Dame Juno—or any one else, 'I ne roghte who'—a fine reward, if they would only put him to sleep. He had scarcely expressed the wish, when, inexplicably, he did fall asleep.

Any one, of course, who wishes to regard the manner of the narrative just reviewed as unsophisticated or childlike is entitled to that privilege. My present purpose is served if it be granted merely that it is unnecessary so to read it. Up to the point where the narrator falls asleep, it would, I think, be difficult to prove any significant difference in character between him and the narrator of the other dream-visions. If there is naïveté in the tone of the narrative, it is such a naïveté as we find in the *Parlement*, the *Hous of Fame*, the Prologue to the *Legend of Good Women*, and, indeed, woven into the very texture of all this poet's work. It is a simplicity and freshness of statement that continually tricks us into discounting the subtlety of perception and genuine human wisdom behind it.

But the problem of the narrator increases in complexity as soon as we enter the dream. The dreamlike quality of the narrative sequence has not passed unnoticed: due praise has been paid to this aspect of the poet's ordonnance. The way in which one episode opens into another without the logical connections or transitions: the Dreamer awakened *into* his dream by a burst of bird-song, to find himself on his bed with the morning sun making kaleidoscopic patterns through the windows of his chamber, richly stained with the Troy legend, and all the walls painted with the scenes of the Romance of the Rose; sounds outside of preparations for a royal hunt; the Dreamer's taking his horse at once and joining the party; the recall from the hunt; the disappearance of his horse ('I was go walked fro my tree'); the appearance and vanishing of the puppy— no hunting-dog, certainly; the flowery path through the woods full of wild creatures; the discovery of the handsome knight sitting against a huge oak and lost in grief—all this has the familiar but unforeseen and strange air of a dream.

We may also note subtle differences between the Dreamer's waking and sleeping states of mind. He does not lose his sense of humor nor his lively awareness: for example, his remarks on the heavenly singing of the birds on his chamber-roof—they didn't just open their mouths and pretend to be singing! Each one of them, without considering the cost to his throat, really exerted himself to show his best and happiest art. The Dreamer takes himself quite comfortably for granted as he is. It does not occur to him to reflect—but *we* notice the fact—that he is no longer carrying any of that load of oppressive sorrow under which he fell asleep. By a wonderful leap of psychological insight, and in strict accord with truth rediscovered in our own century, his private grief has been renounced by the Dreamer, to reappear externalized and projected upon the figure of the grieving knight. The modern analyst, indeed, would instantly recognize the therapeutic function of this dream as an effort of the psyche to resolve an intolerable emotional situation by repudiating it through this disguise. The knight is the Dreamer's surrogate; and in this view it would be significant that the force which keeps the surrogate from his lady is the far more acceptable, because decisive and final, fact of death. The train of analysis would lead us to assume, of course, a kindred connection between the lady of the dream and the fair but cruel 'physician' who refuses to work a cure in the Dreamer's waking life. And here it would be noted that the knight's long and rapturous eulogy of his lost lady would serve, in the Dreamer's unconscious, to discharge the latter's sense of guilt for the disloyalty of wishing the death of that Merciles Beaute. The disguise is rendered complete by the surrogate's having perfectly enjoyed his love before death severed them.

Some one will exclaim, ironically, How fortunate for the foregoing argument that Gaunt's Duchess had actually died, so that what the Dreamer desired could correspond with the facts! The taunt, of course, is irrelevant. What we are praising here is a depth of psychological truth that stands scrutiny on the level of basic human nature, making its silent contribution to the strength and consistency of the artifact. The historical Blanche and John of Gaunt and Chaucer await attention; but for the present we are concerned with elements inside the poem—connecting tissues, implicit but latent relations, that work below the surface to establish a convincing artistic unity.

The implied identification between the Dreamer and the knight is confirmed by parallels of repetitive description. Of himself, the Dreamer declares that he marvels he still lives:

> For nature wolde nat suffyse
> To noon erthly creature
> Nat longe tyme to endure
> Withoute slep and be in sorwe.

Of the knight, he says:

> Hit was gret wonder that nature
> Myght suffre any creature
> To have such sorwe, and be not ded.

The vital spirit of each of them has deserted its seat. For himself,

> Defaute of slep and hevynesse
> Hath sleyn my spirit of quyknesse;

and the knight is in the same case:

> his spirites wexen dede;
> The blood was fled for pure drede
> Doun to hys herte, to make hym warm—
> For wel hyt feled the herte had harm.

The Dreamer before falling asleep and the knight when he meets him show a kindred stupefaction, a grief so unrelieved that they fail to make contact with what is passing around them:

> I take no kep
> Of nothing, how hyt cometh or gooth . . .
> For I have felynge in nothyng,
> But, as yt were, a mased thyng,
> Alway in poynt to falle a-doun.

And the knight failed to observe the Dreamer who stood in front of him and spoke:

> throgh hys sorwe and hevy thoght,
> Made hym that he herde me noght;
> For he had wel nygh lost hys mynde.

Both men are hopeless, and the lesson of resignation is one which each has yet to learn. The knight's sorrow is momentarily assuaged by reminiscences, but it keeps recurring, floods back as he ceases to speak, and surrounds the episode of the meeting. The Dreamer likewise has surcease through the dream; but, as we have remarked, the beginning of his narrative, which is also in a sense the ending, encloses the poem with his melancholy. Each has a psychological and as it were biographical relation with Alcyone, and through her with each other. The story of Alcyone is thus a valuable unifying element in the poem as a whole; and, as we shall see, it is much more.

Out of the Dreamer's instinctive sympathy with the knight is developed the mechanism, subtle but with a surface simplicity, that carries the poem through to its conclusion. The Dreamer observes at once that the knight is in mourning and, approaching him silently, receives the sufficient explanation through the knight's overheard lament, that Death has stolen his bright lady. This is information to which, as a stranger, he has no right; but he cannot bear to leave a man in such grief without making any attempt to comfort him. He comes before him, therefore, and greets him quietly, and as soon as his presence is acknowledged, apologizes for disturbing him. He receives a gracious reply, and proceeds to invent conversation on indifferent matters, carefully avoiding reference to the other's state of grief until he has sanction from the knight's own mouth. 'The hunt is over,' he says; 'so far as I can judge, the hart has escaped.' 'It matters not a whit to me,' replies the knight; 'my thoughts have been far otherwise engaged.' 'That is evident enough,' replies the Dreamer: 'you appear to be sorely oppressed. If you felt like telling me about your trouble, I would do my best to relieve you, believe me; and just to talk might help.'

The Dreamer's tact leaves nothing to be desired; his etiquette is unimpeachable. In reply, the knight makes a long figurative statement of his woeful condition, full of rhetorical paradox, but rather unpacking his heart with conventional words than telling his grief directly—partly, perhaps, out of courtesy to a stranger, and partly because he shrinks from uttering the bare truth. He comes close to it in the avowal that death has made him naked of all bliss. But he prefers to stalk his pain rather than confront it immediately. Yet he is not deliberately concealing his meaning, and certainly expects to be understood. He rails on Lady Fortune in set terms, and says he has played a game of chess with her and lost. She made a sly move and stole his 'fers,' checkmating him in the middle of the board ('nel mezzo del cammin') with an insignificant stray pawn. She has left him destitute of joy and longing for death.

The Dreamer finds his tale so pitiable that he can hardly bear it. He fully apprehends the meaning of the figurative language, which after all only confirms what he has already overheard. To suppose him mystified at this point were to credit him with rather less than the intelligence of a normal dog. Yet some of Chaucer's critics appear to have done just that. They write as if the Dreamer thinks the game was an actual chess-game, that the 'fers' was a literal piece on a literal board. How the Dreamer would understand the knight's opponent in a literal sense they do not explain. Fortune in person would be something to see! Obviously, the naming of the knight's opponent forces a figurative meaning upon the game. If the Dreamer fails to understand this, he understands nothing at all. He *must* take 'fers' in a figurative sense; and the reason he accepts the figurative term instead of abandoning it is that the knight as yet has given no sanction for the familiarity that a substitution would imply. Decorum, not bewilderment, forbids the Dreamer's referring to the lady in more literal terms.

With all the necessary facts in his possession, the Dreamer realizes that he must try to rescue the knight from this abject submission to misfortune. He sees two possible ways of proceeding. One is to rouse a spirit of endurance in the sufferer; the other, to seek to reduce the proportions of his loss. He tries each of these in turn, not forgetting but taking advantage of the fact that he yet has more specific knowledge than the knight's conversation so far has justified his admitting. At the very least, he must keep the knight talking, to save him from black despair. 'You mustn't give way like this,' he exclaims; 'remember how Socrates despised Fortune.' 'It's no use,' says the knight. 'Don't say so,' insists the Dreamer; 'even if you had lost the *twelve* ferses, you would still be guilty of the sin of self-murder if you gave in utterly to sorrow. You would be just as surely condemned as all those other unwise people who ended their lives because of disappointment in love: Medea, Phyllis, Dido, Echo, and Samson. But no man alive in these days would go to such lengths for loss of a fers.'

And here we cannot avoid brief discussion of the term 'fers,' as used by the knight and the Dreamer. Fortunately, we can borrow the assistance of some very learned counsel, of whom the son of Sir James Murray, Mr. H. J. R. Murray, is best of all. Originally, it appears, the piece we now know as the Queen was a masculine figure, in Arabic 'firzān,' meaning counsellor or wise man—an appropriate and useful companion for a Shah or King on the field of battle. 'The fact,' says Murray, 'that *firz* was adopted and not translated in some of the European languages proves that the meaning of the Arabic name was not understood.'⁵ This doubtless facilitated the shift in the sex of that piece. An alternative nomenclature arose pretty generally throughout Europe in which the feminine gender of the piece was left in no doubt: e.g., *femina, virgo, domina, dama, frauw, dame, lady.* Also, and apparently commencing earlier, another series: *regina, reina, reine, quene.* But these did not entirely supplant the old term of *fers,* howsoever they may have affected its denotative and connotative significance, until two or three centuries after the time of Chaucer. The power of the piece in Chaucer's game was not nearly so great as the power it acquired later. Chaucer's fers could move only one square at a time, diagonally, and therefore hovered for the most part defensively about the king. The other pieces had much their modern power of movement: hence the rooks, bishops, and knights were all stronger pieces than the fers, and their loss would be relatively more serious. But in giving the fers such importance in the knight's imaginary game, Chaucer may have had in mind the especially close connection between it and the king in actual play, as well as the fact that all the rest were unequivocally male. That the original meaning of the name *fers* was everywhere completely lost at the moment of the game's introduction into Europe, even where chess-men were representatively carved, cannot be proved; and that some traces of that earlier tradition survived alongside the feminizing influence of the newer nomenclature, is surely not improbable. Moreover, the fact that the masculine pawns, on reaching the eighth row, became ferses, would make for further neutralizing of the feminine concept.

This possibility may have a bearing on the meaning of the Dreamer's curious reference to 'the ferses twelve.' Skeat's interpretation of this phrase, adopted by the *Oxford English Dictionary*, is 'all the pieces except the king.' To arrive at this explanation, Skeat reckons: 'pawns, *eight;* queen, bishop, rook, knight, *four;* total, *twelve*.'[6] The King, according to Skeat, does not count, because he cannot be taken; and the bishops, rooks, and knights are counted three instead of six. To justify the latter count, Skeat takes refuge in the game of Shatranj (Chaturamga), out of which chess evolved; and to escape from applying the same principle of *kinds of pieces* to the pawns, he appeals to the old differentiation of individual pawns as shown after Chaucer's day in Caxton's illustrations. This is desperate pleading, in view of the fact that Chaucer's game had, undeniably, two each of bishops, rooks, and knights; that there is no evidence (I believe) of those pieces ever being called ferses; and that the eight pawns however differentiated were all called pawns. The total, with the fers, and without the king, comes to *fifteen* every time, unless we apply Peter's reasoning in the *Tale of a Tub.*

I am tempted, therefore, to suppose that the solution of the crux must be sought outside the game of chess; and, if the concept of the fers was sufficiently heterosexual to permit, I can think of no twelve companions more famous as a king's defenders than the Twelve Peers of Charlemagne, though I cannot prove that 'Doucepers' was ever corrupted into 'Doucefers.' If some one brought forward twelve equally famous *hetairai* who traditionally went together, I might, I suppose, have to give way. Certain it is, at any rate, that the Dreamer expects his phrase to be understood, that he uses it in a figurative sense, and that the MS. authority never omits the article. 'Defy Fortune,' urges the Dreamer,

> for trewely,
> Thogh ye had lost the ferses twelve,

And ye for sorwe mordred yourselve,
Ye sholde be dampned in this cas . . .

Skeat himself, it may be added, accepts, and goes beyond, the crucial assumption in our conjecture. 'As,' says he, 'the word *fers* originally meant counsellor or monitor of the king, it could be applied to any of the pieces,' that is, was not necessarily understood as feminine.

'No man alive,' says the Dreamer, 'would yield to this suicidal woe, for a fers.' Medea, Dido, and Samson, who all died on account of their 'ferses,' are his comparative cases; and he is not thinking of literal chess-men. He is challenging the knight to justify his extreme grief, knowing well that to do so will force him to recall evidence of his lady's excellence and deflect his self-absorption. The ruse is successful. 'Little you know what you are talking about,' says the knight: 'I have lost more than you suppose.' 'Then, good sir, tell me the whole story, how and why you have been divested of bliss.' 'Gladly, if you will give me your undivided attention.' 'I promise you, there is nothing I'd rather do: I am wholly at your disposal.'

As the Dreamer had anticipated, the knight's memorabilia of his love, once stirred, begin to pour out in a flood: her gracious demeanor, her dancing, her laugh, her look, her hair, her eyes, her soft speaking, her fair dealing—on and on, as if he could never stop. He finally does, however, declaring: 'This was she who was all my joy, my world's well-being, my goddess; and I was hers wholly and entirely.'

The impetuous panegyric has been good for him, as the Dreamer can see. But ecstatic praise without the personal history still leaves the burden undischarged; and it will be yet better if the knight can be got to tell the story of his love, and perhaps be brought to realize it as a treasure that is his to keep, in the teeth of Time and Fortune. 'By our Lord,' says the Dreamer, 'I don't wonder you were wholly hers. Your love was certainly well placed: I don't know how you could have done better.' 'Done better?' exclaims the knight, forgetting logic at the sacrilege of an implied comparison: 'nor could any one have done so well.' 'I certainly think you're right.' 'Nay, but you must believe it!' 'Sir, so I do,' replies the Dreamer, with the reservation in agreement that will keep things going at this critical juncture: 'I believe that to you she was the best and any one seeing her with your eyes would have seen her as the loveliest of women.' 'With *my* eyes? Nay, but every one that saw her said and swore that she was. And had they not, it wouldn't have changed my devotion. I *had* to love her. But *had to* is silly: I wished, I was bound to love her, because she was the fairest and best; it was a free but inevitable offering. But I was telling you about the first time I ever saw her. I was young and ignorant then, but I determined to do my whole devoir in her service. It did me so much good just to see her, that sorrow couldn't touch me the whole day after. She so possessed my mind that sorrow could make no impression.'

The Dreamer's reply is charming and adroit. Here is the man who has claimed to be Sorrow himself, the essential personification of that state, describing how the idea of his love could heal him of all sorrow. The Dreamer leads him toward self-realization by suggesting, figuratively, how much he had to rejoice over, since he could still think of her. 'You seem to me,' says the Dreamer, 'like a man who goes to confession with nothing to repent.' 'Repent!' cries the knight indignantly, rising to the bait: 'far from me be the thought of repenting my love. That were worse than the worst treason that ever was. No, I will never forget her as long as I live.' The Dreamer does not press the logical victory, but turns back to ask again for the narrative, still not forgetting that the lady's death is a fact that the knight does not know that he possesses. 'You have told me,' says he, 'about your first sight of your lady. I beseech you to tell me how you first spoke to her, and the rest; and about the nature of the loss you have suffered.' 'Yes,' says the knight, 'it's greater than you imagine.' 'How so, sir? Won't she love you? or have you acted in a way that has caused her to leave you? Tell me everything, I pray you.'

With this urging, the knight at last abandons indirections and moves straight down the autobiographical road until he reaches the point of perfect felicity. 'Al was us oon,' he says.

withoute were.
And thus we lyved ful many a yere
So wel, I kan nat telle how.

Too plainly, this is not the end. 'For ever after,' the story-books
would say. But in life it is not so, and the Dreamer must help him
to his conclusion. 'Sir,' he asks gently, 'where is she now?' 'Now?'
repeats the knight, his grief suddenly overwhelming him. 'Alas
that I was born! That is the loss I told you of, remember? It was
herself.' 'Alas, sir, how?' 'She is dead.' 'Oh, no!' 'She is, though.' 'So
that is it. God, how sad!'

There is nothing in this narrative, nor in the dialogue which
punctuates it, that need be taken as insensibility or forgetfulness
or egregious simplicity on the part of the Dreamer. To the contrary,
it is hard to imagine the situation being handled with more awareness and delicacy by Geoffrey Chaucer, courtier, man of the
world, and poet, *in propria persona,* had it confronted him so in
actual life. Never presuming on his private knowledge, the
Dreamer leads the knight from point to point to disclose everything, and at the knight's own pace and pleasure.

The unwillingness of most critics to accept the narrative on
trust, merely because they are not explicitly told that Chaucer
knows what he is doing and that he is doing it deliberately, is very
churlish. Why must we assume his incompetence, when the contrary assumption points to an explanation both natural and artistically satisfying? To take the intelligence of the Dreamer for
granted is to remove the difficulty, for his intelligence and tact
dictate his whole procedure.

When we bethink us that the poet would in the first instance be
present in person to mediate between his work and his audience,
we realize that the critical difficulty must have arisen since his
time, as a result of altered relations between author and public,
owing to the far-reaching effects of Print.

An author who addresses an *audience,* in the primary sense of
the word, and who introduces himself overtly as one of the *dramatis
personae* in his work, must naturally expect that his physical
presence will color the self-portrait and contribute inevitably to its

artistic effect. In fact, he cannot employ the autobiographical method, using the first person but meaning another than himself, without giving unmistakable indications that he is *quoting*—unless his audience is to be sadly misled. This is not to say that he may not present himself, or aspects of his total self, in such fashion as he pleases, and with such emphasis or bias as he wills or cannot avoid. But it is still himself that he is representing, however posed and semi-dramatic; and comparison follows inevitably.

When Chaucer read his poem to the circle for whom it was first intended, he was understood to be referring to himself when he used the first person. His audience, according to their private knowledge or degree of familiarity, might consider that he was distorting facts or truth, deliberately or unconsciously; but they would not leap unaided to the assumption that he was speaking in a fictive personality that had no relation to himself nor any reality outside his poem. When, therefore, Kittredge says that the Dreamer 'is as much a part of the fiction in the Book of the Duchess as the Merchant or the Pardoner or the Host is a part of the fiction in the Canterbury Tales,' we must protest that this is true only as we consider that Chaucer himself is everywhere and throughout an essential 'part of the fiction' in the Canterbury Tales, and elsewhere; the fiction being Chaucer's Chaucer, meeting and responding to characters and scenes in his work, and being reported on to his audience by that other Chaucer, of flesh and blood, then and there present before them.

In such a sense, therefore, it is necessary to contemplate the first personal representation that meets us in *The Book of the Duchess*. And it is not too difficult to approximate the two, Chaucer and Dreamer, bearing in mind the high and low lighting, the qualifications and emphases and omissions due to the perspective of an accepted literary convention and to the poet's own choice. We do not have to believe that Chaucer was suffering the extremes of unrequited love in actual fact; but we may well suppose that his neglect to present himself in attitudes of abject self-abasement and vermiform humility is a touch of self-definition regarding the love-conventions; and we may read our knowledge of him into the statement that he got more pleasure out of reading than out of backgammon or chess.

The question of identity becomes most acute where it touches Chaucer's relations with John of Gaunt, both within and without the poem. As John of Gaunt, the Man in Black raises delicate considerations with regard to the deportment of the Dreamer as Geoffrey Chaucer. Hitherto, we have been able to limit discussion to the fictive aspects of the two characters. But Chaucer cannot afford to forget that he is dealing with a most sensitive area in his patron's personal life. When we look at the poem as his solution of this human problem, our admiration for the poet's tact and wisdom is greatly increased; and our sense of his artistic skill is much heightened.

Concerning the stroke of genius that prompted Chaucer to put the eulogy into the mouth of the bereaved man, Kittredge has spoken with shrewd appreciation, and of the major artistic contribution which thereby ensues:

> The substance of the elegy, by this adjustment, is spoken by the lady's husband, who can best describe her beauty, her charm of manner, and all her gracious qualities of mind and heart. Thus we have in the Book of the Duchess, not a prostrate and anxiously rhetorical obituary, from the blazoning pen of a commissioned laureate, but a tribute of pure love from the lady's equal, who can speak without constraint,—from her husband, who has most cause to mourn as he has the best knowledge of what he has lost. [And again:] The mourning knight is not describing his lady: he is giving voice to his unstudied recollection—now of her nature, now of her beauty, now of her demeanor, now of her speech—spasmodically, in no order, as this or that idea rises in his agitated mind.

Little more need be said. It is worth noticing, however, that there is a special propriety about the charming portrait of Blanche. Although she is described, ostensibly, by her husband, it is actually the poet who has to find the terms in which she is to be described. Chaucer has the problem far more difficult than penning a simple eulogy, of imagining what a husband might say of his deceased wife, and expressing it in such a way as may be neither too intimate nor too reserved and cold. Thus, he really has to speak simultaneously for Gaunt and for himself, to find the precise point at which the husband and the friend may unite in expressive agreement. If Chaucer was the immature artist the critics have usually found him in this poem, he had surely tackled a problem of the last degree of difficulty, both artistic and human. He solves it with a skill and tact beyond praise. The materials employed are nearly all such as could be compiled and uttered by an interested observer who had had opportunity of watching the lady's appearance and bearing and ordinary conduct over a space of time. The elements are objective and external, conventional in kind and expression, the inner qualities being suggested in terms so general that they seem more a statement of the observer's faith, an act of devotion, than a private and intimate portrait. There is no charge of presumption that can be laid against the poet; and yet he has also cast a glow of genuine emotion over the whole picture, partly through its very hyperbole, partly through the disconnected manner of its delivery, which makes it seem the true language of recent bereavement. In its sensitive awareness, its manipulation of literary as well as psychological components, its modulations of tone between reticence and confidence, it is a triumph of controlled artistic intention. C. S. Lewis has caught better than any other critic the prevailing mood that it succeeds in establishing: 'How fine and fresh [Chaucer's] treatment is' writes Lewis, 'may be judged from the very remarkable fact that though the poem is a true elegy, yet the abiding impression it leaves upon us is one of health and happiness . . . Not because the poem is a bad elegy, but because it is a good one, the black background of death is always disappearing behind these irridescent shapes of satisfied love.'[7] In truth, the poet comes not to bury Blanche, but to praise her.

He comes also to offer consolation to the bereaved. And in this aspect of his poem he exhibits possibly his supreme artistry and greatest human wisdom. The poem ends, some critics have felt, too abruptly. 'Is that youre los?' asks the Dreamer. 'Be God, hyt ys routhe!' It is the last word in the long interchange between himself and the knight. To some it has seemed lame and impotent for a man who earlier gave hopes of so much more comfort.

> But certes, sire, yif that yee
> Wolde ought discure me youre woo,
> I wolde, as wys God helpe me soo,
> Amende hyt, yif I kan or may.
> Ye mowe preve hyt be assay;
> For, by my trouthe, to make yow hool,
> I wol do al my power hool.

But, apart from the fact that sympathy is the only effective kind of help that can be offered directly in the face of bereavement, Chaucer has been offering indirect consolation from the very commencement, and this is one of the unifying elements of his poem. He well knew that the best advice in the world would be inappropriate when served up to his patron as the last word in such a conversation, on such a topic. It would be socially impudent and out of place, as well as ineffectual; also, and inevitably, inartistic. Yet he does have something to convey, if he can, to his grieving friend. And his lesson is the age-old one of resignation and human acceptance of life and death, of thankfulness for past felicity, of the comfort of precious memories, of the dignity of self-mastery in spite of Fortune's 'false draughtes dyvers.'

At the very opening of his poem, he has sounded the note of resigned acceptance that contains its deepest meaning. 'But that is don,' he says of his own case: 'that wil not be mot nede be left.' This truth will be more evident for the knight in the sequel. Here is a foreshadowing: but the fullest statement is the conclusion of the Alcyone episode, where Chaucer conveys by anticipation the human lesson for his patron which he is unable to express at the end directly. Indeed, this is the most important function of the episode, and that which effectually integrates the work when looked at from a formal point of view. The true conclusion has had to be thrown forward from the end to an inconspicuous point where it can insinuate its meaning unobtrusively and without risk of antagonizing, carried as it is not by the poet but by a third spokesman, the figure of Ceyx. Here is the message, put with exquisite and simple beauty, a message from all dead lovers to their bereaved loves, a tender voice from the grave:

293

Awake! let be your sorwful lyf!
For in your sorwe there lyth no red.
For, certes, swete, I nam but ded:
Ye shul me never on lyve ysee . . .
And farewel, swete, my worldes blysse!
I praye God youre sorwe lysse.
To lytel while oure blysse lasteth!

'My worldes blysse': It is hardly accidental that the phrase is almost identical with the one that the knight is later to use of his own love:—'al my blesse, My worldes welfare, and my goddesse.' The verbal echoes, the carry-over of phrase and idea from one part of the poem to another, the inner harmonies, subtly communicate the underlying relation between its parts, binding it in ways all too frequently ignored. The elements of the work come together and are fused at a level of experience, human and artistic, where likeness melts into a closer unity, and where, in the presence of death, Ceyx and Blanche, Gaunt and Alcyone, the Dreamer and Chaucer and his audience, too, of which we now form a part, are become essentially one.

NOTES

1. G. G. Coulton, *Chaucer and his England* (1927), p. 37; Clemen, *Der junge Chaucer* (Köln, 1938); Kreuzer, 'The Dreamer in *The Book of The Duchess,' PMLA,* LXVI (June 1951), 543–547.

2. G. L. Kittredge, *Chaucer and his Poetry* (Cambridge, 1915), pp. 48–51, 51–52.

3. Allan Ramsay, *Poems* (1877), II, 5.

4. The suggestion (cf. Robinson, p. 884, n. to ll. 445 ff.) that 'foure and twenty' may be a scribal error (xxiiij for xxviiij) infers to my mind, in view of the context, an unduly factual reporting.

5. *A History of Chess* (Oxford, 1913), p. 423.

6. W. W. Skeat, *The Works of Geoffrey Chaucer* (Oxford), I, 481–482. Articles on the *fers* in this poem that do not affect the suggestion here offered are: S. W. Stevenson, 'Chaucer's Ferses Twelve,' *ELH,* VII (1940), 215–222; F. D. Cooley, 'Two Notes on Chess Terms in *The Book of the Duchess,' MLN,* LXIII (1948), 30–35; W. H. French, 'Medieval Chess and the *Book of the Duchess,' MLN,* LXIV (1949), 261–264. Cooley would omit *the* in 'the ferses twelve.' He observes that *twelve* is a number common in familiar reference, as twelve apostles, *douzegers,* etc. I had neglected his article until mine was written, but in any case our readings do not agree.

7. *The Allegory of Love* (Oxford, 1936), pp. 167–170.

PAUL G. RUGGIERS

The Unity of Chaucer's *House of Fame*

In many ways the most tantalizing of Chaucer's vision poems, the *House of Fame* continues to present a serious problem of interpretation to students of medieval poetry. The views of many writers who have dealt with the poem have tended to leave its meaning unresolved, and the steady accumulation of theories, while not obscuring the intention of the work, has unfortunately not clarified into a unified whole a poem in which Chaucer's rapidly developing powers are revealed at every turn.[1] The often repeated charge against the *House of Fame* that it lacks a clear plan, and Coghill's remark that it seems the least successful of Chaucer's longer poems sum up, in spite of more appreciative words, the general attitude of perplexed dissatisfaction with it.[2] A close reading of the work should convince the most reluctant reader that Chaucer was here, if not in complete possession of his artistic powers, nearing the goal of facility and force such as are to be seen in the structural strength and psychological validity underlying his major poetry. A comparison of the *House of Fame* with the *Book of the Duchess* and the *Parliament of Fowls* offers a clue to the problem of its unity, and in spite of the stumbling blocks in the way of a totally satisfactory analysis of the poem as an organic whole, I should like to present what I consider its binding principle in terms of the progressively universalizing impulse which determines its form.

Reprinted, by permission, from *Studies in Philology*, L (1953), 16-29.

I shall attempt to show that the first book of the *House of Fame* presents us with a love story in which Fame, much like Fortune, plays an important role in the lives of two lovers; that the second book, while maintaining both the motive power of a love-vision and the force of a quest, gives us a view of an orderly universe, of which Fame is a part, in which all things seek and find their proper resting place; that the third, satisfying the demands of the quest and the love-vision, reveals the actual distribution or withholding of renown in such a universe. Book II, while transitional, is of great importance because it establishes the philosophical formula for the poem; with Book III it provides a kind of commentary on the exemplum of Book I.[3] Whatever was to have been announced in the grand climax by the man of great authority may have been intended to provide an answer to the common consideration of the Middle Ages, the relationship of men to the mutable world through the agency of Fame.

I

The first of the enigmas of the poem seems always to have been the first book, with its emphasis upon the story of Dido and Aeneas. Does Chaucer devote this book almost entirely to the story of the *Aeneid* and in particular to the ill fortune of Dido simply because the poem is a love-vision? Why then call the poem *House of Fame*? What is the connection between this book and the books that follow? What, for that matter, is the relation between the activities of Venus and those of her sister Fortune?

Two writers, W. O. Sypherd and Howard Rollin Patch, have amply demonstrated these connections for us. Sypherd's argument, stated briefly, is that Chaucer's conception of the Goddess Fame was greatly influenced by the current notions of the goddesses of Love and Fortune, and that the idea of Fame or Rumor was enlarged by adding to her simple functions of hearing tidings and spreading them abroad, the more powerful attribute of sitting as a divinity to decide on the worldly fame of mankind. Chaucer would find some authority for such an equation of the three deities in love-visions and in his own reading and translation of Boethius.

Even the companies of suppliants at the court of Fame, Sypherd writes, are ultimately dependent upon the general notion of the court of the god and goddess of Love.[4] To these identifications Patch gives his further support: 'Fortune is never quite free from the charges of those who are discontented with their fame. As her gifts include glory, so we find her pretty much responsible for our reputation, good or bad.' And again: 'Fortune actually does or undoes the work of the God of Love. We may remember that in many ways her traits . . . resemble those of the love deity. . . . These divinities, Fortune and Love, become sufficiently identified for Venus to take over the characteristics of her sister goddess, and by the time of *Les Éches Amoureux* we find Venus turning a wheel and exalting and debasing mankind.'[5]

What I am suggesting is simply that the functions of the three goddesses are so similar as to result in a conflation of their activities and the effects of their power over men. There is sufficient practical identification of these important deities in the House of Fame ('Geffrey' himself is going to the House of Fame, sister of Fortune, for love tidings) to warrant the recounting of a fateful love story in a poem which is to be concerned chiefly with the meting out of fame. Further, by structural analogy with the *Book of the Duchess* and the *Parliament of Fowls* where Chaucer's method is to juxtapose a preliminary reading from a book with the ensuing vision for purposes of profounder implication and meaning, the *House of Fame* provides us with a specific account of Dido caught in the contrivances of Venus, or the fortunes of love, and of Fame, as an introduction to what 'Geffrey' is to behold in the third book, the goddess Fame doling out her favor and disfavor with random caprice to mankind, in matters of love as well as in the countless other pursuits of men. It is important to notice that when Dido cries out against her fate, her complaint is specifically lodged against wicked Fame, the lament being a neat blend of the two phases of Fame's functions, rumor and reputation:

> O wikke Fame! for ther nys
> Nothing so swift, lo, as she is!
> O, soth ys, every thing ys wyst,

Though hit be kevered with the myst.
Eke, though I myghte duren ever,
That I have don, rekever I never,
That I ne shal be seyd, allas,
Yshamed be thourgh Eneas,
And that I shal thus juged be,—
'Loo, ryght as she hath don, now she
Wol doo eft-sones, hardely;'
Thus seyth the peple prively.

The evil fortune of love, the slander, the loss of reputation, all of which Dido laments in the first book, point towards the third book where Fame is seen in action. There is in Chaucer's epitome of the *Aeneid*, with its emphasis upon the story of Dido and Aeneas a sufficient foreshadowing of his theme to warrant the long so-called digression of the third book where Chaucer relates the method by which Fame distributes her dubious favors. For his purposes the unhappy catastrophe of love is the work of a divinity whose name might easily be Fortune, or Fame, or Venus; their roles are interdependent; they operate in similar circumstances. We need not complain that Chaucer has not told us that this is an exemplum; we need not look for the explicit moral drawn in the manner of Gower or Machaut or Jean de Meun. In none of the early love-visions does Chaucer state the purpose of the pre-liminary reading, for as Bronson, Clemen, and most recently, Malone have shown, all that follows the reading from a book is in a sense a commentary on what has gone before.

The presence of the eagle at the end of Book I and his subse-quent role in the poem raise the old question of Dantean influences upon Chaucer, a question that has a certain importance in an interpretation of the work. The eagle which appears at the end of Book I is generally acknowledged to be derived in part from the eagle which carries Dante aloft in *Purgatorio* IX. If this is so, we cannot very easily dismiss the possibility that Chaucer was fully aware of the significance of this episode for the *Divine Comedy* as a whole. It will be remembered that in the valley of negligent princes Dante is assailed by thoughts of the corruption and decay of Empire. A golden eagle, aptly the symbol of empire, law and justice, Jove's bird, snatches the dreaming Dante into the fiery sphere; the dream is a prophetic one, or as it has been called, a prefatory one, and whatever specifically was revealed to Dante in it, Dante falls away from the purging vision with a sense of the disparity between the ideal of the empyrean and the defective milieu of this earth. The eagle itself is but a forecast of another eagle which Dante is to see, the lecturing, rebuking eagle of Paradise, the bird of God formed by the just rulers who collectively represent Divine Justice. In this circle of heaven Dante is confronted with the great mystery of God's justice with special regard to whether or not the righteous heathen were saved. The question is answered after the manner of St. Paul; that is, it is declared unanswerable. Divine Justice must always remain a mystery beyond the reach of human knowledge; Dante must be content to see that some of the righteous heathen are saved, and that the will of God, embracing and exceeding ours, is its own standard in the choice of the elect. Both the eagle of Jove in Purgatory and the eagle of God in Paradise seem implicit in Chaucer's talking bird. He appears to have adopted the device of the flight from the *Purgatorio* and the meaning of that flight from the *Paradiso*. Chaucer's eagle, the agent of high comedy, not of serious moral drama, and the messenger of Jove, enables him to approach an understanding of the activities of Fame, her casual bestowal or withholding of favor; her caprice, or in short, her injustice is apparently her only standard. The implication for Chaucer, as it was an open rebuke for Dante, is the same: Who is Chaucer that he should attempt to judge this mystery and to fathom its operations? The eagle comes, in the conclusion to Book I, at a calculated moment. Just as Dante needed to be presented with his reassuring vision, so Chaucer now needs his reassuring answer to what he has just recently seen. He prays,

> 'O Crist!' thoughte I, 'that art in blysse,
> Fro fantome and illusion
> Me save!'

Is he perhaps asking how this cruel love which he has just witnessed can be the magnificent love of which Boethius and Dante both speak, ordering the stars in their courses and binding men and women in a sacred tie? The eagle comes miraculously to lead him to an answer.

Such seems to me to be the relationship between Book I and the remainder of the poem. And if we can perceive that relationship, then we will also discover that from the very beginning of the poem Chaucer's genius has taken hold of its direction; it comes more and more to life in bursts out of the very core of his subject, which is a facet of the problem of evil, the role of capricious circumstance in men's lives, whether in the realm of the passions or elsewhere. And as we shall see, he yields himself up to his scheme with an enthusiasm that is always sufficiently held in check to make the poem conform to the requirements of his guiding principle. It seems presumptuous to assume that Chaucer did not learn from Geoffrey de Vinsauf and Boethius, if not from his own hard application to the art of poetry, that the creative artist refrains from plunging carelessly into his task, but first 'aperceyveth in his thought the forme of the thing that he wol make' before he shapes his idea and clothes it with words.[6]

II

There can be little disagreement over the purpose and function of Book II of the *House of Fame*. Its clear statement by the eagle that 'Geffrey' is to be carried away from the uninspiring daily rounds of his life to the House of Fame where he may hear tidings of love, indicates the motive of the dream. The chief difficulty of interpretation has arisen, of course, from our inability to adjust what is promised in the long list of love's circumstances cited by the eagle to what Chaucer actually sees in Book III when he is in the House of Fame. Our general tendency is to feel that the author has lost the main thread of his narrative and has abandoned, if only in part, his original direction. As I have stated above, it is my belief that Chaucer has not relinquished his theme, the reward of love tidings for the weary poet; in the universalizing process, in the conflation of the three goddesses, the love motive has been absorbed into the larger scheme of the mystery of adverse circumstance, and in particular into the accident of fame. All that evolves after the promise of the eagle does so naturally and smoothly: Chaucer protests that he cannot understand how so many items of news could reach the goddess Fame, whereupon the bird launches into his long explanation of the basic order of the universe, and with it, the analogy between the widening circles resulting from throwing a stone in water and the widening circles of sound (which is merely broken air) seeking their natural resting place in Fame's palace.

The function of the book is of course to serve as a statement of purpose, the quest for tidings, and to provide in Boethian terms the basic scientific and theological formula of the orderly universe. Its narrative thread is spatial, and thus the book is structurally, as well as geographically, transitional.

The generally accepted notion has been that at the time of the writing of the love-visions Chaucer had as yet only imperfectly assimilated the substance of his reading, abundant as it was, in continental sources. And yet, one of the satisfying aspects of Chaucer's art has always been his ability to coördinate into an interesting and artistic whole the most heterogeneous materials. This creative synthesis is perhaps best seen in the *Nun's Priest's Tale* where we find the humors, dream psychology, Bradwardine on God's foreknowledge and man's free will, and a parody of Vinsauf's elegy— all cleverly subordinated to his main scheme. One may wonder on occasion whether Chaucer's audience must not have been impressed and bewildered by the confusing array of Chaucer's gifts alongside those of other writers, and whether those who were well-read would not find that they were forced to adjust their recollection of the meaning of a reference in its original context to its new use; but Chaucer's borrowings from Boethius, for example, are extraordinarily successful in the *House of Fame*. The explanation in Boethian terms that 'every thing . . . hath his propre mansyon, / to which hit seketh to repaire, / ther-as hit shulde not appaire,' is beautifully absorbed into the scheme of the passing of report to the House of Fame where it finds its natural resting place. And when, following his exultant little prayer at God's mighty creation, Chaucer resorts to a direct quotation from the

Consolatio, the reference is peculiarly apt and corroborates the tone of subtle irony throughout. The lines read:

> And thoo thoughte y upon Boece,
> That writ, 'A thought may flee so hye,
> Wyth fetheres of Philosophye,
> To passen everych element;
> And whan he hath so fer ywent,
> Than may be seen, behynde hys bak,
> Cloude,' and al that y or spak.

The poem he is referring to occurs at a point in the *Consolatio* where Boethius is about to learn from the lady Philosophy her views on the existence of evil in the world. Through her tutelage he has been gradually freed from the taint of earth and is now to be made 'parfit of the worschipful lyght of God' in a sphere to which one day his soul will return as to its natural home. Chaucer must have liked the passage for its power as well as for its adaptability to his narrative: he too is, in his dream, surmounting the earth; he too has beheld the order and beauty of God's creation; he too will receive an answer, in the form of a demonstration in the House of Fame, to one phase of the problem of evil in God's world. Indeed the whole flight through the upper air is so closely supported by the Boethian references that one catches a hint of the sublime usually denied to Chaucer, the sublime of high comedy. The eagle's amusing disquisition on order in the universe set side by side with the passage of report to the House of Fame, the retreating of the earth beneath them as they mount higher and higher, the precarious relationship of poor Geoffrey to the eagle form the substance of Book II in a lively sweep of narrative related with great deftness and comic awareness, an extraordinary sample of the literature of the journey. Chaucer seems here really to have enjoyed his work, for in its lines he had lavished most of his energy in creating the learned bird and the simpleton foil. The general interest is high because the book serves as a transition from earth to heaven and because the journey, with its scientific apparatus, becomes Chaucer's primary object.

III

The 'lytel laste bok' is the source of most of our difficulties in interpreting the *House of Fame* as a unified whole because it contains the second of the so-called artistic blemishes (the Dido-Aeneas story is the first) in the poem, and because in it Chaucer seems to have lost the original direction of the narrative and shifted his emphasis from love tidings to the vicissitudes of fame. This emphasis upon the granting or withholding of fame constitutes no real difficulty if we consider that Dido and Aeneas are part of the human comedy and that their relationship is conditioned by the intermingled activities of Love and the two sister goddesses, Fame and Fortune. One cannot shake off the conviction that in this book Chaucer has his mind set squarely on his goal. The extravagant invention, the embellishment of glorious names, the energy and the enthusiasm with which the poet pushes towards a conclusion would seem collectively to indicate his singleness of purpose; the fact that the poem does not in its present state fulfill its earlier promise of tidings of love is no warrant that such tidings were not to be forthcoming. The long account of the nine companies of petitioners in the court of Fame, suing for their desired reputation or oblivion, it is entirely possible, is not a digression at all but an organic part of the action, the logical demonstration of Chaucer's ideas about Fame and her influence upon the lives of men. The relationship to Dante which I have indicated earlier suggests that the mysterious and capricious injustice of the Lady Fame is to Chaucer's poem what the impenetrable mystery of God's justice is to the *Divine Comedy;* both poets are led to the threshold of an answer by an eagle who is the messenger of the Almighty. In his own poem, he deals with the problem not so much of God's justice working itself out in the world (although he may have meant that to be a part of the final resolution), but with a collateral consideration that may have had its genesis in his reading of Boethius, the subjection of men to the capricious circumstance of Fame. It is my persuasion that the third book says what Chaucer intends it to say, that Fame and her influence, like that of her sister Fortune, is ever present as a conditioning factor in men's lives, and that men should fasten their hopes on something more stable, over and above this capricious power. Chaucer knew well from Boethius and Dante that there is a tremendous gap between the fame that the world offers and the personal satisfaction in abiding by the laws of his art and eschewing the lures of the inconstant Lady Fame. His own humorous and dispassionate attitude towards the influence of Venus in his life is too well known to mention here; humorous though it be, Chaucer's position with regard to Fame is stated in his answer to the passerby who asks him if he has come in search of fame for himself:

> Sufficeth me, as I were ded,
> That no wight have my name in honde.
> I wot myself best how y stonde;
> For what I drye, or what I thynke,
> I wil myselven al hyt drynke,
> Certeyn, for the more part,
> As fer forth as I kan myn art.

This is Boethius' own lesson well learned, that inner peace cannot be bought on the world's terms. To it Chaucer adds a faith in oneself, which in his words suggests a faith in God-given talents. He refuses to be overwhelmed by the accidents of fortune or fame.

Chaucer has not forgotten his original purpose, the eagle's promise of love tidings as his reward. He falls away easily from the larger theme of Fame's injustice. I have always known, says he, that men desired fame, praise, reputation, but until now, I knew nothing of her house, her appearance, her method of passing judgments. These are not the tidings I mean. And he is led to the nearly whirling house of tidings with its many openings to let out sounds and its open doors to let in all kinds of news. The catalogue of the kinds of tidings which are to be found in the whirling house deserves to be compared with the earlier rehearsal of tidings cited by the eagle in Book II, for in the list of Book III, it should be noted, Chaucer has passed from his emphasis upon love and its phases to life itself, in which love and its various circumstances form only one small part of the picture:

And over alle the houses angles
Ys ful of rounynges and of jangles
Of werres, of pes, of mariages,
Of reste, of labour, of viages,
Of abood, of deeth, of lyf,
Of love, of hate, acord, of stryf,
Of loos, of lore, and of wynnynges,
Of hele, of seknesse, of bildynges,
Of faire wyndes, and of tempestes,
Of qwalm of folk, and eke of bestes;
Of dyvers transmutacions
Of estats, and eke of regions;
Of trust, of drede, of jelousye,
Of wit, of wynnynge, of folye;
Of plente, and of gret famyne,
Of chepe, of derthe, and of ruyne;
Of good or mys governement,
Of fyr, and of dyvers accident.

And it will be remembered too that of the nine companies of petitioners, only two of them, the sixth and seventh, are made up of those who desire fame 'as wel of love as other thyng,' a sign that the love element has been absorbed into a larger framework. This departure from the motive of love tidings exclusively seems to my mind to be the inevitable result of the universalizing impulse behind the broader concept of Fortune in any of her cults. The steadily expanding compass of the successive books of the *House of Fame* demonstrates in small Chaucer's whole development as an artist as he masters a literary type, absorbs a new and liberating philosophy from Boethius, and creates a new form. Book III is an attempt to stay within the tradition of the love-vision while at the same time widening its scope to include more direct observation, more invention and detail. None of Chaucer's early poetry seems so clearly to discover to our eyes the poet utilizing convention but putting it aside for larger and profounder patterns of thought.

The remainder of the poem, its description of the House of Rumor, the final scrambling in a corner of the House where men are talking of love tidings, is a fulfillment of the eagle's promise (never quite lost from view) that Chaucer was to have as his reward a journey to the House of Fame where he would hear such tidings. More than that, it is Chaucer's method of disassociating his enlarged and more grandiose conception of Fame or reputation from the meaner view of her as mere rumor or report, as she had been in classical literature. By supplying the poem with a House of Rumor where reports are received and intermingled before Lady Fame decides what will be done with them, he preserves the grander picture of Fame by subordinating rumor to a mere device in her hands, no longer equating her with it.

As for the name of the man of great authority who was presumably to present the tidings, the guess of triumph which Bronson looks forward to is yet to be made. The identification of the man of authority with an actual historical personage, with Richard II or John of Gaunt for example, has been so unsatisfactory as to lead Robinson to write that the 'identity of the person and the nature of the connection seem now beyond the range of conjecture.' A recent and interesting suggestion, offered in the form of a question by R. C. Goffin, is that Boccaccio may be the man of authority,[7] but the suggestion of a literary figure raises the ghosts of other writers from whom Chaucer borrowed or who turned from the matter of books to the matter of life for their subjects. There is, however, another figure whose influence is manifest not only in this poem but in all of Chaucer's major work and whose philosophy might have supplied a resolution for the demand for tidings. I mean, of course, Boethius himself.

Coghill has written that Chaucer's liberation from the influence of the love-vision was the result of his reading and translation of Boethius in whom he had found his new formula, the turn of Fortune's wheel.[8] My own impression is that Chaucer had already discovered the formula and was in the *House of Fame* prefiguring the many subsequent uses to which it could be put. Perhaps had we the completed poem the precise use of the formula would have been revealed by the man of great authority in a sane and dispassionate pronouncement incorporating the theme of the untrustworthy fortunes of love into the larger picture of the instability of fame in general, a pronouncement voicing the conviction that only disillusion must result from an abuse of the passions and the folly of trusting the inconstant goddesses.[9] That Boethius could supply Chaucer with an answer to suit the needs of the *House of Fame* may be seen from the long concluding speech by Theseus in the *Knight's Tale* where Chaucer has borrowed from the *Consolatio* a part of the Boethian love song to bring his tale to an end. Boethius himself could certainly have supplied a statement on the falseness of the glory that the world offers; and there is a sufficient broadening of the meaning of 'love' in his philosophy to warrant the assimilation of the earthly passion of Dido and Aeneas into the 'fayre cheyne of love' established by the 'Firste Moevere' in whose plan for the world good and evil fame, like good and evil fortune, are a part.

Would Chaucer's high comedy support such a conclusion? My feeling is that it would, for though Chaucer knew that men desired fame and praise, and then came to know where Fame dwelt and how she dealt out her favors, he did not know that like her sister Fortune, Fame is part of a system by which the 'purveiaunce' of God is carried out, and in which even the personal tragedy of Dido has meaning. And this the man of great authority might have told him. Our task is to recover something of the vision implicit in Caxton's words: In the *House of Fame* Chaucer 'towchyth . . . ryght grete wysedom & subtyll understondying. . . . For he wrytteth no voyde words / but all hys mater is ful of hye and quycke sentence.'

NOTES

1. For a summary of the various theories which have accrued to the *House of Fame* the reader is directed to F. N. Robinson's edition, *The Complete Works of Geoffrey Chaucer* (Boston, 1933), pp. 886–87, and to Bertrand H. Bronson, 'Chaucer's *Hous of Fame*: Another Hypothesis,' *University of California Publications in English* III (1932–1944), 171 ff. All quotations from Chaucer are from Robinson's text.

2. Nevill Coghill, *The Poet Chaucer* (Oxford University Press, 1949), p. 49. Coghill is far from alone in this attitude. For Emile Legouis, *Geoffrey Chaucer*, trans. L. Lailavoix (London, 1913), pp. 87–88 and for W. C.

Curry, *Chaucer and the Mediaeval Sciences* (New York, 1926), p. 233, the poem lacks careful selection of materials or demonstrates an incomplete assimilation of Boethius and Dante. Percy Van Dyke Shelly, *The Living Chaucer* (The University of Penn. Press, 1940), p. 84, feels that Chaucer had more matter than he could digest, and Marchette Chute, *Geoffrey Chaucer of England* (New York, 1946), p. 110, surmises that possibly Chaucer had no clear plan in mind and merely intended to ramble along in the 'easygoing medieval way on the general subject of "fame" until he was through.' The most recent expression of this view is that of J. S. P. Tatlock, *The Mind and Art of Chaucer* (Syracuse University Press, 1950), p. 59, who writes that the first part of the poem is undefined and motiveless, and that only in the latter parts of the work is there any concentrated aim.

3. Critics have come more and more to accept the introductory reading from a book in the early love-visions as having the full force of an exemplum. Perhaps the fullest treatment of this rhetorical device in the vision poems is that of Wolfgang Clemen, *Der Junge Chaucer, Kölner Anglistische Arbeiten* (Bochum-Langendreer, 1938), pp. 39–42, 96–99, and 168–70. Clemen's views have been anticipated in part by Bronson, 'In Appreciation of Chaucer's *Parlement of Foules,' University of California Publications in English* III (1932–1944), 199–201, and have been followed for the most part by Kemp Malone, *Chapters on Chaucer* (The Johns Hopkins Press, 1951), pp. 28–29, 51. Needless to say, I am in debt to all of these.

4. W. O. Sypherd, *Studies in Chaucer's 'Hous of Fame,'* (Chaucer Society, 1907), pp. 16–17, 71, 114 ff.

5. Howard Rollin Patch, *The Goddess Fortuna in Mediaeval Literature* (Cambridge, Mass., 1927), pp. 112 and 96.

6. *Boece,* IV, pr. 6, 90–95; cf. *Troilus and Criseyde,* I, 1065–69.

7. 'Quiting by Tidings in *The House of Fame,' Medium Aevum,* XII (1943), 44.

8. *The Poet Chaucer,* p. 64.

9. Cf. the similar conclusion drawn by Paull F. Baum, 'Chaucer's *The House of Fame,' ELH,* VIII (1941), 255–56. 'The ultimate tidings of love from the man of authority would have inevitably been a . . . disappointment and disillusion.'

CHARLES O. McDONALD

An Interpretation of Chaucer's
Parlement of Foules

THE main lines which any investigation of the *Parlement of Foules* must follow have been firmly traced out,[1] and disagreement is limited to the interpretation and weight assigned to specific details. However, such disagreement concerning details may effect considerable alterations in our judgment of the unity and value of the poem.

To describe briefly the unity of the *Parlement of Foules* before beginning a detailed analysis, I would say that the poem has as its subject matter love, but love considered from a very special point of view—that of an entire spectrum of varying types of love experience which the poet is trying to define and analyze. Through the use of contrasted pairs—the golden *versus* the black side of the garden gate, the lush natural beauty of garden *versus* the sterility of the abstract personifications, Priapus *versus* Venus, and the birds of low degree *versus* the 'foules of ravyne'—this spectrum of love experience is set up. Through the idea of 'commune profyt,' and particularly through the figure of Nature, a norm is established by which these types of love can be viewed in their proper perspective and the extreme ends of the spectrum may be treated with a delicate humor and irony. This is the essence of the poem in which Nature plays the rôle of a tolerant mediator between apparently contradictory points of view, and in which the usual rôle

---

Reprinted from *Speculum*, XXX (1955), 444-57, by permission of The Mediaeval Academy of America.

of the naïve and sophisticated are delightfully reversed. These statements are the barest summary of what follows.

The poem opens with an aphorism, *Ars longa, Vita brevis,* usually applied to writing in general and poetry in particular, but which here applies as well to the art of love:

> Al this mene I by Love, that my felynge
> Astonyeth with his wonderful werkynge
> So sore iwis, that whan I on hym thynke,
> Nat wot I wel wher that I flete or synke.

When the poet thinks of the complex emotion he has set out to analyze, consternation arises within him at being so innocent of knowledge of it. The poet's perplexity in the presence of Love is underlined by the following stanza in which he reads both 'Of his myrakles and his crewel yre'. All that the poet can say at the present time is that if Love *will* be Lord, then, 'God save the King,' and with this wryly humorous dismissal of the problem he turns to other things. However the keynote of all the subsequent action is hit in this initial presentation of love's 'myrakles and his crewel yre.' Love immediately suggests a double-standard to the poet, or at any rate two extremes which may result from cultivating his acquaintance. We shall see both these aspects presented at some length before the poem concludes.

The poet tells us of his habit of reading which has led him to read this day an old book for the purpose of ascertaining 'a certeyn thing.' What this thing is he does not tell us, and we must not be too hasty in identifying it. The thing he seeks must have some relationship to that 'newe science,' which he, as well as others, seeks from books and which, probably, has connections with the art of love which he has already characterized as so puzzling to him.

His reading has been 'Tullyus of the Drem of Scipioun' which in seven chapters gave him a complete conspectus of heaven, hell and all the intermediate stations of the universe, so that, theoretically at least, he is in good case to find what he is looking for. He summarizes the dream so as to emphasize the function of the narrative as a way toward salvation for the desiring soul, which, according to Africanus, can make its way to heaven immediately upon death only by working for the 'commune profyt,' a phrase he uses twice. The souls which belonged to transgressors of the law or 'likerous folk' shall be whirled about the universe in torment, until, finally forgiven, they too, come into heaven. Although we cannot yet, with any certainty, say what the 'certeyn thing' is, we may agree with R. C. Goffin in saying that the *Drem* does establish a partial concern with salvation as one of the *motifs* of the poem, and a salvation to be attained most easily through working for the common good. We need not say that this regimen of conduct necessarily excludes all lovers. It rejects only those, as Macrobius says, 'qui se corporis voluptatibus dediderunt,' but it certainly puts limitations on the conduct of all others in a variety of ways as we shall see.

All of this moral reading-matter is very well, but the poor poet prepared for bed when darkness fell,

> Fulfyld of thought and busy hevynesse;
> For bothe I hadde thyng which that I nolde,
> And ek I nadde that thyng that I wolde.

Macrobius had let him down; a way of salvation he had seen, but evidently that was not what he sought. Of what use is a mode of salvation to a poet of love in full pursuit of his trade? The answer comes back quickly enough when Africanus appears and tells the poet that for so diligently perusing his old book, 'sumdel of thy labor wolde I quyte.' There may, after all, be a really direct connection between love and salvation.

Before we begin to follow Africanus we come to the stanza which more than any other has puzzled the commentators:

> Cytherea! thow blysful lady swete,
> That with thy fyrbrond dauntest whom the lest,
> And madest me this sweven for to mete,
> Be thow myn helpe in this, for thow mayst best!
> As wisly as I sey the north-north-west,
> When I began my sweven for to write:
> So yif me myght to ryme and ek t' endyte!

To list the interpretations made for this stanza would take more space than it would be worth, but it seems most likely to me that Manly's interpretation of the words 'north-north-west' as meaning 'in an unpropitious position' (cf. Hamlet's 'I am mad but north-north-west'), or, as Bronson suggests, 'hardly at all,' thus giving the stanza an ironic cast in which the poet is slighting Venus rather than asking her for inspiration, is the correct way in which to read it in view of the treatment accorded Venus later in the poem.

At any rate, we quickly return to Africanus, and as the Roman takes the poet by the hand, we begin to get echoes of Dante's excursion under the guidance of Virgil, gently ironic in tone. The garden-gate definitely recalls the gate of Hell in Dante's *Inferno*, but here the verses inscribed over the door are tantalizingly ambiguous; one side in gold boding good to the wayfarer, the other, in black, boding ill.

The gate however is more important than this simple explanation would suggest; it is one of the key elements in the poem. The phrasing of the mottoes is important. The golden one:

> 'Thorgh me men gon into that blysful place
> Of hertes hele and dedly woundes cure;
> Thorgh me men gon unto the welle of grace,
> There grene and lusty May shal evere endure.
> This is the wey to al good aventure.
> Be glad, thow redere, and thy sorwe ofcast;
> Al open am I—passe in, and sped thee faste!'

The black one:

> 'Thorgh me men gon,' than spak that other side,
> 'Unto the mortal strokes of the spere
> Of which Disdayn and Daunger is the gyde,
> Ther nevere tre shal fruyt ne leves bere.
> This strem yow ledeth to the sorweful were
> There as the fish in prysoun is al drye;
> Th' eschewing is only the remedye!'

This gate seems to symbolize two distinct kinds of love to be found in the garden; love according to Nature, which promises ever-green joy, and love of a more courtly kind which leads to barren sorrow and despair. A further dimension is thus added to the poet's concern with Love's 'myrakles and his crewel yre' which began the poem. The golden inscription uses no words reminiscent of the French courtly romances, and the 'welle of grace' clearly suggests a kind of love which is holy, is approved of by God. The joyful side of love could have been pictured in much more specifically 'romance' or 'courtly' terms if the poet had so wished by the expedient of introducing the opposite numbers of Daunger and Disdayn—for example, Bialacoil and Pleasaunce—but they do not appear; instead 'grene and lusty May shal evere endure'; an entirely different order of description than that lavished on the sorrow-causing allegorical abstractions because of whom 'never tre shal fruyt ne leves bere.' The elements of natural beauty, used also by the French courtly poets, are here given a new and vital function as symbols serving in themselves as a vivid contrast to the allegorical personifications of the courtly tradition rather than as mere ornamental surroundings for them. 'Grene and lusty May' defines a kind of love differing not only in results but in essence from that defined by Daunger and Disdayn.

The poet is inspired to enter by the first inscription but deterred by the second. This is a critical moment for one who has read, as the poet has, so many tales of Love's 'myrakles and his crewel yre,' and Chaucer capitalizes on the inherent drama of the situation in a humorously ironic fashion. Africanus claps the poet on the shoulder, and whisks him through the gate not at all in the manner of Dante's Virgil, commenting that the inscriptions do not apply to the poet, 'For thow of love hast lost thy tast, I gesse, / As sek man hath of swete and bytternesse.' This is only half-true as the poet has already shown us by saying, as he viewed the inscriptions, 'That oon me hette, that other dide me colde.' The concept of love, fostered by Nature, has definite appeal for the poet while the concept of love beset by Daunger and Disdayn has not.

The moment the poet steps inside, the feeling of apprehension leaves him, and he exults in the natural beauty around him:

> But, Lord, so I was glad and wel begoon!
> For overal where that I myne eyen caste

Were treës clad with leves that ay shal laste,
Ech in his kynde, of colour fresh and greene
As emeraude, that joye was to seene.

Obviously this is a garden in which 'lusty May' predominates and where Daunger and Disdayn have little inhibiting power upon the fecundity and growth of the vegetable inhabitants of the region at least. Again the contrast in the use of natural and allegorical imagery is quite different from that of the French poems in which natural objects were just so much more allegorical furniture, undifferentiated in purpose from the personifications themselves.

Then begins the description of the garden, drawn from Boccaccio's *Teseida* but not without certain changes which entirely alter the effect of the original.[2] One may note after Emerson[3] that lines 188–189 and 199–210 are original with Chaucer. Each of these passages is a picturesque addition to the natural detail of the garden which enhances its character as an 'ideal state of nature,' and Chaucer elaborates Boccaccio's list of trees with characteristic delight while altering and subduing the allegorical figures of the *Teseida*. One may note also that Chaucer has transposed the stanzas in Boccaccio's poem dealing with Venus to a position directly after that which describes Priapus, and has placed the two intervening stanzas, which describe the bows of Diana's maidens that decorate the temple and the paintings of the famous lovers upon the walls, at the very end of his account. If we were to agree entirely with R. A. Pratt[4] that Chaucer was translating from his source in a hurry and without much care, such alterations in the placement of whole stanzas would be completely inexplicable, but if we credit Chaucer with some sense of design in his own poem then the reason may become apparent. Chaucer has increased the natural detail of the garden considerably, and we may attribute this solicitude on his part to that preference for a joyous love in accord with nature which we have noticed in the preceding passages. Let us begin to take note of the changes in the personnel of the garden and the way in which they are described in Boccaccio:

E poi vide in quel passo Leggiadria
Con Adornezza ed Affabilitate,
E la ismarrita in tuto Cortesia,
E vide l'Arti ch'hanno potestate
De fare altrui a forza far follia,
Nel loro aspetto molto isfugurate:
Della immagine nostra il van Diletto
Con gentilezza vide star soletto.

And Chaucer:

Tho I was war of Pleasaunce anon-ryght,
And of Aray, and Lust, and Curteysie,
And of the Craft that can and hath the myght
To don by force a wyght to don folye—
Disfigurat was she, I nyl nat lye;
And by hymself, under an ok, I gesse,
Saw I Delyt, that stod with Gentilesse.

Note how *Leggiadria* (Grace) becomes in Chaucer the Romance
'Pleasaunce,' and *Affabilitate* (Affability) becomes 'Lust,' although
Arti is given a relatively literal rendering, 'Craft.' However, when
Chaucer comes to *Diletto* ('Delyt'), he inserts the natural detail of
the 'ok,' consistent with his other uses of natural objects in referring to the joyous aspects of love. In the next stanza of Boccaccio, after literally rendering *Bellezza* as 'Beaute' and *Giovenezza*
as 'Youthe,' but omitting *Piacevolezza* (Attractiveness), he translates Boccaccio's *Ardire* (Audacity) by 'Foolhardynesse,' then renders literally *Lusinghe* as 'Flaterye,' and finally *Ruffiani* (Pimps)
is completely deserted in favor of 'Desyre,' while two more figures
corresponding to nothing in the original, 'Messagerye' (the sending
of messages) and 'Meede' (Merit, Desert), both commonly associated with courtly love concepts are introduced into the company. We note the use of or substitution of as many romance words
in these personifications as possible. The poet is telling us that all
the elements of courtly love allegory are present in this garden,
but he makes them generally as unattractive as possible by allowing them few qualifying adjectives with which he was so lavish in
listing the trees which grew in the garden or which he will use

again to such charming effect in the list of birds. By contrast the picture here is bleak and cold, but we must not think that it is cold, as C. S. Lewis contends,[5] because this is Renaissance, not medieval allegory, for we have seen Chaucer go out of his way to give the common courtly names to his figures. The result of the changes is plain. Only 'Delyt' rates the natural detail of the 'ok.' Indeed, these personifications are 'barren'—with the barrenness of Daunger and Disdayn, who inhibit all fertility and growth.

However, when Chaucer turns to Priapus—a figure who, incidentally, had, since Roman times, in statuary adorned Italian Gardens as their tutelary deity—he alters Boccaccio to a more favorable and humorous light. In place of the Italian, which reads to the effect that the observer in the temple went on, seeing as she progressed many flowers adorning the place, he gives the lines,

> Ful besyly men gonne asaye and fonde
> Upon his hed to sette, of sondry hewe,
> Garlondes ful of freshe floures newe.

Priapus has a place in the temple of courtly love even in Boccaccio, but it took Chaucer to grasp the full potentialities of the situation. Certainly Priapus represents love and fertility at its most natural, and his description is in humorous harmony with what we have noticed before.

Then comes the major change in the passage; the transposition of the three stanzas of the Italian devoted to Venus to their present position where they contrast directly with the picture of Priapus just presented. It has been noticed by other commentators that Chaucer here subdues Boccaccio's verse. Bronson gives the best analysis of the changes which I shall summarize here:

1. Boccaccio dwells on Venus' beauty; Chaucer does not mention it;
2. Boccaccio discovers her virtually naked in bed; Chaucer focuses on the bed;
3. Boccaccio gives her loose golden hair; Chaucer binds it with a band;
4. Chaucer does not dwell on the beauty of her face as does Boccaccio;

5. nor does he mention the beauty of her arms, her bosom, or the apples of her breasts as does the Italian;
6. in Chaucer she is satisfactorily covered; while in Boccaccio it is as if she had nothing on;
7. Chaucer transfers the fragrance which Boccaccio has assigned to her person to the temple itself;
8. Boccaccio dwells on the apple and the victory over Pallas and Hera in the valley of Ida which Chaucer omits;
9. Chaucer wholly invents the phrase with which he dismisses her, 'But thus I let her lye,' which Bronson says is proverbially applied to dogs.

Even if we discount the ninth 'change,' which some might challenge, it can be seen from the above that the portrait of Venus, when compared with the original, or even when compared with the brief picture of Priapus, who occupies 'sovereyn place' in the temple, is far from the lushness or flattery of Boccaccio. Again the sterility of the courtly conventions is suggested to the reader, and certainly to the writer, who had a description far richer than the one he gave in the very source from which he was translating.

This, then, is a very special garden, as we have suspected ever since we came through the strange gate with its double inscription. It is clearly not the garden of the *Romance of the Rose* nor of any of the conventional 'May Morning' poems of courtly love; in fact, in the very real presence of the natural beauty here abounding, the common personifications of the French courtly tradition are put to shame and merely tolerated. The poet is emphasizing what gave him his initial thrill of delight as he entered upon the scene and only fleetingly indicating the presence of those things which threatened pain in the legend in the dark side of the gate. The balance is delicate and subtle, but the position of the heaviest weight is undeniably clear, and produces time and again effects of ironic humor and mild satire at the expense of courtly love.

Again we are in the open, and the poet catches sight of a majestic figure of the 'noble goddesse Nature' upon a hill of flowers. As the poet tells us, it was completely fitting that she be here,

> For this was on seynt Valentynes day,
> Whan every foul cometh there to chese his make,

> Of every kynde that men thynke may,
> And that so huge a noyse gan they make
> That erthe, and eyr, and tre, and every lake
> So ful was, that unethe was there space
> For me to stonde, so ful was al the place.

The fowls have come on Saint Valentine's Day, as is their yearly custom, to choose their mates. This again may seem like unnecessary underlining of a relatively simple point, but it is an important one nevertheless, and has definite bearings upon what comes afterwards. Chaucer himself takes pains that no one shall miss it, for he repeats himself: 'Benygnely to chese or for to take, / By hire acord, his formel or his make,' and once more when Nature says, 'Ye come for to chese—and fle youre wey—/ Youre makes.' We shall soon see how this develops when the very first to choose, the royal tercel, paying no heed to Nature's instructions or to the acknowledged custom, says,

> Unto my soverayn lady, and not my fere [i.e., mate]
> I chese, and chese with wil, and herte, and thought,
> The formel on youre hand, so wel iwrought,
> Whos I am al, and evere wil hire serve,
> Do what hire lest, to do me lyve or sterve; . . .

For the moment, however, let us return to the description of Nature in her glory which contrasts sharply with that of Venus. Her seat on flowers in the open air is susceptible to contrast, with the dark bed of Venus 'in a privie corner,' and her

> aray and face,
> In swich aray men myghte hire there fynde,
> This noble emperesse ful of grace, . . .

seems almost like cognizance on Chaucer's part of the details he had subtracted from Boccaccio's Venus, although he tells us he was thinking of Alanus' description of Nature in the 'Playnt of kynde.' Next the catalogue of the birds is given, and anyone who is not yet convinced that the courtly abstractions are barren and frigid in the list which Chaucer gives of them should read that passage, and then quickly turn to the one now under discussion of which the latter is six lines longer but infinitely richer. Again the contrast is meant deliberately, and our feeling for the natural beauty of the scene increases, while our feeling for the courtly-love elements within it grows less and less.

We are introduced to the 'formel' eagle which perches on Nature's hand. Our expectancy is aroused: 'formel' is not a generic term for a single species of eagle, but merely means a female eagle arrived at mating age. When Nature explains the rules of choosing her introduction becomes clear, for the 'foules of ravyne,' being the ranking members of the assembly, are to have first choice. Immediately, however, a 'sour' note is hit with the speech of the royal tercel already quoted. With a swiftness and ironic humor not often matched in poetry, we are transported by this one line back into the center of the courtly love tradition which the poet has been subtly criticizing. The speech of the tercel, perfectly consonant with his rank, and sympathetically presented, must have aroused in Chaucer's audience some of the same feelings in this setting that Madam Pertelotte's learned disquisition to Lord Chauntecleer elicited in them at a later date. The formel's 'blush' in now clearly apropos since the protestations of a courtly lover were subject to the strictest secrecy, and here they are mentioned in the face of the whole company. No doubt she as a 'formel' had expected the more natural speech of a petitioner to Nature for her as a mate. No respite is granted the blushing formel, for a second tercel of 'lower degree' breaks in vigorously as befits his comparative lack of 'gentilesse,' and continues with a protestation of his continued faithfulness. Now the merriment must have been general as the audience realized that here in perfect form were all the elements of the *demande d'amours* with which French literature abounded, but used so differently! A third eagle with an argument all his own joins in the dispute, and between the three, 'from the morwe gan this speche laste / Tyl dounward drow the sonne wonder faste'. The purpose of the scene is done, and Chaucer does not attempt to draw it out. Instead he introduces a new but highly natural development in the course of events; the agitation of the other birds at this strange turn of affairs:

The noyse of foules for to ben delyvered
So loude rong, 'Have don, and lat us wende!'
That wel wende I the wode hadde al toshyvered.
'Com of!' they criede, 'allas, ye wol us shende!
When shal youre cursede pletynge have an ende?
Have sholde a juge eyther parti leve
For ye or nay, withouten any preve?'

Surely no courtly audience ever reacted this way in the serious French *demandes*! The birds are not only angered at being deprived of their natural rights by all the speechifying, but they are suspicious of speeches themselves as based more on convention than conviction—an issue which has been in the back of our minds ever since the inscriptions over the garden gate. This general uproar is the signal for the richest development of the poem in terms of its irony, the point toward which it has been working from the beginning.

The three eagles have certainly shown little concern for the 'commune profyt,' or for the behests of Nature. For a moment pandemonium reigns as the goose and cuckoo chip in with irreverent proposals for ending the dispute—the cuckoo specifically mentioning the 'commune spede'. Nature rises to the occasion and, with, for her, an unwonted sternness, speaks out,

'Hold youre tonges there!
And I shal sone, I hope, a conseyl fynde
Yow to delyvere, and from this noyse unbynde:
I juge, of every folk men shul oon calle
To seyn the verdit for yow foules alle.'

This speech brings into sharp focus the feverish excitement of the moment and the exasperation of Nature herself as she searches for a way, 'Yow to delyvere, and from this noyse unbynde'—'noyse' referring as much to the courtly pleas as the general commotion. Even patient Dame Nature can stand only so much from her children, and there is the *motif* of the common good to be served.

The birds assent to Nature's judgment, and the 'foules of ravyne' elect a tercelet as their spokesman. True to his class, he mentions

320

first the tested expedient of trial by combat among the three suitors, and they, in a kind of musical-comedy chorus, answer with alacrity, 'Al redy!'. Taking no notice of their eagerness, which is fitting to their chivalric characters, he continues to pronounce his judgment that the formel should chose,

> the worthieste
> Of knighthod, and the lengest had used it.
> Most of estat, of blod the gentilleste.

This amusingly naïve practicality in the spokesman of the idealistic aristocracy is ironically contrasted with fully conscious lower-class practicality as the goose steps forward:

> Pes! now tak kep every man,
> And herkeneth which a resoun I shal forth brynge!
> My wit is sharp, I love no tarynge;
> I seye rede hym, though he were my brother,
> But she wol love hym, lat hym love another!

Such eminently practical advice (couched in such eminently impractical rhetoric) does not set well with the noble sparrow-hawk who takes the goose sharply to task, 'Lo here a parfit resoun of a goos!'.

There is a rather delicate combination of attitudes involved in these developments. We are relieved to hear the spell of the courtly sentiments broken by plain practical realism, and yet we realize that the conventions are not entirely conventions, and that what the birds of prey have been saying has attractions which far outweigh the 'resoun of a goos.' Chaucer has contrived to enlist our sympathy in part for the noble birds, and when the turtle-dove steps forward, 'Nay, God forbede a lovere shulde chaunge!', and blushes, we are in sympathy with her cause as reflecting more clearly the 'commune profyt' than what has been said by the goose.

Still the voice of practical considerations will not be denied, and the duck drawls out sarcastically enough to break the mood:

> Daunseth he murye that is myrtheles?
> Who shulde recche of that is recheles?

'Ye quek!' yit seyde the doke, ful wel and fayre,
'There been mo sterres, God wot, than a payre!'

This last has a double significance; 'There are more fish in the sea than just two,' agreeing with the goose's sentiments, and 'There are others waiting here for this to be settled; let's get on with it!' recalling yet another aspect of 'commune profyt.'

The tercelet feels called upon to defend the proceedings which have thus far occupied all the time, and, in rebuttal to him, the cuckoo puts a point to the second interpretation of the duck's speech which I gave:

'So I,' quod he, 'may have my make in pes,
I reche not how longe that ye stryve,
Let ech of hem be soleyn al here lyve!'

The cuckoo, it may be remembered, spoke previously of the 'commune spede,' but his interpretation of it is more warped than any we have met so far. In answer to him the 'merlioun' succeeds only in proving by his invective that gentility as well as the cuckoo can be 'lewed whil the world may dure.'

The argument has passed the amusing stage, and Nature intervenes quickly to restore peace, ordering the formel to make her own choice. Nature turns to her 'favorite' who is still perched upon her hand:

'But as for conseyl for to chese a make,
If I were Resoun, certes, thanne wolde I
Conseyle yow the royal tercel take,
As seyde the tercelet ful skylfully,
As for the gentilleste and most worthi,
Which I have wrought so wel to my pleasaunce,
That to yow hit oughte to been a suffisaunce.'

The irony of 'If I were Resoun,' Nature's opposite number in the allegorical tradition, must not have been lost on Chaucer's audience after all that had gone before, as well as that of Nature's return to the idea of choosing a mate rather than a paramour. Quite the best is yet to come as the formel, still 'sore abasht' by all

322

that has happened, begins to speak 'with dredful voice.' After begging a boon, which Nature kindly grants, she requests a year to think over the whole idea! The irrelevance of the debate is crowned with a solution more irrelevant than anything that has yet occurred. The formel's reply, however, is not entirely devoid of significance in the general scheme of the poem, for she concludes, 'I wol nat serve Venus ne Cupide, / Forsothe as yit, by no manere weye.' She is specifically rejecting, for the time being at least, the personages in the garden most commonly associated with courtly love poetry. The inversion of values which the poet set out to perform is complete, and the poem may now progress toward its goal of the common good achieved through natural married love for the rest of the birds.

Nature, however, kindly goddess that she is, is unwilling to see anyone completely unhappy, and so to the eagles goes a speech of consolation rich in its humor and irony:

> 'To yow speke I, ye tercelets,' quod Nature,
> 'Beth of good herte, and serveth alle thre.
> A yer is nat so long to endure,
> And ech of yow peyne him in his degre
> For to do wel, for, God wot, quyt is she
> Fro yow this yer; what after so befalle,
> This entremes is dressed for yow alle.'

Starting in a tone of consolatory advice, 'Be good little eagles all,' the situation begins to get the better of Nature, and the gentle sigh of relief inherent in the parenthetical 'God wot' which turns into a broad smile as she continues 'for quyt is she / Fro yow this yer; what after so befalle,' is as brilliantly conceived as anything in the poem.

It is but the work of three stanzas to settle the issue for the rest of the birds and send them happily off caroling the praises of 'Saynt Valentyn.' The irony as well as the thankfulness embodied in the lines of the roundel, 'Wel han they cause for to gladen ofte, / Sith ech of hem recovered hath hys make,' should not be missed. They certainly do have cause to rejoice after the ordeal they have been put through!

We return to the poet,

> And with the shoutyng, whan the song was do
> That foules maden at here flyght awey,
> I wok, and othere bokes tok me to
> To reede upon, and yet I rede alwey.
> I hope, ywis, to rede so som day
> That I shal mete some thyng for to fare
> The bet, and thus to rede I nyl nat spare.

The dream is at an end. This simple conclusion returns us to the beginning and the 'certeyn thing' for which the poet sought in his books, and upon which his dream has, presumably, shed some light, having taken him into one realm of love-experience and shown him its charm. I cannot think that Chaucer here expresses any dissatisfaction with the dream-vision itself such as he felt with his reading upon going to bed. Whether or not he found what he sought he leaves the reader to conjecture, but certainly the concept of 'commune profyt' which impressed him so in his reading has provided a perspective through which he has been able to impart his vision to his audience in a unified and effective way.

What those who have attempted to interpret the entire poem as a serious moral problem presented allegorically have missed, I think, is the genial irony—the 'good nature'—which infuses the whole. A genuine love of nature and natural conduct is balanced against the artificialities adopted by those who consider love a fit subject for rules and regulations according to an arbitrary, 'sophisticated' pattern of courtly conventions. The garden of May and Nature promises joy; that of 'Daunger' and 'Disdayn,' sorrow; the service of Venus and her porter 'Richesse' is conducted in a 'privie corner' here, while Priapus, in the highest place, is decorated with flowers from the world of Nature by his followers. Nature *in propria persona* reigns, and the birds appear before her to choose their mates, a sharp contrast to the satire embodied in Chauntecleer, who, as 'Venus sonne,' had his Pertelotte 'Moore for delit than world to multiplye.' There is no doubt; the common good has been served and through a subtly gentle irony of tone.

Chaucer was to return to this theme and write the tragedy of conventionalized love in *Troilus*, with its austere conclusion in which the artifices of the courtly love tradition are exposed in tragic contrast to the Natural Love of God, and obedience to His commands. In the *Parlement* Chaucer lays his stress upon Love's 'myrakles'; in *Troilus* upon Love's 'Yre,' and the techniques of the two poems differ accordingly, comedy giving way to tragedy, and genially ironic to starkly ironic contrasts between reality and artifice, Nature and convention.

There is, thus, a considerable element of criticism directed against the artificialities of courtly love and the 'foules of ravyne' in the *Parlement*. But what of the claims that have been made concerning the ridicule of the lower classes by other critics? It would certainly be a mistake to deny the existence of such an intent on Chaucer's part. The duck, goose, turtle-dove, and cuckoo are richly comic figures, representative, if we may trust the commentators, of various social classes in Chaucer's England. Naturally there is a covert criticism of their characteristic modes of thought inherent in their speeches. The goose is literally a 'goose' in matters courtly, but her type of thought would do well in the practical business world of mercantile London or any of the port cities of England to which it is conjectured that the *personae* which she and the duck represent belong. The duck, with his rich vein of sarcasm, betrays an even greater degree of sharp hard-headedness along with a commensurate dulling of feeling on the subject of courtly love. The glutton cuckoo, if by worm-fowl luxury-loving clergy are meant, is in a fair way of being an archetypal figure of the man of the cloth who no longer 'eats to live, but lives to eat' and whose notion of the common good is what is good for himself. The turtle-dove who blushes and admits her unworthiness to 'give sentence' may represent a kind of country virtue, perplexed in the presence of courtly conventions, but illustrating the gentility and faithfulness which transcends social status as does the fidelity to his congregation of the 'Povre Persoun' in the 'General Prologue.' These are the barest outlines of the possibilities which Chaucer had at hand and which he may have utilized to create a memorably comic cast of characters.

Through admitting that Chaucer has ironically and satirically treated both the 'high' and 'low' comedy figures of his poem, the central problem of the poem's over-all unity is raised in its sharpest terms. What prevents the poem from splitting into halves? I have tried to suggest that the poem in effect defines a 'natural' norm, a perspective from which the author may satirize mere 'profyt' on the one hand and mere 'romance' on the other. Part of the norm is suggested by the theme of 'commune profyt,' but that abstract semi-philosophic notion would not suffice to weld the whole together if taken alone.

The figure of Nature herself is the greatest single unifying factor. The combination of 'natural' traits given to the goddess is irresistible. She is beauty personified; she has a real sympathy and understanding which all the other characters lack, and she can be exasperated with her children and then laugh herself out of her mood before really chastising them. She can listen with patience to the whole irrelevant *demande* and can seriously consider the possibilities which the lower birds suggest, and she can stop the whole procedure when it threatens the common welfare. She is, in fact, the mediator in the poem spiritually as well as physically. Her position as 'the vicaire of the almyghty Lord' refers not only to the Lord Love but also the Lord God and further enhances her stature as an intermediary. It is her depth as a character who would appeal to any audience which made the rest of the poem acceptable to every audience from Chaucer's time to our own. The portrait of her which Chaucer has presented is astonishing in its range; she is capable of embracing 'courtly love,' 'the love between perfect mates' and 'sexual love' within her understanding and within the compass of the garden in which she rules. She is the source of all the harmony in the poem and her character is the essence of the avoidance of any and all pretence. Only against the gentle background which she provides could Chaucer have constructed his double-edged comedy so as to please his listeners. Love, under Nature and within the bounds of sincerity, varying as they may be for the individual, can lead to 'commune profyt.' Utilizing such a doctrine, Chaucer was able to please his audience by the tolerance of his vision which included not only the individual portraits of the birds but of Nature herself and that for which she stands.

Considered in this way, the poem becomes the end-product of a remarkable genius exercising itself in the realms of sympathetic understanding and broad humor.

NOTES

1. The critical literature connected with the *Parlement of Foules* is roughly divisible into two parts: (a) proposals of various historical allegories for the situation commemorated in the poem; (b) critical analyses based upon the text itself. A selected bibliography:

(a) Historical allegories; J. Koch, 'The Date and Personages of the *Parlement of Foules*,' *Essays on Chaucer*, IV (Chaucer Society, 1877); O. F. Emerson, 'The Suitors in Chaucer's *Parlement of Foules*,' *MP*, VIII (1910), 45–62; 'The Suitors in the *Parlement of Foules* again' *MLN*, XXVI (1911), 109–111; 'What is the *Parlement of Foules?*' *JEGP*, XIII (1914), 566–582; S. A. Moore, 'A Further Note on the Suitors in the *Parlement of Foules*,' *MLN* XXVI (1911), 8–12; M. E. Reid, 'The Historical Interpretation of the *Parlement of Foules*,' *University of Wisconsin Studies in Language and Literature*, XVIII (1929), 60–70; T. W. Douglas, 'What is the *Parlement of Foules?*' *MLN*, XLIII (1928), 378–383; E. Rickert, 'A New Interpretation of the *Parlement of Foules*,' *MP*, XVIII (1920), 1–29; H. Braddy, 'Chaucer's *Parlement of Foules* in its Relation to Contemporary Events' (New York University dissertation, 1932).

(b) Critical analyses; J. M. Manly, 'What is the *Parlement of Foules?*' *Studien zu Englishe Philologie*, L (1913), 272–290; C. S. Lewis, *The Allegory of Love* (Oxford, 1948), 171 ff.; B. H. Bronson, 'In Appreciation of Chaucer's *Parlement of Foules*,' *University of California Publications in English*, III, 193–224; R. C. Goffin 'Heaven and Earth in the *Parlement of Foules*,' *MLR*, XXXII (1936), 493–499; R. M. Lumiansky, 'Chaucer's *Parlement of Foules*; A Philosophical Interpretation,' *RES*, XXV (1948), 81–89; N. Coghill, *The Poet Chaucer* (Oxford, 1949), 57 ff.; Marchette Chute, *Geoffrey Chaucer of England* (New York: E. P. Dutton, 1946), 129–135.

2. The pertinent passages from the *Teseida*, VII, 51–66, are printed in Skeat's *Oxford Chaucer*, I, 68–73, to which the reader may refer for greater detail than space here allows.

3. O. F. Emerson, 'Some Notes on Chaucer and some Conjectures,' *PQ*, II (1923), 81–96.

4. R. A. Pratt, 'Chaucer's Use of the *Teseida*,' *PMLA*, LXII (1947), 605–608.

5. C. S. Lewis, *op. cit.*, p. 174.

J. S. P. TATLOCK

The People In Chaucer's *Troilus*

THE silhouette of the *Troilus,* the kinds of poem behind it that it approximates, are essential and not difficult to perceive. Mr. Young . . . has shown its pervasive elements from the romances.[1] Chaucer hardly set out deliberately to write a poem in the line of Chrétien de Troyes or *Floris,* or what not, but the usages and assumptions of such poems, the commonest kind of serious secular narrative he knew, he adopted as a matter of course. There is vast variety in medieval romance, and the word itself (meaning at first merely a poem in French) is vague, to say nothing of the rarefied air which we reach when we try to grasp the romantic in the abstract. Medieval romance and the romantic in the abstract are not the same, though historically and essentially allied. I turn to the second. One of the essentials of the romantic, the satisfying a taste for the strange, Chaucer provided plentifully for his own day in the intentional ancient coloring, which affected his readers (and not us at all) just as the inevitable and unconscious medieval coloring affects us. He here aimed however no less at satisfying his own informed awareness that the remote past was very unlike his own present than at creating a romantic impression. The emotionalism which belongs to romance also in good sooth is plentiful. What Mr. Young is especially combating is the summary labeling the poem as a psychological novel, a phrase now almost a *cliché,* taken too literally, though no doubt meant by its first user[2] as a mere simplification to assure the momentum of a fresh idea. The

Reprinted, by permission, from *PMLA,* LVI (1941), 85-104.

word *novel* is onesided, even misleading. The hazy word *psychological* implies lifelike portraiture of complex people with internal conflicts, which allows us with probability to descry undercurrents and motives. This is true of the *Troilus*. The facts are, as most critics will admit, that the poem is an intricate blending of romance on every side with delicate and perceptive truth to humanity (though emphatically not a mere 'page out of the book of modern every-day life'); that the two are not contradictory, though more intense and more commingled here than in almost any other English narrative one can think of; that though it is stimulating to guess briefly, it is impossible to decide how much would fall into each category for Chaucer and his readers. Emphatically he no more mediaevalizes than he humanizes his chief source; he complicates and intensifies it.

The novelty most marked here among medieval narratives is lyric, not so much brief penetrations into emotion with a few intense words such as make bits of Shakspere and Dante memorable (though these do occur), as prolonged fanciful and often repetitious embroidery; what anybody in such a general situation might tacitly feel and might express if literary fashion favored. Some readers find the superabundance of this a blemish, the chief reason for the excessive lengthiness of the poem, and also in too violent contrast to the keen reality of so much; the chief element here of contemporary literary fashion which tends to alienate those living under a new dispensation. Boccaccio's *Filostrato*, the main source, has more of the lyric, amounting to nearly a fifth of the poem, mostly in Troilo's mouth; in the *Troilus* it only approaches an eighth, with less from Troilus. But it is utterly uncritical to make a strong antithesis between the two in the matter. The *Troilus* is at bottom a poem of feeling rather than incident, the feeling in part permanently human, partly a product of literary fashion (though sincere enough). Even though there is much more incident than in Boccaccio, and more natural picturing of human beings, Chaucer did often abandon himself to a lyric mood. Not unlike the lyrical pauses is the *sentence*, impersonal intellectual epigrams, proverbs or proverb-like, or expositions on general truths. These even more than the lyric are characteristic of the middle ages, with their avidity for the edifying and the universal. Everyone in the poem (not Pandarus only,—even Diomed) utters *sentence*, even at emotional moments and without regard to congruity. The modern reader may like it not because human but because so coolly medieval. It is one of the things which forbid us to estimate the people solely on the basis of timeless reality.

The attitude and assumptions about love are those of the romantic love which became accepted in literature in the twelfth century and remained in a general way orthodox till the twentieth. In essentials it must have always occurred now and then, but there were conditions about the eleventh century which explain its becoming vocal in literature, and also largely illicit. Aristocratic marriage in general was *mariage de convenance;* the husband very likely far older than his wife, often long absent, interested in affairs, warfare, religion, perhaps mistresses, ignorant, a rough diamond (if diamond). On the other hand with the progress of culture there would be in a castle young men, less manful perhaps but less rude, well-read in Ovid's amatory poems, gifted in music and verse-writing. Complimentary attentions, literary as well as others, are a good way to commend oneself to a patron-lady, and may grow into any of the varieties of love-relation. The new literary expression of love largely came about as a means of flattering aristocratic women by ambitious or sensual young men. Sometimes both were silly, sometimes bad, sometimes genuine, occasionally idealistic. Sometimes it was just 'for fun.' The best of the poetry (such as the *Vita Nuova*) may be regarded as sincere in the sense that St. Augustine's *Confessions* are sincere; both are primarily literary works which voice emotion conceived in the imagination and intensifying the emotion genuinely felt in the heart. A fundamental modern error has been identifying the expressed romantic love with what is at present habitually called 'courtly love.' Definition of what involves emotion and custom is very difficult. I do not define 'courtly love,' or discriminate exactly between it and the mid-medieval romantic love, or any supra-sensual love. But the only justification for the phrase is in distinction from the two latter, and to indicate the kind of love defined in the rules of Andreas Capellanus. Why treat as peculiar to 'courtly love' what everyone recognizes as belonging to any romantic and the higher modern love? And must have occurred now and then centuries before appearing in literature? This wrong identification, and attention to literature and not to human nature, not only dry and chill reading the *Troilus,* but vitiate much recent writing about the whole subject.[3] When we find romantic love analyzed and codified in the late twelfth century by the egregious Andreas Capellanus[4] in the form of 'courtly love' we are not to suppose that any except the very young and foolish took this seriously; but many adopted its usages and assumptions, and in both narrative and lyric these so merge with the natural language of the heart that the two are impossible to distinguish. Most human hearts are not eloquent, and welcome help to express themselves. The point is that 'courtly love' was merely a rather silly outgrowth of the overt emotional romanticism beginning earlier, and that which belongs with the latter must not be identified with the former. An illuminating comparison could be drawn (to disregard of course many differences) between 'courtly love' and the sentimentalism of the eighteenth century,—each an exaggeration and a refining of what had always existed among certain kinds of people, each extending a film of delicacy over the gross (the sentimental often coexists with grossness), each getting its fullest expression in artificial literature, each seriously taken in the main only by the weak and suggestible, but each contributing stereotyped phrases and feelings to the relations of everybody. It may well be doubted whether Chaucer's deep love of reality would ever have let him seriously surrender to what was chiefly a mere literary pose.

Troilus himself is in some measure a 'courtly love' hero; and there are many little reflections of those 'courtly love' ideas which were in the *Filostrato* and much literature known to Chaucer. But there is far less 'courtly love' in the poem than is often vaguely said. Illicit love has always existed, and is not always 'courtly'; the clashing of the love in *Troilus* with Christian morals, about which Chaucer at the end felt so uneasy, is no more 'courtly' than illicit love was in the tenth century or the nineteenth. Out of human truth in a strong or generous nature, not specially out of 'courtly love,' come such ideas as the nobility and ennobling effect of honest love, the humility and pains of the lover, zeal in service, jealousy, feminine slowness and caution, every woman's liability to love, the importance of constancy, the compelling effect of beauty. Anyone who has not observed these things among his acquaintance must be inexperienced indeed. Secrecy in a *liaison* is always important unless in a very lax society. To regard all these as belonging entirely to some bygone esoteric technique is merely ludicrous. The extreme emotional expressiveness and uncontrol in the poem may owe something to the specific 'courtly love' tradition, but they belong also to the popular romanticism which was beginning in the later middle ages, and also to everyday medieval life. It is impossible to say how much of all this might without the 'courtly love' tradition have appeared in a poem by a man of Chaucer's perceptiveness. In some points the poem flatly contradicts 'courtly love' ideas. To pass over Pandarus, who is assuredly no 'courtly lover,' merely an unlucky one, Criseyde expects to be under Troilus' good governance; she never deliberately tortures him, is never a tyrant, nor cold and scornful for a moment, and towards the end suffers as much as he does. Through and through the love is the romantic love fresh in general to literature within two or three centuries, but what is vastly more valuable, contains some of the timeless and most charming realities of human nature. Chaucer was a poet of high imagination, and also richly warmhearted, but he was a hard-headed man; just as later he showed complete disaffection to the traditional 'courtly lover,' so here he had difficulty in surrendering himself completely even to Troilus. To call the *Troilus* a poem of 'courtly love' is far too simple, and indeed is throwing dust in the eyes.

All this bears on a question which ought not to be asked, but often is asked by inexperienced readers who have no grasp of the background assumptions,—why this young widow and bachelor do not marry. Many medieval love-stories do result in marriage; medieval literature was not obsessed with an unreal code in real human emotion. Enough has just been said to show that Chaucer was not so bound by notions of 'courtly love' that he rejected the idea of marriage because that was thought incompatible with them; this was not the reason. And marriage was rejected no more because of fourteenth-century prejudices; it is not a fact that such a marriage, between a prince and an aristocratic subject even with a discredited father, and even in a doomed city, would have been thought unfitting in the fourteenth century. But it is a fact that fashionable readers in the literary swim would not have preferred a tame marriage to something clandestine. The very mystery and furtiveness imparted a charm; and also a complexity, without which there would have been no story, or at most a quite different story. But the chief reason is this. The most esteemed medieval narratives undertook not to convey convincing realities which had never been observed before, but to give a new and piercing momentum to stories which already had the warm appeal of familiarity, and the authority of what at bottom was felt as history. To have sacrificed this appeal and authority would have seemed unintelligible if not absurd. Every reader knew the story in Benoit and Guido, and a few perhaps in Boccaccio. No medieval would have asked the question, Why no marriage?

To approach the subject of the people, the ultimate reality of any person conceived by the imagination is what the conceiver intended. This is the only solid under the feet, however hard to uncover, and whatever any critic may say. Anything else, interpretation which draws largely on the imagination, like Landor's, is legitimate, if as one well may one wishes to surrender himself to it; but it is fancy and poetry, which will vary from critic to critic and age to age, and is not the ultimate reality of the imagined person, which (I repeat) is what the conceiver intended. All this is not to belittle the sudden springing to life which a perceptive reader feels. Interpreting any character in fictitious narrative is radically a different matter from interpreting a person in history. The latter had sides and depths and aberrations which have left no certain record, but may be guessed at; with the former what could not have been in the creator's mind has no place in explaining his creation; nor has (to speak generally) what he would know his readers would be sure not to perceive, to grasp which calls for an understanding of contemporary usage and assumption, and also of the earlier history of the material used in the narrative, if well-known to contemporaries. All this may be self-evident, but it is often and very strangely overlooked by critics of early authors. Even some fairly good critics after absorbing a minimum from a poem will enlarge upon it, with easy eloquence and only too obvious enjoyment, out of their own bowels, following the 'practice of those two prudent insects, the bee and the spider'; stimulating perhaps, but infirm. Especially a critic must be wary about taking subtle though possible implications of word or act very seriously (as he well might with an actual person), unless confirmed by what is more overt. But there is another side to the matter. It is also true that an author may have had in mind something more private, something which while in no wise contradicting the broad outline will fill it in, and which secretly pleases him and which he expects will please readers penetrating enough to see it. *Qui habet aures audiendi, audiat.* This is notably true of Chaucer, as witness Mr. Kittredge's delightful interpretation of 'The Canon's Yeoman's Prolog,' and also others' studies of the Orleans clerk in 'The Franklin's Tale,' and (less) the characterization in the 'Merchant's,'[5] as well as the strong hints as to the relation of the Pardoner and the Sumner, which have not been discussed in print. How to determine what suppositions of this sort are valid is not always easy. But their validity may be supported by a simile from mathematics. In the analytical geometry a straight line may be determined by an algebraic equation, such as $4x-y=4$; supposing we are given six of these, and find, after plotting them on co-ordinate paper, that they form a regular hexagon, we cannot doubt that this was intended. In like manner, if we find in the account of an imaginary person that a considerable number of perhaps inconspicuous details accumulate to outline a lifelike character such as would have appealed to the author, while contradicting nothing else, it is hard to doubt that the author intended this, even if the character at first reading seems undistinguished. The best example in Chaucer is the Orleans clerk. Though not much noticed by most readers, on scrutiny he turns out to be an exquisitely Chaucerian, subtle, diverting, lifelike outline of a businesslike man of science, humble perhaps in origin, but in feelings a gentleman. Traits and motives true to human nature, likely to have appealed to Chaucer, which give his characters three dimensions, and contradict nothing else, may be accepted as having been intended. Or if we should think of him as conceiving a person as a whole, with a minimum of analysis, but if we can believe he would have instantly accepted such a cooler analysis if proposed to him, we may accept such an outline as valid. Of course an important point of departure is always that which the poet himself most used, in this case Boccaccio's *Filostrato*, which most of the time lay open before him. But the best medieval writers deliberately invented, or allowed to grow out, far more than most moderns realize; therefore additions, omissions and other changes, being a spontaneous generation, are more significant yet. On the other hand, above all I must end as I began, by insisting that we must read nothing into an invented characterization which the author's text does not fully justify. The necessary condition for enjoying imaginary portraits is to know where to stop in one's exactions.

In spite of its length the poem is concentrated; the personages are few, and the central ones only four. Of these the least lifelike is Troilus. Chaucer has done his best, omitting some artificiality, and adding angles and lightings which are not in the *Filostrato*. Troilus can be practical-minded and is consulted on serious matters, which he takes grimly. At times we may be in doubt. Though he is modest about his own wits, the poet in revising put in his mouth a long meditation from Boethius on the relation between free-will and divine foreordination, which, if we could take it as dramatic rather than as the poet's own afterthought meditation on the dramatic situation, would mark him as highly analytical. But though such a man might so have reasoned if he could, it is not in character, and is one of the merely contemporary and artificial passages, similar to the *sentence*-element of the poem. Though evidently by nature sensual, and not always tender-minded, he is a 'clean' sort of man; unlike Troilo in Boccaccio, he even shows no sign of such experience with a woman before. Giving no precise indication of his age, but in view of the fact that people in Chaucer's day reached social maturity something over five years earlier than now (owing to the prolongation of dependence caused to-day by education), the poet would probably not have denied that Troilus was in the early twenties. Needless to dwell on his value and valor as a warrior, next to Hector's, which are traditional, and more emphasized than in the *Filostrato*. Boccaccio's earlier women care little for masculine men. Chaucer saw more fully than he that the more of a man the lover is the more of a tribute to Love is the grip of love upon him, and the more pleasing to readers (English at least) among aristocratic women, romantic men, and indeed Chaucer himself on his romantic side. What makes Troilus' portrait a trifle ill-balanced, we see his valor mostly as conveyed in the background, and in some passages he impulsively rejects such ambitions for something more heartfelt. The purpose is not to sculpture him in the round, merely in high relief. First and last, even before his mistress's departure, he goes through the weakness, prostration, and agony which doubtless in spasms are lifelike, and are reduced from Boccaccio's picture, but which in the main here reflect the social and literary tradition developed to flatter aristocratic women. With Troilus the young lover, from beginning to end there are many moving insights in the poem, unstudied touches of nature, not always without highly sympathetic humor to an older reader. Most attractive of all is his perfect humility about himself. Less moving are his pity and contemplation of himself, and it is still harder to accept the absence of self-reliance for years in this skilled fighter and counsellor, and the several scenes where he talks with Pandarus while one or both lie in bed, like a pair of boarding-school girls. His lack of permanent vitality is forced on us by his constant taking to his bed instead of to other recourse when emotionally disturbed, by the perpetual recurrence of sorrow and death in his own and the poet's words of him, by his obvious satisfaction in planning on the very day of Criseyde's departure for the arrangements at his death, by the prompt descent upon him of characteristics of melancholia. A modern man is excusable for thinking him a poor stick who gets from Criseyde, when she is exposed to Diomed, no more than his deserts.[6] This was certainly not Chaucer's intention, that is, not the essential reality; yet in his heart he may now and then have had a flash of this feeling. No doubt a personality and a behavior (allowing for poetic heightening) exactly like Troilus' are not impossible, even in England, before the days of upper-class cult

336

of impassivity and the resulting monocle of some years ago. He might be reconciled with reality by describing him as extremely high-strung, mercurial, at times gallant, at times (in modern lingo) manic-depressive. But the poet's lack of real grip on a human Troilus is shown by the incongruous ending, his happy flight through the seven spheres and laughter at those who grieved for his death, which one or two have misunderstood as ironical. It may be better to question whether Chaucer was consciously conceiving a lifelike personality,—rather a traditional ideal which he and others liked to see movingly embodied. There is abundance of parallel in romantic literature. To the appeal of this nothing is so important as that the principal characters shall be appealing to the reader, and therefore shall embody traits which with his literary habits he likes to see. Minor characters may be highly differentiated, but usually not the hero and heroine; to perceive this one need look no farther back than Scott, Thackeray, Dickens, and half of third-rate contemporary mystery stories. Chaucer's compliance with this general demand harmonizes with the opinion that the poem was written earlyish in his literary life.[7] Never again has he anyone so like a 'courtly lover' as hero. When he had more fully found his vein in the *Canterbury Tales*, he treated Troilus' analogs Aurelius with negligent lightness and Damian as a cipher.[8] But along with many touches of keen reality he surrendered himself, possibly with some effort as is suggested by the Epilog,[9] to Troilus as embodying the ideal of a lover cherished by fashionable readers, and as the vehicle of the lyric. I end however with a tribute to the beauty of the picture.

The two other principal men are more boldly drawn, with no mysteries and no self-contradictions. Diomed being secondary is more lifelike than Troilus; and also, as a skilled seducer having appealed to the youthfully dissolute Boccaccio, owes almost everything in Chaucer to the *Filostrato:* women always just below the surface of his consciousness, his obvious experience with them, his cool technique as a seducer, his sharpness in detecting Troilus' emotion. The desire to outrival another man, already a military enemy, rouses his instinct of the chase, for he shows a streak of what some would call 'meanness,' and here is no case as with

Troilus of love (though doubtles of fancy) at first sight. His powerful physique is in both poets, a trifle more marked than Troilus' in Chaucer, but gives no excuse to think the fastidious Criseyde subdued by a mere bruiser. The principal change from Diomede in Boccaccio is interesting—that Chaucer's gives Criseyde to understand that he is hers for life,—and that 'Thus seide I nevere or now to wommen born,'—and has never had a passion for a woman before; this pretense goes well in contrast with Troilus' genuine inexperience with women, and with the restraint of English life compared with Neapolitan.[10] An inexperienced lover would have had no advantage with Boccaccio's Criseyda or his readers,—or with his Fiammetta. The momentum of Diomed's courtship Chaucer conveys in his highly original line:

The wordes of this sodein Diomede.

But such is his cool-headedness in both poets that Robert Henryson's *Testament of Cressid* shows the inevitable course of events in his tiring of her and abandoning her. No woman could have held Diomed unless one like Shakspere's Cleopatra. Criseyde was too soft.

The two other chief personages have more complexity and also far more of Chaucer's originality. He had accepted Troilus with little change, and had no need to change Diomed. Pandaro in Boccaccio, Criseida's cousin, except in his situation, cynicism, and enterprise is hardly distinguishable from Troilo. In Chaucer Pandarus may well be thought decidedly older than his friend; he is Criseyde's uncle,—probably Victorian critics were right in thinking the purpose here to take some of the responsibility off Criseyde's frail shoulders, but there is not another syllable to suggest that he belongs to a different generation, as there assuredly would have been had Chaucer meant to discard the chum in *Filostrato*. Everyone knows cases when an uncle and niece or nephew are much of an age. Chaucer invented the 'uncle,' but made no further use of it. Several recent critics are quite wrong in calling him 'elderly'; perhaps this is mere irradiation from Shakspere's Pandarus, totally different, degraded, and vulgarly comic. Chaucer's is not a 'comic figure,' but broadly human after his fashion, though

338

with a comic side conscious and unconscious, and of course without much personal dignity. He is still a youngish man carrying on a very heartfelt and open, if unlucky, love-affair, going in for athletic sports with Troilus, and in general leading the same sort of life. Nearly twenty times one of them calls the other 'brother.' But of course he is more experienced and cleverer, and evidently has brains for more than practical matters. Though the part he plays has always struck the world as so ignoble that his decline in respectability and likeableness was inevitable in Shakspere and his contemporaries, Chaucer evidently tolerates and even rather likes him, with a person of his lightheartedness, interest in other people and ardent vitality, the world is not extreme to mark what is done amiss as to morals or even honor. Pandarus is always in a hurry, scarcely ever walks, he runs and leaps, like the Cook's Perkin the reveler. This shows what a living person he was to Chaucer. He loves to talk, possibly more than some readers relish; his enjoyment of the proverbial sort of epigram, though not confined to him among the personages, and part of the *sentence* element, is what Thackeray ascribes to domestic servants' mentality. One hesitates to admit that sometimes to a modern he is tiresome. His motive in playing his peculiar part is simple in Boccaccio, merely friendship for Troilo; the only motive avowed (and often) in Chaucer. But Chaucer's people are so living that we are justified in filling in with more, which perhaps Pandarus would not wholly have admitted even to himself, but which Chaucer would have accepted as a part of the character he had created. Pandarus' 'betwixen game and ernest' admits the complexity. He is thoroughly good-natured and warm-hearted, and he truly believes he is not only making everybody comfortable but is doing an unmixed service to both Troilus and his blighted and widowed niece. We need not deny him a certain pleasure in second-hand sentimentality and voluptuousness with an attractive couple. Being obsequious to the great with whom he is not intimate, his kind of person is likely to be a snob, and it is doubtful if he would have worked so hard except for a royal prince. Perhaps we should believe him when he volunteers a solemn denial of any actually mercenary motive, though the volunteered denial in real life might make one suspicious. He is thoroughly enjoying himself in something which exactly suits his tastes and powers; his skilful but disillusioned stage-management shows experience and gusto; he has a lively sense for the dramatic, and for directing and giving other people hints and cues, and his enjoyment of the assumed seriousness of his little sermons at two critical moments is unmistakable. Above all, having a shallow insight into people, a relish for power without personal risk, and a nearsighted eye for detail, he functions at his best in intrigue, for he is a born intriguer and the father of it.

The only due way to judge of Criseyde's personality is before and after her departure, separately. Boccaccio's Criseyde is an attractive, sensual Neapolitan aristocrat, capable of any trivial impulsiveness, little more than a lay-figure to carry her part, therefore without any great conflicts, personality, or interest. Criseyde on the other hand is the earliest full-figure Portrait of a Lady in English literature. Having a splendid house and a large household, she is used to complicated human relations, and always perceives what attitude and conduct are fitting in the circumstances. It is in the second book that she most emerges sculptured in the round. This is the most original part, and assuredly one of the best; Chaucer being an older and more humanly discerning man than Boccaccio, with a keener love of reality and more delicate taste, here shows his heroine far more charming and dignified and less easy to win than Criseida. She is not intellectual or probably highly-educated (why should a patrician woman be?). Pandarus does not think her intelligent; this might be ascribed to his own self-conceit, for she uses her brains, is shrewd and perceptive, fertile in plans, and cautious, critical, and cool-headed; as to the consequences of a simple flight together she is as clearsighted as Pinero's Paula. It is the greatest mistake in the world to think her the kind of woman who has to have a lover; there has been no breath to tarnish her reputation; though she has been married, she talks as if untouched by love; her simplicity and innocence about it, and her prolonged anxious hesitation and her soliloquy about Troilus, suggest the kind of woman who might have remained alone for years had no one arrived to rouse her. It is only after some time that she begins to suspect impending action, and there is no reason to doubt her words that what first won her was in the broadest sense Troilus' 'moral vertu, grounded upon trouthe.' Unlike him she does not love at first sight, even though forewarned that she is loved; the poet takes pains to show her as at first much less impassioned than he; she takes it rather coolly at first, though conflict of feelings makes her emotional and even capricious. The picture of the growth of her love is perfect, with a wonderful balance of feeling and good sense; a cool head and a warm heart are not inconsistent, and make a poised character. Yet unquestionably she is apt for love, takes to the thought and to Troilus at once, and has plenty of spontaneous coquetry. It is the antithesis here which makes her one of the most appealing and deeply touching women in all poetry. The only trait which in the least prepares us for her undoing is her softness. She is no more fearful or even timid than any woman of her general type would be—in all the circumstances; softness is the word, and together with tenderness is her most endearing trait. There is no strand of steel in her make-up; and no 'courtly love' affectation, for she expects to be under Troilus' governance. But with her loyalty and balance in dealing with people there is no reason to think her anyone's immediate victim, or to doubt her ability to carry out her warning to Troilus that, prince though he is, he shall have no undue sovereignty over her, nor will she forbear to anger him if he does amiss. She makes her own decisions, and trusting the managing Pandarus as she does she has no need of more enterprise. There is no other sign of a weak character than her softness, and no forewarning of her speedy decline. There is no better phrase for her personality than that she has every trait which makes woman attractive to man. It is true that the approaching ruin of Troy (far more than in Boccaccio) gives the poem at the end a mood of fateful grandeur, a crumbling into doom of all that is bright and fine, but fate has nothing to do, so far as Chaucer shows, with Criseyde's trivial infidelity.

In the first half or so of even the final book, still the same Criseyde, day after day, she grows pale and thin with longing. Then we hear moral strains and cracks, and then she collapses out of sight. 'Sliding of corage' we are told, the first hint of the sort in the whole poem; on the tenth day after her departure in a deeply pitiful passage we see her unresistingly swaying towards Diomed, and even losing her usual conscious poise; then on the tenth day we are told quite baldly the origins of her decision to remain,—the peril of the town, her need of friends, what Diomed had said, and his high station; reasons laughably inadequate compared with the interior warmth of the earlier picture. None of this is mere coquettish pastime, for which she is in no mood, but there is also no love, nor even desire,—it is mere calculation. Ignominies accumulate fast. On the eleventh day Diomed stops her sighing and cures most of her pain; next she gives him things which had come from Troilus; drips with moving but abject self-pity and deception; worst of all, she descends to downright meanness, lying excuses and promises and deliberately lying blame cast on Troilus. Much of this of course is due to bad conscience about her own falsity; but the main thing is that, though Chaucer will not say within how few weeks after her falsity is completed, it has distinctly begun the eleventh day after her heartbroken farewells with Troilus. Her character has deteriorated with a speed which almost dizzies us. Chaucer's purpose here may well have been to promote not the lifelike but the dramatic. Yet a second purpose is also possible. This fastidious if soft woman was in no wise compelled to take a second lover; the circumstances left her as free afterwards as before—it is nothing less than absurd to read them otherwise. It is customary to pooh-pooh the idea that the furtive and therefore more sensual nature of the first affair caused the deterioration which led to the second, and to hold the first quite blameless by the 'code of courtly love'; but if there is little 'courtly love' in the poem this has little relevance. Only a few hundred lines later comes the author's religious disavowal of 'feigned loves,' 'worldly vanity,' which has so surprised some readers, and most certainly refers to the kind of loves portrayed in this poem. I am not at all sure that the fundamentally Catholic Chaucer, in spite of his earlier surrender to romance, and even in consequence of its intensity, half-through the last book of this intensely earnest poem had not come to the feeling that it really was the nature of the first *amour* which led so quickly to the second. With his firm personality and inherited Christian ideality, perhaps he ceased to be content with fashionable irresponsibility. Never again does he accept seriously such a case as Criseyde's. This view will probably find little favor at the present moment.

Nothing is more notable than her fading into invisibility near the end. After the minute tracing of her love for Troilus, and after the first warnings of coming ruin, we are left to take her submission to Diomed on faith and behind the scenes. Why the poet did thus we can only guess. Boccaccio did, but his purpose in writing was other than Chaucer's. There is actually a suggestion that Chaucer meant to cut the painful part even shorter than he did. The whole poem had grown exceedingly, far beyond the extent of the *Filostrato*. But besides brevity there are other explanations for Criseyde's disappearance and the summary speed here of the narrative. The Englishman was almost in love with his heroine himself; he never wrote more heartfelt words than his refusal to chide her,—'I wolde excuse her yit for routhe.' No poet was ever more masculine and chivalrous than he. It is not unlikely that he simply had not the heart to follow the degrees of her deterioration, and that he gave the reason for his policy when he wrote

> Ye may her gilt in othre bokes see;
> And gladlier I wol write, yif you leste,
> Penelopees trouthe and goode Alceste.

Undoubtedly the charm of the heroine would be spoiled for anybody if he had to watch a slow descent; bad enough to look here upon this picture—and on this. Further, in early literature human character is apt to be conceived and presented as static and not changing; to be given two Criseydes (as we pretty much are) is unusual, and a whole series of steps would be amazing. It is surprising that moderns should expect this, or a complete preparation. But the chief reason is still more medieval. History and story had not yet made their declaration of mutual independence, and this traditional story to all practical intents was history. The first and only thing everyone knew of Criseyde is that she was faithless; Boccaccio announces the final lesson bluntly:

Giovane donna è mobile, e vogliosa
È negli amanti molti.

Chaucer announces the essence in the very first four lines of the
poem, and also a little later:

The double sorwe of Troilus to tellen, . . .
In lovynge, how his aventures fellen
Fro wo to wele, and after out of joye.

. . . .

In which ye may the double sorwes here
Of Troilus in lovynge of Criseyde,
And how that she forsook hym er she deyde.

He felt no demand to analyze distressingly the course of what
everybody knew, any more than to show why there had been no
marriage. By any moral principles, Christian, pagan or chivalric,
she was blameworthy, and the modern feels that the fascination
and beauty of her earlier personality only makes the unexplained
promptness of her defection the harder to acquiesce in. But his
undertaking, as I have said elsewhere, was not to explain how an
attractive woman became faithless,—had he meant to do this, there
could have been no mistaking it,—but how infinitely appealing a
woman notoriously to become faithless could be. His matchless
contribution is in the first four and a half books; thereafter he
takes her as he had found her. No doubt many readers weary of
analysis, and would prefer to snap into a less attractive makeshift
conception of Criseyde which makes her a whole, even though
ignoring part of the picture. But if one is interested in the real
Criseyde, which is the poet's whole picture of her, it may be
doubted if the above can be much corrected.

Several persons in the poem are extremely lifelike sketches as
far as they go. Three are of men best described as princely, developed by Chaucer from their personalities in the *Filostrato* and
earlier tradition. Hector is generous, considerate and gracious, as
well as gallant, staunch, resolute, beyond him of the *Filostrato*. To
pass over Sarpedon of the fifth book, in Troilus' favorite brother
Deiphobus there is a like princely graciousness, as well as valor.

344

Calchas is an abject; a great and skilled lord whose compliance with the will of the gods learned from his science does not save him from the degeneration caused by violation of human honor, or from his daughter's disrespect. Chaucer adds touches of degredation not in Boccaccio. The sketches of women (inferior or lacking in Boccaccio) are even more lifelike and charming. I merely glance at one of the most enchanting of all passages, Chaucer's creation, ending with the song of the nightingale and Criseyde falling into dreams of love, and of an eagle exchanging his heart for hers; the most winning touch of all is Criseyde's niece the lady Antigone's hymn to love, her frank innocence in idealizing love. No hint here of the 'courtly' variety. More realistic are two other sketches. Helen, ideal like Troilus's two brothers, is the *bas relief* of a princess, the earliest in English poetry, also in a scene added by Chaucer. She is discerning, sympathetic, sufficiently sincere, responsible, with the gentle gracious acts and words which high-bred women often value giving and receiving. Dry humor is not absent when Deiphobus says of his tactful and beautiful sister-in-law, 'She may leden Paris as her leste.' Cassandra is more individual and even diverting. No wild sybil but evidently prepossessing, she has a gift of prophecy which is supported by knowledge of history and human perception but no sympathy. Her smile before telling Troilus his fate has as complex a content as La Gioconda's, and her epigrammatic close has no mercy,—'This Diomede is inne, and thou are oute.' Her use of the symbolism of dreams is almost startling to a modern who has heard anything of some modern psychology.

The emotional half-unreal Troilus, the confident Diomed, the intriguer Pandarus, the soft Criseyde (besides the minor personages) all have one thing in common,—they are aristocrats; are free from sordid care, know the code, and in minor matters go right by instinct. The *Filostrato* also is high-bred and sensitive according to its standards, but these are far less deeply human. Hardly another so aristocratic narrative exists in English; with scarcely a trace of superciliousness, its concentration simply excludes the humdrum, cheap, dirty, and coarse. The smoothly-running attractive quality of life among such people, felt so strongly by moderns like George Meredith and Henry James, Chaucer felt also. Not for nothing had he for years of his impressionable earlier youth lived with the royal Countess of Ulster and in the King's chamber. The poem tells us (if we need to be told) that the best fourteenth-century patricians were no different from twentieth-century.

In manner too as well as content he follows an aristocratic direction, not only that of the politer medieval romance, as Young has shown, but the equally refined literary example of the ancient Roman poets. In spite of the keen human reality, his effort to realize the ancients as unlike men of the fourteenth century,[11] his stately invocations and prologs, and many a minor touch put the *Troilus* on a more aspiring level than anything else he ever wrote. All these, the insight into actual people and the traditional literary usage, the loftiness and the every-day dialog, the unreal ideality in Troilus and the keen even prosaic naturalness of the others, the immersion in unchristian ethics and the abjuring of them in the Epilog, give the poem a clashing discord, which however adds to its appeal. Later he left this rarefied yet stormy atmosphere, returning first to the polite contemporary French style, then in the *Canterbury Tales* to the penetrating and wider human naturalness which he had so relished at times in the *Troilus,* and in which by genius as well as origin he most belonged.

NOTES

1. Karl Young, 'Chaucer's *Troilus and Criseyde* as Romance,' *PMLA*, LIII (1938), 38–63.

2. G. L. Kittredge, *Chaucer and His Poetry,* pp. 109, 112.

3. *E.g.,* W. G. Dodd's *Courtly Love in Chaucer and Gower* (Boston, 1913), pp. 129–208, and also C. S. Lewis' more brilliant and mature *The Allegory of Love* (Oxford, 1936), e.g., pp. 183, 192, 194. Miss C. B. West's *Courtoisie in Anglo-Norman Literature* (Oxford, 1938) though clearer in thinking would gain through still clearer definition. Long after this paper was written, the secretary of the MLA sent me an advance copy of T. A. Kirby's *Chaucer's Troilus: A Study in Courtly Love,* well-informed and meritorious (La. Univ. Press, 1940).

4. *De Amore Libri Tres;* the most accessible edition is by Amadeo Pagès (Castellon de la Plana, 1929).

5. *Trans. Roy. Soc. of Lit.,* Ser. 2, xxx, 87–92; *Kittredge Anniv. Papers,* pp. 340–341; *MP,* xxxiii, 367–373.

6. See J. S. Graydon, 'Defense of Criseyde,' *PMLA* (1929), 141–177. But he writes of the pair as if they had really lived, with little regard for the literary climate where their ghostly existence belongs.

7. Though some have wished to think a much later date settled, I gave in 1935 many further reasons for this opinion in *MLN,* L, 277–289.

8. See *MP,* xviii, 123–128.

9. See *MP,* xxxiii, 370–371, 373–374.

10. See my article in *Anglia,* xxxvii, 81–85, 107–108.

11. *MP,* xviii, 128–134.

ARTHUR MIZENER

Character and Action in
The Case of Criseyde

A GOOD deal of attention has been devoted to the question of Chaucer's intention when he created the character of Criseyde. Almost all answers have as their starting point a common assumption: that Chaucer was doing his best to create a unified character in the modern sense of the phrase. They start, that is, from the assumption that Chaucer meant Criseyde's character and actions to appear all of a piece and from the fact that he made her false to Troilus in the end. Only two conclusions are possible on the basis of these premises: either Chaucer intended Criseyde's character to appear compatible with her betrayal of Troilus from the first, or he intended it to appear to change during the course of the narrative in response to the events. The first of these conclusions, with its assumption as to Chaucer's conception of things, is the one most frequently encountered.

Professor Root, for example, concludes that Criseyde was intended to appear calculating, emotionally shallow, and a drifter from the first. Concrete evidence for hypotheses of this general type can be provided only by making very subtle psychological analyses of carefully selected details of the poem, on the tacit assumptions that Chaucer (1) thought of Criseyde as living a very complex inner life and (2) deliberately chose to reveal the nature

Reprinted, by permission, from *PMLA*, LIV (1939), 65-81.

of that inner life clearly only by the most indirect hints. Professor Root speaks of the line 'Tendre herted, slydynge of corage'[1]— which Chaucer took over from Benoit—as if this were the key to Criseyde's character.[2] It is difficult enough to believe that Chaucer would put the whole burden of clarifying Criseyde's motive for betraying Troilus on a half line near the end of the poem, and even more difficult to believe that he could have meant it to outweigh the import of the preceding five and one half lines, even if it be assumed that this passage is intended as an explanation of Criseyde's motives rather than a simple listing of the general qualities of her character.

But the main difficulty with this type of explanation is not the doubtfulness of these interpretations of details. It must be shown either (1) that Chaucer meant them as the essence of his intention, the rest of the poem to the contrary notwithstanding, or (2) that the hypothesis which is in accord with these interpretations fits the implications of the rest of the poem. The first of these alternatives is manifestly impossible. And it is impossible, too, to show in detail that the calm, essentially innocent but prudent, and finally deeply moved woman of the early part of the poem was intended to appear so morally instable that her betrayal of Troilus is a natural consequence of her character.

Professor Kittredge's more convincing explanation also suffers from the fact that he tries to find in Criseyde's character the cause of her unfaithfulness: 'As Cressida is at the beginning, such is she to the end; amorous, gentle, affectionate, and charming altogether, but fatally impressionable and yielding.'[3] Is it possible to believe that Chaucer intended to convey such an impression when he lengthened Boccaccio's period of wooing, when he was so careful to point out that Criseyde did not fall in love suddenly and to describe her admirable conduct in her difficult situation in Troy? Are not all these changes made so that Criseyde shall not appear 'impressionable and yielding' at the beginning? Yet only by believing that she is meant to appear some such thing as this can we explain her unfaithfulness on the assumption Professors Root and Kittredge make.[4]

It may appear gratuitous to say that Criseyde is unfaithful because the story makes her so, but it is just the insufficient attention given to this possibility which has made it seem necessary to prove that there was from the start some tragic flaw in her character which motivated her betrayal of Troilus.[5] The purpose of this essay is to suggest a different hypothesis of Chaucer's conception of character and its relation to events from the one which previous critics have used, and to test that hypothesis by analyzing Criseyde. This hypothesis is that for Chaucer a character consisted in a group of unchanging fundamental qualities, and that the relation between such a character and the events of the narrative was one of congruence rather than of cause and effect. This hypothesis is the outgrowth of a conviction that Chaucer's chief interest was in the action rather than in the characters.[6] If this conviction be valid, the arrangement of his narrative was determined primarily by a desire to develop fully the dramatic possibilities of the action, not by a desire to reveal the characters of the personages in the narrative by making motivation the significant aspect of it. The subtlety and richness of such a narrative, in so far as it is a matter of character alone, will be, not in the reader's sense that each episode is a further revelation of profoundly analyzed motives, but in his sense of how perfectly Chaucer has visualized a character of unchanging fundamental qualities in a series of situations which are there because they are necessary to the action. Certainly everyone will agree that Chaucer knew, and knew how to show the reader, precisely how a character of a certain kind would respond in a given situation. The point in question, therefore, is not the subtlety of Chaucer's observation of humanity but only whether he intended us to take each observation as a hint toward the efficient causes of the successive situations of the narrative or as part of the adequate realization of the character in a situation the efficient cause of which lay elsewhere. It is a question of whether Chaucer does not, for the sake of the action, sometimes omit what is necessary for a complete explanation of events in terms of characters, sometimes distort what needs to be clear for that purpose, and even put into the mouths of various characters remarks which are appropriate to them on no theory of character.

Chaucer's method of characterization is, in this view, essentially static: a character is presented, that is, shown as made up of certain characteristics such as pity or generosity; and then, by the events of the story, it is placed in various circumstances in which it always acts in accord with these characteristics. Chaucer's characters do not change or develop under the impact of experience; they display various aspects of an established set of characteristics as the progress of the narrative places them in varying circumstances. Conversely, the events of the narrative are not determined by the particular moral qualities ascribed to the characters. It would not occur to a mind which conceived of the relationship of character and event in this fashion to ask how a person who exhibited a certain character in one set of circumstances could possibly have acted so as to get himself into certain other circumstances; because in this conception the personages of the narrative do not get themselves into circumstances; the circumstances are primarily determined by the necessities of the action.

Whatever the advantages of the modern method, devised for a narrative in which the primary interest is the revealing of character, there can be no question that it involves the sacrifice of many of the dramatic effects which were possible with Chaucer's method. One such effect of major importance is the tragic emphasis Chaucer is able to manage in the Fifth Book; but on a smaller scale such effects are to be found everywhere in the poem.

Our conviction that in real life or in a psychological novel the Criseyde of the Fifth Book must have been different from the Criseyde of the early books to act as she did is no doubt true. And that Chaucer should have intended to imply no causal interaction between what Criseyde does and what she is therefore runs counter to all our habits of thought on this subject. Yet Chaucer's poem, looked at without prejudice, offers, I believe, no evidence that he intended Criseyde's unfaithfulness to appear either the cause of a change, or the consequence of an established vice, in the character he presents to us. In fact, there are grounds for an initial presumption to the contrary, for it is only if there is a contrast between what she is and what she does that Criseyde's fate is tragic. A Criseyde whose fall is the product either of an inherent vice or of a change for the worse in her character is at best an object of pathos. The argument here is, then, that from the beginning to the end of the poem Criseyde, whenever described or shown in action,

> sobre was, ek symple, and wys withal,
> The best ynorisshed ek that myghte be,
> And goodly of hire speche in general,
> Charitable, estatlich, lusty, and fre;
> Ne nevere mo ne lakkede hire pite;
> Tendre herted, slydynge of corage; . . .

Criseyde's first prolonged appearance in the narrative is the interview with Pandar in the Second Book. Before that her beauty is described and a brief account is given of her conduct at the time Calchas left Troy. Chaucer departs radically from Boccaccio in this scene when he introduces the long preliminary skirmish between Pandar and Criseyde. This addition permits him, among other things, to present at leisure Criseyde's character: her charm, intelligence, feminine simplicity, and sensitiveness. Having established the character, Chaucer then returns to Boccaccio for the main outline of the action.

In the matter of character, as in so many other matters,[7] an adequate explanation of Boccaccio's poem is not necessarily an adequate explanation of Chaucer's. By this time Chaucer has created a fixed character and, even when he translates directly, the effect against such a background is very different from that in Boccaccio, for what Chaucer borrows operates in a different context. This different effect is no accident, but the deliberately planned consequence of Chaucer's art. In the scene where Pandar reveals Troilus's love, for example, Chaucer's Criseyde senses that Pandar is about to say something important and lowers her eyes just before he tells of Troilus's love; in Boccaccio the revelation is made before Criseyde exhibits any signs of embarrassment.[8] By this slight change Chaucer makes his heroine appear, unlike Boccaccio's, both modest and sensitive to the implications of a social situation. In Chaucer's account, too, Criseyde's subsequent question as to how Pandar discovered Troilus's love impresses the reader as a typical example of the innocent curiosity which is generally believed to be characteristic of women under these circumstances. But in Boccaccio Criseyde, having just subscribed heartily to Pandar's 'gather ye rosebuds' speech, then adds:

> But let us now stop thinking of this, and tell me whether I may still have solace and joy [giuoco] of love, and in what way thou didst first take note of Troilus.

Boccaccio's Criseyde is a practical young lady arranging an affair. Chaucer, using much the same material, so arranges it as to convey a very different impression of his heroine. The delicacy and complexity of this scene can hardly be exaggerated, and it is difficult to see how anyone can find evidence in the character presented for Criseyde's later action. Only the supposed necessity for finding weaknesses in her can have led people to read them into this fine rendering of an admirable woman.

The implications of the next scene are not so obvious and will probably be determined ultimately on the basis of the reader's conception of Chaucer's main intentions. A great deal has been made of it as evidence for Criseyde's cold-blooded, calculating nature. But to call Criseyde's consideration of all the factors involved in her acceptance or refusal of Troilus calculating seems to me possible only if one fails to recognize the difficulty and complexity of her situation. She would not appear either sober or prudent if she were to rush into the affair without considering that in her precarious situation in Troy, Troilus might easily have her 'in despit,' or without thinking over carefully the disadvantages of the change.

A more significant point about this scene, however, is the fact that Chaucer does not motivate Criseyde's falling in love. In Boccaccio Troilus does not go by her house until after her meditation and only then Criseyde 'praised to herself his manner, his pleasing actions, and his courtesy, and so suddenly was she captivated that she desired him above every other good.' This apparently struck Chaucer as producing an undesirable effect, for he shifted this scene so that it comes before Criseyde's meditation. It was not that Chaucer saw any psychological inadequacy in love-at-first-sight, for he used it without hesitation in the case of

Troilus. Nor does he, in Criseyde's case any more than in Troilus's, describe a gradual change in her psychological attitude leading eventually to her being in love. He simply states, quite flatly, that the process was gradual. This change was not made, then, so that Chaucer might describe Criseyde's development from one state of mind to another.

Chaucer is anxious, however, that Criseyde's attitude in this scene should appear congruous with her established character, and that is the positive consequence of his shifting the location of Troilus's ride past Criseyde's house in the sequence of the narrative. In Boccaccio Criseyde's meditation follows immediately upon Pandar's revelation that some one, not known to her personally, is in love with her. She thus appears to be weighing the joys of love (of a sort) against its risks, and the reader gains the impression that she is a shrewd and sensual young lady for whom the sight of Troilus's elegant person in the end turns the scales. In Chaucer's poem, on the other hand, despite his protest that Criseyde's glimpse of Troilus was only the beginning of love, we come to her soliloquy with a vivid memory of Criseyde gazing out the window at Troilus and wondering 'who yaf me drynke?' This soliloquy, as a result of Chaucer's change in the narrative sequence, is bound to be read as the thoughts of a person already in love with Troilus. If Chaucer's purpose was to reveal the development of Criseyde's character, then he has either deliberately and unaccountably tried to confuse the reader at this point or he has without deliberation blundered into doing so. For he has created an impression of Criseyde's feelings the existence of which he himself denies. If on the other hand his purpose was to make us read Criseyde's soliloquy, not as 'cool calculation' but as the meditation of a prudent but tender-hearted woman in love, and at the same time to make us remember her as having fallen in love slowly, then this shift in the sequence of the narrative is masterly.

The first exchange of letters between Troilus and Criseyde also raises the question of how Chaucer intended the reader to interpret Criseyde's attitude. Critics have believed that this scene was intended by Chaucer to illustrate Criseyde's tendency to drift into things. There is no drifting earlier in the poem, for no one with a

354

knowledge of courtly love can doubt Criseyde's sincere belief in Pandar's threat that unless she yields a little both he and Troilus will die. Criseyde yields there quite deliberately to what appears to her serious necessity; she does not drift. And in this scene she conducts herself as any intelligent but modest lady would. When she accepts Troilus's letter she consciously takes the first step on the long road to the goal of courtly love; the way in which she at first refuses this letter shows she is perfectly aware of what it means to accept it. And when she writes Troilus she takes quite consciously again (as Chaucer himself tells us) another.

In both Chaucer and Boccaccio Troilus's letter is given, and then Criseyde laughs; in Boccaccio she laughs at this speech of Pandar's:

> A strange thing is this to consider that at what is most desired by her sex each lady should, in the presence of others, show herself annoyed and vexed. I have spoken to thee so much of this matter that thenceforth thou shouldst not play the prude with me.

No such speech is the cause of Criseyde's laughter in Chaucer, given her established and now familiar character in this situation it is very evident that she is incapable of the light-hearted cynicism of Boccaccio's heroine. At the same time she must act deliberately. Chaucer's task is to make her appear definite but neither cynical nor immodest. The definiteness is there, for not only the embarrassment at the moment when Pandar gives her the letter, but the tacit assumption on his part after dinner that she has read it are evidence that they both clearly understood the implications of Criseyde's taking the letter. Yet even in Chaucer's times those implications had their embarrassing side for such a genteel if unhypocritical lady as Criseyde. She therefore attempts to prevent their appearing as it were naked between Pandar and herself by smiling and remarking

em, I preye,
Swich answere as yow list youre self purveye;
For, trewely, I nyl no lettre write.

And Pandar, realizing that this is not really a refusal at all but an exhibition of tact, accepts the turn Criseyde is trying to give the conversation and replies in kind with an equally tactful little joke. 'Therwith she lough, and seyde: "go we dyne." ' The subtlety with which Chaucer visualizes and communicates the attitude of his character in this situation can probably not be exaggerated. But there is nothing in that attitude which suggests a character capable of the ultimate betrayal of Troilus, and nothing in Chaucer's narrative which justifies the assumption that he intended it to suggest such a character.

The decorous slowness with which Criseyde falls in love is further emphasized by Chaucer's introducing a second scene in which Troilus passes by her house and by his carefully pointing out that it is far too soon for Criseyde to consider yielding to Troilus, a thing she does not do for a considerable time. Criseyde, when she sees Troilus pass by for the second time, definitely becomes very much in love, and from this point on Chaucer assumes that we understand that fact.

When Criseyde encounters Troilus at Deiphebus's house she acts exactly as we should expect, calmly and with a complete understanding of the situation and the meaning of all that is said. She loves Troilus and she is perfectly clear as to what that involves. It is difficult to imagine how Chaucer, short of showing her making the advances, could have done more to prevent her appearing to 'drift genially with circumstance,' for the progress in the relations of the two lovers made at Deiphebus's house is almost entirely due to her. Her acceptance of Troilus is characteristically deliberate and unambiguous, for all its delicacy. Certainly there was no question in the minds of Pandar and Troilus of Criseyde's meaning or of the magnitude of her decision.

As a question of character there is no necessity for Pandar's elaborate scheme for bringing Troilus and Criseyde together. But by inventing this scene Chaucer adds a tensely dramatic situation to the action. The introduction of this material is justified on these grounds; it cannot be justified on the grounds that the development of the character demanded it. For if Chaucer had been interested in the changes in Criseyde's mind which led up to her attitude at the moment Pandar came in with his cock and bull story about Orestes, he would have centered his attention in that. But he does not, and the result for the reader who does is unhappy. Chaucer, so the explanation runs, makes it clear that Criseyde sees through Pandar when, while inviting her to his house for supper, he implies that Troilus is out of town. But if Criseyde's action through the events of the night at Pandar's house must be explained in terms of a Criseyde who knew all along that Pandar was manoeuvering her into Troilus's arms, then her attitude, when Pandar comes in with his tale of Troilus's jealousy, must be put down as pure hypocrisy. Can any one read this last passage and believe that Chaucer meant Criseyde to appear hypocritical in her protestations?

If, however, we assume that this scene was introduced primarily because it is necessary to the complete development of the action, and not because it plots a point on the curve of Criseyde's gradual demoralization, and look at Chaucer's portrayal of Criseyde in this scene, not as his attempt to reveal what characteristic in her caused the scene to occur, but as his attempt to visualize how a woman of the type he has shown Criseyde to be all along would act if placed in this situation, then, it seems to me, the full subtlety of Chaucer's portrayal becomes clear. Every single word and gesture fits Chaucer's fixed character perfectly, reasserts with apparently inexhaustible variety of detail one or another of the qualities which he has already ascribed to her. She is seriously concerned at Troilus's jealousy and eager to explain to him. For, believing Pandar's tale, she assumes that an explanation is what is required. It is her affection for Troilus which finally makes her do what Pandar says will satisfy Troilus, however foolish it may seem to her. Her eagerness to help Troilus when he faints is again not the acting of hypocrisy but the result of sincere and affectionate anxiety. And at last there is her famous flash of humor when Troilus takes her in his arms.

Every word of Criseyde's in the scene is just what would be expected from the woman Chaucer has described, were she placed in the situation of the story. In that sense, psychology of the subtlest kind abounds, but in the sense that what she says is an explanation of her past or future behavior it does not. If an attempt, for example, is made to consider Criseyde's statement that she would not be there had she not yielded long before as an explanation of her state of mind during what has preceded, rather than as a reassertion of her sense of humor, there is again the necessity of explaining her attitude when Pandar tells of Troilus's jealousy. Once again only the assumption that she was playing the hypocrite will serve, and Chaucer has given us every reason to suppose Criseyde is quite sincere when she offers to see Troilus the next day and explain everything. There is not an ounce of hypocrisy in Criseyde up to this point; what reason could there be for Chaucer's making her suddenly acquire it? And yet there is no escaping a belief in her hypocrisy unless it is accepted that Chaucer had no intention of revealing Criseyde's motives here, but only of keeping her attitude consonant with her established character.

Somewhat similar motives have been read into the scene the next morning when Pandar comes to Criseyde's room and asks with assumed anxiety if the rain has disturbed her sleep. This beautiful presentation of two witty but tactful people has been considered as evidence that Criseyde was not much in love with Troilus,[9] since she can joke about it. But to this Professor Kittredge's answer is sufficiently devastating: 'It is ridiculous to accuse her of insincerity in her love for Troilus. To be sincere, it is not necessary to be either solemn or stupid.'[10]

The ending of the poem, especially the Fifth Book, shows most clearly Chaucer's method and its purpose. It is Criseyde who, true to her character, offers most of the practical suggestions when it comes to making plans for her return, it is she who brings hope and wisdom and a plan to the final meeting of the lovers; while Troilus, true to his character also, does little except tell of his love and sorrow. That Criseyde is to be thought of not as a deliberate hypocrite or facile optimist, but as perfectly sincere and determined to return soon cannot be questioned, for Chaucer is careful to tell us these things in his own words. That is, the woman in this scene is exactly the same as she is in every other place in the poem, just as the man is. Yet in the face of Chaucer's word that Criseyde means all she says, she says a great many things which, while they are exactly what we expect from the character, cannot be brought into accord with her later conduct. They are true to her character in the circumstances in which they are spoken, and they both heighten the tragic effect of the parting and emphasize by their very sincerity the tragic irony of the scene.

But if Criseyde's words here are not meant as hypocrisy or the self-deception of a weak and shallow nature, perhaps the discrepancy between her professions and subsequent actions may be reconciled (and the tragic irony removed) by arguing that she encountered overwhelming obstacles to her plans when she got to the Greek camp and that it was impossible for her to return to Troy:

> ... she soon discovers that she has matched her woman's wit, not against her dotard father merely, but against the doom of Troy. No pretexts avail, not because Calchas suspects her plot, but because he knows that the city is destined to destruction.[11]

This line of reasoning, unfortunately, ignores Chaucer's poem. For it is after Criseyde has realized the hopelessness of persuading her father that she finally determines to return to Troy in spite of all the difficulties she has been running over in her mind.

Mr. Graydon has worked out with great ingenuity the most probable chronology of the Fifth Book; Chaucer (for good reasons) deliberately obscures the evidence for it and once even professes ignorance of it. But if Chaucer had any chronology in mind at all, it must have been some such one as Mr. Graydon suggests. As nearly as can be determined Criseyde's second letter, which practically states she will not return, is written more than two months after her departure, and her yielding to Diomede comes about two years after her departure.

But all through the Fifth Book Chaucer avoids this chronological sequence. His purpose is to describe the sorrow of Troilus, and to heighten the tragic appearance of that sorrow, and the arrangement of the narrative for that purpose inevitably involves what seems to the reader who is looking for an orderly development and explanation of character, an unaccountable confusion of the chronology of events. The whole story of Criseyde is presented at the beginning of the Fifth Book down to the time she gives herself to Diomede, a period of about two years. Chaucer then goes back to the ninth day after her departure from Troy and takes up his description of Troilus's sorrow. By concealing such chronological references as he gives and by telling of Criseyde's fall in comparatively few words, Chaucer gives the impression that that fall is very rapid. With this defection and its apparent undignified haste fresh in the reader's mind, he describes Troilus on the Trojan walls sighing his soul towards the Grecian tents, pathetically confident that each approaching figure is Criseyde. Chaucer has arranged the sequence of the events in the narrative in the order which will give the maximum effectiveness to the tragic scene. This arrangement hopelessly muddles in the reader's mind any possible chronology, so neccessary if we are to follow the development of Criseyde's character. Yet Troilus's sorrow would be infinitely less pathetic if Chaucer were to say: 'And as a matter of fact, just about this time Criseyde was courageously determining to return to Troy.' If Chaucer had centered his purpose in the development of the characters, something like that would have been necessary, but since his purpose was to create a tragic action, it was not only unnecessary but highly undesirable.

All through these final scenes this purpose is apparent. Criseyde, rather surprisingly, has by far the larger number of protestations of love and loyalty. They were not meant to prove her either a hypocrite or a moral weakling. Each of them is true to Chaucer's static characterization of her, and each of them, against the background of the reader's knowledge of the future, has an ironic effect in terms of the action. Troilus accuses Criseyde of disloyalty long before she has actually contemplated any such thing. This accusation was certainly not intended by Chaucer to prove Troilus's unreasoning jealously, as Mr. Graydon argues, but merely to give the impression that the fatal conclusion of the action was rapidly and irresistibly approaching. As soon as Criseyde is out of Troy, Pandar suddenly becomes certain she will never return. No reason for this opinion is given, and it utterly contradicts his previous serious and considered praise of Criseyde's integrity. This change of front is unmotivated. It serves the purpose of heightening by contrast the tragic irony of Troilus's confidence that Criseyde will return; it is not a hint of Criseyde's motive for not returning.

There is, finally, the crux of the poem so far as this question of Criseyde's character is concerned, that is, her unfaithfulness. Her soliloquy on the ninth night in the Greek camp is so similar to her earlier meditation on whether she ought to yield to Troilus or not that it is difficult to avoid comparing them. In each she considers carefully all the facts involved and in each reaches a definite decision; in the latter soliloquy her decision is that she will go to Troy in spite of all the difficulties. It is not easy to see how the woman presented in this soliloquy differs in any fundamental respect from the woman of the earlier parts of the poem. And the difficulty of believing Chaucer meant this speech to be taken as an indication that Criseyde was 'calculating' is as great as the difficulty of believing that that was his intention in writing her soliloquy on love in Book Two. Furthermore, instead of describing a change in her attitude subsequent to this soliloquy which we are to take as the cause of her staying with the Greeks, Chaucer merely states in five brief lines that she did stay, that two months later she was still in the Greek camp. Criseyde's failure to return to Troy is one of the necessary events in the story Chaucer is telling. The whole structure of the poem at this point shows that he did not ᵩhink of it as determined by Criseyde's character.

Nor does Chaucer, in any serious psychological sense, motivate Criseyde's physical betrayal of Troilus. She betrays Troilus because the action requires it, because she had to if the tragic possibilities of the main action, 'the double sorwe of Troilus,' were to be worked out completely, and not because of anything in her character which made that betrayal inevitable. Chaucer says she is guilty, but he never shows us a woman whose state of mind is such as to make the reader believe her capable of betraying Troilus. In fact, Chaucer carefully avoids showing the reader Criseyde at all from the time when she makes her last statement of loyalty to Troilus to the time when she expresses her grief at her betrayal of him. He even refuses to say that 'she yaf hym [i.e., Diomede] hire herte,' and there is what appears to be a conscious effort on Chaucer's part to blur Criseyde's inconstancy in the reader's mind as much as he can without destroying belief in it altogether. The nearest Chaucer comes to offering on his own account (as apart from dramatically presenting) a reason for Criseyde's betrayal of Troilus is to hint at one in the stanza in which he explains why she did not return to Troy. But this reason is not psychologically reconcilable with the character displayed by Criseyde. No conceivable character capable of acting as Criseyde did for this reason can be brought into accord with the woman presented in the first four and one half books of the poem or with the woman who was griefstricken 'whan that she falsed Troilus.'

The Criseyde we are shown, both before and after the event of her yielding to Diomede, displays exactly the same characteristics we have associated with Criseyde since the beginning of the narrative. It is difficult to believe that Chaucer was not conscious of the consequences of this arrangement of the narrative. It leaves us knowing that Criseyde has betrayed Troilus and yet visualizing her, as we have from the start, as gentle, tender-hearted, loving and honorable. In other words, Chaucer's arrangement is calculated to leave our sense of Criseyde's character as little affected as possible by our knowledge of her act, it does the best it can to prevent our substituting for the Criseyde we have known all along the character we must invent if we are successfully to imagine Criseyde's yielding to Diomede.

The hypothesis that Chaucer meant to ascribe to Criseyde a character calculated to explain her betrayal of Troilus seems to me to break down most completely at this most crucial point. For one thing, it is so incompatible with Chaucer's treatment of this part of the narrative that in order to set it up in the first place the critic must rewrite the poem in his imagination, at least to the extent of adding a new scene. For another, it requires proof that Chaucer has shown Criseyde as consistently 'impressionable and yielding' or psychopathically terrified from the first, and it seems to me impossible to present this proof without distorting the implications of the first four books of the poem. Finally, such an explanation prevents the reader from seeing Criseyde as a tragic figure. If Criseyde's character is such as to be a complete explanation of her betrayal of Troilus then she is at best merely pathetic;

it is only if there is a contrast between what she seems to the reader to be and what he knows her to have done that she becomes tragic. It may be argued, of course, that Chaucer invented her only as an instrument for producing the tragedy of Troilus, but if he intended Criseyde, in addition, to be tragic in her own right, then he must have aimed at this contrast between what she is and what she does, a contrast which we destroy if we insist on seeing her as no better than she should be.

In real life as we believe it to be or in a psychological novel that contrast would be impossible. For in these worlds deeds are the outward manifestations of a process of which the inward manifestations are congruous thoughts and feelings. In them, therefore, people cannot approach and look back upon an act of inconstancy rebelling against it with their whole natures, any more than they can take this attitude while committing murder. But Chaucer's Criseyde, not living in such a world, can and does rebel against her own act, Chaucer shows her as horrified at her disloyalty, regretful of the loss of her good name and greatly admiring Troilus. Is not this precisely the attitude to be expected from the woman portrayed in the first four books of the poem had she to face the situation in which Criseyde finds herself? Chaucer could scarcely have portrayed her in this fashion had he meant us to think of her character as now degenerated to the point where her betrayal of Troilus is the perfect manifestation of it, and he certainly would not have so portrayed her, here or elsewhere, had he meant us to think of her as capable of that betrayal from the start.

From this point forward Chaucer's arrangement of the narrative is governed by his wish to emphasize the sorrow of Troilus. Criseyde's suffering and her hope that she may yet return to Troy, even though she has overstayed her ten days, are presented just before Chaucer describes her thoughts as she decides—Troilus and Troy being forgotten—to remain in the Greek camp. This sequence is incongruous, so far as any explanation of her character goes, but it strengthens the pathos of her peroration on Troilus which follows and so heightens the tragedy.

When Criseyde's first letter from the Greek camp is summarized, Chaucer very definitely gives the impression that the letter is not quite honest, and advises Troilus to give up any hope of Criseyde. This impression is contrary to what we can, if we wish, prove to be the 'facts,' for Chaucer tells us elsewhere that the letter was written about two months after Criseyde's departure, and on Chaucer's own say-so she was at that period not at all entangled with Diomede and probably had not yet ceased to hope she might return to Troy. But these 'facts' must not be allowed to obtrude here, for they would interrupt the steady and fatal progression of Troilus's tragedy. The 'false' impression that Chaucer gives furthers that tragedy; it makes us sympathize with Troilus's growing belief that Criseyde has been unfaithful to him, and that is Chaucer's purpose.

The same method is followed with Criseyde's second letter. There is no way of knowing exactly when it was written or whether Criseyde is lying. Chaucer does not even bother to provide this information so vital to a complete understanding of Criseyde's character. The letter is part of Troilus's fate; it completes his tragedy.

So, it seems to me, Criseyde is meant to be taken. Her character is a combination of subtly observed characteristics, and the illusion of reality that character leaves on a reader's mind is the result, not of Chaucer's painstaking motivation of every event from within the character, but rather of the variety and concreteness with which he puts these characteristics on display in any scene in which the character is presented. The character of Criseyde is primarily an instrument for, and a unit in, a tragic action; it is therefore statically conceived and is related to the action by congruence rather than by cause and effect. For both Troilus and Criseyde are the victims of an act determined, not by Criseyde's character, but by the dramatic necessities of the action.

NOTES

1. v, 825.—All references are to *Chaucer's Troilus and Criseyde*, ed. R. K. Root (Princeton, 1926).

2. *The Poetry of Chaucer* (Boston, 1922), p. 114. 'Slydynge of corage' is interpreted as meaning emotionally shallow and inclined to be fickle (see Professor Root's note to this line in his edition of the poem).

3. *Chaucer and his Poetry* (Cambridge, 1915), p. 135. 'Baffling alike to us and to herself' (*ibid.*, p. 126), he adds elsewhere, as if Chaucer intended us not to be able to understand her.

4. Mr. C. S. Lewis's more recent analysis of the meaning of Criseyde (*The Allegory of Love*, pp. 179–190) is of this general type. According to Mr. Lewis we are meant to see Criseyde as from beginning to end governed by an almost pathological fear ('a dash of what is now called mazochism'); this theory leads him to argue that Chaucer meant the reader to see Criseyde's remarks at the last meeting of the lovers as 'desperate speeches in which Creseide, with pitiful ignorance of her self, attempts to assume the role of comforter . . .' and that he meant her resolutions to return to Troy after she had reached the Greek camp to be seen by the reader as 'desperate efforts to rise above herself.'

5. 'Emphasis cannot be too strong when placed upon the fact that in *Troilus and Criseyde* an absolutely inescapable necessity governs the progress of the story.' W. C. Curry, 'Destiny in Chaucer's *Troilus*,' *PMLA*, XLV (1930), 152.

6. The allied problem of the connection between Chaucer's conception of character on the one hand and of Fortune and Destiny on the other is far too complex to be taken up here. But see W. C. Curry, 'Destiny in Chaucer's *Troilus*,' *PMLA*, XLV (1930), 129–168; H. R. Patch, 'Troilus on Determinism,' *Speculum*, VI (1931), 225–243; and William Farnham, *The Medieval Heritage of Elizabethan Tragedy* (Berkeley, 1936), especially pp. 155–157. Professor Patch, if I understand him correctly, argues that any narrative in which there is not 'the interplay of free motivation' is 'the spectacle of the action of irresponsible puppets.' If this line of reasoning be valid, then it must follow from the argument of this essay that Chaucer was a complete determinist, a conclusion which is certainly open to question. But Professor Patch's line of reasoning seems to me not only to involve a confusion of literal and metaphorical statements (it is only by metaphor that one can speak meaningfully of any characters as 'irresponsible puppets' since literally speaking all characters are just that) but also to over-simplify the problem by assuming that there must be a direct connection between an author's narrative method and his philosophic opinions. Some kind of connection no doubt always exists, but surely it is not such that one can conclude that all narratives except those which provide a tight cause-and-effect relationship between the characters and the events are evidence of their author's disbelief in the freedom of the human will and the responsibility of human beings for their own acts.

7. See Karl Young, 'Chaucer's "Troilus and Criseyde" as Romance,' *PMLA*, LIII (1938), p. 39.

8. II, 38. The references to Boccaccio are to *The Filostrato of Giovanni Boccaccio*, trans. N. E. Griffin and A. B. Myrick (Philadelphia, 1929).

9. Joseph M. Beatty, Jr., 'Mr. Graydon's "Defense of Criseyde,"' *SP*, XXVI (1929), 472.

10. G. L. Kittredge, *op. cit.*, p. 133.

11. G. L. Kittredge, *op. cit.*, p. 120.

HOWARD ROLLIN PATCH

Troilus on Predestination

A CARDINAL sin of the middle ages according to the average modern
critic is its long-windedness; another is its proneness to digression.
As a beautifully flagrant example of both these faults is usually
cited the long speech on predestination in the fourth book of
Chaucer's *Troilus*. Professor Lounsbury's statement of the case
may serve as typical. He is talking of the 'poet's passion for
dialectics'[1]:

> With the grossest instance of the failure on the part of Chaucer
> to comply with the requirements of his art, I pass from this branch
> of the subject. His special fondness for the questions connected
> with the doctrine of free-will and predestination has been men-
> tioned in a previous chapter. It is not always a misfortune. In the
> Knight's tale it is made conducive to the general effect. In the tale
> of the Nun's Priest it relieves the situation by its contrast between
> the greatness of the questions involved and the pettiness of the
> incidents upon which it is brought to bear. But in 'Troilus and
> Cressida' it is an intrusion of the worst kind. The hero is in an
> extremity of grief at the enforced departure of his mistress from
> Troy. He is so fallen into despair that he cares not whether he lives
> or dies. But his method of deploring the coming calamity is un-
> exampled on the part of a lover. He enters into a discussion with

Reprinted from *The Journal of English and Germanic Philology*, XVII (1918),
399-423.

himself upon the doctrine of predestination. Fully one hundred
and twenty lines he takes up with establishing the proposition that
everything that happens, happens by necessity. The passage is a
versification of the argument on the subject of God's foreknowledge
and man's free-will that is contained in the fifth book of the treatise
of Boethius. It utterly interferes with the movement of the story.
It is tacked to it by the flimsiest of fastenings. It is lacking in some
manuscripts, though unfortunately not the best ones. Still, its absence from these makes it reasonable to suppose that its addition
was an afterthought which in this case was not of the wisest. The
bad taste exhibited by the poet in such passages will be conceded
by all. His most fervent admirers would be the readiest to admit
the justice of the censure.[2]

From the attacks, of which Lounsbury's criticism is representative,
we hear that the monologue of Troilus has little to do with the
main thread of the plot; that it hinders the progress of the narrative; that it is absurd in the mouth of its speaker; and finally that
the passage is an anachronism. I shall try to answer these points
separately, but they may all be summarized as taking issue with
the dramatic fitness of the speech.

Most critics will agree that Chaucer seldom rambles on to no
purpose. That he very well knew the principle of selection in art
is made evident again and again in his poetry when he brings us
sharply back to the main issue. On this matter we may quote
from the *Troilus* itself:

> But now, paraunter, som man wayten wolde
> That every word, or sonde, or look, or chere
> Of Troilus that I rehersen sholde,
> In al this whyle, unto his lady dere;
> I trowe it were a long thing for to here;
> Or of what wight that stant in swich disioynte,
> His wordes alle, or every look, to poynte.

Compared with the verse of some of his contemporaries Chaucer's
lines are crammed; and he cannot, he says, waste time by setting
down every detail of the speeches of Troilus to his lady. Yet in
the very next book he gives up one hundred and twenty lines to the

argument on predestination which Troilus utters to himself. Nothing even remotely corresponding appears in the *Filostrato*, and, as Lounsbury has said, we find it in the best manuscripts of the *Troilus*.

Still it is possible that Chaucer's style may be terse enough and that he did not insert the passage with total unconsciousness of any motive. Interested in a certain conception of philosophy, he may have seized an occasion to preach. After the story itself had grown cold for him, he picked up his manuscript and saw in one of the most intense scenes of the tragedy a splendid opportunity to point a moral. The passage has been defended in this way, and from various appreciations we learn that the poet is here trying to edify his readers or that he is here giving us his own spiritual doctrine. For example we are told that the monologue 'has a special interest in showing us the settled determinism of Chaucer's philosophical conception of human life.'³ Views of this sort presuppose, to my mind, a most remarkable idea of Chaucer himself. But no matter how the critics imagine the poet, the views themselves rest on several assumptions which can be readily tested: first, that the monologue is so placed that we are justified in lifting it from its context and in regarding it as one of the moral conclusions of the poem; secondly, that in Troilus's speech the poet does give a proper and adequate statement of the problem; thirdly, that in whatever he presents here, he is perfectly serious.

In support of these assumptions we have what is extremely important—almost contemporary evidence. In the *Testament of Love*, the lover asks the Goddess of Love whether, since everything happens through God's knowledge and takes its being from Him, God is not therefore the author of bad deeds as well as of good:

'Quod Love, "I shal telle thee, this lesson to lerne. Myne owne trewe servaunt, the noble philosophical poete in Englissh . . . in a tretis that he made of my servant Troilus, hath this mater touched, and at the ful this question assoyled. Certaynly, his noble sayinges can I not amende; in goodnes of gentil manliche speche, without any maner of nycetè of storiers imaginacion, in witte and in good reson of sentence he passeth al other makers. In the boke of Troilus, the answere to thy question mayst thou learne." '⁴

368

Two centuries later, Speght, in his second reprint in 1602 of Thynne's edition of Chaucer, puts at the head of the *Troilus* as its argument: 'In which discourse Chaucer liberally treateth of the divine purveiaunce.'[5] These quotations seem to indicate that Usk and later Speght thought that Chaucer was pretty much in earnest in the discussion. This view complicates my problem; for if Chaucer intended to present a really adequate account of the question of predestination and if he intended the monologue to be sufficient unto itself, then he was not so likely to keep the passage true to its dramatic setting. Therefore, while this general defence in a measure would answer the criticism that Chaucer's lines are meaningless in themselves, it would not in any way refute the objection that the monologue is totally out of place where we find it.

What is the relation of Troilus's speech to the main thought of the poem? To decide this point we must first make very sure of just what Troilus has in mind. What he says may be summarized as follows: (a) he gives the various attitudes taken by different clerks toward the subject of predestination and free will; (b) then he comes to his own conclusions on the subject—viz. (1) whether God has divine foreknowledge of events, or whether He foresees things because they are foreordained, events are surely destined to happen; and therefore (2) man has no free will. In the course of his argument Troilus is not vitally concerned whether God or fate is responsible for the 'necessity' of affairs, but he seems to incline to the former view.

It is often pointed out that in the passage we are studying Chaucer merely versified parts of Boethius, which he already knew in the original and had himself translated. There in the *Consolatio* the speaker asks whether there is any such thing as free will. Lady Philosophy assures him that there is. The speaker then proceeds to oppose this idea with the doctrine of divine prescience and predestination in much the same manner as Troilus; but he goes even further and carries the idea to what seems its logical conclusion:

. . .'in ydel ben ther thanne purposed and bihight medes to gode folk, and peynes to badde folk, sin that no moevinge of free corage voluntarie ne hath nat deserved hem . . . and it sholde seme thanne,

that thilke thing is alderworst, which that is now demed for alder-
most iust and most rightful, *that is to seyn,* that shrewes ben pun-
isshed, or elles that gode folk ben y-gerdoned: the whiche folk, sin
that hir proppre wil ne sent hem nat to that oon ne to that other . . .
but constreineth hem certain necessitee of thinges to comen:
thanne no shollen ther nevere ben, ne nevere weren, vyce ne vertu,
but it sholde rather ben confusioun of alle desertes medled withouten discrecioun . . . than folweth it, that oure vyces ben referred
to the maker of alle good. . . . Thanne is ther no resoun to hopen
in god, ne for to preyen *to god;* for what sholde any wight hopen
to god, or why sholde he preyen *to god,* sin that the ordinaunce of
destinee, which that ne may nat ben inclyned, knitteth and strein-
eth alle thinges that men may desiren?'[6]

Removing the burden of sin from mankind in this way would, I
say, seem to be the logical goal of Troilus's speech; but Chaucer,
who must have been aware of this, prevented any such interpretation by a touch that proves itself to be quite deliberate. He omitted
the sentiments which I have quoted, and borrowed instead, for
the beginning of Troilus's speech, some of the sound doctrine from
the discourse of Lady Philosophy herself:

> . . . 'god seeth every thing, out of doutaunce,
> And hem desponeth, thourgh his ordenaunce,
> In hir merytes sothly for to be,
> As they shul comen by predestinee.'

This passage is lifted from a section in Boethius different from that
required for the rest of Troilus's speech, and it shows how carefully
Chaucer composed the long monologue. Troilus, then, believes that
although ruin is his destiny, God has so arranged matters that it
is also what he deserves; although mankind is not originally responsible for its merits, or defects, yet ultimately punishment or
reward are quite *apropos.* In other words Troilus wishes to indicate
that he is not responsible for the present disaster, but he wishes to
do so piously. There is a kind of self-pitying humility in his attitude.
He will not trouble to blame anybody else, God or man, so long
as it be acknowledged that he himself has been opposing unfair

odds and that he has never really had a chance—with all due respect to the Creator's sense of justice.

We need not be disturbed by the logical inconsistencies involved in this view. In a way they are no worse than those involved in the greater issue—that of divine prescience and human free will—but even if they were it would not matter, for, if I am right, the speech is not intended as a sample of dialectic fireworks but as an outburst of human emotion.

In still another place Chaucer deviates from his source. Although it does not seem to be generally remembered, ten Brink has already observed that the ultimate conclusion of the whole problem in Troilus's speech differs from that reached in Boethius, that in the *Consolatio* when the speaker has finished, Lady Philosophy gives a rather striking reply:

> . . .'I axe why thou wenest that thilke resouns of hem that assoilen this questioun ne ben nat speedful y-nough ne sufficient: the which *solucioun, or the whiche resoun,* for that it demeth that the pre-science nis nat cause of necessitee to thinges to comen, that ne weneth it nat that freedom of wil be destorbed or y-let by prescience.'[7]

The speaker finally admits his mistake, but Troilus in contrast holds to his fatalistic views and Chaucer does not give us any further solution of the problem.

It used to be held, however, that in this passage Chaucer had more prominently in mind another work on predestination and free will, and that there he borrowed his theories of determinism supported by a more or less orthodox scholastic. This different authority was Thomas Bradwardine's ponderous treatise *De Causa Dei,* written against the surviving heresies of Pelagius. But the passages in Bradwardine which suggest something like the argument of Troilus are only vaguely similar and then similar in content not in style. Furthermore there are some serious discrepancies between the thought of Troilus and that of Bradwardine in general. The latter does subordinate the human will to Necessity and both of these to the Divine Will:

'Si vis omnium quae fecit *et* quae passus est veram scire necessitatem, scito omnia ex necessitate fuisse, quia ipse voluit, voluntatem verò eius nulla praecessit necessitas: voluntatem, inquam, eius diuinam nulla parecessit necessitas, sed humanam.'[8]

But he proceeds to demonstrate that necessity and freedom, and merit, chance, and fortune, are not mutually exclusive. He states his thesis as follows:

'Necessitas et libertas, ac meritum casusque et fortuna invicem non repugnant; de fati quoque praescientia, praedestinationis et gratiae cum libero arbitrio ac merito concordia generali.'[9]

In this view he is clearly in opposition to Troilus and he continues more and more emphatically to be so. For example, Bradwardine says that Necessity attains moral power only as man submits his will to it, and sin and virtue are matters directly connected with the willing:

'Ex his autem euidenter apparet, quod licet quis necessitatus fuerit ad faciendum quicquam boni vel mali, si tamen necessitationem illam ignoret, et faciat hoc voluntariè et liberè, quantum in *eo* est, meretur.'[10]

At times, perhaps, Bradwardine seems to place more emphasis on the power of God than on the freedom of the human will, but that is because his work is directed especially against the Pelagians. This sect believed on the one hand that where man had no power he was sinless: obligation was, they said, in accordance with ability, and so they diminished the sinner's responsibility. On the other hand they laid great stress on the freedom of man's will, and in so doing went to heretical extremes, diminishing the power of God. It is against this latter element in particular that Bradwardine writes.

Chaucer might have been influenced by such a placing of emphasis, did not Bradwardine bring out very clearly and emphatically too his belief in free will:

'Quare manifestum est, quia si virtus coelestis vel fatum, vel quicunque alius motor extrinsecus moueret animas humanas ad volendum vel nolendum, non aufert eis dominium *et* imperium, vel autoritatem suarum voluntatum et actionum, cum nec vim, nec violentiam nec coactionem eis inferre ad haec possunt: *et* hoc est' propter libertatem atque imperiositatem voluntatis, propter quas nec coactionem sustinet, nec receptibilis est vllo modorum ipsius.' [11]

It lies not in our stars that we are underlings; we have a complete and free choice to do what we will. Bradwardine reconciles this choice with divine prescience in the following manner:

'Atque ita qui omnes rerum causas praesciuit, profecto in eis causis etiam nostras voluntates ignorare non potuit, quas nostrorum operum causas esse praesciuit.' [12]

God can foresee not only our actions but the causes of them: he knows our wills. So Bradwardine answers the argument of Troilus.

Let us remind ourselves at this point that Bradwardine's lifetime was not so very long before Chaucer's, that in fact it extended well into the fourteenth century. Orthodoxy had lasted as long as that at least. In opposing the Pelagians, the Church did emphasize the grace of God, but still it maintained a belief and a very pronounced belief in human free will. The Church Fathers held to a faith in divine predestination of human affairs, but they reconciled it with human free will none the less. Those who held independent views on these points would be considered heretical and, like the Lollards, would be marked extraordinary. If Chaucer introduced such alien doctrines into the moral of his poem, he must have been deliberate in the fact and he must have been conscious that he was thereby making his work conspicuously revolutionary. The fourth book of *Troilus and Criseyde* would indeed be a strange place to tuck away such a heterodox confession!

Does the prevailing sentiment of the poem bear out this view? Is the doctrine at the end of the poem consistent with Troilus's fatalism? After finishing his revision of Boccaccio's story, Chaucer added a passage from another tale by the Italian poet, borrowing from the *Teseide* to describe the ascent of Troilus to heaven and thus giving us Troilus's final realization of his own mistake. The youth sees that here on earth our deeds follow our 'blinde lust' (pleasure) when we really ought to set our hearts on heaven; and the poet warns 'yonge fresshe folkes' to realize the emptiness of worldly frivolity and turn from it to God. Evidently, then there was some choice in human affairs and Troilus suffered from having chosen to meddle in things that were not worth-while. In his early speech at the crisis of his tragedy, he merely gave utterance to what seem to be extremely typical ideas for such a time: he exonerated himself of all guilt for his disaster so that he might pity himself the more justly. This after all is but 'the excellent foppery of the world, that, when we are sick in fortune,—often the surfeits of our own behavior,—we make guilty of our disasters the sun, the moon, and the stars, as if we were villains on necessity, fools by heavenly compulsion.' There is no reason for thrusting this foppery upon Chaucer himself. Furthermore it is quite characteristic of Troilus, who all through the poem, at every turn of the plot, blames Fate or Fortuna for whatever occurs.

The speech is, therefore, dramatically appropriate to Troilus but does not voice the moral of the poem as a whole. To take this passage as representative of Chaucer's own ideas is as logical as to take Shakspere's 'Out, out brief candle' as evidence that the dramatist believed in universal suicide. Troilus denied the existence of free will, but in reality his only bondage has been the subjection to his own folly. As Boethius puts it:

'For after that they han cast away hir eyen fro the light of the sovereyn soothfastnesse to lower thinges and derke, anon they derken by the cloude of ignoraunce and ben troubled by felonous talents; to the whiche talents whan they aprochen and asenten, they hepen and encresen the servage which they han ioyned to hem-self; and in this manere they ben caitifs fro hir propre liber-tee.'[13]

Obviously, however, Chaucer could not state his moral in this fashion; for the *Troilus* is not a gloomy, heavy tragedy, nor does the love affair consist in complete abandonment to 'lowe thinges

and derke'! Such things are a matter of degree. I have no doubt
that Chaucer's own sympathies were with his hero, and that he
enjoyed the lovers and was heart and soul with them in their difficulties; but I believe that his sense of moral values was never
jostled by his emotional interest and that he never dreamed for an
instant of a code of 'higher morality.' He does not say, to be sure,
that Troilus had cast his 'eyen fro the light of the sovereyn
soothfastnesse,' but he does bid young folk to do the opposite:

> 'And of your herte up-casteth the visage
> To thilke god that after his image
> You made.'

We are now left with the problem of Usk's complimentary
reference to Troilus's speech. Usk's comment that here Chaucer
has 'at the ful this question (of predestination) assoyled,' must
mean one of two things, if it is sincere. Either Usk must refer to
the solution given by the entire poem and so not specifically to
the monologue of Troilus, and this seems improbable; or he must
have taken the speech to be sufficient unto itself because he,
Thomas Usk, was a fatalist. The latter possibility is not promising
when we read one of the speaker's remarks in the *Testament*: 'So
that now me thinketh, that prescience of god and free arbitrement
withouten any repugnaunce acorden.'[14] The safest inference, to
my mind, is that Usk's reference is not based upon any deep consideration at all, but that it is merely a sample of his skill in
unctious flattery. As to Speght's reference later, it is obvious that
that does not bear on the question either way except in so far as it
shows Speght's own interest in the passage.

What, then, were Chaucer's own ideas on the subject of fate
and free will? I cannot here enter into this problem fully, because
it would require a study of his use of Fate, Fortune, and divine
predestination in the schemes of all his works. He certainly seems
to have had a steady interest in the question, perhaps stimulated
by the vivid discussion in the *Consolatio*. It might be urged that
Troilus's speech is not the only place where he gives utterance to
deterministic doctrines: in the *Knight's Tale* we read in the speech
of Arcite:

'Allas, why pleynen folk so in commune
Of purveyaunce of God, or of fortune,
That yeveth hem ful ofte in many a gyse
Wel bettre than they can hem-sel devyse?'

Here again we find, it might be said, that 'purveyaunce of god' or
Fortune actually do give man's destiny to man, and although this
passage too may be fitted dramatically to its setting yet this is the
second time that the poet has found an opportunity to express
these views. This argument proves unsound, however, when we
remember that no one denied that much of man's destiny did come
from God: the Church in fact laid stress on this point as a part of
the doctrine of God's grace. The essential part was not to omit the
doctrine of man's free will, and it is this omission of which Troilus
is peculiarly guilty. In general in regard to the poet's own views,
if impressions are to count for anything, I suspect from Chaucer's
dismissal of the subject in the *Knight's Tale,* his turning of the
argument in the *Troilus,* and his humorous reference to it in the
Nonnes Preestes Tale, that so far as laymen were concerned, he
thought that the subject had been laboured a good deal more than
was necessary or fruitful.

I have now dealt with all the points proposed at the beginning
of this paper except one. No one apparently has ever felt that
Troilus's speech is anything but an anachronism, even if a for-
givable one. A distinction should have been made in this criticism,
however, in its relation to subject-matter and to method. In regard
to the former, I very much doubt whether the accusation is just;
for it seems reasonable to suppose that in Trojan times, as much as
in the middle ages or in our own day for that matter, there was a
discussion of something corresponding to fate and free will. In
regard to the method of the speech, one must admit that the system
of logic employed seems more characteristic of the Church Fathers
than of the Trojan youth. But it must be remembered that the
young man of the middle ages probably adopted some of the
methods of the scholastics when he had a particular reason to
strive for soundness: in his day those methods seemed after all to
be the best form, and they certainly represented the form with

which he was most familiar. And can we not go even a step further? If the speech shows a peculiar earnestness which would naturally express itself in the unusual care in detail and in the repetitiousness so common to the scholastic writings, but which might reveal those same traits in any age even without scholastic influence, its appropriateness then becomes a question of its relation to the mood of the speaker and the charge of anachronism falls to the ground.

To establish this final point in regard to the monologue of Troilus requires considerable delicacy. It must be observed that if I fail to make myself clear in this particular, the points already made will be in no way affected. I have the double difficulty of tracing Chaucer's steps in the operation of a piece of alchemy and of persuading my readers that the final product is gold. I have also that worst task of all—the discovering of humor where none has been seen before. I can only ask the reader first to follow my discussion closely and then with my interpretation in mind to reread the passage in its proper setting in Chaucer.

Let us now see how the speech develops. In his despair Troilus feels that he is 'but loren,' he goes to the temple to pray and finds no consolation, and his first outburst comes from his feelings, not from his intellect:

> 'For al that comth, comth by necessitee;
> Thus to be lorn, it is my destinee.'

First the feeling of his destruction and then of the inevitableness of it; one thought has suggested the other and here is the germ of all that follows. He is glad to have something, especially something external, to accuse; for his chief purpose is to exonerate himself in order to justify his self-pity. So he proceeds, 'For certaynly, this wot I wel,' and the whole game is begun: he remembers the scholastic discussion on the subject, the opposing views, and the possible inferences and conclusions. It is a splendid beginning, humanly real in every way.

He remembers the paradox between the dogma of divine prescience and that of human free will, and he applies it at once to his own case:

'That for-sight of divyne purveyaunce
Hath seyn alwey me to for-gon Criseyde.'

Then, as I have shown, he points out that doubtless God takes
human merit into consideration; but the inference of this statement
is that, merit or no merit, God has doomed Troilus to destruction
and he has had no real fighting chance in the matter. After all, he
says, clerks are divided on this subject of destiny and free will:
some hold to the one and some to the other. Thereafter follows
almost to the end of Troilus's speech a pretty close rendering of
the section from Boethius, and sometimes Chaucer echoes the
very language of his own translation, which probably he had
already made.

'What clerks,' says Troilus, 'am I to follow? For some of them
say that if God has foreseen everything, then everything must
happen according to the way he has foreseen it, and so we have no
free will.' The next two stanzas are devoted to an elucidation of
this argument: if God has perfectly foreseen our deeds and our
thoughts, we can have only such deeds and thoughts as He has
known we were going to have; otherwise His prescience would
be imperfect and we must not believe such heresy as that. Although
practically the same statements are found in Boethius, the setting
here is of course different and the effect is that of Troilus becoming perhaps wordy and even repetitious but extremely anxious
to be logically clear and correct. 'Other eminent clerks,' he continues, and his reference to them is perhaps just a trifle flippant or
bitter:

'Somme
That han hir top ful heigh and smothe y-shore,'

'other eminent clerks hold that prescience is not the cause of the
happening of events, but that since something is going to happen,
therefore God must foreknow it.' 'So necessity falls on the other
side of the proposition; and the whole issue reduces itself to a
matter of the order of causes—whether the prescience of God is
the cause of the happening of events, or whether the necessary
happening of events is the cause of the prescience.'

'But,' he says, 'I will not bother with the order of causes. The upshot of it all, whichever way you take the causes, is the same: I know surely that the happening of things which are foreseen, is necessary, although it may not seem that prescience causes them—for better or worse.' This stanza introduces the first marked touch of what I have called the dramatic quality of the speech; but if this quality is not clear already, I must make it clearer by analyzing the psychology of Troilus at this part of his argument. Roughly put, his course of thought is as follows: 'One school of clerks says that prescience makes the happening of events necessary; another says that the necessary happening of events causes the prescience. In either case (waiving all fine logic) I am sure of one thing anyhow: what is known ahead of time *must* happen—whether foreseeing it causes it or not.' The first proposition (of which he says he is sure) he states with dogged determination because it is about that truth that he most cares; and his second proposition— 'although it does not seem that prescience causes the events'—is uttered in deference to the logic of the case: in fact, is added somewhat as an afterthought. The total effect to the casual listener is indeed strange: 'The fact that something is foreseen means that it must happen, although, if logicians are right, it does not happen because of the fact that it is foreseen'! Such a verbal contradiction, surprising in itself, suits splendidly the dramatic effect of which I am speaking; and yet at the same time, we are able to see by what mental processes Troilus got there. A man does not wilfully leap into such a contradiction. Troilus is arguing very solemnly indeed, determined not to slip, and although perhaps a little conscious that he may seem confusing, he is all the more grim about it. His last desperate 'Al falle it foule or faire,' shows that he thinks he has gained his point.

He then proceeds to give the figure of one man's sitting on a seat and another man's observing him there. Whether this figure be considered logically sound or not (Troilus substitutes the necessity of the fact of sitting and of seeing for the sureness of divine vision which has no place in this general application of the argument), the figure in each of its two forms must certainly seem highly ludicrous—especially in the wording into which Troilus occasionally stumbles. And here for once, Troilus gets thoroughly confused himself. 'If you see a man sitting on a seat, and if he is actually sitting there, then your opinion that he is sitting there must be true.' He is now up to his neck in the complexity of the argument; stating the reverse of this case will take very careful thought indeed to make no error in the argument:

'And ferther-over now ayenward yit,'

he says. 'Beside, notwithstanding this point, however,'—the jargon of a self-conscious beginner in the study of logic and coherence, as any teacher of first-year English will recognize. In Boethius the transition to the other half of the argument is quite simple: 'And on the other hand it is also true of the reverse case'—'And ayenward also is it of the contrarye.' [15] Troilus, however, fights on: 'Beside—now—on the other hand—still, just see!—it's exactly the same with the counterpart of this—that is to say,' (he gulps once more) 'now listen, for I'm not going to take long,' (he is talking aloud to himself and forgets the character of his audience),—'I *say*,' and at last for a moment he is on his feet again.

'And ferther-over now ayenward yit,
Lo, right so it is of the part contrarie,
As thus—now herkne, for I wol not tarie—

I seye, that if,' etc.

If I exaggerate, it is only slightly and I do it to make my point thoroughly clear; for it seems to me a distinct and subtle dramatic touch which should be more generally appreciated.

The figure of the man sitting and of his observer is used, from a logical point of view, to illustrate the argument drawn from the two opposed schools which has already been cited; and the result is the same. 'The fact of his sitting may be the cause of the truth of one's seeing him, but necessity plays a part on both sides of the proposition. So in the same way I may reason about God's pre-science.' Then Troilus adds (not from Boethius), 'Wherefore men can see that what happens on earth, happens necessarily.'

Having shown the strong element of necessity in human affairs Troilus goes back to the order of causes. To make the conclusion that is of most importance to him, he must restate the whole situation: 'Although a thing is foreseen because it is going to happen and does *not* happen because it is foreseen, yet it follows necessarily either that what is to come be foreseen or else that what is foreseen necessarily happen.' This statement would certainly be a staggerer for the casual listener—or we may say, reader! He is simply pointing out once more the necessary part that necessity plays (!), but he does it in what certainly sounds like rubbish or, at best, self-contradiction. The last clause certainly seems impossible after what is granted in the first. Muddled as he seems, however, Troilus is working his way through the involutions and we can see both his way into and his way out of the apparent contradiction. The boy is having a hard time of it, but he gets there! 'This necessity in either case destroys our free will. And to return to the order of causes, it would be wrong to say that the happening of temporal events causes God's prescience. What kind of thinking should I be guilty of, if I thought that all the events of the world that have ever happened were the cause of that sovereign Foreknowledge?'

He has now made his point and made it definitely. But he continues:

'And over al this, yet seye I more herto,'

and he puts this with rather broad confidence, having achieved his goal in his own mind. Then he goes on apparently to repeat the gist of the whole matter once more! 'Just as when I know there is a thing, that thing must necessarily be true; so when I know of a coming event, it must likewise come. And so the happening of events which are foreknown, cannot be avoided.' He repeats all this, to be sure, to take up the alternative problem as to whether God's foreknowledge causes the events, since the reverse is not true; but the proposition is put so weakly that it sounds fallacious (how certain is the knowledge that 'I,' the speaker, know? Troilus does not give the corrective to this that is found in Boethius) and it gives merely the impression of stating the old argument once more: God foresees events; therefore they must happen; therefore man has no free will.

This argument Troilus has found occasion, for one reason or another, to state about four times. To one who cannot follow his thought closely (and it would be an unusual reader or listener who could at the first reading!) he seems to repeat his idea of the part played by necessity at least six times. In a way his logic is straight enough; but the effect of it is at times very much tangled as a result of its presentation in a time of emotional stress. To all intents and purposes he contradicts himself at least twice, although by careful analysis we can see how his mind is moving. In other words, Chaucer shows amazing power in keeping both the dramatic effect and the psychology of his character true. There is the same effect of happy fallacy in Troilus's speech that we find in a solemn and earnest malapropism. Once the boy has succeeded in clearing his mind to his own satisfaction, he stops his argument to call on Jove to have pity on his sorrow or kill him straightway. He has satisfied himself that Jove is running all the affairs of this world: why, then, does not the great god run them *properly!*

Nothing, it seems to me, could be more beautifully adapted to the scene than this speech by Troilus. It is his way of saying 'I've never had a chance,' and he sets out bravely to prove his case. It is involved and confusing, but the boy gets bravely through with it. He is extraordinarily conscientious at every step, and develops his argument with the most elaborate, the most scrupulous care. *Of course* he would be verbose and repetitious and longwinded. Pandarus does not take the speech (so far as he hears it) as instructive, but comments, 'Ey! who seigh ever a wys man faren so!' Troilus has certainly been 'going on'; and nothing could be more delightful, and, I feel, nothing under the circumstances could be more like a young man—like Troilus.

Certain objections to this interpretation will occur to everyone. It might be urged that we moderns find more fault with this speech than a man in the middle ages would have found. Let us remember in answer to that point, however, that Chaucer himself saw the humor of the tedious *Tale of Melibeus*. Again, I may be reminded that all this speech was taken pretty much as we find it from

Boethius. In reply to that, I must say that I have not denied all virtues to the passage. That the argument seems involved or repetitious in the speech of Troilus does not mean that one is to find fault with it for the same reasons in its setting in the *Consolatio*. Chaucer has not represented the full argument as the speaker in Boethius gives it; and in Boethius the full scholastic apparatus was necessary for logical reasons—there the speaker is fully justified in being so painstaking. Besides, although Chaucer does show a sense of the humor of the *Tale of Melibeus*, he had once seen enough value in it to bother to translate it entire.

I cannot maintain that I have wholly removed the grounds for the charge of anachronism. Troilus refers to 'clerks' and mentions a discussion which was really in the air in Chaucer's time. But I hope to have reduced these grounds to a minimum: merely so to say, to the fact that Chaucer does use certain mechanical properties, which to be sure were not genuine antiques, but for the use of which he is no more to be censured than for the fact that Troilus speaks English rather than Aeolic Greek. He takes a discussion which is redolent of the scholastic treatises, although its subject was a common topic of controversy among laymen; but he metamorphoses it into a completely adequate expression of Troilus's personality and feelings. It is one of those obvious and yet felicitous strokes of which a genius is so strangely capable and in the effecting of which it is worth while to watch the genius at work. The result shows an almost unparalleled example of Chaucer's balance in his just comprehension of tragedy and his gentle sense of humor.

NOTES

1. *Studies in Chaucer*, New York, 1892, vol. III, pp. 372 ff.
2. *Ibid.*, III, p. 374 f.
3. T. R. Price, *PMLA*, XI, p. 311.
4. *Test. of Love*, III, ch. IV, ll. 248 ff. in Skeat, *Chaucerian and Other Pieces*, p. 123.

5. *Wks. of Chaucer*, 1602, sig. Bb 5 recto.

6. Chaucer's translation, Skeat, *Complete Works*, II, Boethius, Book v, Prose III, ll. 109–133. I have omitted most of the glosses.

7. Boethius, Book v, Prose IV, ll. 16–21.

8. III, cap. I, p. 460 B.

9. Page 640, *Corollarium*.

10. III, cap. I, p. 644 B.

11. III, cap. I, p. 644 A and B.

12. I, cap. XXVIII, p. 267 B.

13. Chaucer's Boethius, v, pr. II, ll. 24–30.

14. *Test.*, III, chap. IV, ll. 236–38. (Cf. also III, IX, ll. 5–7. Usk was no profound thinker, as one may gather from his account of the origin of evil (ll. 264–7, ch. IV); but after all he was not deadly in earnest in any part of his treatise.)

15. B. V, pr. III, l. 41.

JAMES LYNDON SHANLEY

The *Troilus* and Christian Love

O yonge, fresshe folkes, he or she,
In which that love up groweth with youre age,
Repeyreth hom fro worldly vanyte,
And of youre herte up casteth the visage
To thilke God that after his ymage
Yow made, and thynketh al nys but a faire
This world, that passeth soone as floures faire.

And loveth hym, the which that right for love
Upon a crois, oure soules for to beye,
First starf, and roos, and sit in hevene above;
For he nyl falsen no wight, dar I seye,
That wol his herte al holly on him leye.
And syn he best to love is, and most meke,
What nedeth feynede loves for to seke?

CRITICS have seen these lines of the *Troilus* as no part of the whole and perfect deterministic tragedy;[1] as a completely unexpected return from the Renaissance to the Middle Ages;[2] or as the repudiation of an immoral code which Chaucer had pretended to uphold.[3] This paper will attempt to show that these views are wrong and that the correct one is: that the epilogue is no mere tacked-on moral but is implicit in the whole poem.[4] It will seek to show that there is a more fundamental connection between the story and the epilogue than Professor Robinson suggests in his introduction:

> It [the epilogue] expresses . . . exactly the feeling by which Chaucer might have been possessed at the moment when he was deeply moved by his tale of 'double sorwe.' . . . The artistic propriety of the epilogue may always be a matter of dispute, and its

Reprinted, by permission, from *ELH, A Journal of English Literary History,* VI (1939), 271-81.

acceptability to the reader will depend in some measure upon his attitude toward explicit moralization. But it is not necessary to find any deep conflict between the epilogue and the story.[5]

We should not consider the *Troilus* as simply a romance of courtly love, a psychological novel, or a drama, even though it has characteristics in common with all these types. Most simply stated, what Chaucer did was to recast a narrative poem; and he caused a fundamental difference between the *Troilus* and *Il Filostrato* when he retold the story in the light of an entirely new set of values, determined not only by this world and man's life in it but by the eternal as well. He did not merely retell the story of an engaging young man who, because he trusted in a woman, was made unhappy when she proved faithless. The ultimate reason for Troilus's woe was not that he trusted in a woman but that of his own free will he placed his hope for perfect happiness in that which by its nature was temporary, imperfect, and inevitably insufficient.

We shall not be surprised at the suggestion that Chaucer meant his thoughtful readers to understand this fact long before Troilus did if we remember that at the heart of mediaeval philosophy and religion was the conviction of the inherent insufficiency of things earthly, no matter how noble and good, and, on the other hand, of the reality and completeness of heavenly bliss and the individual's responsibility in attaining it. But the statement of these ideas, in the light of which I think the moral Gower and the philosophical Strode would have read the *Troilus,* points only to a possibility. An examination of the poem will perhaps make it appear a probability.

Accustomed to the conventions of courtly love, Chaucer's readers would have found nothing unfamiliar in the early stages of the love affair. They would have accepted Troilus's great misery and sorrow as natural in one who had not yet gained the love of his mistress; further, Chaucer had assured them that Troilus's worthiness would be rewarded. But the readers also knew that Criseyde would forsake Troilus before she died. Therefore, when Troilus, on his return from the temple where he first saw Criseyde, willingly and completely gave himself over to Love, the pity and the irony of the situation marked the tale as no ordinary courtly romance.

Yet all proceeds favorably for the lovers, and there seems to be no reason why they should not possess happiness when, after Criseyde decides to remain at Pandar's the consummation of their love is made certain. The reader knows, however, that it is to be only temporary, that the lovely and gracious Criseyde will forsake Troilus. And the reader is not only reminded of this but is also shown the lovers' fundamental error just as they are apparently to have their utmost desires fulfilled. For, when she is told of Troilus's supposed jealousy, Criseyde cries that worldly happiness, called false felicity by the learned, is mixed with bitterness because it is unstable, and her conclusion is:

> trewely, for aught I kan espie,
> Ther is no verray weele in this world heere.

The word of Troilus's jealousy seems to bring home to her for a moment the quality of earthly joy and shows to the reader the reason for Troilus's pathetic situation: it is not that he thinks Criseyde and love good, but that he has made them the things upon which all his happiness depends.

As soon as she has allayed the stings of jealousy and all is well, Criseyde herself quite naturally forgets the warning she gave. But the reader does not and what follows only heightens the irony. For, after the fashion of courtly lovers, Troilus and Criseyde describe their joy and give thanks to Love in the religious terms constantly used in speaking of God, the everlasting good:

> Benigne Love [says Troilus]
> . . . .
> Yet were al lost, that dar I wel seyn certes,
> But if thi grace passed oure desertes.

And Criseyde, as deeply in love as Troilus, replies to his protestations of entire love:

> Welcome, my knyght, my pees, my suffisaunce.

Nothing remained to be said after this; both gave themselves completely to love. Following Criseyde's surrender, Pandar attempted to make Troilus see that worldly joy 'halt nought but by a wir,' but in vain; for Troilus and Criseyde had such joy that 'felicitee' could not describe their state, wherein 'ech of hem gan otheres lust obeye.' But before the mediaeval mind seriously and religiously concerned with life and happiness were divine peace and felicity, perfect and eternal, to be achieved not when individual wills were drawn to one another, but when they were drawn to God's, for it was His will that was peace.

Brother, the quality of love stilleth our will, and maketh us long only for what we have, and giveth us no other thirst.

. . . .

Nay, 'tis the essence of this blessed being to hold ourselves within the divine will, whereby our wills are themselves made one.
So that our being thus, from threshold unto threshold throughout the realm, is a joy to all the realm as to the king, who draweth our minds to what he willeth;
and His will is our peace; it is that sea to which all moves that it createth and that nature maketh.[6]

Nothing could break the peace of which Dante was told and of which the reader is reminded by Criseyde's words. But the peace of Troilus and Criseyde, the reader knows, is to be broken. Criseyde once more recalls this fact to his mind when she exclaims, on learning of the parliament's decree:

Endeth thanne love in wo? Ye, or men lieth!
And alle worldly blisse, as thynketh me.

But again she forgets, and later in the Grecian camp, bemoaning the delay of her return to Troy, she resolves to take no heed of gossip and censure but to return to the city, for, she says:

Felicite clepe I my suffisaunce.

Love was too strong to allow her to remember, but her glimpses of the truth and Pandar's hints at it were enough to make Chaucer's more serious readers understand why, after his complete surrender to love, Troilus was inevitably to go from weal to woe.

But they would hardly have been satisfied with the conduct of the story and the fate assigned to Troilus if in his world he had never had the opportunity to choose the way to felicity. If Destiny had had complete control over him, then, according to the *Troilus,* 'yonge, fresshe folkes' would have little choice as to where they would place their hearts; and Chaucer's appeal, however pious and sincere, would have been vain. The control of Destiny is not complete, however, in the life of either Criseyde or Troilus. We cannot deny its importance in their lives: because of the 'lawe of kynde' Troilus must love; Troy is destined to fall; Criseyde must leave and Troilus live thenceforth in pain because of fatal destiny; and it is Fortune's decree that prevents Troilus and Diomede from killing one another. Forces and events completely beyond the lovers' control affect their lives greatly.

But the story does not depend on destined events alone, nor is the final unhappiness of either owing only to fate. They are free to choose what they wish, and as they choose they determine their lot. (Chaucer's philosophical reconciliation of these elements we do not know; the *Troilus* is not, as are the *Divine Comedy* and *Paradise Lost,* a philosophical poem; but it is controlled by Chaucer's philosophy as *Tom Jones,* for example, is controlled by Fielding's conception of the natural goodness of man.) When Pandar is preparing to reveal Troilus's love for Criseyde, he tells her that every one has a chance to have good fortune and that she should take hers before it slacks. And when he tells her of Troilus's plight, and asks for her pity at least, she says that since one ought to *choose* the lesser of two evils, she will give Troilus some encouragement rather than endanger her uncle's life. Destiny has no hand here, but the interplay mentioned above is seen when we seek the reason for her loving Troilus. 'Who yaf me drynke?' she asks as she sees him ride by; but that she will love him is not determined then; there follows her clear and deliberate meditation as to whether or not she will give him her love. From her words to Troilus when he first enters her closet at Pandar's, we know that such thought did influence her. As well as the excellence of love, which none may or should attempt to resist, the sight of his loyalty and service also led her to have pity on him. Moreover, as Troilus takes her in his arms, at last able to see the pleasant side of life, he says to her:

> Now be ye caught, now is ther but we tweyne!
> Now yeldeth yow, for other bote is non!

But Criseyde snatches the last word to impress upon him that she is there only because she is willing.

Finally, when Criseyde is untrue to Troilus, although sorrowful, she acts deliberately. In order to heighten the dramatic effect of the betrayal through suspense, Chaucer tells us, at the beginning of Book Five, that Destiny sends Criseyde from Troy and decrees that Troilus must thenceforth live in pain. But Destiny does not make Criseyde faithlessly turn to Diomede. She deliberately gives up her intention of returning to Troy because she enjoys Diomede's clever talk, respects his great estate, fears the perils of Troy, and needs help. Later

> the bet from sorwe hym to releve,
> She made hym were a pencel of hire sleve.
>
> . . . .
>
> And for to helen hym of his sorwes smerte,
> Men seyn—I not—that she yaf hym hire herte.

In both instances she acted for a definite purpose, in itself a good one but not when related to all other ends. No one knew better than she that the fault was hers, and the pitifulness of her last lament lies in her clear-sightedness accompanied by an equal blindness:

> Al be I not the first that dide amys,
> What helpeth that to don my blame away?
> But syn I se ther is no bettre way,
> And that to late is now for me to rewe,
> To Diomede algate I wol be trewe.

Earlier, as she left Troy, she accused the constellation of her birth for her forced departure from the city, but here she recognizes that the fault is her own. And Chaucer, in spite of his pity which will not allow him to chide her further, could not excuse her guilt, which he mentions again at the end of the story.

When we turn to Troilus, we find that if we took his own word, we should look no further. When Criseyde's departure is almost certain, although he desires above all things to prevent it, Troilus is unable to do so. Forces beyond his control make his will of no avail; so great is his despair that he prepares to die, for he is lost since, as he sees life at the time, 'al that comth, comth by necessitee.' To prove his statement he reviews the arguments of the 'clerkes' on the subject of divine providence and free-will; he decides that those who deny the existence of free-will must be right. Dramatically the soliloquy is perfect, but it reaches the wrong conclusion to fit the facts of the world Troilus lives in. He decides the question as he does because his will is thwarted; his philosophizing started from its conclusion.

His trouble was not that he lacked free-will but that he had used it unwisely. Once again we see the interplay of necessity and free-will in his world, and we see that his unhappiness depended on his own choice. To love was inevitable, and Troilus loved by 'lawe of kynde'; yet the individual could control the love born of nature. Pandar set forth the doctrine when he told Troilus that Criseyde was suited to love a worthy knight and that he would hold it for a vice in her unless she did. She was free to and did choose Troilus. And we know from his own words that Troilus once had the power to control his own love for Criseyde. When he returned from the temple where he first saw her, he not only 'took purpos loves craft to suwe' and 'gan fully assente Criseyde for to love.' He also sang of his love and acknowledged that he had no right to complain of its burning, for only if he consented could it be as strong as it was in him. After his song, he acknowledged the god of Love's mastery of his spirit, thanked him for his favor, and vowed to live and die in the service of Criseyde.

Thus his 'sorwes' began, and serving as the background against which this action took place for the reader was the fact that no human pleasure, however good, could be sufficient for the individual's complete happiness. Professor Gilson has pointed out that on this fact rested the whole Christian conception of love.[7] Later than Chaucer, Thomas à Kempis wrote:

How small soever anything be, if it be inordinately loved and regarded, it keepeth thee back from the highest good, and defileth the soul.[8]

And Dante had learned in Purgatory:

Nor Creator nor creature, my son, was ever without love, either natural or rational; and this thou knowest.

The natural is always without error; but the other may err through an evil object, or through too little or too much vigour.

While it is directed to the primal goods, and in the secondary moderates itself, it cannot be the cause of sinful delight.

. . . .

innate with you is the virtue which giveth counsel, and ought to guard the threshold of assent.

. . . .

Wherefor suppose that every love which is kindled within you arise of necessity, the power to arrest it is within you.[9]

It was with this in mind, it was according to this scale of values that Chaucer retold the tale of Troilus's unhappy love. Boccaccio's treatment of the problem was not satisfactory. He showed how Troilus, who led his life according to the dictates of the tradition of courtly love, ultimately found only sorrow because Criseyde, like most young women, was vain and fickle:

O youths, in whom amorous desire gradually riseth with age. I pray you for the love of the gods that ye check the ready steps to that evil passion and that ye mirror yourselves in the love of Troilus, which my verses set forth above, for if ye will read them aright, and will take them to heart, not lightly will ye trust in all women.

A young woman is fickle and is desirous of many lovers, and her beauty she esteemeth more than it is in her mirror . . . she hath no feeling for virtue or reason, inconstant ever as leaf in the wind.[10]

But as this description will not do for Chaucer's Criseyde, so Boccaccio's solution will not do. Even as Chaucer told of Criseyde's guilt, he had only pity for her:

> And if I myghte excuse hire any wise,
> For she so sory was for hire untrouthe,
> Iwis, I wolde excuse hire yet for routhe.

At no time do we feel that Criseyde is unworthy of love; she was gracious and kind, neither desirous of many lovers nor unmoved by virtue; we cannot feel that Troilus was well rid of her. We can only accept the fact that, gentle and lovely as she was, Criseyde could not stand fast in 'trouthe.' Because she did not and because he had placed all his hopes of happiness on her, Troilus suffered. Although he did nothing ungentle or ignoble, although 'he loved chivalrye, trouthe and honour, freedom and curteisye' and was faithful to all that he thought best, yet his portion in life was pain.

> Swich is this world, whoso it kan byholde,
> In ech estat is litel hertes reste.
> God leve us for to take it for the beste!

Chaucer's comment is not that women are fickle and men foolish to love them, but rather: *Sunt lacrimae rerum, et mentem mortalia tangunt*; for he saw men seeking lasting peace and happiness in things unstable by nature and moved by forces beyond their control. But Troilus could not be blamed or scorned for caring; Pandar's Horatian acceptance and warning of inevitable change was no sufficient substitute for the joy which Troilus thought to have. And it covered only half the problem as Chaucer saw it and as a modern poet has stated it:

> Teach us to care and not to care.

Pandar could not, with all his kindly and worldly wisdom, keep Troilus from sorrow. But the solution was clear since the tale was told in reference to the beliefs and ideas of the Christian tradition. St. Augustine, in his *Confessions*, wrote of his seeking for peace:

> Be not foolish, O my soul, nor become deaf in the ear of thine heart with the tumult of thy folly. Hearken thou too. The Word itself calleth thee to return: and there is the place of rest imperturbable, where love is not forsaken, if itself forsaketh not. Behold,

these things pass away, that others may replace them, and so this lower universe be completed by all his parts. But do I depart any whither? saith the Word of God.[11]

It was in contrast with this conception that Troilus's woe was seen. Chaucer's conclusion was but the direct statement of the ideas and beliefs which gave full meaning to Troilus's situation and sorrows. And it is, I think, aesthetically essential as well as intellectually consistent, for by these lines only is the final emotional resolution achieved. Not only is the appeal to 'yonge, fresshe folkes' consistent with the implications of the tale; it also completes and fulfills them. Chaucer was not finished until he had written the epilogue, for the Troilus was not a completely objective representation left to speak entirely for itself, but a tale with comment as was Boccaccio's.

Chaucer found in Boccaccio an artistic guide, but in his story and comment no adequate treatment and explanation of the experience set forth. The case of Troilus was but part of a whole in which, as Theseus said in the *Knight's Tale*:

> spéces of thynges and progressiouns
> Shullen enduren by successiouns,
> And not eterne, withouten any lye.

And one part of wisdom was, he added:

> To maken vertu of necessitee,
> And take it weel that we may not eschue,
> And namely that to us all is due.

The whole of wisdom Chaucer set forth in his *Balade de Bon Conseyl*

> That thee is sent, receyve in buxumnesse,
> The wrastling for this world axeth a fal.
> Her is non hoom, her nis but wildernesse:
> Forth, pilgrim, forth! Forth, beste, out of thy stal!
> Know thy contree, look up, thank God of al;
> Hold the heye wey, and lat thy gost thee lede;
> And trouthe thee shal delivere, it is no drede.

This is the summary of the attitude of the man who wrote the *Troilus* and the *Canterbury Tales*. The epilogue of the *Troilus* is not, as some have seen it, an inconsistent repudiation of life by one who seems to have enjoyed and accepted it. It is rather, like the *Balade de Bon Conseyl*, the expression of the belief and feeling on which Chaucer's acceptance of life was based. The 'trouthe' that will deliver one is the 'trouthe' placed in Him who, as the poet said in the epilogue, 'nyl falsen no wight, . . . That wol his herte al holly on him leye.' It was because he did believe 'trouthe' would avail in the end that Chaucer, in spite of sorrow which he saw and felt, could accept life as he did in the *Canterbury Tales* and would have Troilus say for him as did another earthly lover in Dante's Paradise—

Non però qui si pente, ma si ride.

NOTES

1. W. C. Curry, 'Destiny in Chaucer's *Troilus*,' *PMLA* 45 (1930), 168.
2. J. S. P. Tatlock, 'The Epilogue of Chaucer's *Troilus*,' *MP* 15 (1920–21), 146.
3. G. L. Kittredge, *Chaucer and his Poetry* (Cambridge, 1915), p. 143.
4. Geoffrey Chaucer, *The Book of Troilus and Criseyde*, ed. R. K. Root (Princeton, 1926), p. 1.
5. *The Complete Works of Geoffrey Chaucer*, ed. F. N. Robinson (Cambridge, Mass., 1933), 452–3. All references to the text of Chaucer are to this edition.
6. *Paradiso*, 3. 70–2, 79–87. Trans. the Rev. P. W. Wicksteed (J. M Dent & Sons, *The Temple Classics*, 1930).
7. Etienne Gilson, *The Spirit of Mediaeval Philosophy*, trans. A. H. C. Downes (New York, 1936), p. 271.
8. *Of the Imitation of Christ*, Bk. 3, ch. 42 (New York: Thomas Nelson & Sons, 1926).
9. *Purgatorio*, 17. 91–9, 18. 62–3, 70–2. Trans. Thomas Okey (J. M. Dent & Sons, *The Temple Classics*, 1930).
10. *Il Filostrato*, 8, st. 29–30, trans. N. E. Griffin and A. B. Myrick (Philadelphia, 1929).
11. *Confessions*, 4, 11, trans. E. B. Pusey (J. M. Dent & Sons, *Everyman's Library*, 1932).

D. D. GRIFFITH

An Interpretation of Chaucer's
Legend of Good Women

FOUR times in the F Prologue of the *Legend of Good Women*
Chaucer declares that his poem is a legend, while the Man of Law
refers to it as the 'Seintes Legende of Cupyde.' Other references
show that Chaucer's followers understood the poem as a legend.
In Hoccleve, Chaucer's *Legend* is referred to as Cupid's 'Legende
of Martres,' in Lydgate as 'the Legend of Cupide,' and as a 'legende
of parfite holines,' and in the Lay Folks' Mass Book as 'The holy
legende of martyrs of Cupydo.'[1] To modern taste, this title seems
paradoxical, as all the stories concern heathen women and as the
medieval and technical meaning of the word 'legend' is the life of
a saint who is often also a martyr to the Christian religion. The
solution of the difficulty lies in the very conception of the poem.
Chaucer has borrowed from the Court of Love literature the idea
of a religion of love of which Cupid is the god. Just as Christian
saints have suffered martyrdom for their religion, so those whom
the worship of the God of Love has brought to their deaths may
be thought of as martyrs to the god Cupid. Just as the stories of
Christian saints are called legends, so the stories of those who
died because of their devotion to love become legends of the
saints of the god Cupid. In this poem, Chaucer is creating a collection of the legends of Cupid's saints and martyrs.

The following notes will show how completely Chaucer's *Legend
of Good Women* has for its organizing motif the presentation of
good women, who were martyrs to love because of devotion to a
definitely conceived religion of which the god Cupid is the head.[2]
This worship has its god, its mediator and intercessor (Alceste), its
saints, its legends, its martyrs, its relic, and its shrine, with a sys-

---

tem of repentance, penance, and satisfaction—all created in analogy to the Christian worship of Chaucer's time. This paper will also point out that this organizing motif dominated the F Prologue, but that Chaucer changed his attitude toward this religion of Cupid and omitted from the G Prologue the most noticeable analogies to Christian worship. The study of all the alterations that Chaucer made in the F Prologue seems to show that the poet made his revision with the intention of removing unorthodox references to Christian service and, especially, of canceling the presentation of himself as a votary of Cupid.

In tho F Prologuo tho poot's attitudo toward 'oldo storios' as devotion and his worship of the daisy as the incarnation of the God of Love are plain. It is also plain that in the G Prologue he has abandoned this attitude. In F, l. 27, he says, 'Wel oghte us than honouren and beleve' 'olde bokes,' 'And on hem yeve I feyth and ful credence' (l. 31), but, in G, the words, 'honouren' and 'feyth and ful credence' are omitted. 'Farwel my book and my devocioun!' (l.39, F) becomes, in G, the colorless 'Farwel my studie, as lasting that sesoun!' In F the reading of 'olde bokes' is devotion which he leaves seldom on holy days; in G this reading is study which he leaves only on holy days. In the F Prologue this devotion to love's literature is the reason for the worship of the daisy—'Now have I than swich a condicioun'—but in G the connection is broken by the statement that besides his study he loves the daisy.

In F the poet worships an individual flower, while in G this individual worship is removed by the expression of the poet's admiration for 'these floures,' that is, for daisies in general without any symbolism. In F, then, the poet enters the fields in May to see this flower open to the rising sun and to worship the daisy as the incarnation of love after his devotional reading in love's literature. He says he is glad 'whan that I have presence Of hit, to doon al maner reverence.' In F he addresses the daisy personally, without name, as often in the hyms to the Virgin, for she is 'of alle floures flour,' 'Fulfilled of al vertu and honour,' 'ever y-lyke fair and fresh of hewe.' In G these words are not personal, nor are they addressed to a nameless and adored person designated as 'she' but are descriptive of the beauty of the daisy as a flower. In F the poet pledges eternal devotion and says that no creature loved 'hotter in his lyve.'

In the F Prologue Chaucer runs at sunset to see the flower close for 'so hateth she derknesse.' He does this in honor of love for she is 'clernesse and verray light,' that leads him through this world, the mistress of his wit, whom he obeys as the harp the hand. She is his guide, his sovereign, his earthly god. He says he cannot praise the flower sufficiently and calls upon the French poets as 'Ye lovers' to aid his labor. In F the poet does this 'in service of the flour, Whom that I serve as I have wit or might,' but in G he is neutral in the contentions between the flower and the leaf. In G none of this fulsome adoration is retained. The poet does not say that his spirit moved him 'with so gledy desyr That in my herte I fele yit the fyr.' The adored one does not hate darkness nor is she clearness and 'verray light.' She is not mistress of his wit, his guide, his sovereign, his earthly god. The French poets are not addressed as 'Ye lovers' but as folk that have gone before. With the removal of the poet's religious adoration and his joy in the flower's presence, which is like the sacred presence of a shrine, the G Prologue has eliminated the worship of the daisy as the incarnation of love.

In the F Prologue, 'With dredful herte and glad devocioun' the poet rises to witness the 'resureccioun' of the flower. He kneels before it and remains kneeling until the flower uncloses. He greets the flower in worshipful and religious fashion. The poet remains in the fields all day worshiping the flower for she is his 'emperice and flour of floures alle.' At home he has his bed strewn with flowers and dreams that when he is lying in the field, the God and Queen of Love come to him. In G these religious words have all been omitted, and the worship of love by the birds has been placed in the dream to remove this worshipful adoration from the poet's waking moments. In the F Prologue the poet's religious adoration of the daisy as at a shrine is very skilfully presented and becomes the reason for Alceste's intercession in his behalf later in the poem.

In the vision described in both prologues, the Queen is habited in semblance of a daisy. The God of Love wears a halo and his face shines so brightly that the poet cannot look upon him. This description is practically the same in the two prologues, except that in G the poet avoids the religious significance of the halo by substituting a garland. In praise of this 'lady fre' in F the poet sings a balade, but in G the God stops at the flower, his ladies kneel as at a shrine, then dance, and sing the balade. In this way the balade in G is not a hymn sung by the poet as worship in a religion of love. Also, in F the lines 'So passeth al my lady sovereyne That is so good, so fair, so debonaire' lose their personal adoration and become 'Hir name was Alceste the debonaire.' The song of the ladies, 'Hele and honour,' which is reminiscent of the songs to the Virgin, is omitted in G.

In both prologues Cupid and his train worship the daisy and seat themselves in a circle about it, but in F the poet remains kneeling by the flower, while in G he is 'lening faste by under a bente.' Cupid accuses the poet of effrontery in kneeling 'So nigh myn owne flour.' He asserts that the daisy is his relic. The poet has broken the law of god Cupid; he has hindered folk in their 'devocioun'; he holds it folly to serve Love; he spreads heresy and encourages schism; in the *Romance of the Rose* and the *Troilus,* he has violated God's law and, 'By seint Venus,' he shall repent. In G, while the frame of the episode is the same, the poet's worship of Love is removed. He is blamed for being in the god's presence and not for his worship of the daisy. In G the flower is not given the religious name of relic. Instead of holding it folly to serve love, as in F, the poet has, in G, personally offended Cupid by preventing folk from trusting in him. The difference between the prologues is further emphasized here by the statements of Cupid, added in G, that 'he nis but a verray propre fool That loveth paramours' and 'Thou beginest dote As olde foles, whan hir spirit fayleth.' In F the poet is a votary of love and a worshiper of its god at the shrine of the daisy. In G Chaucer has carefully removed the definite references to an analogy between Christian service and the worship of the god Cupid, and presents himself as an old man out of sympathy with the religion of love.

In the G Prologue at this point occurs Cupid's list of reading which is accessible to Chaucer. The god declares that women are true not 'for holinesse But al for verray vertu and clennesse.' This statement is a retraction of the F Prologue, in which the women were true because of devotion to a religion of love. The G Prologue states that these women were not true to love through a religion but through virtue which is inherent in the nature of women.

By analogy with the position of the Virgin, the Queen of Love becomes the mediator and intercedes for the poet in return for his devotion and his worship of her. In her intercession in F, she presents Cupid as a god and characterizes him as a king who is just, who must rule his court and beware of slanderers, and who should show mercy to unfortunate people. While this characterization applies well to the duties of an earthly king, it is also ecclesiastical and shows the position that a god should hold as the head of a religious system. In F the Queen says, 'if ye nere a god,' but in G the expression is omitted. The Queen, as intercessor, says that the poet has repented utterly of his works against love, but Chaucer omits this statement from the G version. Besides referring to balades, roundels, virelays as hymns for holy days of Cupid, the Queen refers in F to Christian writings as holiness of another kind. This distinction between the holiness of Christian writings and the holiness of Cupid is removed in G by the weak line 'And for to speke of other besinesse.'[3]

In both prologues, at the intercession of the Queen and because of her grace, Cupid forgives the poet. The poet then kneels to her and gives thanks for her mediation in his favor. The Queen assigns his penance that he write a glorious legend of good women and tell of false men that betrayed them. She says that she will pray the God of Love to aid him in his work and, in F, commands that he present a copy of the legends in her behalf to the Queen at Eltham or at Shene.

In both prologues, after the poet has declared that he has always sought to further truth in love, the Queen speaks the formula, 'Thou hast thy grace.' Even in this part of the poem, however, some analogies to Christian worship have been removed in the revision of F. The part of Cupid's speech omitted in G, ll. 552 ff., says, 'Ne shal no trewe lover come in helle,' and tells of twenty thousand women true in love that make up the god's company. Cupid must go home with these true women to 'Paradys,' but, in parting, he commands the poet to serve always the 'fresshe dayesye,' his relic.

In the legends themselves that follow, Chaucer's conception of a religion of Cupid analogous to Christian worship is maintained. A saint's legend often describes the martyrdom of the saint and contains a declaration of faith at the end of the story. In writing of his saints who were martyrs to Cupid, Chaucer tells of their sacrifices for love and places at the end of his legends a declaration of devotion to faith. The place of the heathen opposition to the Christian martyr is taken by men who are faithless in love or, as in *Thisbe,* by the fathers who oppose love. This opposition and untruth is wickedness against the divine law of god Cupid. Professor Dodd, by an analysis of each of the legends, has shown that Chaucer changed traditional incidents and characterization and reorganized his stories to suit the fiction of the religion of love. In *Cleopatra,* for example, Anthony is belittled to make him a heathen as regards love and the Queen of the Nile is made a model of virtuous devotion to love. The dying Cleopatra shows the fortitude of a Christian martyr and glories in the most terrible death of a pit of serpents in sacrifice to her worship of Love's religion. This pit of serpents is a conscious addition by Chaucer out of analogy to Christian martyrdom, as this form of torture is often used in Christian saints' legends.[4] Professor Dodd has proved that in a similar way the succeeding legends emphasize the fortitude and the faithfulness of the women who suffer for love and the treachery and wickedness of the men who oppose Love's law.

The present study of the legends and the alterations that Chaucer made in the F Prologue shows that the organizing motif of the *Legend of Good Women* was the presentation, with delightful skill, of a definite religion of Love in analogy to Christian worship. By analogy with the conception of God, Cupid is made a divine judge, loyal to his followers, and approached through an intercessor, who, because of her wondrous grace and vicarious suffering, may plead for divine mercy. In the F Prologue are added the slightly offensive parallels that the god wears a halo, that his worshipers do not come to hell, and that he and his saints dwell in paradise.

The function of Alceste is the same as that of the Virgin in her position as mediator and intercessor, in which she is the embodiment of mercy. Through her may be secured the grace of the God of Love for sins against his law. She is the fairest among women and is to be worshiped at her shrine with hymns that address her personally without name and with postures of Christian worship. The daisy is the relic of this religion, with which Alceste is identified because of her dress. It, too, is worthy of worship as at a shrine and is addressed personally as the embodiment of the living presence of the god. Possibly the same relation existed between the daisy and Alceste as existed between the Virgin and her image.

The religion of Cupid had its system of repentance, penance, and forgiveness, just as the Christian worship had. As it was a work of Christian devotion to read saints' legends and to write stories of martyrdoms, so it was a work of devotion to the God of Love to read 'olde stories' and to write legends of the saints of Cupid. Cupid had his holy days and his worship was holiness in contrast to the holiness of Christian service. This religion had its devotions, its reverence, its heresies, its penance, and its absolution. To write of untruth in love with sympathy was wickedness and sin against God's law. This religion had its hell and its saints lived with their god in paradise. This God of Love had his martyrs who died for his religion of love, as did Cleopatra, Thisbe, Dido, Medea, and Lucretia, and their stories, as in Ovid's *Heroides*, were devotional literature.

In the G Prologue Chaucer changed his attitude, not toward the larger conceptions of the poem—the nature of Cupid, the intercession of Alceste, and the assignment of the legends as penance, if they might be represented in a dream—but toward the details borrowed from Christian worship that might give offense to a strictly religious person. The poet also removed the passages that would show him as a votary of the religion of Love. This revision of the F Prologue removes analogies to the Christian religion in four different ways. (1) He omitted the poet's words of personal adoration and his attitudes of worship. (2) Chaucer removed expressions that had a definite religious significance in the Christian church. These expressions are of three kinds: Christian words of definite significance,[5] words of adoration,[6] and the hymns, which are very reminiscent of the usual worship of the Virgin in Chaucer's time, in that they are sung as to the living presence at a shrine and contain, in the song 'Hele and Honour,' the commonest word of address to the Virgin and such expressions as 'trouthe of womanhede' and 'flour that berth our alder prys.' (3) Beside the attitudes and words of worship, Chaucer has omitted from G other Christian elements—the reference to hell, the god's departure to paradise, and his halo. (4) This avoidance of religious analogy is further emphasized by the organization of the G Prologue. By placing the dream earlier in the revised prologue, Chaucer has caused such religious elements as are retained to fall in the dream and not in the poet's waking moments. In F the poet is a sympathetic worshiper of this religion of love. In G he is an old man unsympathetic to love and has fallen into an adventure with the God and Goddess of Love in a dream and not because of any personal devotion to their religion.

This very significant change in religious attitude suggests a reason for the revision of the F Prologue. It seems tenable that Chaucer in his maturer life became more formally religious and regarded the analogies between the service of the Roman church and the service of Cupid as blasphemous. The main impulse for the revision of the F Prologue probably came from the request of Venus in the last book of Gower's *Confessio Amantis*, where are many parallels to Chaucer's poem and a message to the poet himself asking that he continue his work.[7] Chaucer was pleased with the use Gower had made of old age and revised his poem using this 'old age' motif and some of Gower's stories. He had grown displeased with his own bold analogies between the Christian service and the worship of Cupid and with the representation of himself as a sympathetic votary of that religion. Hence, he reorganized the poem, removed the obvious use of the Christian service and his adoration of the religion of love from his waking moments, and retained, in an impersonal way, much of the material from the French poets.[8] This view is based upon a study of the elements that Chaucer removed from the F Prologue in its revision and would place the revision late in Chaucer's life, at least, after the completion of Gower's *Confessio Amantis* in 1390.

NOTES

1. See E. P. Hammond, *Chaucer, a Bibliographical Manual*, p. 379.

2. That the *Legend of Good Women* has echoes of Christian worship has been noted by J. S. P. Tatlock, *Studies in Philology*, xviii (1921), 421–22, note, and by W. W. Skeat, *Chaucer*, iii, 139. W. G. Dodd, *Courtly Love in Chaucer and Gower*, pp. 208–32, has discussed the general influence of ecclesiastical elements upon the *Legend*.

3. See Professor J. S. P. Tatlock, *Studies in Philology*, xviii, 422, for the medieval meaning of the word 'Holynesse.'

4. See, in addition to the common reference to Dante and Professor J. S. P. Tatlock's article in *Modern Language Notes*, xxix, 98 ff., *Herrig's Archiv*, lvii, 253 ff.; and lxii, 453 ff.; *Vision of Peter* (Robinson and James, London), sec. 10, p. 50; *St. Patrick's Purgatory*, E.E.T.S., Orig. Series 87, p. 206; *An Old English Miscellany*, E.E.T.S., Orig. Series 46, pp. 149, 224, and 227.

5. These words are: (all in F) 'feyth and ful credence' l. 31; 'devocioun,' l. 39; 'reverence,' l. 52; 'hateth she derknesse,' l. 63; 'dredful herte and glad devocioun,' l. 109; 'resureccioun,' l. 110; 'relik,' l. 321; 'if ye nere a god,' l. 348; 'holynesse,' l. 424.

6. Aside from the adoration, which is in itself reminiscent of worship, such expressions as 'of alle floures flour,' 'fulfilled of al vertu and honour,' 'y-lyke fair and fresh of hewe,' 'clernesse and verray light,' 'maistresse of my wit,' 'lady sovereyne', and 'erthly god' would, in the mind of a medieval worshiper, have a definite association with the prayers and hymns to the Virgin. The kneeling of the poet before the flower, his day long worship as a votary at a shrine, and his greeting of the flower in religious fashion, all in F and omitted in G, make clear the analogy between the Christian worship of the Virgin and the poet's adoration of the daisy which was omitted in the revision of the F Prologue.

7. See G. L. Kittredge, 'Chaucer's Medea and the Date of the Legend of Good Women,' *Publications of the Modern Language Association*, xxiv (1909), 343 ff.

8. Other reasons for the revision of the F Prologue have been suggested. Professor J. L. Lowes, 'The Legend of Good Women,' *PMLA*, xx (1905), 780 ff., suggests that better organization is the reason for the revision. It is somewhat difficult to determine, however, just what would be the medieval conception of 'better organization' in dream poems, but, to modern taste, the organization of F is more logical in the early parts of the poem.

The removal of the extravagant elements of French poetry is not the reason for the revision, as many of these elements are retained in G in the dream.

The view (Professor J. S. P. Tatlock, *Development and Chronology of Chaucer*, pp. 102 ff.) that the personal elements of F were removed after Queen Anne's death, because they referred to her personally, does not explain the removal of the religious analogies. If the F Prologue were personally complimentary to Queen Anne, its revision, in any form, would surely have given offence to King Richard. The complimentary verses of the F Prologue are, however, only commands that a copy of the legends be given to the Queen in accordance with the custom of incorporating such verses in a presentation poem. In any case, the occasion for the reference would be past.

BERNARD L. JEFFERSON

Queen Anne and Queen Alcestis

CHAUCER's Prologue to the *Legend of Good Women* has long had its riddles requiring solution. The question most discussed recently has been that of the allegorical interpretation of Chaucer's fervid worship of the daisy and of his devotion to the mythical heroine, Queen Alcestis. In 1890 Ten Brink advanced the theory that both the daisy and Alcestis were intended to represent Queen Anne. This view was generally accepted until Professor Lowes challenged it in 1904.[1] Since that time the question of the identification of Queen Anne with Alcestis and the daisy has been much discussed and argued pro and con.[2] When we read version B[3] for internal testimony, we are indeed somewhat bewildered with the array of evidence that can be gathered on both sides of the case. It is almost paradoxical, as the following summary of some of the arguments will show. We shall first review the arguments for identification, and then those against it. Our final purpose is to offer a solution which attempts to reconcile to each other the conflicting groups of arguments.

First of all on the side of identification, we have conclusive proof that Queen Anne was in Chaucer's mind when he wrote the Prologue. Lines 496-7 tell us that the *Legend of Good Women* was to be presented to her in her palace at Shene. Secondly there is described in the Prologue a queen, much like Queen Anne, although she bears the name of the mythical heroine Alcestis. She

Reprinted, by permission, from *The Journal of English and Germanic Philology*, XIII (1914), 434-43.

is young, beautiful, merciful, and an exemplary wife. These are all characteristics of the living Queen. In the next place Alcestis in the Prologue is indentified with the daisy, just as ladies then living, were identified with that flower in the *marguerite* poems of Chaucer's distinguished French contemporaries, Machault, Froissart, and Deschamps. To be identified with the daisy was the kind of honor which would be particularly pleasing to Queen Anne. She was young and presumably a lover of fashion. Symbolism by flowers was one of the fads of the time, as is attested by the prevalence of the flower and leaf *balades*. An introduction of a *marguerite* poem into the English court by Chaucer, one of the court poets, would attract general attention. In a poem, presented to her, perhaps written at her express command, if we may believe Lydgate, Queen Anne might well expect to receive the chief honor. Everyone, who had intelligent interest in such matters, would be asking who the flower was, for we need not suppose that the fourteenth century Englishman was less likely to make conjectures than we are today.

The view that Queen Anne was meant to be identified with the daisy gains additional confirmation in an examination of lines 84–96, the lines which Mr. Lowes shows to have been borrowed from the *Filostrato* of Boccaccio. The latter wrote the passage in honor of a living lady. But Chaucer uses it to honor a lady through the medium of the flower. He refers with almost passionate fervor to the daisy as his light, the mistress of his wits, the guide who leads him in this dark world, his lady sovereign, his earthly god. It would seem absurd for Chaucer to lavish such extravagant homage upon the pale figure of a long forgotten mythical heroine, like Alcestis. Chaucer, staid and forty-five, would become a visionary, a chaser after moonbeams. Moreover we must not disregard the transition which later leads to the dream. Alcestis has not been introduced as yet. She is distinctly a figure of the dream. We should hardly expect Chaucer to make Alcestis the guiding star of his life here in the waking day in the field.

After reading this passage, if we go on in the poem, we find another, which not only tends to confirm the impression of Queen Anne's identification with the daisy, but also induces the belief that Queen Anne is to be identified with the lady of the dream as well. The dream has begun, and a lady has been led in by the god of Love. She is not mentioned here by name. Chaucer merely alludes to her as 'a quene.' The specific name Alcestis is not introduced until much later in the poem. Chaucer thus describes the effect made on his dazzled eyes. He says, 'If men were to seek over the earth, they could not find a creature one-half so beautiful as she.' Now Queen Anne was not only on the earth, but, what is more, she was in Chaucer's mind, for he dedicates the poem to her. This would seem a sorry compliment to Queen Anne, when she came to read it, if Alcestis and Alcestis alone is meant.

These words are scarcely out of Chaucer's mouth, before he is moved to express the same sentiment in the form of a *balade*. The burden of his song is, that the approaching lady is fairer than all other fair and peerless ladies. She may disdain them all. No name has been mentioned. Yet Chaucer seems not to doubt who the lady is. It is 'his lady' as we learn from the refrain thrice repeated. And so we are inclined to identify her with the lady praised through the daisy in the working day in the field.

More tributes to the lady follow the *balade*. Among them we find this line:

I prey to God that ever falle hir faire!

This line strikes us queerly. To judge from the meaning, it is a prayer made for one who is to be subject to future dangers, who is to live the hazardous life of earth. It is not a natural note to arise spontaneously in the mind of a poet, when speaking solely of Alcestis, whose earthly troubles may now be considered to have passed, seeing that she lives with Cupid in the 'Paradys' of the blessed. Chaucer certainly cannot profess to be anxious about her welfare. And so behind this line, we think we see a prayer for the future health and prosperity of the living Queen.

Let us now consider the arguments which militate against identification. They are short but apparently decisive, especially that contained in the following lines, found when we approach the close of the poem:

And whan this book is maad, yive hit the quene
On my behalfe, at Eltham, or at Shene.

These words are spoken by Alcestis. Now if Alcestis *is* Queen Anne, we realize the absurdity of the situation. It is as if Alcestis should say 'on my behalf give the book to myself,' nonsense for which we cannot easily give an explanation.

This presentation ordered by Alcestis is followed up a few lines later with a vivid allusion to the descent of Alcestis into hell. Again if Queen Anne is Alcestis, it certainly is not a pleasing picture which associates her with so gruesome an event. Rather than believe Chaucer so tactless, so entirely without discrimination, we would almost entirely discard the identification.

Then over and above these facts, when we conclude the Prologue, we are left with this inquiry in our minds: How would Chaucer have told the story of Alcestis among the number of the legends, if it were encumbered with the allegorical trappings which connected it with the name of Queen Anne? It would have been embarrassing to attempt to carry on the allegorical interpretation throughout the rather dismal events of the life of Alcestis. But Chaucer, once having identified the two queens, would have found it a delicate matter to disentangle Alcestis from the double identity. So the conclusion is that the identity never existed, for originally he certainly intended to incorporate the tale in the *Legend*.

When we recall all that has been said above, it will be seen that a fairly good case can be made either for or against identification. There is only one path out of the maze, and that is to make the explanation as shifting, as self-adjustable, as the identification itself seems to be. And after all the problems of the Prologue are not the problems of mathematics. If Alcestis=the daisy, and Queen Anne=the daisy, it is not necessary to assume that Queen Anne= Alcestis=the daisy, for ever one, and inseparable.

It will be noted that the arguments, based on internal evidence, *for* identification come almost entirely in the early part of the poem; the arguments against it, in the latter part. We have reached by a deduction from the distribution of the passages on which the arguments above are based, from the scattered allusions to the daisy throughout the poem and from considerations soon to be enlarged upon, the following conclusions. Till the beginning of the dream, Chaucer's worship of the daisy in the field does honor to Queen Anne and Queen Anne alone. Then from the beginning of the dream until the first mention of Alcestis by name is a neutral zone, where Queen Anne, Alcestis and the daisy merge one into the other by an almost indefinable and dreamlike process. We feel the residual influence of Queen Anne from the first two hundred and ten lines and the forecasting of the influence of Alcestis to come. In the last one hundred and fifty lines of the Prologue, Alcestis stands practically alone. Queen Anne enters only in so far as the daisy enters and that is only to a very small extent. During the course of the poem, the prominence of Queen Anne and the daisy gradually diminishes to the vanishing point, whereas the prominence of Alcestis correspondingly increases.

A solution for such an interpretation of the Prologue is not to be found by emphasizing the study of it as a type of allegory. It is entirely possible to conceive that Chaucer was not deeply interested in allegory for its own sake but that he was using it rather as a tool for accomplishing two definite purposes which he had in mind, the first to compliment Queen Anne, the second to introduce the *Legend*. For these two purposes Chaucer had on hand two types of allegory; for the first purpose he had the machinery of the *marguerite* poems wherein ladies were complimented through the medium of the daisy, for the second, he had the conventional dream allegory wherein he was enabled to unfold the graceful fiction of the 'good Alceste' who enjoins upon him the task of writing his poem. It was his business, after he had decided upon the two themes of the Prologue, to couple them together as smoothly as possible. If he could so unite them that the one would lend aid in heightening the effect of the other, so much the better. If he could make anything out of the fact that both Anne and Alcestis were good and beautiful queens, well and good; he would take whatever advantages accidentally happened to arise. And so well has Chaucer succeeded in blending his two *motifs*, that one is hardly aware that the earlier part of the poem, and the prolonged adoration of the daisy through almost two hundred lines is really irrelevant in the sense that it contributes nothing essential to the introduction of the *Legend of Good Women*. It now becomes our purpose to find more exactly the respective parts which Queen Anne and Queen Alcestis play in the Prologue.

We take a step toward the truth, if we can realize that all which pertains to the daisy relates primarily to Queen Anne. The Prologue is to be read with the thought in mind that Queen Anne *is* the daisy. When Alcestis first appears in the dream, she looks *like* a daisy. She wears daisies in her crown. Her hair is covered with a fret of red gold above which the white crown rises. She is clad in a garb of green. Why? Merely to suggest the flower which Chaucer worships and to honor it further. When Alcestis and the god of love first accost Chaucer, he is still kneeling over the real daisy; the living Alcestis stands above him. Cupid fiercely rebukes Chaucer, the scoffer at love, for profaning the flower with his presence. Cupid alludes emphatically to the daisy as 'myn owne flour.' From Cupid's point of view, depending on his knowledge of events soon to be disclosed, the allusion may be to Alcestis, but Chaucer and the reader have no reason for differentiating the flower over which he is now kneeling from the one originally introduced. Indeed it is almost as if Chaucer and Cupid had a misunderstanding as to whom the flower really did represent. When Cupid says what business have you near my flower, Chaucer, evidently seeing no reason why he should not be near it, replies with some spirit: ' "And, why sir," quod I, "and hit lyke yow?" '

Then we pass on in the poem. Any classical learning that we may happen to have receives somewhat of a shock. The god of Love, incidentally to explaining who the lady really is, casually drops the remark that she, Alcestis, had once been turned into a daisy. He does not explain the why nor the wherefore of this transformation, nor does he explain how, once having been turned into a daisy, she was there, a living queen. The only explanation for these surprising mysteries is to be found, it would appear, in an old book that lies in Chaucer's chest. That old book has never been discovered. Nowhere in the whole range of classical or mediaeval literature has evidence ever been found that Alcestis underwent such a transformation. So far as can be discovered, it was Chaucer's imagination which produced it. And why? The invention suggested itself to Chaucer as another bond between the two queens and another sweeping compliment to Queen Anne. But it is only here at the very end of the poem that Alcestis is identified with the daisy in the literal sense that Queen Anne is identified with it.

We may consider farther the lines where Chaucer a moment later recognizes Alcestis:

> Now knowe I hir!   And is this good Alceste,
> The dayesye, and myn owne hertes reste?

The transitional word between 'Alceste' and 'myn owne hertes reste' is to be noted. Why was Alcestis Chaucer's own heart's rest? Not particularly because she was Alcestis, but because she was a daisy, and the daisy represents Queen Anne.

We said a little while ago that there was a neutral zone in the middle of the Prologue, where the two Queens are blended. Let us look more carefully at the method of this blending. We recall Chaucer's enthusiastic praise of the approaching queen, before the mention of her name. It has often been argued that Chaucer purposely reserved the mention of the name Alcestis until very late in the Prologue, so that meantime he could leave the impression that he was praising Queen Anne. But it would be a very poor compliment to her majesty, if the lady praised turned out after all not to be she, but some one else. Suppose, however, that Chaucer intends to picture *himself* as at first mistaken in the identity of Alcestis. It would be a distinct compliment to Queen Anne to be mistaken for so glorious a lady as Chaucer describes in Alcestis. In this case all the praise showered on Alcestis, applies equally to her. There is evidence to support this view, that Chaucer pictures in the dream that he was thus mistaken. In presenting this view, we shall not think of the Prologue as a dream allegory essentially. We shall suppose, for example, that Chaucer did not bring in the belated recognition *motif*, blindly and because he thought no dream allegory would be complete without one. We shall consider that the allegory afforded him material, in his hands more or less molten, so that he could shape it for his own purposes.

Let us examine first the *balade* wherein is found the outburst of praise of the approaching queen. It runs, somewhat as follows 'hide your tresses, Absolom. Ester, lay down your meekness. Isould and Helen, hide your beauty; for *my lady* comes that all this may bedim.' Chaucer says 'my lady,' as to him, in his enthusiasm for her beauty, it can be only one person, the lady of his own adoration. Really, as later becomes apparent, he was mistaken. It was Alcestis who approached. But he does not realize this until events begin to develop. Then the recognition gradually draws on him. In line 432 he for the first time hears the name Alcestis. She speaks of herself as 'Alceste, whylom quene of Trace.' He is puzzled. The first time he has an opportunity to speak to her thereafter, he takes advantage of the opportunity to explain that he does not know who she is. After thanking her for her intercession in his interest with the God of Love, he says:

> And yeve me grace so long for to live,
> That I may knowe *soothly* what ye be,
> That han me holpe and put in this degree.

After Chaucer has finished, Alcestis replies in a speech which concludes with the injunction for Chaucer to present the book that he is to write to Queen Anne at Shene. Then the God of Love, at this allusion begins to smile:

> 'Wostow,' quod he, 'wher this be wyf or mayde,
> Or quene, or countesse, or of what degree,
> That hath so litel penance yiven thee.'

Chaucer, now, stoutly insists that he knows nothing about her. Cupid explains to his satisfaction. Finally Cupid, in his parting words, calls Chaucer's attention to the fact that he had neglected to put the name of 'Alceste' in the *balade*. Chaucer had indeed forgotten her. In a list of noble heroines of old, Alcestis should have been named along with Ester, Isould, Helen, and the rest. Cupid's rebuke shows clearly that in his mind, at least, the 'my lady' of the refrain meant not Alcestis but some unnamed lady of Chaucer's devotion. In this rebuke of Chaucer by the God of Love, we see Chaucer, the literary craftsman, using a device to stress the idea that he, in his dream, had thought the lady upon her first approach Queen Anne.

It is to the extent just described, we believe, that Chaucer has blended the two Queens. Whether we accept the explanation as the true one, depends on whether we can think of the Prologue as a record of human feeling, involving the pride of the young queen of twenty and Chaucer's ability to comply gracefully with her wishes, or whether we think of it as an elaborate example of the dream allegory, wherein little weight may be attached to what is actually said and done.

NOTES

1. *Publications of the Modern Lang. Ass. of America*, xix, 593 ff.

2. Compare the argument of Professor Tatlock in *The Development and Chronology of Chaucer's Works,* pp. 102 ff; of Professor Kittredge in *Modern Philology*, vi, 435 ff; and of Professor Moore in *Modern Language Review,* vii, 488 ff.

3. In this article, I approach the question of identification from the standpoint of version B, since the priority of that version over version A, thanks to Professor Lowes and Professor Tatlock, seems to be generally accepted. All references, therefore, will be to version B, unless otherwise stated.